Donald Macdonald

The Asiatic Origin of the Oceanic Languages

etymological dictionary of the language of Efate, New Hebrides

Donald Macdonald

The Asiatic Origin of the Oceanic Languages
etymological dictionary of the language of Efate, New Hebrides

ISBN/EAN: 9783337313647

Printed in Europe, USA, Canada, Australia, Japan

Cover: Foto ©Andreas Hilbeck / pixelio.de

More available books at **www.hansebooks.com**

THE ASIATIC ORIGIN OF THE OCEANIC LANGUAGES.

THE ASIATIC ORIGIN

OF THE

OCEANIC LANGUAGES:

ETYMOLOGICAL DICTIONARY OF THE LANGUAGE OF EFATE (NEW HEBRIDES)

WITH AN INTRODUCTION.

BY

THE REV. D. MACDONALD,

EFATE, NEW HEBRIDES.

Melbourne:

MELVILLE, MULLEN AND SLADE,

262 AND 264 COLLINS STREET.

LONDON: 12 LUDGATE SQUARE, E.C.

1894.

PREFACE.

———◆———

THE following work gives, in the first place, a Dictionary of the language of Efate, New Hebrides, as accurate as I can make it after upwards of twenty-one years' constant study and use of the language in the performance of my duty as a missionary stationed on the island of Efate. But, as is noted in the introduction, a vast number of derivative words have, for the sake of brevity, not been inserted. In the second place, the dialectical variations of Efatese words are given in a considerable number of instances ; the cognate words in other languages of the Oceanic family are usually put within brackets, and are chosen purposely from its four great branches—the Papuan (or " Melanesian "), the Maori-Hawaiian (or " Polynesian "), the Malayan, and the Malagasy (or " Tagalan "). These, which embrace the fundamental elements of Oceanic speech, have been found of great use in determining the radical meaning and original forms of words, and also, it may be remarked, in illustrating the homogeneity of the great insular family, properly called Oceanic, since it extends from Madagascar in the Indian Ocean to Easter Island in the Pacific, from the Hawaiian Islands in the North Pacific to New Zealand in the South, and from Sumatra through the Eastern Archipelago and New Guinea to the New Hebrides and Fiji. In the third place, and usually after the bracket, are placed the Asiatic—*i.e.*, the Semitic—words to which all the preceding Oceanic words are traced. Arabia, which borders on Oceania, has always been, and is to this day, the principal home of this, the most important family of Asiatic languages.

For a short Efatese grammar the reader is referred to the work entitled " Three New Hebrides Languages: Efate, Eromanga, Santo ;" for short grammars of other New Hebrides languages, to that entitled " South Sea Studies ;" and for some general outline of Oceanic grammar, to that entitled " Oceania: Linguistic and Anthropological." Any remark on a particular point in the present work which differs from any similar remark that I had made in the works just named is to be regarded as correcting it. Even in the present work, as, *e.g.*, in treating of the formative particles, many of the main elements of Oceanic grammar are dealt with ; in a work treating of the whole material of a language of a family so extremely analytic as the Oceanic, it could not well be otherwise. While fully convinced of the importance of grammar in comparative philology, I have for many years been equally convinced that, to establish the Asiatic origin of the Oceanic languages, the whole material of one Oceanic language must be dealt with, as in the present work.

The work of Gibbon has been described as the splendid bridge from the old world to the new. The work presented to the public in this little volume is a bridge of an immensely wider span than Gibbon's, connecting two worlds less known than his, and throwing light, as I believe not otherwise obtainable, on both, especially on the newer—the world, so interesting to modern science, of the existing savage, which can be thoroughly known only through his language. This bridge, indeed, makes no pretension to "splendour," but, while perhaps more deeply sensible of its imperfections in details than anyone else can be, I trust it will be found to be in all substantial respects well and faithfully built, and durable even to indestructibility. However that may be, it is certain that the building of it has taken more than the twenty years which the building of Gibbon's took.

I may here explain that, as no Arabic or Ethiopic type are in the establishment where this work is printed, I have been reluctantly obliged to re-write all the Arabic and other Semitic words in Roman characters. For this reason I have not printed at all, as I originally intended, the second part of the Dictionary, or Asiatic-Oceanic. Whether the complete work, with proper type, will appear hereafter will largely depend on the reception accorded to the present volume.

LIST OF ABBREVIATIONS.

a., adjective.
ad., adverb.
art., article.
c., with.
c. art., with the article.
cg., cgg., cognate, cognates.
conj., conjunction.
cf., compare.
d., dd., dialect, dialects.
d. syn. c., dialect synonymous with.
den., denominative.
dem., demonstrative.
der., derivation.
i.q., the same as.
inf., infinitive.
inter., interrogative.
interj., interjection.
imp., imperative.
mid., middle voice.
n. a., nomen actionis (infinitive).
n. ag., nomen agentis (active participle).
n. p., nomen patientis (passive participle).
nom. suf., nominal suffix.
num., numeral.
opp., opposite, opposed.
part.. participle.
pers. pron., personal pronoun.
pl., plural.
pref., preformative.
prep., preposition.
prob., probably.
pron., pronoun.
ps., passive.

q.v., which see.
redup., reduplicate.
s., substantive.
s.v., under the word (sub voce).
sing., singular.
syn., synonymous.
syn.c..synonymous with.
t., transitive.
v., verb.
v. c..verb causative form.
v. i., verb intransitive.
v. r., verb reflexive, or reciprocal.
v. t., verb transitive.
verb. suf., verbal suffix.
voc., vocative.

A., Arabic.
Amh., Amharic.
Am., Ambrym.
An., Aneityum.
Arm., Aramaic.
Assy., Assyrian.
Bu., Bugis.
Ch., Chaldee.
E., Ethiopic.
E. Mai, East Mai.
Ef., Efate.
Er., Eromanga.
Fi., Fiji.
Fut., Futuna.
H., Hebrew.
Ha., Hawaiian.
Ja., Java.
Ma., Maori.
Mg., Malagasy.

Ml., Malekula.
Ml. A., Malekula Aulua.
Ml. P., Malekula Pangkumu.
Ml. U..Malekula Uripiv.
Mod. A..Modern Arabic.
Mod. S..Modern Syriac.
My., Malay.
Pa., Paama.
S., Syriac.
Sa., Samoan.
Soc., Socotra.
T., Tigre.
Ta., Tanna.
TaSa., Tangoan Santo.
Tah., Tahiti.
To., Tonga.

Ct., Catafago's Dictionary of Mod. A.
Freytag, Freytag's Arabic Lexicon.
Ges., Gesenius's Dictionary of Hebrew.
Nm., Newman's Dictionary of Mod. A.
St., Stoddart's Grammar of Mod. S.
After an Arabic verb 1, 2, 3, 4, 5, &c., denote its different forms, and 1), 2), 3), &c., its different meanings.
After a Hebrew verb Pi. denotes Piel, Pu. Pual, Hi. Hiphil, Ni. Niphal.

INTRODUCTION.

Tʜᴇ Aʟᴘʜᴀʙᴇᴛ.—The Ef. alphabet used in this work differs from that used in the Ef. version of the New Testament only in the use of *b* instead of p. The letters are a, b (and *b*), e, f, g, i, k, l, m, n, o, r, s, t, and u. The vowels a, e, i, o, u have the Italian sounds: i and u are also used sometimes for y and w, thus uo is pronounced wo, but i is very rarely used for y. B stands for both b and p, f for f and v, g for ng in sing, and k, l, m, n, r, s, t are sounded as in English. In one dialect of Efatese h represents the s of the other dialects. In My. d· is nearly the same as d, ch is like ch in church, â like short e, and g is hard, as in give. In the New Hebrides languages, Fiji, and Samoan, g represents ng as in Ef. In Fi. c represents th, and in Malagasy o stands for u. The Samoan ' is a click, or half-expressed k, and the Hawaiian k stands for the t of the cognate dialects. Ef. au sounds like ow in now, and ai, or ei, like i in sigh, or ei in height. Ef. *b* is sometimes like bw, sometimes like kb: a more rare variation of m is *m*, or m̃, like mw, or gm. The alphabet of the Asiatic group of languages to which the Island group of languages is traced in this work is represented thus:—' (Elif), b, g, d, A. d, h, w (u, o), z, h, A. h', t, A. t', y (i), k, l, m, n, s, ' ('ain), A. " ("ain), p (f), s, A. s·, k, r, s', th (t), A. t. Of these the ' represents a quiescent consonant, or spiritus lenis, like the h in hour; b, b and sometimes bh or v; g, g and gh; d, d and dh; w (u, o), w and v; h, a guttural h, like hh; t, a guttural t; ' is related to ' and to h; s represents ts; k, a guttural k, some

times confounded with ' : s', sh. Of the Arabic letters d, h', t', ",
and s', d is sounded like th in that, with ; s', somewhat like th in
this ; and t' (an aspirated t, or th) is sometimes like a strongly-
articulated palatal z (somewhat like s), sometimes like s' ; while h',
and " are stronger guttural sounds than h and ', the former like ch
in Scotch loch. The Arabic t is a grammatical ending, and is
represented in Arabic by an h with two dots over it. In Mod. A.
only when it is followed by another word is it pronounced t, otherwise it is a quiescent h. It should be noted that ' in the middle or
at the end of words represents also an omitted letter or vowel
sound.

LETTER CHANGES.—The Ef. vowels u and o are frequently
interchanged : in many words—as kori (kuri), bonoti (bunuti), loko
(loku, luku)—it is equally correct to use either u or o. The vowel
a is very often pronounced and written e, as in set, bet, the My. â.
The short sounds of i and e are practically identical. The diph-
thongs ai, or ei, and au, are sometimes contracted to e, or i, and o,
or u. Generally when w (u) and y (i) come between two vowels
they may be omitted in writing and pronunciation, thus mauora
(mawora) or mäora, uui (uwi) or üi, noai (na-uai, na-wai), and nai,
ia (iya). The labials b, f, m, are thus often elided, being first
changed into u (w), as in the examples given mauora is for mabora,
noai for na-fai (d. ni fai), and uui for ufi or ubi.

The labials are very frequently interchanged, as m to b or f,
and *vice versâ*, as munuti, bunuti ; mago, bago ; mai, bai, or bei,
and be. B and f are constantly interchanged, especially when
occurring at the beginning of verbs, thus ba fano go thou, i bano
he went, bare, redup. barefare ; and bano to go, nafanoen the
going. As already noted, m, b, and f are often changed to w (u),
and then elided : at the end of a word preceded by the vowel a,
they readily become w or u, thus baram, barab, baraf, barau are all
Ef. forms of the same word ; and in the same position, preceded by
the vowel u, they are apt to be simply elided, thus num, nuf, nubu,

nu are all **Ef.** forms of the same word. B and *b* are interchanged, and also m and *m* : *b* (like b) readily changes into w (u, o), as *b*ota ia, redup. botauota, and uotauota (wotawota), na*b*otān, or nauotān, mauota (mawota) or mäota.

G (ng). This sound in **Ef.** usually stands for k (see generally words beginning with g in the Dictionary) ; more rarely it stands for n, as in finaga and rāg (rān), and still more rarely for m, as in sugi (sumi). G (ng) is not one of the original stock of Oceanic consonants.

K. The **Ef.** k is sometimes elided, as in ālia for kali a, usi for kusi, nosoafa and soafa for nakosoafa, nāra for nakoro, buti for bakauti ; sometimes changed to g (ng), and sometimes interchanged with b, as bui na and kui na, bisi na and kihi na, makus and mafis (cf. My. bawa and gawa, &c.)

N. This letter is sometimes elided, as a for ani or an, ma for man, sometimes interchanged with g (ng) q.v., t, as ni ki, ti ki ; s, inuma, isuma ; l and r, nag, lag, rag, and nagusu, läusu.

R. This letter is interchanged with l, as rag and lag ; with t, as baki ta for baki ra to them, and very commonly ta for ra in both the nom. and verb suf. 3 pl ; with s, as busi for muri, gusu na for gore na, and, s to r, muri na for mesau na. It is also sometimes elided, as ĕu for ĕru, u for ru. In one d. r is often pronounced tr, which in others is nr, t, and nd.

L. See r and n. L and r in some Oceanic dialects are identical, and l is sometimes pronounced somewhat like d.

T. See r and l. This letter is sometimes in **Ef.** pronounced ts, as tsi ka for tika (also rika and nika), and is found changed to s, as sa for ta.

S. See t, r, n. In one **Ef.** d. it is changed to h, as latĕha for latesa, &c.

NOTE.—The gutturals kh, hh, gh, in some of the New Hebrides sister dialects, have been lost from the **Ef.** The Oceanic inter-dialectical letter changes are in general so self-explaining and well known (My. and Ef. k, Mg. h; Fi. c (*i.e.*, th), Ef. s, &c.) as to require no treatment here.

LETTER CHANGES IN THE ASIATIC LANGUAGES OF WHICH THE ALPHABET IS GIVEN ABOVE.—The sounds represented by ', h, h, h', ', and ", may have been all distinct from each other in the Semitic mother tongue, but the uniform tendency of the Semitic languages is, as they become developed analytically, to confound them all into one or two. Thus in Assy. ', h, h, ', and ", all became like ' (*i.e.*, spiritus lenis), and even h' became either a mere spiritus lenis or k. So in Ef. these are all a mere ', or spiritus lenis, except h, and h', which are sometimes k.

G, k, and k were not only sometimes interchanged with each other, but also with ', h ; and, as above remarked, k is sometimes treated in pronunciation as a mere ', or spiritus lenis.   In Ef. they are usually represented by k, and sometimes elided (*i.e.*, spiritus lenis).

The labials b, w, m, p.   These were interchanged with each other : b (or v) in Mod. S. has sometimes a sound varying from w to v ; in Assy. m and v are interchanged, in Himyaritic m and b (or v) ; in Assy. m was also sometimes changed to n and ng ; p is either p or f in II., in A. it is f ; b following a in Mod. S. is pronounced o, and f (or p) following a is pronounced au (*i.e.*, ab or av becomes o, af or ap au).   Compare the remarks on the Ef. labials above.

N.   This letter, especially when the first consonant of a verb, was often dropped.   Accordingly in Ef., &c., such verbs are often without the initial n.   It was also interchanged with l, m, and y.

R, l.   These are interchanged with each other, and with n : they are also sometimes elided ; l is interchanged with d, and r with the sibilants, as with z and s.   Compare the Ef. above.

SIBILANTS AND DENTALS.—These were sometimes interchanged with each other ; and see r, l.   They were also sometimes elided. See Ef. r, l, t, s, above.

See concluding remarks, *infra.*

THE ARTICLE.—The forms of the article illustrate some of the foregoing remarks on letter changes. Its common form in Ef. is na, nĭ, n', in Mg. ny, Sa. le, E. Mai. re, Meli and Ma. te. But in Ef. it not only occurs in some words with its consonant elided (A. al, hal, l', H. ha) as a, ĕ, or ĭ, but also as la or l' (or ra), as in lausu, lag (also rag, ran, nag), and lífāru (also rãfālu, libuis), lobu, laso na, lima, and rakum, rarua ; as ta, as in tanekabu (and nanekabu, see ate, *infra*), taliga; and as s, as in suma (My. rumah). In such words the article has been prefixed in very early times (in lífāru certainly before the word left Arabia), and has come by later generations to be regarded as a part of the word. By looking up these words in the Dictionary it will be seen that they illustrate more than one of the above noted letter changes. The article is regularly prefixed to the abstract substantive that may be formed from every verb or adjective in the language by the ending an (ana, usually written en, ena) as nakasuana the being strong, strength, from kasua strong, nafamiena the act of eating, food, from bami to eat : in My. the article (or dem. particle) ka is thus used (Mg. ha). This ka or k' occurs in Ef. only as an " unconscious " article, and the former, l', r', or n', occurs in My. only as an unconscious article. Both of these articles were also prefixed to verbal nouns (substantives or adjectives) without the formative ending an, as in kalumi spider, lit. the sweller, or that which swells, kalau spider's web, lit. the woven, or that which is woven, kolofa bent (Fi. kalove), lit. the bent, that which is bent. To a word of this kind—with the unconscious article ka—the causative preformative was attached, and hence baka (see ba, c. pref., and baka, Mg. maha, *infra*). In the same way—to words with the unconscious article n' (ng)—was prefixed the same c. pref. ma (in My. and Mg.), forming man, mana, mang, &c. Thus Mg. be is " great," habe greatness, lit. that which is great, mahabe to make great, but also manabe to make great (na, modern form ny, the article, and also used in the sense of a relative = ha = that which, &c.) The r in My. bâr (ber, be), the reflexive preformative, is a form of the same article (Fi. ra, forming so called passives like ka) which in Ef. occurs as l', n', and r', &c., and the prefixed bâ or be, Mg. mi, Ef. bi, Sa. fe, is the real r. pref. : hence My. bâr is equivalent to Mg. miha, the difference being that the former has the art. r, the latter the article ha. The fact that in Mg. maha is the causative and miha the reflexive preformative shows that there is nothing either reflexive or causative in the ha. But of course baka, man, &c., came to be regarded, when their origin was no longer remembered, as simple formatives.

THE PERSONAL PRONOUNS AND NUMERALS.—For these see two papers in the *Journal of the Polynesian Society*, on " The Asiatic Origin of the Oceanic Personal Pronouns" and " Oceanic Numerals" respectively.

THE VERB.—The Semitic verb had two bases, the one that of the perfect, being the "concrete" or participial, the other that of the imperfect (or "future"), with which was connected the imperative and infinitive, being the "abstract" or verbal substantive. In the Oceanic languages the ancient inflexion of the perfect and imperfect has disappeared, its place being supplied by analytic substitutes. The Oceanic verb is really a participle, or verbal substantive used as a participle, and represents, or is, either the ancient participial base, as afa ia, āfa ki, ba, laba or leba, and (passive) būra, tuk or toko, or the ancient infinitive base, as tao, taru (or toro), soko, saki, or a derived participle or infinitive of the ancient verb. The ancient participle (or verbal adjective) had two forms, the active and passive, and was sometimes used as a substantive; the ancient infinitive had numerous forms, each of which could be used either in an active or a passive sense, and was sometimes used as a participle or verbal adjective. Every adjective in Efatese is a verb when used with the verbal pronoun (the analytic substitute for the ancient inflexion of the perfect and imperfect), and every verb is an adjective when used without the verbal pronoun. The following are examples of verbs representing ancient participles and infinitives:—Active participle, mita; passive participle, mitela, barua, bau ; infinitive, roko (loku, luku), borau, mauri (moli). It will be observed that these examples involve both the Semitic modes of inflexion, by internal vowel change and by external addition.

In the Semitic languages the simple verb usually had three radical letters, but a very large number of these were, or became, always pronounced as having only two, and a good many were sometimes so pronounced, as those one of whose three letters was ', ', ", h, h, h', k, w, y, and (initial) n. Generally, but not always, it is the briefest form of the ancient word that is found represented in Efatese. In some instances the three strong radicals of an ancient verb are still found in its Efatese representative, as in salube, sekof, serab, surut, sumat. The final n of an ancient verb is sometimes found elided in Efatese, as in asua, and m, b, or p (f) vocalized or elided, as already pointed out, as in nu (num), nu ē a, rā (or tā), barau (barab), bolau (uolau), sau, galau, balu-sa (and balu-saki).

The "forms" of the Efatese verb, or derivative verb forms, are the causative, having the formative prefixes ba (or ma), and baka and sa ; the reflexive or reciprocal, having bi or fi ; the reflexive passive, having ta; the passive, having ma (mi, &c.): see the Dictionary for these particles and words beginning with them. Among "forms" of the verb may also be placed the reduplicate forms, as when the whole verb is doubled, as magamaga ; when the initial syllable is doubled, as sasabo ; and when the final is doubled, as tafagka or tafakāka (or tafak'ka). Reduplication modifies the meaning of the verb in various ways, expressing intensity or repetition of the act, and sometimes giving a diminutive sense.

THE SUBSTANTIVE.—From every verb, whether simple or derivative, is or may be formed a verbal substantive by adding to it the formative suffix ana, or an (usually pronounced ena, or en), and prefixing the article na (ni, &c.) This formative suffix is common generally to all the Semitic and to all the Oceanic languages, forming infinitives or abstract verbal substantives denoting the action or

state and various related ideas. In Efatese, when used without the
article, this verbal substantive is used in a passive sense as a verbal
adjective, thus bami to eat, nafamiena the eating, the act of eating,
eating, food, and famiena to be eaten, eatable, for eating, as nafinaga
famiena food to be eaten, eatable, or for eating. These, to save
space, are not given, except in a few instances, in the Dictionary.

A number of Efatese substantives analytically represent the n.
ag., or active participle, of the simple form of the Semitic verb, as
kălĭ, from kili a, līta, or tīla, from tila ia, so sār', lĕt, lōfa, lāga,
lūma, nīfe, ōri, sĕru, sīko, sīl, tūnu, sōro, &c. A number of Efatese
verbs become substantives by prefixing the article, as mitela broken,
i mitela it is broken, namitela that which is broken, a fragment,
manaki to remain as a guest, namanaki a guest: see above on the
article. In the same way, as already observed, some nouns were
formed by prefixing ka, k'; but no new substantives can thus
be formed. On the other hand, a new substantive phrase can
be similarly formed from every verb in the language by prefixing
the particle te (for which see the Dictionary), as te fami what eats,
eater, te kili what digs, a digging thing or person. A number of
Efatese substantives simply represent, or are, the ancient Semitic
substantives, whether primitive, as fai or ai (water), āfa or āb'
(father), or derivative, as ātĕ (liver), tua (leg), kuli (skin). A few
Efatese verbs become substantives by suffixing a, as namisakia
sickness, namatakua fear, namitiria a writing, namaietoa anger: this
a represents the ancient abstract ending H. ah (for ath), A. at, Mod.
A. a (or ah).

THE ADJECTIVE ENDINGS.—The first of these to be noticed is a,
as in samā, koa, sulia, lebalebā, lasoa, litia, bulia, buria, oroa. This
in Assy. is a (originally ai), Mod. S. a, E. i, awi, ai, A. iyy'. It was
originally pronounced iya, or aya (Dillmann). Sometimes in Ef. it is
i, as in tuai. Another a. ending is na, or 'na, as in barbarutena,
bibilena, telatelana, sasana, rana, rarana, oraorana. This in Assy.
is an', or en', Arm. ana, an, na, A. an'. These are found in the

Oceanic languages generally. The former, a, is exceedingly common in the Maori-Hawaiian languages, and the latter in Malagasy. The so-called passives in Samoan, &c., formed by the ending a, are not passives but adjectives : sometimes in Samoan they are actives, and they always seem to be so in Futuna, and they sometimes turn a substantive into an adjective. The Efatese adjective tunitunia is formed from tuni (i.e., tu ni, tu, v., and ni, t. prep.) exactly after the manner of the so-called Maori-Hawaiian passives, which in a vast number of instances suffix the ending a to a verb having a transitive preposition. A third a. ending is ak, k, or ka, as in katak, kanoka (also syn. kanoa), sikai (and sikatika), Malagasy isaka, iraika. This in Assy. is ak', which may be the same as the Mahri ending k, which forms adjectives, as safaik healed, taimak thirsty, sebak full, hark hot, heberrek cold : this ending in Mahri formed also in earlier times verbal substantives.

OTHER ENDINGS.—The ending t (or th) in the Semitic languages is very common in Malagasy, and pronounced tra, which is often changed to ra. This occurs in all the Oceanic languages generally as in bătĕ, 4, My. ampat, Mg. efatra, Sa. (elided) fā, and also in Sa. fitu, Mg. fito, 7 ; and in Ef. fuata, barbaruta, lebalebara, fuluara, bulora, sikara, and (elided) in bau head, for batu (as the neighbouring dialects prove), also in batu, bate, buta. Sometimes the t. prepositions are found suffixed to the verb, as if they were a part of it, and have to be carefully distinguished from the formative endings above treated of. In bau, fitu, lifāru, &c., we have also the ancient Semitic ending u.

THE TRANSITIVE PREPOSITIONS.—These are simply the prepositions coming immediately after, or suffixed to, the verb, connecting it with its object. The construction is exactly the same as in the Semitic languages, and the prepositions are identical, and occur in all the Oceanic languages, forming a marked feature of them. The verb with its t. prep. is construed as one word, and to it is or may be suffixed the substantive formative ending an, or ana, or the adjective ending a, or na. The three most frequently used preps. are bi, or fi, or mi (also ba, fa, ma), li, or ni, or ri (also la, na, ra), and ki (also ka). The two former are the most frequently used in all Semitic languages, and the latter very frequently used in Himyaritic (or Sabaean) and Amharic. The double t. preps. usually have the latter, as maki, faki, raki, naki, &c., but not always, for there occur also nusi, nus (as in bunusi and banus, My. panas), bisi (as in libisi), noti or nuti (as in bonoti, munuti). In the Dictionary the t. prep. (or preps.) is usually given with the verb, see, *e.g.*, under the words sili, v. t., and alialia, and the a which is often suffixed to the prep. is the verbal suffix pronoun, 3 person, see, *e.g.*, under bamau ria (d. bamau sa). The na after many substantives in the Dictionary, see, *e.g.*, under balu, is the nominal suffix pronoun, 3 person. Thus balu na denotes his brother, bamau ria to find him, her, or it, le-kā see him, le-baia see him, le k'baia see him, li-bisia see him ; these are all practically synonymous, but le-kā is lit. look *to* him, le-baia look *upon* him, le-k'baia look to—upon him, and li-bisia look upon him (the transitive prep. si being in this case without definite meaning and merely directing more emphatically to the object).

CONCLUDING REMARKS.—Taking the letters of the above-given Asiatic alphabet in their order, and, for the sake of brevity, taking them here only as they occur as the *initial* letters of the words compared in the Dictionary, we may observe the changes these letters have undergone from the time they left South-Western Asia till the present time when they are found in Oceania :—

'. Always found as spiritus lenis, generally dropped, sometimes retained (*i.e.*, its accompanying vowel retained). Number of words large.

b. Nearly always b, rarely m. Number of words large.

g. Nearly always k (or its variant g, *i.e.*, ng), rarely elided. A good number of words.

d. Nearly always t, very rarely r, rarely s, and still more rarely elided. A good many words.

d. Always t, except in one instance s (d. h). Very few words.

h. Always spiritus lenis, and sometimes its accompanying vowel elided. A good many words.

w (u, o). Always retained only in its accompanying vowel (as a for wa), and sometimes that vowel elided. A good many words.

z. Always s. A good many words.

ḥ. Nearly always spiritus lenis, but in a considerable proportion of instances k (or g), and rarely its accompanying vowel elided. Number of words large.

ḥ′. Generally k (or g), sometimes spiritus lenis, very rarely its accompanying vowel elided. Not very many words.

t. Generally t, rarely r, l, or n. A good many words.

t′. Always t. Words very few.

y (i). Always retained only in its accompanying vowel, and that usually is elided. Not many words.

k. Generally k (or g), rarely elided. Number of words large.

l. Nearly always l, rarely r, t, and (see the prep. ni) rarely n or elided. A good many words.

m. Usually m, often b (or f), very rarely (through w, u) only its accompanying vowel retained. A very large number of words.

n. Usually elided, n when retained as it sometimes is. Number of words large.

s. Nearly always s, in one instance t, and in one instance n. Not many words.

ʿ. Always spiritus lenis, and retained only in its accompanying vowel, which is sometimes elided. Number of words large.

ʻʻ. Always spiritus lenis, and as preceding letter. A good many words.

p (f). Generally b, or f, rarely m, *m*, sometimes *b*. Number of words large.

s. Generally t, or s, oftener the former, sometimes (rarely) r, or l. See futum, busuf, and tiu, riu, tutu, lulu, luma, luba. Number of words large.

s'. Generally t, sometimes l, in one instance s, and very rarely r. A good many words.

k. Nearly always k (or g), rarely spiritus lenis. Number of words large.

r. Generally r, very often l. Number of words large.

s'. Nearly always s, rarely t, and more rarely l, in one instance n. Number of words large.

th, t. Usually t, sometimes n, rarely r, l, or s. A good many words.

Certain words and particles, owing to their very frequent use, undergo greater changes, as the pronouns, numerals, formative particles, and prepositions; thus the Ancient Semitic interrogative and indefinite pron. ma (Sabaean ba) in Ef. occurs as ma, fa, and a, and the same word, m', used as a preformative in participles and infinitives in the Ancient Semitic, in Ef. occurs as m', b', and f', Mg. m', f', mp', My. m', b', and p'; and see the preps. li (original form), ni, ri, i, &c., and with a, ani, an, a, and bi, fi, or mi, with dem. suffixed bai or bei. See also, above, the article, and the negative adverb in the Dictionary.

DICTIONARY

OF THE

LANGUAGE OF EFATE

(NEW HEBRIDES).

A, verbal pron., I : d. ni, q.v.

A, v., contraction of ani, q.v., to be, or dwell in.

A, prep., contraction of ani, an, q.v.: sometimes e, or i, in, at, to, of. Used prefixed to nouns, as ataku, etaku, or itaku, at the back, behind ; and to the suffixed pronoun of the possessive, as agu my, ana his, dialect enea, or inea his, inu my. [The same contraction is found in Mg. ahy my, azy his, and in Sa. ana his. The Mg. a is contracted for any, an, and the Sa. is probably the same particle.]

A, art., or dem., prefixed to certain words, as to some nouns, pronouns, akamus ye, and prepositions, ani of, aki or agi of ; and to verbs, nikam, d. agau, that which nips, or grasps. [Fi. a, an article, prefixed also to prepositions, as a nei, a kei, denoting the possessive case as in Efatese. The Fi. a is a form of the article na, and the Efate a, being the same as the Fi., must in that case be a form of the common article na (ni, ne, &c.), q.v. Agi (a gi)

of, in Efate in one dialect is nag or nagi (na gi) of, and akam, ye, in another dialect is nikam ye. The same article is found in Ma. and To. as a. In Fi. and Ef., prefixed to possessive prepositions, it has somewhat of the force of a relative pronoun.] H. ha for hal ; A. al, sometimes hal, dem. art., used also sometimes as a relative pronoun prefixed to verbs and prepositions: compare ha, according to F. Muller identical with hal for al, the article, Arm. ha this, as an interjection, lo ! H. hē.

A, interj., O ! lo ! [Ha. a, Tah. a, lo ! o !] See under preceding word.

Ab, s., d. voc., father. [Ma. pa, My. pa, pak, Mg. aba.] A. āb, H. āb, Ch. aba, father.

Aba, v. See ofa.

Abab, s., father. [Ma. papa, My. bapa, bapak, Mg. baba.] See āb.

Abu, v., to heal, get well (a sore), d. au, id., d. mau, to get well, recover from sickness. [Sa. mafu, to heal up, Mg. miafu, to recover from sickness.] A. afa, 3, 4, restore to health.

2

Abu, s., ashes, also afu, au. See following word.

Abuobu, v. redupl., to be dusty, to fly in the air (dust), also afuafu, id.; naob dust, ashes, lime (ashes of coral), na, art., and ob, noba (nōbwa), s., id., nobanoba, v., to be dusty, become dust, fly in the air (dust), tano afu, tano abu, tano au ashes; libu, v., to be ashy, ash-coloured, dirty, or covered with ashes, as in mourning for the dead, hence malibu; v., to be a mourner thus, especially for a deceased husband or wife, and hence malibu, s., a widow or widower, that is, one so mourning : libu, v., is also found (Bau d.) as lifu, lifulifu ; mafu, s., a thick vapour like dust; uncleanness (ritual). [Sa. efu, s., efuefu, s., dust, efu, v., to become dust, efu, a., reddish-brown, To. efoo, s., dust, ashes, efooia, a., dusty, covered with ashes, Sa. lefu, a., s., lefulefu, s., ashes, Ma. nehu, s., dust, nehunehu, a., dusky, whakanehu, v., reduce to powder, My. abu, s., Ja. awu, s., dust, ashes, My. dabu, labu, id., kalabu, v., a., ashy, ash-coloured, also klabu, Ja. kluwu, Mg. vovoka, s., dust, ashes, mamavoka, v., to dust, sprinkle with dust, mavo, a., brown, manavo, v., despise, blacken, sully, mavoana, a., unadhesive (applied to mortar), Fi. dravu, s., ashes, dravudravua, a., ashy, of the colour of ashes, poor, hence vakadravudravua-taka, v., to make poor.]

A. haba (habu), v., rise, float-in the air (dust), become like dust, de carbone igne extincto, die, 4, raise or excite dust, habwat dust, colour of dust, Ct. habut dust, dust mixed with ashes, a thick vapour like dust, Nm. hebwa fine dust, powder, mutahabbi weak in sight.

Abuera, and abura, s., d. for kabuer, q.v.

Āfa (āva), s., father, an afa his father. See āb, d. voc. afa.

Āfa, v., swim (man, or animal), d. ofa.

Afā ia, v. t., carry (him, or it), d. ofēa. The first meaning seems not connected with the second, to a European, but a native connects them thus : a man afa natas swims or floats on the sea, the sea afa natamole bears or carries the man; so a man afa ki nakasu swims holding a floating stick, but if he gets on to the stick and lets it float him ashore the stick is said to afa ia carry him. The sea or the stick carry him thus, hence afa, v. t., denotes carry a man on one's back, then to carry anything on the back : and as a man so carried clasps with his arms the carrier round the chest the head of an axe is said to afa its handle, and as one carrying a basket on his back holds the string of it over his shoulder, so a man drawing a log by a string thus over his shoulder is said to afa it, and a tug steamer is said to afa or tow a ship. A dog afa a piece of meat, carrying it off firmly held by its teeth, and a man afa a pipe or a twig, i.e., carries it held by his teeth. A messenger afa, carries, his message, a horse its rider, and a warrior afa, carries, i.e., leads his troop ; also a person afa narogitesan bears a disease or infirmity or trouble. (See bāfa.)

Afāfa, v. redupl., dd. ofaofa, ofafa. [My. apung, s., a float, ampung, a., buoyant, kambang, v., to float. Sa. opeope, to float, Epi mava, d. mia, to swim ; Sa. fafa, v., carry a person on the back, faafafa, s., a burden carried on the back, Mg. baby, a., carried on the back, mibaby, v., to carry on the back (as children and others are carried), Fi. vava, v., to carry on the back, va-ya, to make a bundle, as of sticks, to carry on the back, ps. vai, cf. bai a, fai a, infra.] A. 'āma, swim (man), go (camel), 2, dispose in sheaves or bundles : Nm. float, swim. 'Amat a bundle, a float, or raft, for carrying things across water. In this A. word there is the idea of connecting together (as things in a bundle, &c.) Cf. the cognates under bau, mau, &c., infra, viz., 'amma, &c. In afaia, carry him, as a floating stick carries a man in the water, or a horse carries him on land, the transitive preposition = bi (afai = 'āma bi) gives the verb its

transitive force, make to swim, to go, i.e., carry.

Afa ki, v. t., and ōfa ki, to bury, Maka tāfaki, pr. n., name of the person who buried the first men who died in the beginning of the world, according to native story. [Sa. ufi, v., cover, conceal, ps. ufitia, with instrumental particle ufita'i, ufi, s., a cover, ufi, s., the yam, Efate ui, or uui (pronounced uwi), the yam, Mg. afina, vo'afina is concealed, miafina to conceal oneself, manafina to conceal, to bury, My. buni to conceal, concealed, mámbuni to conceal, tàrbuni, sambuñi, &c. See bei, infra.] A. "āba be concealed, 2 to conceal, to bury, 5 be absent. See egg. s. v. bei, infra. "Ayāb" roots (so called because buried in the ground or covered with earth), Sa. ufi, Ef. uwi, Ja., My. uwi, ubi, Mg. ovy (uvi) yams.

Afaru na, s.,d. ofari, wing, wings. [Ero. evlok, Tidore filafila, Torres Islands perperi, wing, My. mibar, mabur, to fly with wings.] H. 'abar, Hi. to soar, mount upwards in flight, 'eber and 'evrah wing feather (with which birds soar).

Af ia, v. t., to be near to, d. ōf ia, A. wahafa to approach, draw near to.

Afin ia, v. t., afan ia, afen ia, also dd.

Afis ia, and afit ia, to put or carry under the arm or arms, held between the arm and the side; to cover with its wings, as a bird its young, clasping between the wing and the side, and afini na, s., armpit, axilla, and d. afili na, id., also the groin. [My. kâpet, mângâpet, carry under the arm, Sa. afisi, carry under the arm.] A.'Ibit', pl., ābat' armpit, axilla, abt, 5, place, or carry under the arm, 'ibat' what is put under the arm, anything put or clasped to the side.

Afiti, s., a slave. This word occurs with the article as nàfiti. [My. beta, Ja. patik, a slave.] H. 'ebed, Ch. 'abad, a slave. See bati, v.

Afo, s. See foga.

Afuafu. See abuobu.

Agau, d. nikam, s., a, or ni, art., and kam, or gau, nippers, tongs: from the verb kamu, q.v. [Fi. ai qamu, id., My. angkub forceps, nippers, pincers.] See kamu, kamut.

Aga (anga), for anka, art., a., and prep. ka, literally that or the to, or that which to; a particle prefixed to the nom. suf. pron., forming a poss. pron. Without the art. it is pronounced ka, q.v. See kagu, &c., for meaning.

Agana, poss. pron., 3 sing.; aga, na. See kana, kakana, kanana, and for meaning and use see under kiana.

Agama, poss. pron., 2 sing.; aga, ma. See kama.

Agagu, poss. pron., 1 sing; aga, gu. See kagu.

Ag'gami, poss. pron., 1 pl., excl.; aga, gami. Kagamî.

Agagita, poss. pron., 1 pl., incl.; aga, gita. Kagita.

Agamu, poss pron., 2 pl.; aga, mu. Kamu.

Agara, poss. pron, 3 pl.; aga, ra. Kara.

Agam, pron., 2 pl., you, ye; dd. igam, nigami, nigkam (gk for g), akam, egū, art., a, or i, e, or ni, and the pers. pron. 2 pers. pl. kam, gam, gami, which in one dialect, without the art., is kumu, in another is kami, q.v.

Ag, pron., 2 sing., you, thou; dd. nāgo, nīgo, nēgo; a, or na, ni, ne, art., and g. go (for k, ko). See k, ko, ku, ki.

Agi, or aki, particle consisting of the art. a, and prep. gi (for ki, q.v.) to, of; dd. nig', nag', nigi or nigki (ng for g), in which the art. is na or ni. Agi is often equivalent to ani, q.v., but not always: ani or ini sometimes means "of" nearly in the sense of "from." as rarua ini sū? a canoe of (from) what place? which cannot be expressed by rarua agi sū? See the preps. ki and ni. Agi is often equivalent to the simple prep. gi, or ki, but sometimes it means the, the (thing), that which of, the art. having the force of a relative pronoun.

Agiēgi, s., c. art. nagiegi, the air, breeze: lagi.

Aginago, poss. pron., 2 sing., thy, of thee; agi, nago.

Aginai, poss. pron., 3 sing., his, her, of him; agi, nai.

Aginami, poss. pron., 1 pl. excl., our and theirs, of us and them; agi, nami.

Aginara, poss. pron., 3 pl., their, of them ; agi, nara.

Aginau, poss. pron., 1 sing., my, of me ; agi, nau.

Agita, poss. pron., a, prep., and nom. suf. gita ; a, gita. [Sa. a tatou, Mg. antsika.]

Ago, pron., 2 sing., you, thou ; ag, nãgo.

Agu, poss. pron., 1 sing., my ; a, gu. [Sa. aʻu, Ma. aku, Mg. ahy, my.]

Agumu, poss. pron., 2 pl., your ; agi, kumu.

Aheka, d., tasila, d. tasiga ; sila ia.

Ais, or eis, ad., here, d. ieta ; a, or e, or i, prep., and is, see sa, se, s, this, here ; d. esas, q.v. [Mg. aty, ety, ato eto, Ta. yesa. My., without prep., sini, sika, and with preps. di and ka, disini, kasini.] H. zeh, without prep., here, properly this, Ef. se, this, here, E. zĕya here. Also H. bazeh, E. bazya, c. prep. ba, with which is to be compared Ha. ma in manei here, and also generally. The prep. a, e, or i was also similarly used. See examples of this under the word igin, infra.

Ai, s., c. art. nai, water, d. for nifai, q.v.

Aime, s., c. art. naime, a stream : preceding word, and me, q.v.

Aka, a., d. koa, and koakoa, a., stringy, fibrous, as a yam when cooked (bad to eat) ; akoa na, or ako ana, root, its root, lit. and fig. ; aka, a relative, family connection (considered as root or off-shoot

from), aka na, d. ek, eka na ; in one place ek or eka denotes great grandfather, and great grandmother (which in another place is denoted by tai la, or tai, q.v.), in another place aka denotes mother (used by a child addressing its mother), d. iak (i, art.), mama; aka na, or uaka na (waka na) fissure, inside of fissure, as of the mouth, of a canoe (hold), of a bag or basket, or of anything ; kaka naniu the fibrous substance like coarse cloth that grows round the top of the stem of the cocoanut tree (naniu) ; makaka, to be ragged or fissured, as cloth ; mako, or maka, offspring, in pr. nn. as mako naru, &c.; taumako, the wild yam growing on the hills, so called because koa or fibrous. Koa has the a. ending a. [To. aca, Fi. waka, My. akar, Mg. faka, root, Ma. long and thin roots, akaaka fibrous roots, kaka a fibre or hair, a garment, a kind of net, Ha. aa niu = Ef. kaka naniu, also roots (small), offspring, a pocket, a bag, a coarse kind of cloth, Sa. aa fibres of a root, family connection. Mg. kaky, ikaky (i art., cf. Ef. aka, iak) father, papa, Tah. aa root, sieve, &c., aaa the stringy substance in any kind of food or vegetable, native cloth that is not well worked.] A. ʻakka, n.a. ʻakak, to be split, fissured, ʻakko, a fissure, ʻakikaʻ a bag (pera viatoria, Ha. aa), also like ʻakiko and ʻikkaʻ, hairs of a fœtus ;

'awako, small shoots sprouting from the upper part of a palm, 'ikkano. shoots sprouting from the roots of palms and vines, 'akka, 4, to send forth such shoots from the roots *(palms or vines)*, cf. Mg. faka root, caus. verb mamaka to send forth roots, and My. akar roots of a plant, scandent plant, parts of a plant that climb.

Akam, d.; a, art., and kam, you; pers. pron., 2 pl. See kumu.

Akamus, preceding word, with dem. s suffixed, as it is in E. to pers. prons.

Akē, interj. See ako, ako ri. [Mg. akay!] A, interj., and ke, q.v.

Akē ri, interj., akē or aki and *ri*, as in ako ri.

Aki, prep., i.q., agi, q.v.

Akit, d., pron., 1 pl., incl., we and you. [My. kita, Tag. kita, Fut. akitea, An. akaija.] See nininta.

Akoa na, or ako ana, s., root. See aka.

Ako, interj. For ri, dem. particle, used also as an expletive, and la, ad., see these words.

Ako ri la, interj.

Ako ri, interj. Ako expresses surprise, wonder, admiration, also mourning, commiseration. A, interj., and ko, q.v.

Āl, d., syn. with ēlo, d. āli, the sun. See ali.

Alat ia, v. t. (and let, q.v.) to press together, nip as with scissors, or with the teeth, press between two things drawn together, to press, urge, persist, be importunate with, to grasp.

The final consonant is often dropped ;

Ala, s., c. art. nāla, a basket or purse the edges of whose mouth can be closed by being drawn or pressed together, women's carrying basket ;

Alati, s., scissors, nippers, clippers ;

Alaterabati, also alati bati ore, to gnash the teeth, lit., press the teeth together creaking. See bati and ore ;

Ala goro ki, v. t., press, urge. See goro ;

Alāla, a., compressing. [Mg. lasitra, mandasitra to pinch.] H. Lahas to press, squeeze, 'alas to urge, S. 'elas coegit, arctavit, A. lahis' angustus, arctus (drawn, pressed together).

Alalu, i.q. elalo, q.v. See alo na.

Alau, s. ; a, prep, and lau, sea ; also elau, d. elà, the sea, on the sea, seawards. [Malo a lau, Epi lau, My. laut, Ja. lahut, lot, Tag. dagat, Marshall Islands lojet, the sea, My. lauti, v., and malaut, v., to put to sea, be at sea in a boat or ship.] A. logg', and loggaǔ', or lojjaǔ', middle and depth of the sea, ocean, lajja, or lagga, 8, the sea was wide and deep, or such a sea was sailed over, 2, he entered the vast and deep sea.

Alekabu, c. art, talekabu, d. for arekabu.

Ali, s., c. art., nāli, leaf, leaves : ulua.

Ali, s., day (d. ali sun, d. ali

light, see lina). Sera ali, every day, toko ali, stay at home during the day, not going to work. Usually this word is doubled, as

Aliati, s., day (for aliali). [An. adiat]. And

Aliati, v., to day, to dawn, to lighten as the dawn. See al, alo, elo, the sun, also meta ni al, meta ni elo, the sun, lit., eye, *i.e.*, source of day or light. [Mg. andro, Malo alo, My. ari, hari, Sa. la, Ma. ra, day; Sa. la, Ma. ra, My. mata-ari, Mg. maso-andro, the sun.] A. nahār', daylight, day (from sunrise to sunset), H. nharah, light, daylight, S. nhār, A. nāra, to shine, be light, 2, to dawn, lighten as the dawn.

Al ia, v. t., for gal ia, or kal ia, q.v.

Ali, and alia, s., place, part, alia n, its place or part, d. male n, or mile n; luān, that place, there, for alia uan, li bān, d. lo bōn, there (li for alia); mala, and malo, a place, a part, malo, time, *i.e.*, a part of time, as malo ni aliati a part of the day, malo uan, that time, or that place, malo, trunk of the body, or of a tree, mala malala, an open place or plain, also the village dancing and public worship ground, mal-mal, redup., a small place or part; mālu, malumalu, to be bare, clear, as a piece of ground, to be bare, devoid of hair, as the face, malamala naked. [Fi. mala a part, Sa. malae the open space where public meetings are held, Tah. marae the sacred place formerly used for worship, marae, a., cleared, as a garden, or a place of worship, Ma. marae enclosed space in front of a house, a yard, maramara, a small piece.] A. 'ariya to be naked, 'arā', 'arā', 'arat', an open place, tract, part, mo'rai, and mo'rat', naked part of the body not covered with clothing, H. 'arah to be naked, 'arah a naked or bare place, ma'ar a naked space, void space, ma'ārah a naked place, *i.e.*, a plain or field devoid of trees, 'A. mo'arrai, naked, bare.

Aliāli, v. i. (doubled), to delay, be slow, and taliali, id., intensive. [Cf. Ha. alia, v., to wait.] A. āla (alu), and, 2, alla', and, 5, to delay, be slow.

Alialia, v. i., or a., insane, to be insane : connected with this is ululia inspired, possessed, or entered by a deity (natemate) or demon, and, therefore, as a matter of course, out of one's senses. Alialia is not used in some places where ululia (for uluuluia) is used in both senses ; this latter word is also pronounced luluia, and lulia. It is a reduplicate and has the a. ending ia, and literally means entered (*i.e.*, by a spirit), possessed. [Sa. ului-tino enter the body, possess (as by an *aitu*), ulu to enter, and tino body, Ha. uluia and uluhia to be inspired, possessed by a spirit, ulu to have spiritual possession, good or bad, ulala insane, out of one's senses, Tah. uru to be inspired, uruhia inspired. This last word corresponds to Sa. ulufia, which simply means entered, being the passive of ulu to enter. Tah. taura a pretended prophet or some-one inspired by some god or goddess. Corresponding to Sa. ulu to enter is Mg. idi*tra* to enter, and with this latter is connected the reduplicate ad-ala insane, senseless, a lunatic, a fool (cf. Ha. ulala). Ef. lāla an idiot, senseless person, fool, may belong here also, and cf. Fi. lialia foolish, crazy, an idiot.] Ch. 'alal to enter, S., id., 'al he entered, imp., 'ul enter, A. "alla he entered.

NOTE.—The A. is followed by prep. fi, the S. by b and also l (A. li): the first of these preps. is used in Mg. (amy), as in Jno. xiii. 27, Satan nidi*tra* ami*ny*, entered into him ; and the second (any, sometimes contracted to an and a), as in Lu. xxii. 3, and often : in Sa. we have the first in the fi of ulufia, hi of Ha. uluhia, and the second in the i of ulu-i-tino and of Ha. uluia. This is the verb constantly used in S., Mg., and Sa., to denote the entering into a man of a spirit. The Ef. and Fi. use another and synonymous verb, Ef. sili to enter, Fi. curu, id., which is used also in A. to express this idea, and the first of the above preps. is sometimes used in all three languages, as in Lu. xxii.

3, Ef. sili-fi, Fi. curu-mi, A. fi : for the A. verb corresponding to sili, curu, see sili, *infra*. In the three languages both verb and prep. exactly cor-respond, and express (that Satan) entered into (Judas).

Alo, s., d., the sun. See ali.

Alo-fi a, v., wave (with a circular and rolling motion) to him, beckon to by so waving the hand, or a branch of a tree ; alo, and prep. fi : bialo, v. r., wave often, or wave to each other, alo-alo wave repeatedly, tālo go round, avoid, turn round, taloalo keep going round (as on a zigzag or crooked path), turn round. See next word.

Alo n, or alu n, s., belly, abdo-men, the front, before, d. al' naru na, belly, *i.e.*, palm (or front) of his hand; reduplicate lalo n, or lalu n, id., elalo, be-fore (e prep., and lalo front), d. elol, in the belly, inside, an enclosure, d. lōga. [Fi. yalova, Ml. P. oruvi, Ml. U. oluve, TaSa. lobe or iove, Malo alovi, to beckon, To. taloo to beckon, Sa. alo to fan, talo to fan, to beckon, to wave a piece of *tutuga* over the dead, begging him to take calamities and diseases with him, alofi to sit in a circle, alofilima palm of hand (*i.e.*, front or belly of hand), Sa. alo belly, under side, Ma. aro face, front, Ha. alo belly, face, Ma. arohi to look for, arohirohi to turn round and round, Ha. aloalo to turn this way and that, alo to elude, to oppose (face, front), to swim (wave hands), double (as a cape, *i.e.*, go round).] H.'ul belly, abdomen, so called from its roundness, A. alo : the root is 'ul, and 'il, not used as a verb in H., and its primary notion is to roll, turn round, as is seen in its (derivatives and) cognates, as H. ḫul, gil, galal, 'agal, &c., and A. alla (awl, &c.) The meaning of Ef. elalo in front, before (e = in) is secondary, the radical meaning being in the belly, inside, and it is as opposed to etaku (e taku) behind, at the back (taku radically denoting back, as na taku natamole a man's back), that it has the former meaning. It should be noted that Gesenius points out that a secondary meaning of the root 'ul is to be strong, powerful, whence, el, strong, God ; and that thence arises a third notion, that of pre-eminence (A. awila to go before, precede), whence H. 'ulam prop. *front*, then *vestibule*.

Al' (naru) (for alo naru), d., palm (belly) of the hand. [Ml. P. aro, Malo lolo.]

Alo ana, or aloa na, s., maternal uncle ; vocative (reduplicate) lolo (cf. abab, mama). [In Ef. dd. syn. auaua, bau. Malo taura (ta art.), maternal uncle.] A. ḫ'alo maternal uncle. See next word.

Aloara, a. ; alo, and a. ending ara or ra ; and

Aloaloara, a., redupl., spotted,

marked. [Sa. ilaila, a., spotted, marked, ila, s., a mother's mark, a mark in the skin, To. ila a mole or mark in the skin.] A. ḫ'alo, pl. ḫ'ilān, mole or mark in the skin, aḫ'yalo, a., having such marks in the skin, spotted, marked.

Alo-fi a, v., rub on (to) it ; alo, v., and prep. fi. See loa, and lo-fi a. A. ḫalā, ḫalū, or ḫalō, rub, smear.

Alikas, s., c. art. nālikas, for na uli na kasu, leaf or leaves of trees. See uli, and kasu.

Alsēr, s., c. art. nālsēr, dried or withered cocoanut leaves, so called because jagged : from nal for na uli, leaves, and sere, jagged.

Alu na, s., for alo na, q.v.

Ama, poss. pron., 2 sing., thy : a prep., and nom. suf. ma. [Sa. au, Mg. anao, thy.]

Amau, a., true : in loamau, q.v., lo a thing, and amau, also mau, mori, mauri, true. H. aman. See mau.

Amos ia, v., to carry on the shoulder, to bear, to carry. Often the final s is dropped ; hence

Amo, v., to carry, to put a load on the shoulder ; and

Amo-taki, d., id. ; and

Amo-rua, am'rua (rua two), to carry two (burdens), one on each end of a stick (as a Chinaman carries two baskets) ; the word also occurs in tak'amo, d. takiamo to carry a burden on only one end of such a stick ; and

Amoamo, c. art. namoamo, s., a burden, lit., that which is carried. [Sa. amo, v., to carry on the shoulders, amoga, s., a burden, Ha. amo, to carry a burden on the shoulder, to carry.] H. 'amas, bear, carry, especially lift up a load and put it on a beast.

Amo, s., c. art. namo na, the lungs, but also

Am' kanoa, the heart, and

Am' insat, the lungs (see kanoa, insat); and

Am' molu, the spleen. [Fut. ama, Sa. mama, the lungs, To. mama, id., Ha. akemama, the lungs, from ake liver, and mama. In To., Sa., Fut., and Ha., mama (a reduplicate) means light, to be light (opp. of heavy), but this is not the stem to which the word mama denoting the lungs belongs, and does not occur at all in Ef., though the Ef. amo is manifestly the same as Fut. ama, and Sa. (reduplicate) mama, the lungs. For analogues of akemama see under the word ate, the liver. In Ef. uateam', q.v., the kidneys, is ua ate am', lit., fruit of the liver (or inside) of the belly (am', the belly): uateau (d. uateaf) is d. for uateam', and balau, q.v. (for balam'), the common Ef. for inside, is lit. the hollow of the am' (amo), i.e., belly. See following—

Amo, s., c. art. namo, the soft forming kernel of a young cocoanut: so called like the internal parts of man or animal from the softness and smoothness:

Amoamo, v. i., a., reduplicate, to be soft and smooth, as the forming kernel of a young cocoanut, or the intestines or viscera, or any smooth or polished surface: d. momoa. [Sa. mama, a., clean (i.e., smooth), Tah. clean, not soiled or polluted, To. and Ma. ma clean, white.] A. ma'y', pl. ām'a' intestinum; also, a level place between two rugged places (Ef. na momo, or na amo'mo, a smooth and level place between the rocks in a reef), ma'a, 4, to have dates ripe or ripening (a palm), ma'w' dates on the tree, ripe or growing ripe, ma'i soft, smooth (of food), ma"y' softness of skin, H. me'eh only in pl. me'im or m'ey intestines, the belly, then the bosom, heart: eg. is A. maha to gleam with whiteness, to gild, whence mahw' new soft dates. Gesenius gives the radical meaning as "flowing down softness," see H. ma'ah.

Amo'mo, or am'mo, c. art. nam-omo, or nam'mo; see s. preceding word: d. momo.

Amori. See mori.

Amos ia, v. t., to rub, to rub in order to make smooth: mos ia, mus ia. A. wamasa to rub (a thing), to rub (a thing) that it may be smooth.

Amu, poss. pron., 2 pl., your: a, prep., and nom. suf. mu.

Ana, form of pers. pron., 3 sing., he, she, preserved in aneana: other forms nai, enea (inia), gā (nga).

Ana, poss. pron., 3 sing., his, her, its : a, prep., and na, nom. suf. [Sa ana, id., Mg. azy, has the same prep. a, but pre-fixed to the separate pron. like Ef. anai, d. inea, his, her, its.]

Anagagu, anagama, anagana, anagagita, anagami, anagamu, anagara (or anagata), poss. prons., syn. c. agagu, agama, &c., q.v.

Anaga, in these words, is the same as aga, in agagu, and anaga is related to aga as nagi or nig to agi, that is, the prefix to the prep. ga (or gi) is the art. with or without its n.

Anai, poss. pron., 3 sing., his, her, its : a, prep., and nai.

Anāna, poss. pron., 3 sing., his, her, its, d. for aneana, q.v.

Anĕana, poss. pron., 3 sing., of him, his, her, its : anĕ or anī, q.v., prep., and ana, a form of the pers. pron., 3 sing.

Anekabu, c. art. nanekabu, d. for arekabu.

Anekama, c. art. nanekama, d. for arekabu.

Anekabu, c. art. tanekabu, d. for arekabu.

Anēna, d. for aneana.

Anēra, for anĕara, often pro-nounced anēta, anĕata, d. arĕ-ara, poss. pron., 3 pl., of them, their; prep. anī, and ara, pers. pron., 3 pl.

Anēta, d. for anēra.

Anī, prep., particle consisting of the art. a and prep. nĭ, q.v., and often used for the simple prep. ni, of, belonging to (geni-tive prep.), for (dative, rare, this is usually expressed by

magi, nag', or nig', q.v.) : generally synonymous with agi, q.v. for a difference. Some-times pronounced inĭ (enĭ), and contracted to a, in, i, or e, and having among other meanings that of "in" (cf. the contraction in English of i' for in, as "i' the forest," for "in the forest"), or "at," or "on," as etaku or itaku behind (at the back), elau or alau on the sea, also to the sea, seawards, as ba ki elau, go seawards, or to the sea, ki e being two preps. of similar meaning, the one strengthening the other (cf. My. akan, Mg. ho any, ho a).

Anĭgami; d. syn. c. aginami; poss. pron. 1 pl. excl., of us—them (of us and them): anĭ, prep., and gami (for nani), pers. pron. 1 pl. excl. See nami, kinami.

Anigita; d. aninita, q.v. ; poss. pron. 1 pl. incl., of us—you (of us and you): ani prep., and gita (for nīta). See ninita, nita.

Animu; d., syn. c. agumu; poss. pron. 2 pl., of you, your : a, prep., and nimu (for nikamu), d. nikam, pers. pron. 2 pl.

Aninita, d. obsolete, syn. c. anigita : ani prep., and nita, pers. pron. 1 pl. incl. See ninita, nita.

Anĭ, v., usually pronounced enĭ, d. onĭ, contracted to an, en, a, o ; c. preformative m' or ma, it is mān, mā, bān (and mbān), bā, dd. bon, bēn, bao, baon, maon ; to abide, to be, as i

ani or i an suma he abides or
is at home (in the house), i
man or i ma tafa he is on the
hill, i man or i ma rarua it is
in the ship or canoe, i ma or i
an til ia, but ia, he abides
(continues) or is telling it,
doing it.

NOTE 1. — The verb an
may be thus used before
any verb, like toko (contracted
to) to sit, dwell, be, with
which it is nearly synonymous.
But an tano *lies* or *is* on the
ground, toko tano, or to atano
sits on the ground, tu tano
stands on the ground. Both
tu and toko are used before
other verbs like an, and toko
til ia, tu til ia, like an til ia,
denote to abide, continue, or
be telling it. Another verb,
tau, q.v., is used in the same
way before other verbs, as i
tau til ia, but ia, he abides, or
is constantly, habitually, or
addictedly, or repeatedly, telling, doing it. These verbs
thus used before other verbs
are auxiliaries, not of tense,
but of "form," expressing
continuance, intensity, repetition ; and as in the English
phrases "I do say it," "I
must say it" (where *say* is the
simple infinitive after the
auxiliaries *do* and *must*), the
verb immediately following
them is the infinitive.

NOTE 2.—The preformative
m', ma' (mĕ, mī) is used with
toko, tu, and tau, as well as with
anī, an, as matoko (or mato), dd.
batoko, fatoko (vatoko), matu,

batu, fatu (vatu), mītau or
mĕtau : with this preformative
these verbs have much the
same meaning as without it ;
they have the same meaning
with the added idea of continuance or intensity. [Mg.
monina dwell, reside, inhabit,
onenana, fonenana (a dwelling),
mponina (dweller).] A., 4)
"aniya, to dwell, abide, 8) to
be, ma"na' dwelling, cf. H. 'un
to rest, to dwell, ma'on a dwelling.

Ani na, c. art. nani na, s., child,
son or daughter, dd. ati, atu.
[My. anak, Mg. anaka, id.,
My. kanak (see kanao, kano,
infra), Mg. zanaka, id., c. arts.
k' and z'.] A. wald', walad',
walid', E. waldĕ, Amh. wandĕ,
T. wadĕ, H. yalid, one born,
child, son, from the verb H.
yalad, A. walada, to bring
forth, bear (*a mother*), to beget
(*a father*), A. walid', parent,
genitor, father, walidat' mother,
genitrix (Nm. wêlid, wêlida,
Ct. walidah). My. bâranak
(Makassar, ma-ana), to bear a
child, bring forth any offspring,
have children, be a parent, Sa.
fānau (cf. A., 4) to bring forth,
fananau, fanafanau, fanaua
(ps.), fānau, s., offspring, children, fanauga, s., offspring,
child-bearing.

NOTE.—The word ani, or ati,
atu, son or daughter, probably
represents an original mascu
line (and so that denoting
father, A. walid, Ml. and Santo
tata, voc., reduplicate, Santo d.
tai, Mg. ray), but the word

belonging to this stem denoting mother, the ancient
feminine (wĕlida, walidah).
This is in Ef. d. raite na, or
reita na mother, d. cre na (for
era na), Ta. iti, d. rih, Am. rahi,
An. risi, Ml. risi, d. are, Epi d.
la, Pa. lati, Fila lĕta, Celebes
leyto: Ef. voc. tete (cf. abab, or
mama) a reduplicate; also belong here Ef. atene na grandmother, and d. atia na, id.,
the vocative of which, a reduplicate, is tata. In one dialect
atia means also grandfather.
In Epi mother, in one d. la, in
another is kaine, i.e., ka art.,
and ine (for ina) mother, and
this latter is the prevailing
form of this word in the Malay
Archipelago (see Wallace's list),
Amboyna, Ceram, &c., ina, Mg.
reny and ineny (reduplicate,
voc. Ta. d. nana), Sa. tina ; the
Sa. tina is t' art., and ina,
Fut. jina, Aniwa nana, Epi d.,
without art. ani, Mg. r-eny
Celebes undo, Bu. indok, ina,
My. ind-u, J. id-ung ; also
Ysabel ido, San Cristoval ina,
Motu tina, Mare nene, Duke of
York na.

Ānoï, or ānuï, s., c. art. nānoï,
or nānuï, vir, husband, male :
m has been elided from the
beginning of this word as in
noai, d. nai, d. nifai (nivai),
q.v., water ; d. ñiane (mwāne),
ma'an (mo'an), male.   See
mane.

Anu, d., pers. pron. 1 sing., I.
See kinau.

Ānu na, s. c. art., nanu na, his,
her, its shadow, i bi ān' fŭr
it is an empty appearance,
mere shadow (worthless).
[Epi ununo, Malo unu, Ml. d.
nunu, id.]   And

An', s., a rope, c. art. nān'.
These two meanings are also
found in the A.   A. 'anna, n.
a. 'annu, 'ananu, 'ununu to
present itself, to appear, 2, to
hold with a rein ; 'ānu a long
rope, 'ananu and 'inanu ad-
paritio rei, 'ananu clouds, II.
'anan a cloud.

NOTE.—The radical mean-
ing of H. anan is to cover,
and cognate are kanan and
ganan ; A. janna, or ganna, to
cover, to be dark (of the
night), to be possessed by a
demon and insane, jinnu, or
ginnu, darkness of night, also
demons, spirits, or every kind
of them (this is the jin of the
"Arabian Nights "), hin a kind
of demons, ginniyyu a demon
or spirit, ganunu genii.   In
Ef., d., unu ghost, d. inini
spirit, soul, Ml. P. oni, noni
n, his soul, or his shadow, Epi
d. anunu soul or spirit, Epi
(Baki) unu, c. art. niunu soul
or spirit, ununo shadow ; and
Ml. oni, Malo unu, one's likeness in water or in a looking
glass.   Ef. ate, q.v., denotes
the soul, a spirit, one's
shadow, and one's likeness in
water or in a looking-glass.

Ao (or au), v., d., to bark (as a
dog).   See bakau.   [Sa. ou,
id.]

Āo, ad., yes.   [Ma. au.] See äu.

Ara, form of pers. pron. 3 pl., preserved in areara : other forms uāra, nigara (gara), enera, kiniara.

Ara, s., a fence : c. art. nāra, d. nār : see koro, c. art. nakoro, id. (ara has the initial k elided), Nār fāt, d. for nakoro fatu, a stone fence.

Ara ia, v. t., seek, ara ika search, look for fish, come seeking, ba ara go or come seeking, ti ara press after seeking. [Fi. qara, v. t., seek, qaqara, qaraqara, vakasaqara.] A. ḥala, 3, n. a. ḥawal', v. t., seek.

Araara, or arāra, v., reduplicate of ara, to join to, join together, connect with, arāra naui, attach the yam vines to stakes, arāra nia connect it, arara ni ora naui ki nakau connect or attach the yam vine to the stake : arāra ki nalo na agree to his voice (judgment, opinion, &c.), lit. join on to it, syn. sokari nalona : oraorana, q.v., variegated, belongs to this stem. H. ḥabar, S. ḥbar, E. ḥabara, to join together, connect with ; then, to agree with someone ; then, to be banded, striped, variegated, A. ḥabara, ps. ḥubira to be striped, E. ḥubur coloured, variegated, adorned with various colours, Ch. ḥabarbar spotted. Primary meaning, bind together.

Arāra, s., heat, arāra ni elo heat of the sun : see next word.

Arān, or orān, d. arain, d. on, d. uen, s., c. art. nārān, &c., sand. In on and uen (wen), the r is elided, the n of on, like that of manĕ (male), q.v., is non-radical. [Sa., Ma., Tah., To., Ha, one, and one-one sand ; oneonea (a, a. end-ing) sandy.] A. ḥorr', or ḥorron, sand, from ḥarra to be hot, whence ḥarārat heat, Ef. arāra heat.

Arai, d., dem. pron , this, that. For the final ai, see uai. [Ha. la, Ma. ra there, Fut. ra that, Mg. iroa that, there, ery, ary, there.] S. hal, H. halah there, connected with the dem. H. hal, A. al, the art., Ch. alu, aru, Ch. and Talmud harē, are, dem., lo ! there ! Of this dem. syllable al, hal, ar, har, Gesenius remarks— "It is hard to say which form is the more ancient and primitive ;" it is seen also in Arm. ḥarka, ḥalkah, here, H. elleh, &c., these, those, and in Ef. arog (d.), eri, erik, eru, q.v.

Areara, d., for aneara, anēra, q.v.; the prep. anī, or anĕ, is arĕ in this word.

Arekabu na, s., c. art. narekabu, the liver. See ate.

Arifon, s., c. art. narifon, diviner, magician. A. 'arrafon a di-viner, from 'arafa to know, divine, 2, make known.

Ari(a), v. t., to plane, scrape off, rub off. [Sa, oro, id.] S. gra' to scrape off, shave, H. gara'.

Arog (arong), d., dem. pron., this. See arai and erik. The final g as in nag, naga, dem.

Āru na, s., c. art. nāru na, hand, arm ; fore-foot of a

quadruped : nāru arms, *i.e.*, weapons of war, war; i bi aru uia he is industrious, lit. a good hand, i bi aru sa he is handless, lazy, lit. a bad hand. [New Guinea dd. uadu, dei, Ml. P. fera, Ml. A. verua, Samang tong, Nias tanga, Borneo dd. tongan, lungan, rongo, tangan, My. tangan, Mg. tánana, d. tángana, Madura Bali tanang.] H. yad hand, S. id., A. yadu (and yaddu), dual yadān ; also, adu, dual adān, hand, arm; fore-foot of a quadruped. The Mg. *tàna*-na compares with the A. adān.

Asa, ad., the day after to-morrow. See nāsa.

Aselī na, s., a friend. [Ml. U. selen, Bu. sölao, id.] A. wasīl', intimate friend, from wasala to join, be joined.

As ia, d. uas ia, v. t., cut, cut out, as asi naniu cut out the kernel of a cocoanut (to make a water vessel of it), asi (lua namena na) cut (out his tongue), asi intălĕ cut the roots of taro (while it is in the water, to pull it out of the ground) : hence maseasi, q.v. S hsa, v.t., cut out (as the eye).

Asī na, s., c. art. nāsī na, the part of the face bearded, jaw, jawbone, chin. [Malo ase TaSa. ese chin, Ml. P. fese chin, ese cheek.] The radical idea is that of *cutting, sharp, tearing.* A. h'add' mala, gena.

Asī ta bunu, jaw cutting dead ; Asī tageli, crooked jaw : these expressions denote, the latter crooked talk, the former talk calculated for and resulting in the death of one hated.

Aso, v.i., to burn, be burning (*a fire*), be kindled, to be burnt or scorched (as one's skin, or food in being cooked). [Fi. qesa, qesaqesa, a , burnt or scorched, as in cooking, An. ececsas, a., burned, acas, or cas, to burn ; hot, burning.] A. wakada, n. a. wakdo, H. yakad, S. ikad, to burn, be burning, be kindled.

Āso, s., a kind of crab, the robber crab.

Āso, or āsu, s., c. art. nāso, or nāsu, a bow (for shooting arrows). [Aurora usu, Paama hisu, Ml. P. vus, Ml. U. vis, Amblaw busu, My. busor, Saparua husu, id.] A. kawsu, or kāsu, id. So called from being curved.

Asoara, s., the rainbow. Cloth brilliantly variegated with different coloured bands or stripes is called na kalu asoara, a phrase in which the word is an adjective. Also a stone fence constructed of three rows or bands of stone is described as asoara. See *infra,* soara (or souara).

Asolat, see soli.

Asua, v. i., to smoke, c. t. prep., asuènia to smoke on to it, or him : c. art. it is s., naasua na the smoke of it, its smoke. [Mg. etona, s., smoke, manetona, v., to smoke, My. asáp (probably this word lit. means smoke of fire, api), bârasâp to smoke, Malo asu, s., mo asu-asu, v., TaSa. asu, s., m'asu, v., Ml. P. ese, s., mi es, v., Ml. A. nahamp basua, s., lit. the fire smokes, basua, v., Sa. asu, s., asua, and asuina, v. ps.] H. 'as'en, to smoke, 'as'an smoke, A. 'athana, 1, 2, 4, to smoke.

At, or āts, c. art. nāt, q.v., banana.

Ata (or nata), s., c. art. nata, d. na eta for na ata, a man, a person ; one, someone ; nata nata, every one. See atamole, atemate, ata na, atamani. [Motlav et, Ureparapara at, man. See below, Note 2.] A. nat', for nas', which is the commonly used plural ("pluralis fractus," a collective or abstract, or singular with a collective meaning), of 'insan', man, male or female, a human being, also umbra hominis (the older plural is 'unas', with which corresponds H. 'enos', Arm. 'anas'a, a man, men), and denotes men, also genii, demons.

Note 1.—A. 'insan, for which there is also 'īsan, corresponds to H. 'is'on, which is formed from 'īs' by the ending on, and denotes, when followed by the word eye, "little man of the eye, i.e., pupil in which as in a glass a little image of a man is seen" (Ges.) ; the A. denotes in addition to the meanings given above " the little image appearing in the pupil of the eye : " A. 'insan is from the root 'ans

and H. 'is' vir, 'is'ah woman, from 'ins', 'ins'ah, hence the pl. of 'is'ah is nas'im, corresponding to A. nisā', niswat, and niswan, women. The words 'is' vir, is'ah woman (and their equivalents in the cognate languages) must be carefully distinguished from that given above under ata (or nata) denoting "a human being" whether male or female, though they all belong to the same root or stem.

Note 2.—According to the above, the t in ata, like that in A. nat', represents an original s as in nas'. In Ef. dd. this t is sometimes pronounced nearly as r, and ts. In other New Hebrides dialects this consonant is found as t, s, r, l ; thus corresponding to Efate ata-mani male (vir) are An. ata-maig, Fut. ta-ne (for ta-ane), Ta. yeru-man, Epi dd. ata-mani, su-mano, Ml. U. oro-man, TaSa. la-mani. My orang, Mg. olona belong here.

Ata na, s., c. art. nata na (or nate na) his spirit, his soul ; his shadow : his image (in water or a glass). This is the same word as the preceding, but in this use has the nom. suf. [Sa. ata a spirit, a shadow, Fut. ata a ghost, shadow, image (as in water), picture or likeness, Fila tano ata, his soul, Ma. ata reflected image, shadow, ata po early morning, ata marama moonlight, whaka-ata mirror, Sa. ataga (from ata a shadow) the mere appearance of a thing, atagia to glisten (as from a reflected light), ataata the red sky after sunset, Ha. aka the shadow of a person, figure, outline, or likeness, aka to light up, as the moon before rising, akalani a heavenly shadow, a splendid light, Ef. atalagi, q.v., the moon.] See preceding word.

Ata ia. or atai a, v. t., to know, d. tai, q.v.

Atakasua, a., jealous; suspicious : from ata (soul), and kasua q.v.

Atalagi, s., usually written atelagi, the moon : from ata (see ata na), and lagi the sky, heaven. [Ha. akalani (a heavenly shadow, a splendid light) is composed of the same two words.]

Atamauri, or atemauri, s., the spirit of a living man that has gone out of him during sleep and been seen by someone. This word occurs in one dialect and is composed of ata the soul, and mauri, q.v., to live.

Atamate, or atemate, s., c. art. natemate, spirit of one dead, ghost, spirits of the dead, demons, good or bad spirits, supernatural beings, objects of worship, gods (gen. name). The word is composed of ata (above), and mate, q.v., to die, be dead, a. dead. [Ml. P. demej, Epi dd. atamate, simaro, Ta. yeramis, Ml. A. temes, An. natmas, id.] The primary meaning of natemate seems to be dead man : thus

a corpse may be called natemate, and natemate sometimes denotes "the dead" in a collective sense.

Atamole, s., c. art. natamole, man, male or female, a human being, same as ata, or nata, with the addition of mole, q.v., to live, a. living. Natamole lit. denotes living man. [Mg. olombelona, id. The Mg. is composed of the same two words as the Ef. ; for olona see ata (above), and for velona to live see mole (below) ; and the meaning of the compound word is the same in each case. At least the initial ta in Fi. tamata, Sa. tangata, Tah. taata, id., belongs here.]

Atamani, s., c. art. natamani, male, lit. a male human being, from ata (above), and mani, q.v., male. [For New Hebrides forms of this compound word, see ata (above). Fi. tangane, Sa. tane, id.]

Atatabu, or at'tab, s., c. art. natatabu, or nat'tab, lit. sacred spirits, sacred stones identified with such spirits, and objects of pagan worship : from ata (above), and tabu, q.v.

Atama s., d. syn. c. ore, the pointed rubbing stick for producing fire by its friction with another stick : a, art., and tama ia, q.v.

Atara, aturiei. See natara, naturiei.

Atāta, v. i., or a., a reduplicate, to have white spots or marks

3

such as show where sores have healed. See next word.

Atāta, s., an albino. The radical meaning would therefore seem to be white. [Cf. Mg. hatsatra white, pale, wan, sickly.] A. was'ah' white spot appearing on the head or feet of a horse, was'ah' whitening spots of leprosy, was'ih' very white; from was'aha to be manifest, white (as milk), &c.

Atĕ, c. art. nătĕ na (d. nănte na), the liver (of a shark), the spleen; in arekabu (for ate-kabu) it signifies the liver or principal viscus of the kabu (or kobu, q.v.), inside, and in uateam, q.v., the proper meaning seems to be the middle, the middle and more important part. [My. ati the liver, then the mind, heart or inside, Mg. aty the liver, the inside, Sa. ate the liver.] A. kabd', kabid'. H. kabed, E. kabdĕ, the liver, Amh. hodĕ, the belly. A. kabid' also denotes the belly with its parts, the middle and more important part (of a thing), the middle (of a thing). E. kabdĕ viscus (nom. gen.), stomach, belly, inside, and particularly the liver, as the heaviest of the viscera. (See Ludolf's E. Lex.) H. kabad, E. kabda, to be heavy (primary meaning).

NOTE 1.—Arĕkabu, q.v., c. art. nărekabu, dd. tālekabu, nănekabu, tānekabu, and nănekama, the liver, is composed of āre (for ate) the

liver or principal viscus, and kabu (for which see kobu the belly, the inside), and lit. denotes the viscus (or liver) of the inside; with are (for ate) corresponds Ml. U. ere, and New Guinea, Maclay Kiiste arre, the liver.

NOTE 2.—With Ludolf's statement (above) compare that in the Ha. Dict., where ake (for ate) is defined as "the liver," and also "a general name for several internal organs, qualified by different terms": thus akeloa spleen (loa long), and also akeniau; akepaa the liver, as well as the simple ake; ake-mama the lungs (see above, s.v. amo). In Sa. atepili the spleen, atevae the calf of the leg, Tah. aterima the thick part of the arm. In Ef. uateam' (d. uateau) the kidneys (see above, s.v. amo) ua-nate-natuo, or ua-nate-tuo, the calf of the leg, in one dialect is denoted by uateau natore, lit. kidneys of the shin (i.e., the leg from the knee to the foot, see tore), and uateau laso denotes kidneys of the scrotum. Ua-nate has exactly the same meaning as uate (i.e., ua-ate) the only difference being that in the former ate c. art. is nate; ua, fruit, is used because the parts spoken of are round or fruit-shaped. In Ef. dd. the calf of the leg is uateau natore, ua-nate tuo (or natuo), and nabela natore, of which the last lit. denotes the belly of the leg (below the knee).

Atelaki na, or atelakia na, s., the owner of it, owner: from a, art., and telaki or telakia, q.v.

Atena na (d. atia na), s., maternal grandmother; voc. tata. See ani na.

Ati na, s., c. art. nati na, child, d. ani na, q.v. [Ma., Tah., ati offspring.]

Atia na, s., paternal grandfather or grandmother: voc. tia. See atena na, tata, tematete ta, tia, tematia ta.

Ati(a), d. uati(a), v. t., d. for ari a, q.v.

Atoara, see natoara.

Atu na, s., c. art. natu na, d. ati na, his, her child, offspring. See ani na.

Ātŭ, c. suf. atu-gia (d. uātŭ) beat, smite, break off or divide off (as a piece of a plantation); atu (namauri) utter (an incantation), at' usi utter rehearsing (see us ia), àtŭ saki plop up (of a turtle, also of the sound of the breath in the throat of a man recovering from a faint or dying); and atu taku turn the back (to anyone on being addressed, as if not aware of it), atu taluko turn oneself (from someone); atu tuai break in pieces (a plantation) giving him (a portion); fiàtu, v. r., to be fighting, to be smiting each other: nalagi atu the wind beating, a hurricane; atu nabau kill (by smiting the head); atu

ualubota rout the enemy (smite, break the enemy). With the ending maki the word, atu-maki, means jerk, snap, as atu-maki jerk (as the branch of a tree), balusa atu-maki to paddle jerking (with a jerking motion of the paddle), atu-maki nalō ra jerk their voices, or snap their voices. A. hatā beat, smite, hatiā be bent, stoop (a man), Nm. heti declaim: cf. hatta to break, to beat off (as leaves from trees), to utter (words).

Atuta (see ta atuta ki), s., set time, or place, as i ta atuta ki nia, he declares a set time to (one), i.e., to meet him on a certain day, or at a certain time (to do something), ru tu natūta they kept the set time, i risugi natuta he changed the set time. See ta atuta.

Atu-maki, v. See atu.

Atu saki, at 'saki, v. See atu and saki.

Atu taku, at' taku, v. See atu and taku.

Atu taluko, at' taluko, v. See atu and taluko.

Atua, s., God. Introduced word. In Meli. c. art. the word tētua (East Mai rētua, To: hotooa, he otua) denotes among the heathen the same as atamate, that is, any spiritual being regarded as having supernatural qualities or powers, as a demon, good or bad, a ghost, a god: it is a general name. A human being on dying immediately becomes a tētua or natamate—

that is, not only a spirit, but, among the heathen, an object of superstitious regard. In Sa. aitu a spirit, a god, seems to belong to the same stem, whence, with a. ending a, aitua haunted. Probably both aitu and atua belong to the same stem as ata, q.v. The word in Ha. (akua), To. (otua), Ma. and Sa. (atua) now denotes God in the Christian sense, and it has been introduced with this meaning into Aneityum, Tanna, Efate, Epi, &c.

Atum-kol, s., echo, lit. offspring of the call or shout, and

Atuma, in pr. nn. atuma-neru offspring of war, &c. See kola, and for atuma offspring, see futum.

Atuta. See p. 19.

Au, verb. pron. 1 pl. excl., we, they, d. pu (for mu): separate pron. kinami we—they; kinau I, verb. pron. a I, d. ni.

Äu, ad., yes, d. äo. A, dem. prefix, and u, or o, for which see o. H. hahu' that (is it).

Au, v. i., to heal, get well, d. for abu, id., q.v.

Äu, s., a kind of lizard, d. for käu, id.

Au, v. i., to bark. See ao.

Aüa (āwa), v. i., or a., fatigued, c. art. näüa, one fatigued. H. ya'af, to be fatigued, ya'ef, fatigued.

Aüä (awä), ad., no, it is not: d. eüo, q.v.

Auaua, s. (awawa, a reduplicate), d. bau, q.v., maternal uncle.

[My. uwa, wa, uwak, an uncle or aunt], cf. A. 'amm', an uncle. See bau na.

Aue, interj., surprise, commiseration. [Sa. aue, alas! oh! of wonder.] A. awwi (&c.), alas! ah! oh!

Aui, interj., surprise, commiseration ; a, dem., and ui, q.v.

Auis, interj., surprise, commiseration ; a, dem., and uis, q.v.

Aul ia, v. t., dd. ul ia, ol ia, uil ia. See ul ia.

Aum, s., c. art. naum, d. for aime, q.v.

Aure, s., a singer, bard, a, art., and ure or ore (see ore). [Fut. goro, Ma. whakaoriori, Ha. olo, My. uraura, Mg hira, to sing, &c.] E halaya, to sing.

Aüta, s., or ad., auta, ashore, on land, d. euta, q.v., a, prep., and uta, q.v.

B a-, or fa-, caus. prefix, originally ma. [Mg ma-, fa-, mpa-.] S. ma- (Maphel conj.), Mod. S. ma-, caus. prefix (St., pp. 110, 111): the Mafel or Maphel is simply the participle of the ancient Aphel (H. hiphil, A. 4).

Ba (bwa), and ua (wa), v. i., to rain = d. boua (bowa). [Epi mboba, mbobo, Ta. ufu, id.] A. ba'a to rain continuously, ba'a'a rain, rain water.

Bá, or fa (va), v., to go, enter (a ship, &c.), tread (go upon), with si suffixed, ba-si to tread, tread upon (go upon). [Fi. va-ca, to tread upon, hence va na, and probably yava na, the feet, Mysol bo, to go. This verb in Ef., &c., is often followed by a "directive," or adverb, which sometimes is suffixed to it, and the expression thus formed may signify either to go or to come, thus, An. apan, go there, apam, come here, Ef. ban, or bano, go there, ba be (d.) come here, (d.) umai (in which the ba is corrupted to u), Sa. o mai, Amboyna uimai, oimai, omai, Mysol bo mun, to come here ; My. pàrgi, pai, to go, is perhaps this pa and rgi or i, pàrgi-mari to come, like Ef. d. bano to go (ba and no), bano-mai to come here. The mai in such phrases as the above, Ef. dd. mai, be, has sometimes, from being an abverb or directive so used after ba, come to be used alone, the ba being understood, signifying to come : thus in one Ef. d. mai, in another d. be (mai and be are forms of the same particle) are now verbs used alone denoting to come here. My. mari hither, here, in like manner used alone signifies to come. See under banotu, notu.] H. bo', ba, to enter, come, go (egg. E. bawi', A. bā, to return, &c.)

Bā, v., to come from (from a place), as Ku ba se ? you come from where ? i ba nalia uan he comes from that place, dd. bai, be, bāki (where the prep. ki = from). [Mg. avy aiza ? = ba se ? = come from where ? come whence ? avy to come.] See under banotu.

Bà ki, v., c. prep., to go to (a place) : ba, and the prep. ki to : ki, to, sometimes denotes from see preceding word.

Bai, v., d., bā, q.v., to come from, as bai se ? come from where ? See under banotu.

Bai, v., to be, d. for bi, q.v.

Bai a, v. t., to gather together in order to carry home, as firewood, or fruit, &c. [Fi. va-ya, ps. vai, to make a bundle, as of sticks, to carry on the back.] See afaia.

Ba, d. mba, final conj., that : used in the conjugation of the future and imperative and infinitive of verbs.

Ba, that thou, sign of 2 pers. sing. imperative ; includes pron. 2 pers. sing. [Motu ba, used in the same way in fut., inf., and imp., Fi. me, in imp. and inf., Ma. me, forming a kind of imperative future, Mg. mba that, Ml. P. ba, b' that, used in conjugation of imp., inf., and future.]   A. fa that (final conj.), &c.

Bā, v., d. for mā.   See anĭ, v.

Bāb, s., d., voc., father = āb, bābu, abāb, id.

Ba na (kba na), s., c. art. na ba na, and reduplicated

Baba na, s., hollows, or channels ; and

Baba, s., c. art. nababa, a hollow, channel, or bed of a stream, dry except after heavy rains :

Baba, s., c. art. nababa, a board : [Sa., Tah. papa, My. papan, id.]

Babu na (d. bamu na), s., c. art. na*b*abu na, the cheek : (My. pipi, Tah. papa—uru, id.] H. gabab to be curved, hollow ; to cut, dig. Hence gab the back (see below, bamu), geb a board : egg. having the sense of hollow, curved, are numerous, as gavah, gafaf, guf, or gup (*infra* kobu, kubu, kabu), kafaf (*infra* kau, kai, kaf), na*k*ab (*infra* na*b*ea, *i.e.*, nak-bea, d. nakima, fafine), bub, 'abab, nabab, &c., and the cg. words in A., &c. Mg. ho-boka hollow, concave, pepo hollow, concave, My. âmpa hollow, To. papa the hollow piece of wood on which *gnatoo* is imprinted, lowpapa a board, &c.

Babatrēga, v. i., or a., variegated, versicoloured, as cloth : the formative prefix ba doubled ; said to be denominative from trôga (toga), q.v., a versi-coloured woven basket.

Bābu, s., d., voc., father : dd. āfa, āb, abāb, bāb'.

*B*āfa, s., a small separate house used only by women dwelling apart from men during menstruation, and also at the time of parturition. From afa to bear, carry, c. pref. *b*a (for ma). See bäofa (d.), which is from ofa, d. for afa, bear, carry : bäofa, though etymologically the same as *b*afa, has a different meaning, no such custom as is implied by the *b*afa obtaining among the speakers who say " baofa." It denotes the act of men-struating, not the house for those menstruating.

NOTE.—In Ha. the house for menstruating women was called hale pea.

Bafanau, same as fanau, q.v.

Bafano, or fafano, v., to wash the hands. See bano lia. [Sa. fafano wash the hands and mouth, Fi. vuluvulu wash the hands. See bulu nia, bano lia, balo nia, &c., *infra.*]

Bafatu, or fafatu, v. t., to trust in, confide in, rely upon. See fatu.

Baga, v. c. See bagan ia, to feed, charge, fill ;

Bagan ia, v. c., to feed, lit. make to eat, bagan ià sa, lit. make him eat it ; caus. prefix ba, and kan to eat. With the n elided baga, as baga nata feed anyone, baga sisi load a gun ; baga, absolute, as i baga (of a pig or a fish) to wander about in search of food ; faga (of fire), nakabu faga a burning or devouring fire, i faga it burns, devours, or eats (of fire, and of an ulcer); nafaga a bribe, nafagafaga a bait. [Fi. vakani-a, Sa. fafaga, feed, cause to eat, Mg. mamahana to feed, also load (a gun), caus. pref. ma, and fahana.] See kan ia.

Bagau-nabau, pr. n., c. art. nabagau-nabau : the feeder of the oven with the slain ; baga, ua, nabau.

Baga, s. See bago, a hill, d. mago, d. bega.

Baga, s., d. for maga, the banyan tree.

Bagabaga, v. i. See bagobago.

Bagarai a, v. c., to dry, lit. make
dry : from gara, kara, dry.
[My. mangaring kan, id.] See
gara, kara.

Bagaranu a i, den. v. c. ; from
ran, c. art. niran, fresh water;
to wash with fresh water after
bathing in the sea : d. bakanaru mia, id. (naru, transposed
for ranu). [Sa. faalanu to
wash off salt water, ps. faa-
lanumia; with 'i faalanuma-'i.]
See ran, s.

Bagi, v., to mount, climb, ascend
(a hill, ladder, tree, ship, &c.);
may also have the prep. ki
before the object, as bagi
nakasu or bagi ki nakasu
climb the tree, bagi to go up,
ascend, bagi ki go up on. [Mg.
akatra, miakatra, id., My.
minggah, id., Ma. piki to
climb, pikitia.] A. 'aka', 4), to
ascend.

Bagobago, v. i., or a., to be
crooked. [Sa. pi'o, pi'opi'o,
id., Ma. piko, bent, Mg.
vokoka crooked, My. bengkok,
Ja. bengkong crooked.]   H.
hafak, S. hpak, A. 'apaka
to turn, &c., H. hapakpak
crooked, twisted.   Hence

Bagobagoa, a., crooked, twisted :
-a, a. ending ; and

Bagobagōra, a., id.: a. ending -ra.

Bago, v., to be behind, i bago
asa he is behind it, as i bago
nakoro he is behind the fence
(of a man behind a fence put
up about his house to shut
out the public view), i bago
nafanua it is behind the land
(of a ship taking shelter under
the lee side of an island in a
hurricane). The word bago
na, s., denotes the heel ; the
lower part of the back (syn.
bisi na); bago nafanua west
end of an island, is the opp.
of meta nafanua east end of
an island (fore-end and heel-
end); bago na kelu, or baga
na kelu is the after part of an
army that (kelu) goes in a
circuitous course to surprise
the enemy—and in all these
senses the word in one dialect
is pronounced mago na, which
is the more original form.
The hills behind the villages,
or not far back from the shore,
on which there is no jungle,
are called bega, baga, d.
mago. This word is much
used in names of places, points
or heels of the land : thus
Pagona is the name of west end
of Deception Island, Havannah Harbour, and Pago of the
long point of land on the
south of Fila harbour ; Selim-
baga a place on Tongoa, &c.
The end of anything, as the
land, a stick, &c., is called
meta-bago na, lit. the eye or
point of its end. [TaSa.
pigo na, end or extremity.]
H. 'akab, A. 'akaba to be behind, to come from behind :
the form (in Ef.) resembles
A. ma'kob, mago, bago : H.
'akeb the heel, A. 'akib' id.,
and the end of a thing : H.
'akeb also denotes the ex-
treme rear of an army, and
'akob a hill, acclivity (A., E.,
id.)

*B*ago na, s., d. for mago na, heel of foot ; back part of body ; hinder end (of an island) in opp. to meta na fore end (*i.e.*, east) ; hinder part of an army ; an end (of anything) ; end of a house (the Efatese house has two ends), hence, inside of a house at the far ends, and then generally in one d. inside (of a house) ; end, *i.e.* bottom, of a hole or deep pit. See preceding word and mago.

Bagote fia, v.c., to buy it, purchase it, lit. to break, separate (from its former owner) a thing, d. bakotufia. See koto.

Bagokot, or bagkot, v., reduplicate of foregoing.

Bā gote fia, v., to break a thing (as a stick) by treading (see bā) on it.

Bai, v., d. bā, to go or come from (a place) : ba v., and prep i., d. bā ki, id., has prep. ki.

Bai, or bei, v., dd. bi, mi, to be, as, i bai fatu it is a stone ; also prep. before the object of many verbs, see bei. See bi ; and bei (or bai).

Baibai, or baibaia, v. i., or a., to be large, wide ; said to be d. for bebea, q.v.

Bai na, s., d. for bau na, the head. See bau na.

Bai, s., d., c. art. nabai na, feathers or covering of a bird : d. for mau na, q.v. [Ma. hou, feathers.]

Bai ! baibai ! interj., surprise and pleasure. [Mg. baba, id.] A. baḥ'i baḥ'i id.

Baina, v., to go there (away from speaker), ba go, i to, na there :

d. binēn' : d. syn. banotu, q.v.

Baka, d. sometimes for baki, v., used also as a prep.: ba to go, and ki (rarely ka) to, as v., i baki nalia uane he goes to that place ; as prep., i bisa baki John he speaks to (or unto) John. [Epi beki ; and Epi d., with prep. ni (instead of ki and equivalent to it) bani, Florida vani.] See preps. ki, ni.

Baka, or faka, caus. prefix. This consists of the caus. prefix ba (or fa), q.v., and the dem. particle ka, q v. [Fi. vaka, Sa. faa, Ma. whaka, Mg. maha, faha, mpaha.]

Note.—As this particle ka (Mg ha) has various uses in Oceanic, and as in baka it is manifestly used in a manner not of local or recent origin, the question arises as to what its exact force in this connection is. In My. ka is prefixed to the verbal noun formed by the suffix an exactly as in Ef. na (the common art.) is to the same verbal noun, and in that case it has the force of an article. In Ja. ka is used in the same way, and in addition prefixed to a verb forms a passive verbal adjective, as suduk to stab, kasuduk stabbed, or passive verb (as it is called) to be stabbed. (So in Fi., as, *e.g.*, voro-ta to break, kavoro broken.) And it is thus that, in the case of the numerals, ka prefixed to the cardinals makes them ordinals in Ja., My., Fi., and Ef. These ordinals having been formed as katolu third (that which or he who is three, that (or what) is three) the causative prefix ba added formed bakatolu make third, cause to be third ; this word in Mg., fahatelo (verbal adjective), is "third," in Ef. i bakatolu is (verb) he made the third (time) at it, and the verbal noun from this verb, formed in the usual way, is nafakatoluan the being or doing the third time. Compare in H. the den. verb formed from the numeral three, Piel (causative) "*to do* anything *the third time*," &c., and Pual part. (verbal adjective) "three-fold," &c. In Ef. bakatolu, though really a verb, is translated into English as an adverb of times—thus i bakatolu bat ia he did it three times, but lit. he made the third time doing it.

Baka roa, v. i., to jerk over to the other side (a canoe sail) : boka tia to strike, and roa to turn round.

*B*āka, s., a fence, a fence of stone or wood made for protection or fortification in war. [Ha. pa a fence, Ma. pa a stockade, fortified place, pā to block up, obstruct.] H. ma'ākeh a parapet (surrounding a flat roof) to hinder one from falling off, from 'akah, A. 'aka' to hold back (and 'āka), hinder, impede.

Baka sia, d. transposed for kaba sia, koba sia, to follow.

Bakabasea, v. c., d. syn. c. suer ia, to scold, vituperate : from base a, id.

Bakabātĕ, or bakafāte, v. c., make the fourth time : from bātĕ, 4. [Mg. fahefatra the fourth.]

Bakabulu tia, v. c., nearly the same as the simple verb bulu tia, q.v.

Bakabunuti, bakamānu, &c. See bakaralima.

Bakafakal ia, v., to console, comfort : reduplicate from bakal ia, id., q.v.

Bakafia, d. bakafisa, v., make how many times ? make how often ? See bisa.

I. Bakal ia, v. c., to soothe, comfort, take tender care of (as of a child, or one in sorrow) : see kal. A. 'agila to soothe, comfort ; E. 'egal, a child, Ef. kal, fakal, and d. kekel, id., usually vocative, and much used in proper names of children, as kal nagusu child of the point (promontory), kal or fakal tamate child of peace, &c.

II. Bakal ia, v. c., to sharpen (as a knife, axe, &c.) H. kalal, Pilpel, to sharpen ; to move to and fro, A., E., id. See makal sharpened, sharp, kala little, &c. H. kalal to be light, to be swift, fleet, to be diminished, little, so A. kalla to be despised, H. kalon, shame, pudenda, Ef. makal.

Bakalailai, v. c., nearly same as simple verb lailai, q.v., to be delighted.

Bakalarua, v. c., make the seventh time, or seven times.

See larua, kalarua. [Mg. fahafito the seventh.]

Bakalatesa, v. c., make the sixth time, or six times. See latesa, kalatesa. [Epi vaari.]

Bakalatolu, v. c., make the eighth time. [Epi vaarolu.] See latolu.

Bakalifiti, v. c., make the ninth time. [Epi vakoveri.] See lifiti.

Bakàleba, v. c., make (himself) great, be proud : leba, laba.

Bakalima, v. c., make the fifth time, or five times. [Mg. fahading, the fifth.] See lima.

Bakamataku ki, v. c., to make afraid, to threaten, frighten : from mataku to be afraid. [Mg. mahatahotra, My. mana kuti, manakut kan, Sa. faamata'u.]

Bakamaturu ki, v. c., make to sleep, put to sleep : from maturu to be asleep, to sleep. [My. manidor kan.]

Bakamauri a, v. c., to make alive, save : from mauri to be alive, live. [Sa. faaola, My. mangidupi, Mg. mamelona.]

Bakametà sa, v. c., to direct the eyes to, look at : a bakametà gu is, i bakameta nà sa, &c., seems to mean lit. I direct my eyes, make my eyes upon it, &c. : meta, or mita, q.v., v., and s. Bakamita, id.

Bakamirara. See mirara.

Bakanaru mia, v. c., naru, transposed for ranu : d. for baga-ranu a i, in the one case m' is the t. prep., in the other a.

Bakarairai, v.c. Nearly the same as the simple v. rairai, q.v.

Bakarau sa, v. c., divide it (among a number of persons), distribute it : from rau, q.v.

Bakàrogo, v. c., make (himself) hear or obey, be humble, quiet, meek ; from rogo, q.v.

Bakàru. See bukaru.

Bakarua, v. c., make the second time, or two times. See rua, karua. [Mg. faharoa, the second.]

Bakaralima, or bakarualima, v. c., make the tenth time, or ten times. [Epi vaduñlimo.] See rualima, or ralima, kara-lima.

NOTE. — The caus. prefix baka may be attached to the word or words denoting any number, as bakabunuti (bun-uti, 100), bakamànu (mànu, 1000), make the hundredth, thousandth time, or one hundred, one thousand times, bakaralima lima (ralima lima, 50), bakamanu ralima (manu ralima, 10,000), make the fiftieth, ten thousandth time, or fifty or ten thousand times, &c.

Bakas, or bokas, s., c. art. nabakas, flesh ; then, a pig (not a sow or a boar) specially reared and esteemed for its flesh ; then, Hades, because of the numbers of such pigs killed on occasion of deaths, especially of chiefs, whose flesh was not only much enjoyed at repeated feasts among the living, but supposed in some way to accompany or follow the souls of the deceased to Hades, and give corresponding gratification to the shades of the departed assembled there : with the prep. a, abakas, or abokas, in Hades. [Epi bukahi a pig (not boar or sow), Fut. pakasi a pig (gen. name), Ero. mpokas a pig (gen. name), An. picad, *i.e.*, picath, a pig (gen. name).] A. manhus' having much flesh, fleshy, from nahas'a to denude a bone of flesh, to take the flesh from off a bone.

Bakasa, v. c., bakasa ki, or bakasá ia, to paint (as the face), hence na fakasa, s., a festival (adornment); to clean, make clean (as a place), to clear, make clear. [Fi. ai qisa paint for the face.] A. nakas'a to paint, to colour ; to clear, make clear (as a place) : bakasa, dd. (trspd.) bisaki, biski.

Bakasau, v. c., dd. bisakau ia, bisaui, bisaku tia, to make or build up a fire, lit., make to join on to, *i.e.*, one stick to another, to make a bigger fire. (By joining together the smouldering ends of two fire sticks and then joining on to them the ends of other sticks a fire is built up.) The initial bi or ba in this word is the causative prefix : the simple verb is siku tia, q.v.

Bakaser ia, v. c., to loosen or remove a tabu (as from a place), make common or non-tabu. See ser ia.

Bakasere a, v. c., to treat kindly carefully providing for, to entertain hospitably. See sere a, ps. masere.

Bakasikai (d. fakasikitika), v. c., make the first time, or one time. [Mg. faharaika the first.] See sikai (or isikai), kasikai.

Bakosoro fia, v. c., make to burn : from soro, v. c., to burn.

Bakatabtabu ki, v. c., make tabu, or declare tabu. See tabu. [To. fakatabu to interdict.]

Bakatar ia, v. c. Nearly the same as the simple verb tar ia, q.v.

Bakatau, v. c. Nearly the same as the simple v. tau, q.v.

Bakateba, v. c., caus. form, to watch, to look out or watch for, as bakateba na bai saki ni aliati watch or look out for the rising flush of dawn. [Sa. tepa, tetepa, to look towards.] H. sapah to look out, view, watch, look out for.

Bakatilas ia, v. c., to suffice : from tilas ia, q.v., and see also the simple v. las ia.

Bakatogo ia, v. c., d. for

Bakatoko ia, v. c., to make a show or feint of striking or pushing. See the simple v. togo fia.

Bakatolu, v. c., make the third time, or three times. [Mg. fahatelo the third.]

Bakau, or bakauĕ, v. c., to say or shout auĕ ! auĕ ! or au ! au ! to make a howling or barking noise in a well-known Efatese way expressive of joy, triumph, or derision : the howl or cooee repeated several times, ending in the loud jerking or barking utterance of au ! au ! au ! H.

'avah to howl, cry out, A. 'aui to howl, as a dog, wolf, or jackal.

Bakaul ia, v. c., to make like, imitate, to be like to, resemble: the simple v. is aul ia (dd. ui lia, ol ia) or ul ia, q.v.

Bakauti a, v. c., d. buti a, q.v., make an end, finish. [Fi. vakaoti, To. vakaochi, Sa. faaoti, Ma. whakaoti.] H. kaseh an end, kasah, A. kas'a', 2, to finish.

Bake, d. baku, v., to search, to search for (as to search for insects in the head, or for fleas and such like in mats or cloth). S. bka', or bko', to search.

Baki, v., to go to (a place), ba to go, and ki, prep. ,to: d. bĕ' (nearly beh), id.

Baki, prep., to, unto. This is preceding word used as a prep.

Bāki, v., d., to go or come from (a place), dd. ba, bai: ba to go or come, and prep. ki (to), from. For bā see bai.

Bakē, d. for baki se, go where? bakē is for baki ē, go to where: se, d. e, where? se is e c. art. s'.

Bakilina, v., to go or come into the light, i.e., into view, to appear: baki go or come to, and lina light. See lina, d. ali.

Bakitakita d. for makitakita, q.v.

Bako, s., shark, d. bakĕ. [Malo bacio, Epi bekeu.] Der. uncertain.

Bākor, v., d., to go or come in front of, to appear: ba to go or come, and koro, q.v.

Bakotu fia, v. t., d. for bagote fia, q.v.

Baku, v., d. for bake, q.v.

Baku, v. t., to pluck out, baku sa pluck it out, ps. mafaku plucked out, tafakaka, d. tafagka (i.e., tafak'ka), v. i., to burst, explode. [Sa. fa'i pluck, extract, mafa'ifa'i extracted, Ma. whakiwhaki, and kowhaki, to pluck, My. kopak to burst, break out, Mg. vaky burst out, mitifaka to burst, mitefoka to sound (as the explosion of a gun.] A. faka' to burst, to pluck out, tafakka', 5, to be burst.

I. Bala, v. i., to be smooth. [Sa. molemole, lamolemole, id., Tah. moremore smooth, without branches, as a tree; even, without protuberances; also, hairless, more, v. i., to drop or fall, as piŋ leaves when ripe, Ma. moremore, v. t., to make bald or bare; strip of branches, &c.] A. māra, n. a. maur' to fall off (as wool or hair from the body, feathers from an arrow); to pluck out or off (as hair, wool).

Bāla, i bi bala, it is smooth, level. See preceding word.

Bala-gara, v. i., d., to be poor, lit. smooth (or bare) dry, bare and dry: gara or kara dry, q.v.

II. Bala, v. i., often pronounced bela, d. bola to incline to; be close to: i bala nakasu inclines and keeps close to a tree (hiding), bala sa inclines and keeps close to it, bala-ati nafanua hugs the land (a ship), (see af ia); bala is close to (as a man to a tree, or one board to another), hence to be stuck and inclining from side to side to get through (as a man in the vines of the jungle, or in any confined place, as a narrow door; a bone in the throat, or the branches of a fallen tree in those of another); *bala*-tagoto, or *bala*-goto incline across, hence cross, a., as nakasu *bala*-tagoto (see goto) a cross beam, or cross stick, hence fāla a ship's yards (because they are fixed across or on the mast), and sticks fastened across or on a tree for a ladder to climb it are called fāla, or balafala, and *bala*-galu (see galu) is the upper cross board at the end of a canoe; fāla also denotes a litter, so called because the sticks forming it are fastened across or upon each other. [Sa. pilia to be entangled (as one tree falling against another, &c.), pilipili be near, pipili a cripple, Ma. piri, to stick, come close, keep close, skulk, hide oneself, pipiri come to close quarters, join battle, Ha. pili to cleave to (as to a friend).] A. māla, n. a. mayl' to incline, incline to, bend or lean to (something); to be close or near to; to have a part of the body (vitio naturae) inclined or bent to one side (used also of a building leaning to one side); 3, make a hostile incursion. Nm. miel, v. i., slant, deviate, incline (to-

wards), mail (gerund) slope, inclination, propensity.

III. *Bala*, s., the belly, usually pronounced *bele*, q.v.; *balau*, for *bala* am' (like uateau for d. uateam'), the inside of a man, or of anything (hollow or womb of the am', abdomen), *baloa* (ending a) a hollow, a valley, *balua* a hollow or hole in a rock, falea a cave, *bala*-kutu na the hollow at the back of the head (lit. the hollow of his kutu, q.v.), *balo*-leba the stomach (lit. the big hollow), *bile* na, or *bele* na his mother (lit. his womb, the womb that bore him), na felak a family, tribe, bela-ki, to gird (oneself), to tie or fasten under one's girdle or belly, to take with one, to conceive (*a woman*), *bela* source. [Ma. wharua, a., concave, s., valley, whawharua, s., mother, whare a house, people of a house, wharetangata connection by marriage, Tah. fare a house, farefare, a., hollow, as the stomach for want of food.] II. beten the belly, the womb, the inside, the womb, mother, batan properly to be empty, hollow, vain, i.q. batal (see *balo infra*), A. batn' belly, inside or middle of anything, pl. connections by marriage, a tribe (small), batana to have the belly distended with food, to be intimate and familiar, to be hid, 4, to fasten the girth under the belly (of a beast of burden), to cover, hide, 5, to put a thing under

one's belly, S. btan to conceive, have in the womb, A.
batuna to have a great belly.

*B*alāf ia, v. t., incline to keeping
near to : ala II., and āf ia.

*B*alagote fia, v. t., incline (or
bend) across it : *b*ala II., and
goto, or koto.

*B*alāfis ia, v. t., hug (as a ship
hugging the coast): *b*ala II.,
and afis ia.

Balaga tia, v. c., to lift up (as
the cover from anything) :
laga tia.

Balaga-saki nia, v. c., lift up,
stripping off (as the husk of
reeds) : preceding word, and t.
ending saki. Hence

*B*alaga na, s., husk, scale, or
similar thing that is or may
be *lifted up from* what it
covers or encloses : syn. lagalaga na.

Balafalà sa, v., to be entangled
(as one tree falling against
another). [Sa. pilia, id.]
The radical idea is seen in
*b*ala to be entangled or stuck
in the throat *(a bone)*; the
bone *inclines to one side* and
so sticks. See *b*ala II.

Balafala, s. See fala, s.

*B*alas, c. art. na*b*alas, *i.e.*, na*b*a
las big hollow ; na*b*ua na*b*alas
the road of the big hollow or
gorge behind Utaon.

*B*alau na, s., the belly, inside ;
inside, middle of anything :
*b*ala III., and au for amo :
*b*alau is, lit., the hollow or
middle or inside of the belly.

*B*alaus ia, v. t., to go through or
along a thing lengthwise, not
to go across it (*b*alagote fia) :

*b*ala II., and us ia to follow,
go through or along (as a
road, &c.)

*B*alea, s., d. for *b*aloa, valley :
*b*ala III., and a. ending a.

*B*ale*b*alea, and *b*ele*b*elea, full of
hollows, bellied, large : *b*ala
III., and a. ending a. [Ha.
pele, to have a large belly ; to
be large.]

Bale sia, v. t., d., to husk, strip
off (as the envelope of sugar
cane) ; and

Bala-saki, v. t., id. A. wafala
to decorticate.

Bali, v. i., to fast ;

Bali ki, v. t., to fast from (a
thing) ;

Balifali, v. i., to fast *(many
people)*. [Mg. fady, id.] A.
'abala, or 'abila, to abstain ;
to be devoted to the worship of
God, 2, to mourn (the dead).

Balikau ia, v. t., to go or step
over : *b*a to go, and likau or
lakau, q.v.

*B*alo, v. i., a., ad., to be empty,
vain, null and void, to no
purpose or effect : i *b*alo it is
empty, nasuma *b*alo an empty
house, lo or te *b*alo an empty,
i.e., a worthless thing, a trifle,
nothing, i toko *b*alo he remains
in vain, to no purpose, for
nothing, idle ; d. mole ; hence
sera te *b*alo, or sera te mole,
to deem worthless, vain, to
despise. [Fi. wale uselessly,
for nothing, idly, Ha. wale,
Sa. vale.] A. batala, n. a.
butl', or botl' to be vain,
nothing, to no end or purpose,
in vain, for nothing, idle, H.
batal to be empty, vacant,

idle (cognate baṭan, bala III.),
E. baṭala to be empty, vain.

Bālo, prep. or ad., d., above, up :
see (b') bi, prep., and ulua, v.
[Malo aulu (a, prep. "on "),
Fut. weiluga (see elag, *infra*),
Ha. maluna above, up (ma,
prep., and luna).] Amh.
balai above, and exactly as
Ef. bālo ki (above to), balai
ka, as *above* his house, or
above anything : the prep. ba,
E. ba, on, and lai the upper
part, high, A. 'alu, 'alo, upper
part.

Note.—Compound preps. or
ads. of this kind consist of a
preposition prefixed to another
word, which may be an ad., s., or
a. used substantively (as English *above, aboard, around, i.e.,*
on-bove. on-board, on-round) :
thus Ef. elag, d. bālo, Sa.
iluga, Ha. maluna, Malo aulu,
Amharic balai, above, on high,
on the upper side or part, all consist of the preps. e, i, or a, q.v.,
or bi, b' or ma, mi, q.v., and a
word signifying high, up, or
the upper part and side, for
which see ulua, elag, lua, laga,
infra.

Balo nia, v. t., dd. balo sia, or
bilo sia, bulo sia, bulu gia,
bunu lia bulu nia, bano lia, to
wash (anything) to wash (by
rubbing) : fafano, or bafano,
q.v., to wash the hands. [Sa.
fufulu to rub, to wash, My.
basuh to wash.] A. maṣa n. a.
maus' to wash ; to rub with
the hand.

Baloa, s., c. art. nabaloa, a
valley, lit. what is hollow or

concave, -a being the a. ending.
[Ma. wharua, a., concave, s.
valley.] See bala III.

Baloleba, s., the stomach : balo
cavity. See bala III., and
leba, laba, big.

Balōtu, v. i., d., to go there,
or thither (away from the
speaker), dd. banōtu, bīnōtĕ,
bīnāts, nĕt, to set out, go
away (from the speaker), hence
a common word of farewell to
one departing is Ku balotu
you are going away, to which
the one departing replies Ku
mato you remain. See banotu.

Balua, s., a hole or hollow in a
rock : see bala III.

Balu-saki, v. t., to paddle (a
canoe), row (a boat) ;

Balu-sa, v., to paddle, row, balu-
sá sa paddle or row with it (a
paddle or oar). [Epi dd.
mbeluo ka, mbahua kin, v. t.,
An. aheled (aheleth) to paddle,
to row, to sail, Am. fuloh to
paddle, Fi. ai voce an oar, voce
to paddle, to row, voce-taka,
v. t. (= balu-saki), Pa. palusa,
Ml. d. masu, Ml. A. sua, Malo
mo sua, Ta. asua, Fut. sua,
Mg. voy, act of rowing, mivoy
to row, voizina rowed, fivoy
an oar, My. d'ayung an oar,
d'ayung, bârd'ayung to row.]

Note. — Balu-saki is the
same as voce-taka (pronounced
vothe-taka) the saki or taka
being the transitive termination, *i.e.,* the prep. connecting
the verb with its object, and
consisting of two preps. combined, sa or ta and ki or ka.
The first of these preps. is seen

in the d (th) of abeled, and in
the z or zi of voizina, and sa
of palusa. The verb "to
row" is balu, voce (vothe),
(m)beluo, (m)bahua, voy, masu,
and without the preformative
b' (v', m',) asua, sua, d·ayung,
and the l in balu, c (th) in
voce, h in mbahua, s in sua,
d in d·ayung, all are variations of the same original
consonant which is elided in
voy. The word for "oar," ai
voce, fivoy, is in Ef. uose, d.
uohe (wose, wohe), Fut. foi.
In Fut. the connection between sua to paddle and foi
an oar or paddle is not so
apparent as that between Ml.
P. su to paddle, and bos a
paddle, because in foi, as in
voy (= Fi. voce) the s has
been elided ; and the connection between Ef. balu to
paddle and uose a paddle is
not so apparent as that be-
ween Epi mbahua to paddle,
and voho a paddle, Epi d.
bahua to paddle, boho a
paddle. See uose, *infra*. A.
jadafa, or gadafa, kadafa (or
'athafa), Amharic kazaf (or
'azaf), to propel with oars,
to row, Mod. A. kaddaf, or
'addaf, part. mo'addif (anc.
mo'addif, or mo'azzif, cf. voce
(vothe), bose, uose, voy, foi).
Sua is without the preformative, cf. 'azafa, 'addaf : balu
seems to have the same prefix
as Sa. pale to row, without
which is Sa. ālo (ps. alofia),
and alo-fa'i to paddle, row, and
with another verb, Sa. taualo,

to row, to keep on rowing.
As to the prefix in balu compare that in batok, batu, q.v.
Balu na, or *balu* na, s., relative,
friend ; a brother's brother,
or sister's sister. A. ma'lai
helper, relative, friend, associate, walai to be closely related, to be a friend, helper.
*B*alu-naki, v. t., to be a balu to
a brother or to a sister.
*B*alu gor ia, v. t., help, befriend,
take the part of. See gor ia.
*B*aluk, s., c. art. na*b*aluk, an in-
let or small bay, a cul de sac :
*b*a, and luku.
Bamasokò sa, v. t., come upon,
find : ba go, and masoko, q.v.
Bamau ria, v. t., d. bamau sa,
come upon, find it; ba go, and
mau (sa), q. v.
Bamau, v., to reach to, or term-
inate at, as i bamau nalia uane
it reaches to, or stops or terminates at, that place ; hence,
absolute, i bamau it terminates,
stops, or ceases : ba go, and
mau, q. v.
Bamu na, s., the shoulder blade,
shoulder, d. bau na. [Tah.
papa the shoulder blade]. See
*b*a*b*a a board.
Bamu na, s., d. for babu na, q. v.
Bān, v., d. for mān ; āní, q. v.,
c. preformative m.
Ban, v. i., for bano.
Ban, s., and baniben, s., armlet,
worn between the elbow and
the shoulder, and woven so
that the outer surface consists
of different coloured beads
(carved out of shells) arranged
in regular figures. [Malo ban,
Epi beni]. Der. uncertain.

Banī, v., to act violently, to oppress, as ru banī kiena they violently destroy or take away a man's property (at his house or plantation), as in time of war, or as a punishment for crime; baniban us ia follow him, acting oppressively, persecute him. H. yanah to act violently, to oppress: banī has the preformative as in batoko, balu, &c.

Banako, v. t., dd. bīnako, bunak, to steal. banakò sa, and banak ïa, d. bunako n', steal it. [Ma. whanako, whenako, Fi. butako, Ero. prok, Ml. fenake, My. cholong, Ja. ñolong, Mg. halatra c. pref. mangalatra, id.] A. saraka, n. a. sark', Mahri heriq, heliq, and desoq, to steal. Ef., Fi., and Er., &c., have the pref.

Banaga, s., mats, d. banu ; so called because they are plaited, see bau. [Fi. ibi, Epi yembi.]

Banei, v.i., to come here (to the speaker) ; same meaning as banïmai, or banŏ-mai. [Ml. P. vine, id.]

Banei, s., d. bane, volcano : see bani a, v. t. [Pa. banei id.]

Bani a, or ban ïa, v. t., to burn ; to roast, to cook by roasting on the fire; bēn or fēn cooked or roasted. The n is not radical: dd. beni a, banu sa, whence banus. See banei ; and dd. ubu, upu, of (ov), um, ïïa (uwai. oven (cooking), fireplace. [Sa. faafana, to warm up food, mafanafana, to be warm, To. mafana, heat, warmth, Ma. mahana, warm,

Ta. mahana, warm, the sun, a day, Fi. vavi-a to bake, My. bu to roast, grill, broil, Ja. panas hot, warm, panaskan to heat, Mg. fana, voafana, warm (applied to food cooked and warmed the second time), mafana, mafanafana, warm. hafanana, s., heat, manafana and mahafanafana, v. t., to heat, mihafana, v. i., to be hot, grow hot ; and Mg. memy, Sa. umu, oven.] H. afah, to cook, to bake, specially bread or cake in an oven (Ch., S. id.), A. wafa', whence mīfa', an oven, Mod. S. yafyana, a baker.

Banïmai, v. i., to come here (to the speaker), opp. to banotu go there (away from the speaker) : see banŏmai. [Epi mbinime.]

Bano lia, d. bālo sia, v. t., d. for balo nia.

Bano, v. i., to go, go off, or away. [Malo vano, Epi mbano, mbene, Meli fano, Fut. fano, Ta. uven, An. apan.] The verb ban or bano is composed of ba to go, and an adverbial suffix or directive, for which see under Lanotu.

Banŏmai, banămai, or banïmai, v. i., to come here or hither, dd. ba be, umai, mai, be: bano mai, or without the suffix nŏ, nĩ, ba, be ; with ba corrupted to u, umai ; and, without bano (or ba), mai, d., or be, d., as a verb in the sense of the full expression, bano-mai, or ba-be. See ba, bano, *supra* ; and under the following word. [Meli fano mai.]

4

Banōtu, sometimes pronounced balotu, v. i., to go away (in a direction from the speaker), to go there or thither, dd. bĭnōtĭ, bănāts, bĭnāts, and nōtu, nēt: ba to go, and nōtu there or thither. Nōtu, or nēt, originally an ad. has come to be used in some dialects for the full expression, as a verb. See the similar remark as to mai, or be, under the preceding word.

NOTE on the particles mai, d. be (in banomai, babe), notu (in banotu), and 'no (in bano):—

1. Mai, or be, coming after a verb is an ad. or "directive" signifying here, hither. [So in Fi., Sa., Ha., Tah., To., Ma. (My. mari).] Coming before a verb in Fi. it signifies to come, as au sa mai kauta I have come to take; so in Ef. a mai buati I have come to take, i.e., I (am) here to take: in two Ef. dd. a mai, a be, I have come, or I (am) here; as "to come" is always expressed in other Ef. dd. by banomai, or babe, mai or be in those two dd. may be regarded as a mere abbreviation of bano-mai, babe. So Mg. avy and My. mari are also used as verbs signifying to come. Before a noun or the ad. "where" mai signifies from in Fi., Sa., Ha., To. (mei, or me), Ef. (bai, bā, be), and Mg. (avy), thus Fi. maivei? Sa. maifea? Tah. mai hea? To.

meife? or mefe? Ef. bā se? bai se? or be sabe? Mg. avy aiza? from where? whence? The Mg. and Ef. are verbs—i bā se? avy aiza izy? he comes from where? In the other cases the mai, as in mai hea? is called a prep. Ef. i bā, or bai se? is, literally, he (is) hither (from) where? and in one dialect the prep. ki = from is expressed as i bā ki e? he (is) here (or hither) from where? In Fi. mai is also a prep. signifying in, at. The radical meaning of this particle is here or hither, and it is an ad. consisting of the prep. ma or ba (Ha. ma in, at, to, &c.) in, to, and the dem. i or 'i, this (place), here, hence mai, bai in or to this (place), here or hither. See Ef. d. i this, here; and the prep., in Ha. and Ma. ma, Fi. vei, Mg. amy, under the word bi (d. mi) infra. H. bazeh in this (place), here, Amh. bazih, and with the z elided (bayh, or baĭh), here, lit. in this (place), and with the pron. 3 sing. instead of zch. Mahri boh here, H. poh here, lit., in this place.

2. Nōtu, or lōtu (nāts, nāt, nēt) like mai in two dialects has come to be used as a verb (nōtu, nēt) with the same meaning as banōtu for which it is used, as mai and be for banomai, babe, for the sake of brevity; and like mai it is a compound ad., consisting of the prep. ni, or n' to (or ani,

q.v.), as to which see nĭ, *infra*, and a dem., *that, you* (place), *there, yonder*, and signifying to that or you (place), thither.

3. The no, or 'no, in bano, is the same as the no in notu, but without the tu, *i.e.*, it is the prep. n', and o, dem. The difference between notu and no, or rather between banotu and bano, is slight, banōtu being simply a strengthened bano. The difference between banŏ or banĭ in banŏmai, or banĭmai, and bano in banōtu seems to be that in the former banŏ or banĭ or banĕ the dem. after the prep. n' is wanting, thus banĭmai go to here, banōtu go to there.   T. nyo to there, thither, Matt. ii. 22, nye, id., Matt. xvii. 20, xxiv. 28, xxvi. 36.   Amh. with the prep. wada, to, instead of nĕ (*i.e.*, originally E. la, A. li, to, cf. balōtu), wadaziya, and (z elided) wadiya to there, thither.   The tu in banotu is dem., as in My. itu, that, situ, there, TaSa. natu and atu, that, F. uetu, that, H. zektu, that.

Bānu, s., d. *ba*naga, q.v.

Banu sa, and banus.   See bani a to roast.

Bāo, v. i., d. for mā, mān, bā, bān, bōn.   See anĭ, v. i.

Bāofa, s., d., menstruation, i su baofa mcamea (said of a woman menstruating while still suckling a child) : *ba*fa.

Bara, v. i., to be burned (as food in cooking) : see būria, d. bouria, or bauria, ta*ba*ra. [Ma.

wera burnt, hot, s., heat, pa-wera hot, Sa. vevela to be hot, ps. velasia, vela, done, well cooked, My. parik, marak, to kindle, set on fire.]   H. ba'ar (Ch. bĕ'ar to burn, Pael to kindle), to burn up, to kindle, to be burned.

Bara, v. i., or a., to be barren, d. oro.   E. 'abara to be barren, 'ebur barren.

Barab, v. i., or a., long, high (as a hill).   [Malo barauo, Fi. balavu, Ml. U. periv, long, also wide.]   Ef dd. baraf, baram, barau, birerife (see la*ba*, leba), prop. extended, cf. Ml. U.

Baraf, d. barab.

Baragai, d., transposed for bagarai.

Bara tia, v. t., to beat. . [Fi. waro-ca, My. palu, Ja. pala, Mg. velv.]   A. wabala to beat.

Bara tia, v. t., to bind together. My. barot to gird, to bind round.]   H. hibar to connect, join together.   See farătĭ, *infra*.

Baram, d. barab.

Bara-tuna, s., d. for bura.

Barau, d. barab.

Bārau, v. i., to reproach, speak loudly reproaching.   See rau.

Barĕ, v. i., to be moved, move about, bare ki, v. t., to move, agitate, barefare ki, id.   A. farĕfara to move, agitate.

Bare, or barea, v. i, or a., d. uorea, or orea, to be blind (a man), to have a white speck (of an eye whose sight is lost), to be dirty looking, like a

sightless eye (of half-raw food).
[Ml. A. bar, U. oror, Epi
mbili.] H. 'avar, E. 'awir, to
be blind.

Baretau, a., black and white
spotted (as a pig), also a yam
that has been peeled, or a tree
that has been barked, i bi
baretau : tau white, and bare,
for which see the following
word.

Barea, or borea, d., v. i., or a.,
black, dirty coloured. [My.
biru blue, TaSa. berika black.]
A. 'a'faru dust-coloured.

Baro, v. i., or a., to be heedless, taliga baro deaf, d. na
baro one deaf, barobaro to be
heedless, indifferent, tabaro
to be heedless, refractory,
lawless, bārua free from, as
i tumana bisa bārua ki nia
he declares himself free from
it (as a crime), marua to
cease, leave off, lo bārua kin ia
see the nakedness of someone,
literally, or as to his poverty
or being devoid of food, &c.
See baror, būra. H. para' to
loose, let go. make naked,
pāru'a lawless, unbridled, A.
fara"a to empty, leave off, be
free from (as free from cares
or labour, careless. idle), 5,
tafarra"a to be idle.

Baro, c. art. nabaro, s., one deaf.

Baro sia, or baru sia, v. t. This
verb was used thus in the old
days : to fell a big tree they
burned round the base of it,
then ru baru si, or baru lu
namalitera, that is, smashed.
broke, shaved, chipped, cut, or
scraped off the charred wood :

then burned the new exposed
surface again, smashed or cut
off (with the karau tare) the
charred parts again, and so on
till the tree fell. On E. Mai
barusi naniu := Ef. koi naniu
(see koi). Tea farofaro that
which cuts, shaves, rasps off,
barobaroa (a. ending -a) fit for
rasping off (as sandpaper or a
grindstone). [Fi. varo-ta to
file, saw, or rasp, Sa. valu
scrape out nuts (= Ef. koi), to
scrape (as taro), ps. valua, Ma.
waru to scrape. shave, cut (the
hair), Ha. walu to scratch,
rub, rasp, polish, Tah. varu to
shave, to bark a tree, to scrape,
My. paras to shave, to pare close
to the surface, Mg. fara scrape,
scratch, make smooth.] H.
bara to cut out, carve out, &c.,
A. bara' to cut out, to cut or
pare down, to plane and polish.
(As to the notion of breaking,
cutting, separating, which is
inherent in the radical syllable
H. par, see under H. parad
(Ges. Dict.) The same is
found in the somewhat softened
syllable bar, A. and H.)

Baroaki, d. See boroaki.

Barobaroa, a. See under baro
sia.

Baror, s., one careless, heedless,
lawless, wicked, foolish. See
baro.

Barobaro, v. i., or a. See under
baro.

Bārua, v. i., or a., made naked,
devoid of, clear or free from.
See baro.

Barua, or uarua, v. i., or a., fat,
big, large. [Mg. baribary,

bary, large, full, well made, Fi. vora to grow fat or stout.] H. bara', to grow fat, bari' fat, A. wara' to be fat.

Barubaruta, a., fat ; ending -ta : barua.

Barubarutena, a., fat ; ending -tena: barua.

Ba-si a, v., go upon, tread upon, basi namatuna tread upon something : ba to go, and t. ending si [Fi. va-ca.]

Basa, to speak. See bisa.

Basĕ a, v. t., to break off (as a branch from a tree), to break off with a snap or jerk, basu, id., mafasu d. moàs (mowàs) broken off, basc-raki, takes a different object, as base nara nakasu break off the branch of a tree, base-raki na-usu break off from a reed (the husk or covering, so as to make it bare), basebase raki nia, id., basu li a, t. ending li, to detach, break off, tabasuli detached, broken off, separated. [Fi. basu-ka, or -raka, to break, also to open one's eyes or mouth, basi-a, nearly syn. c. basu-ka. Sa. fati to break off, ps. fatia.] A. fas's'a to break off, fassa detach, shiver off, H. pasah, q.v., to distend, open (the lips), A. fasa' to separate, detach (as flesh from a bone).

Basĕa, v. t., c. verb. suf., scold, vituperate, rail at, d. syn. suer ia : bakabasea, id.   A. nabaza to reproach, blame, rail at.

Basiu, s., a bone piercer. See siu.

Baso ia, v. t., to pierce. See sui. [Fi. veso-ka and sua-ka.]

Bastak, v., d. for bātaka : basi, taka.

Bastufi, v. t., d., to follow, to be like: basi, and tufi. A. tabi'a to follow.

Basu li.   See basĕ a.

Bātaka na, v. t., to be like, equal to, sufficient for (bastufi and mautaka nearly syn.): ba to go, and taka like, similar to.

Batako na, or batoko na, s., the body, d. mole na. [Ta. buti, My. batang, Mg. vatana.] A. badano the body.

Bāte, v., d. for bātu.

Bātĕ, num., four. [Mg. efatra, My. ampat, Sa. fa.] A. arba'at', four.

Batī na, s., the teeth, a tooth, also a shoot (of banana or taro), a seed. [Fi. bati.] See nabatī na.

Batī-gāt, and d. batī-gaut, s., a thorny plant, with crooked, grasping thorns, like hooks: for gaut, see under gau, tagau.

Batī-rik, s., mosquito : batī, and rik, q.v.

Bat ia, or bati a, v. t., to do, make, work at.   [My. buat, or buwat, to do.] S. 'bad, to do, to work, work at, make.

Bātīk, d. uārīk, v. i., or a., few, to be few. See tik or rik.

Batīra, s., precipice, rugged declivity :

Batībatīra, a., rugged and precipitous : batī teeth, and ending ra: nabatira, that which is rugged (as a precipice), syn. na tiroa.

Bātok, v. i., d., to remain : toko.

Bàtu, v. i., d., to remain : tu.

*B*atu, s., na *b*atu, an adult,
young man.   A. fatiy' adult,
fata' young man.

Bātu, v., d. bate, to close up the
roof at the ridge-pole with
reeds : na fātu the ridge-pole.
[Epi bofugo, v., id.]   See fatu,
s., and bau.   A. "amā' to cover
a house, that is, its upper roof,
as with reeds.

Bātua na, s., the knee : prob.
bau (q. v.) the head, and tua
leg.   [Ml. A. lua leg, mbulua
knee, Ml. P. and Malo bau
knee.]

Bātua ki, v. t., to go from (any
thing or person) : ba to go,
and tua ki to place. lay down :
lit. go laying down or leaving.

Bau na, s., d. for bamu na, q.v.

Bau, s., one slain.   [Ha. po,
slain, lost, hidden].   See s. bog.

Bau na, s., the head : a head or
chief, specially, d., maternal
uncle, that is, head of the
family.   [Malo batu, San Cristoval bau, head : Tah. fau a
kind of head dress, a god, as
being head or above, a king
or principal chief. as being
above others.]   A. hamatu the
head : the head and chief of
a tribe or family.   See egg.
under bau sia and mau.

Bau lulu, s., a proud person, lit.
high head : lu.

Baua, or uaua (waua), s., a pillow:
preceding word and ending -a :
also, v., to pillow one's head.

Bau-maso na, s., portion of the
property of one deceased in-
herited by a member of the
family : bau, and maso, q.v.
For bau see s. bau sia.

Bau, v. t., to be above, cover,
surpass, i bau gor ia.   See
tabau :

Bau sia, or fau sia, v. t., to
fasten together ; to plait (a
mat) ; bau rarua fasten together (the parts of) a canoe ;
bau uago fasten a pig to the
carrying pole : ora naui i bau
the yam vine fastens on or
round the stake ; redup. bau-
fau ; bau-maso (maso a portion)
the portion collected or fastened
or gathered together, bau-terag
ia fasten—to dry it (as wet
cloth), i.e., fasten it on something in the sun or before a
fire.   [Sa. fau (Ma. hou) tie
together, fasten by tying, ps.
fausia, To. fau fillet round the
head, turban, Fut. fausia to
fasten, tie, Fi. vau-ca to bind
together, Sa. fau-la'i to be
heaped up, to abound, My.
ubung to join, connect, &c.]
See mau.   H. 'amam to gather
together, to collect, to join together, A. 'amma to put on
the head a fillet, to be a chief,
to be an uncle, "amma to
cover, to fasten (a camel), H.
'amam to cover, hide, fig. to
surpass, A. "amma, 4, to dip,
&c.

Bau gor ia, v. t., to *cover* over :
tabau sa to be above (as
covering a thing), to be over,
surpass him (in dignity or
rank).   See under preceding
word for bau.

Bäu or fäu, bäio or fäio, v. i., or
a., new.   [Malo baro, Ml.
mermer, Motu matamata, My.
baharu, Sa. fou, Fi. vovou, vou,

Mg. vao (havaozana) new.]
A. mahaduth, part. of hadatha
to be new, new. H. hadas',
S. hdath, id., E. hadas, to
renew.

Bauli a, v. c., to buy by exchang-
ing :

Baulu. or faulu, s., the thing
given in exchange wherewith
to purchase something, barter
(wherewith to buy by ex-
changing). See aul ia, ul ia.

Bau-ragia, or bau-teragia. See
bau sia.

Baus ia, and bausus ia, v. t., to
ask him (or her), bausus iä sa,
ask him it (or about it) :

Bausu ki, to inquire about (a
thing), bausu baki to inquire
at (a person), to ask, to question (a person). See us ia.

Bauria, d. for būria, q.v.   See
bara.

Bea (kbe, or bwe), s.   See nabea.

Bē, d. mai, ad., here, hither ; d.
to come here, like mai, q.v.;
also d. for bā, bai, to come or
go from, as i bē sāb mai ? he
comes from where hither ?

Bē emia, v. t., to have it, i be
nalo he has a thing, d. i
bienia he has it: bienia, bi enia.

Bē, or bea, dd. bei, mia (tiamia),
v. i., or a., to precede, go
before, be first, first.   [Sa.
mua, and mua'i first, muamua
to go before, first, Lakon mo,
Volow mag, Arag moana first,
Fi. mada to precede.]   A.
fuhat mouth, entrance (as of
a river), hence the first or
foremost part of anything,
Amh. pat, or fat, fore-part,
and e. a. ending fatanga first.

Be, d., a particle used after
interrogatives, then, now, thus
ua be? sa be (sāb)? where
then? takani aga bat ia be?
how shall I do it then (or
now). In other dialects it is
not used. H. 'epɔ' then, now,
as ayeh 'epo' where then? eg.
'ɔpoh (poh here) where? how?

Bē, fē, conj., if, should; ku fē
bano i fē uia should you go it
were well, i bē fano i bē uia
should (or if) he go it were
well. [Ta. ip, Fut. pe, if.]
Amh. ba, .bē, if, should (repeated in each clause as in
Ef., Isenberg's Gr., pp. 158–9).

Be a, or fe a, redup. befe, v. t ,
to read, also to count.   E.
nabab to speak, recite, read,
eg. H. naba' to prophesy (A.
naba' to declare), from naba',
Hi. hibi'a to tell.

Bē, or bea, redup. bebea, v. i.,
or a., to be great, wide extended. [Mg. be great, large,
Mota poa, Gao bio.] E. 'abya,
or 'abia to be great, wide, extended, 'abiy great, large.

Bega, d. baga, q.v., a hill.

Bei ki, or bai ki, d. bi ki, v. t., to
show : d. syn. bisai ki. A.
baha to appear, be shown,
manifest, show, divulge, indicate ; hence

Beifei ki, make manifest, indicate.

Bei, v., bei ki to watch for (as
for an animal to take or kill
it) : d. bu to see, look at.   A.
ba'a (ba'ai) to watch, observe,
look at, look out for, rush
upon (the prey) from an ambush, seek, &c.

Bei, or bai, a thing hidden, concealed, i bi bei it is hidden. [Mg. afina, My. buni, To. fufu, Ma., Ha. huna, Fut. funa, Epi mbin. Fi. vuni, hidden.] See afa : eg. to the word there given are A. "abai, H. haba', A. h'aba', to hide.

Bei, d. for bē, or bea, v. i., or a., to precede, first.

Bei or bai, d. ba. prep. (in this form as a prep., but see bai, v.), used mostly after verbs, connecting them with their object : lo to look, lo bei a look upon it, see it, d. lekbā (the final a is made long by the absorption of the pron. of the third person) ; taruba to fall, taruba bei a fall upon it, d. ro to fall, ro bei a to fall upon it ; an to be, to lie, an bei a lie upon it ; toko sit, toko bei a sit upon it ; ba to go, ba bei a go or tread upon it (for instance, upon filth in the path, ba bai intai); le ba i look upon it, see it, d. libi sia or lebi sia (i.e., le bi sia look upon it): the final i in bei or bai belongs to the pronoun of the third person. [Fi. vei to, d. va.] E. ba, A. fi, bi, H. b'.

Bei, s., na bei saki ni aliati the ascending cloud of dawn, the dim cloudy or misty appearance preceding daylight at dawn: d. in tei saki the rising cloud. See tai ni lagi. A. "amma (S. 'am) to be covered with clouds, as the sky, "ammai dust, darkness "ammat' cloudy.

Befe, or fefe, s., oven cover (made of leaves) ; a covering trap (for catching fowls). [Sa. veve oven cover of leaves.] See (bofia) bo.

Beigo, or baigo, s., a trumpet (shell) ; d. a kind of flute (cocoanut shell). [Sa. fagufagu a flute, To. fagofago a flute blown by the nose.] A. baka to blow a trumpet, ba'ku, or ba'ko, a trumpet.

Bela ki, v. t., to gird (oneself), bela ki na tali put on one's girdle or belt : to tie or fasten anything or carry anything between one's girdle and the lower part of the belly : hence, to take with one, to have with one or attached to one. See bala III. The s. is nafelaki, d. nabūlai, or bālai, what is fastened or girded round the loins. girdle.

Belaki, v. i., to be pregnant : bala III.

Belaki, s., c. art. nabelaki, d. syn. intamate, great heathen feast or series of feasts periodically held at every village, at which there was *abundance of food*, singing, and dancing : prob. so called because of the *abundance of food*, and friendly feeling : bala III.

Bēla, or fēla, if perhaps, if indeed, conj. bě, and ad. la.

Bela, v. i., to be smooth, level ; bala I.

Bela, d. for bala II., q.v.

Bela-tagot. See bala II.

Bela-galu. See bala II.

Bēle, s., the dead body of a pig : said to be so called because its

belly swells. *Bala* III. [Ha.
pele to swell out, have a large
belly.]
Bele na, s., the belly (or *bălă*
na); the womb: a mother (dd.
syn. eri na, raite na, susu na);
a source, as *bele* ni torogo the
source or master of the torogo
(a species of divination), also
bele nai (naui) kanoa the beginning or feast of the first
ripe yams : *bala* III.
Belbel, d. for bile, bilebile, q.v.
Beles, s., c art. nebeles, a dance
in which the two parties keep
meeting each other. See lasī,
tilasi.
Bĕn, or fĕn. a., cooked, broiled,
roasted : bani a.
Beni a, d. for bani a.
Bĕn, d. for băn. See anī to be,
abide.
Belŭ ki (kwelu ki), v. t., to
fold, to double, tăbelŭ (tak-
welŭ) folded, doubled ;
Bĕlu to be doubled up, as it were
folded together, hence to be
hidden, to hide oneself, *bĕlu*
ki to be hidden from, also
uĕlu ;
Bĕluuĕlu, v. i , or a., folded,
hence limp, doubled up, and
bĕluueluki, a., doubled up,
uneven, limp, limber, weak,
flexible. [Ha. pelu to double
over, bend, or flex, as a joint,
to fold, doubled, folded over,
pelupelu to double over and
over, doubled over, Sa. mapelu,
mapelupelu· to bend, stoop,
Fi. belu-ka to bend, curve,
kabelu bent, Mg. valona
folded, doubled.] H. kapal to
fold together, to double, part.

ps. doubled, Ch. kapel to
double, roll up, S. Ethpe.
'ethkfel, or ethfel, to be
doubled, folded together.
Bera, or fera, v. i., to crumble,
fall to pieces, berafĕra, and
taberafĕra to crumble, fall to
pieces, be scattered about in
fragments ;
Bĕra ki, v. t., to scatter about,
tabĕra ki to scatter about,
make to fall to pieces, and
berafĕraki, v. t., and taferafĕra
ki, v. t., na feroa, s., a crumb,
sabera ki, v. t., to scatter,
saberak, d. saberik, v. i., to
fall to pieces. [Fi. vuru-taka
to crumble, vuruvuru, v. i., to
crumble, and S., a crumb,
Mg. miveraberaka, v. i., to
crumble, mahavera, v. t., My.
âmbor scattered, tabur to be
scattered ; Ja. sâbar to scatter,
to strew, My. sibar to strew,
scatter.] E. farfur a crumb,
Talmud parpor from H. pur
to break, Pilpel pirper to break
in pieces : "this is the original
power of the biliteral par,"
Ges., s. v. parad, then applied
to scattering, &c.
Bera gia, v. t., d. bĭrĭgia, q.v.
Bera kati a. d. bera tia, bera tiki
nia, v. used as ad., fully,
thoroughly, accurately ; also
a., as tea berakati na a thing
fully his, a thing his own.
Probably connected with bura,
d. biri, to be full, full.
Beru, v. d., syn. uma, to clear
for a plantation, to cut down
trees, cut or clear the jungle.
[Mg. firala (fira cut, ala wood,
forest), miferala cut down

wood in order to make some use of the ground, clear the forest, Ja. tipar felling and burning the forest for cultivation, Ma. para to cut down bush, clear.] H. bere', Piel of bara' to cut down—"go into the wood and cut out room for thee there " Josh. xvii. 15.

Bes, or besŭ, s., dry wood, hard dry wood used for fencing. A. yabīs' dry (wood), Nm. yabis dry (wood).

Bes, d. besŭ, s., a young pig whose mother is dead and which is brought up as a pet and is therefore tame and gentle; also a motherless child, syn. mitabusa. So called from being deprived of the mother's milk, and, as it were, arid. See preceding word and busa: A. yabisa to be dry.

Beta, or fetà, s., a tribe, a crowd or lot of people, or of animals, accompanying each other, as nabeta Togoliu the tribe of Togolius, the Togoliu crowd, set, or lot ; a shoal, nabeta naika, a shoal of fish. See bita, bita-naki, ta.

Beti, or bati, s., in proper names, as Togoliu beti, Metanibeti, &c. : beti seems a form of the word bati (see nabati na) and prob. means chief, or head of the family.

Beti, s., a kind of spear pronged with sharpened human bones, and feathered : prob. so called because pronged or *toothed*. See nabati na.

Bi, v., d. for umba ki, q.v.

Bi, or fi, dd. mi, bai, v., to be, only used before substantives, or words used as substantives, as i bi natamole, fatu, nakasu, it is a man, stone, tree, ru bi natamole nia they are good men. [Epi mbe, ve, to be, Ml. P. fe, A. mbe, be, U. vi.] This is the prep. bi, fi (or bai) come to be used as the verb to be, somewhat similarly to E. bo, M. A. fih and fi. But the word is not used impersonally in Ef. as in E. and A.; it is more used in Ef. and Epi than in Ml. Compare Ges. Dict., s. v. be *(Beth essentiae)*.

Bi enia (d. bi emia, or be emia), v. t., to have ; i be nalo, or i bieni nalo he has something : enia is the pronoun him, her, it, suffixed to eni (for ani, q. v.) the prep. or transitive particle, the verb being bi (or be), which (see preceding word) denotes also to be. In E. bo denotes to have, as well as to be, and governs the accusative. Dillmann, Gr., §176, h, §192, 1, b.

The Ef. i bi enia may be simply he is to it, *i.e.*, he has it ; thus i ti-ka ki nia denotes either he is not to it, or he has it not = i ti bi enia he has it not : so (d.) i be (be e) nalo he is to something, *i.e.*, has something, i ti be nalo = i ti-ka ki nalo. he has not anything. Note that ti-ka is written tika, q.v. It is equally correct to say namuruen i tika ki nia he has not laughing (lit. laughing is not to him), and i tika ki namuruen he has not laughing (lit. he is not to laughing) : the former is the order of words in expressing the notion "to have" or "to have not" in H., A., and S., "is to him," or "is not to him."

Bi ki, v. t., d. for bei ki, q v., to show.

Bi, s., only in meta-ni-bi small openings in the ends of a house through which light comes, and which are left uncovered in thatching. Of same stem as preceding word, whence is A. buhu a name of the sun, and buh' the uncovered part of a house or tent.

Bia, or **fia,** d. bīsa, or fīsa [Malo, Santo, &c., visa], v. i., or a., how many? as ru bia? they are how many? natamole bia? how many men? And, not interrogatively, ru bia, they are so many, few, natamole bia so many men, i.e., a few men. [Sa. fia, ad., how many? Fi. vica, ad., how many? Ta. kuva, ad., how many? My. bārapa (apa) how much, or how many, much, many, some, Mg., ad., firy how many? mi-firy, v. i., into how many parts does it divide?] The final part of bia or bisa, namely a or sa, is the interrogative pronoun, as is apa in bārapa. In sa the s is a dem. prefixed to the interrogative pronoun, and probably the r in Mg. ry is likewise a dem. The prefixed bi or fi is the reflexive verb preformative, Ef. bi or fi, Sa. fe, My. bâr, or bä (ber, be),

Mg. mi (fi), as the My. bārapa seems to indicate (and the r of bārapa must in the absence of anything to the contrary be regarded as a dem. like the r in ry and the s in sa). On this reflexive verb preformative bi, My. bä (be), Sa. fe, Mg. mi (fi), see next word following. In support of this view let it be observed that bia or bisa in Ef. is never an adverb and is a verb, being usable as an adjective only as every verb in the language is. In bakatia or bakafisa (q.v.) make how many times? (Fi. vakavica) the causative verb preformative baka has the same effect as in bakarua, bakatolu, &c. In A., S., and H., how many? how much? is expressed by ka, or ke, as, prefixed to the interrogative pronoun, the compound signifying literally "as what"? H. kamah, S. kīma', A. kam, and with a different interrogative, kāy, kain' quot (how many? so many). Compare Tanna keva, d. kuva.

Bi, or **fi,** reflexive verb preformative (ba, or baka, fa, or faka, being the causative verb preformative), as ru atu gia, v. t., they smite him, ru fiatu, v. r., they smite each other, they fight, auli a, v. t., exchange, replace, substitute for it, bauli a, or fauli a, v. c., nearly the same, make to take the place of, barter for it, ru biauli, v. r., they are bartering with each other, or

they are replacing each other
or taking each other's places
(as men at the oar). [Sa. fe
"the reciprocal particle" prefixed to verbs, Fi. vei, My.
bâr (*i.e.*, ber) and be, prefixed
particle sign of the neuter or
intransitive verb, Mg. mi
reflexive verb preformative
(Griffith's Mg. Gr., p. 112),
and with ha (the ka in baka),
miha : the r in My. bâr or
ber (see under preceding word)
is held to be a dem. or pro-
nominal particle like the ha
in miha and maha (ka in
baka), and n (or na) in Mg.
man, mana, My. mâng (the
ba or ma in these being the
causative verb preformative).
See ba and baka.] II.
mith-, mi- (as in middabber),
for the A. it-, i-, see Wr.,
Gr. I., §111, participle, Anc.
muta-, Mod. mut-, Ch. mit-, S.
met-, or meth-; the m- belongs
to the participle, and without
it the prefix is in H. hit or
hith, Ch. it, S. et or eth, A. it
(for ta); and when the t of
this prefix was assimilated to
the initial radical of the verb, as
it often was, it became simply
i- followed by a doubled consonant, as in H. hiddabber,
A. issakata. Of this only the
prefixed i could remain, and it
has become the prevailing
form in such languages as Sa.,
My., Mg., or Ef. It may be
remarked that in Mg. in all
verbs of this reflexive form
this prefix occurs without the
m, in the future and past

tenses, as simply i. As to
signification of verbs with this
prefix in A., H., and S., they
are primarily reflexive, then
reciprocal or passive (intransitive) or transitive, governing
an accusative. In Ef. verbs
of this form are reflexive, or
recip., and intransitive, rarely
transitive.

Bia, bibia, d. biau or beau, s., a
child, youth, bia kiki little
children, bia turiai young
men : and in names of children as bia-nara, &c. [TaSa.
pipi infant, Ml. U. bibi infant, Ml. A. pepe infant, and
Fut. foi, in foimata, eye (but
lit. pupil of the eye), Ja. bayi
infant, child.] A. bu'bu' a
little boy (from bābā to say
papa), the pupil of the eye, (at
Damascus) bubu a little child.

Biau, or beau, s., wave, waves
[Sa. peau, id., My. ombak, id.]
E. ababi, A. 'ubāb', i.q. 'ubāb'
flood, waves, from 'abba to have
broken waves (*the sea*). Hence

Biafiau (for biaufiau), v. t., to be
raised in waves, rough (as the
sea). [Sa. peaua rough (as the
sea), lit. wavy, full of waves ;
peau and the a. ending a.]

Biauli, v. r., d. bioli, barter or
exchange with each other ;
take each other's places, as
men at the oar or other work,
spell each other.

Bialo, v. r., to wave (beckoning) ;
reflexive of alo-fia, q.v.

Bib, s., d. for *baba*, a board.

Bibisinu, v. i., to ring, sing (of
the ears) : sinu ; bibi is the
preformative bi doubled.

Bibe, v. i., or a., for bebea.

Bibila, v. i., or a., big, great: redup. of bila.

Bifera ki, v. t., to show by a fera (or omen): fera.

Bigo. See buigo.

Bikutu ki, v. t., speak to each other (against someone in his absence); decide about (someone). See kutu ki.

Bila, v. i., shine, lighten, gleam, flash, appear; bilafila, redup., to do so repeatedly: lo bilă ki glance at; fila lightning; bulĕ-meta eyeball (gleaming part of the eye). [Sa. pula, pupula, pulapula to shine, may be same.] A. barak, or bara', shine, gleam, flash, glitter, appear; lighten (lightning), 2, open the eyes, glance at, bark' lightning, pl. buruk, H. barak, S. barka: hence bila, or fila, bile, or file, s., lightning: c. art. nafila.

Bila ia, or bilai a, v. t., pick up, gather up (anything, as fallen leaves, fruits, fish lying on the ground, &c.);

Bila guru ki, bili lua, bili sai, &c. See guru, lua, sai. Bilai has the pref. b'. [Fi. vili-ka pick up, as fallen leaves or fruits.] E. 'araya gather (as fruits, herbs), glean (as after reapers): c. preformative.

Bila, also (dd. mbula, bur);

Bibila, redup. (intensive), and

Bilena, bibilena, v. i., or a. (-na, a. ending), big, large, great, [Mg. bolobolo, mibolobolo, a., thick, close, dense.] A. 'abula, 'abila to be thick, big, 'abanbal' strong, great, large.

Bile, or bila, v. i., to be quick; hence sudden, confused, inaccurate, to err, make a mistake: redup. bilebile (d. belbel) quick, sudden, bilieli sudden, quick, hence confused, erroneous: tabile to be hasty, commit an error. Often used adverbially, as ba bilebile go quickly, si bile shoot missing (lit. hastily, erroneously, not hitting the mark), &c. H. bahal, bahel, prop. to tremble, be in trepidation, Piel to hasten, to hasten (as if to tremble) to do anything, Hi. id., Ch. (behal) Ithpeal inf. bithehalah, s., haste, speed, with prefixed bĕ, ad., quickly.

Bile, d. bilĕ, v. i., to dispute, wrangle. [My. babil to wrangle, squabble.] E. behil (2) contradict, tabahala dispute, wrangle, bahl dispute, altercation, wrangle.

Bili, v. t., bili meta shut the eyes, redup. biliuili, id. (of many); hence

Bili, s., a blind person (with closed eyes); and

Bilil, s., a tree (whose leaves at a certain stage of their growth cleave together): d. bilbilo wink, close the eyes. [Cf. Ma. kimo wink, kikimo keep the eyes firmly closed.] A. "amas'a blink, wink, close the eyes.

Bili a, v. t., d. for lelu ki, q.v.

Bilăki, v. i., to be terrified, tremble (as it were) with fear. H. balăh to be terrified, to fear, Piel billeăh to terrify, and suffix ki.

*B*ĭle na, s. See *b*ele na mother.

*B*ile-meta na, s., nephew or niece, child of a man's gore na, that is, his full or uterine sister. Lit. mother, *i.e.*, source, of the tribe or family, such nephew being a man's heir (and not his own son).

Bilāga, v. t., bilāgà sa, seek, search for it. See lāga, lāgà sa, id.

Bilele, v. i., r., to turn hither and thither, to go backwards and forwards, round and round : lele.

Bilele, v. i., r., d. for bitoli, q.v.

Bĭlīāsa, ad., the morning (lit. awaking) of the day after to-morrow : bulo, āsa ; bĭlĭ as in bĭli-bog, bĭlĭ-mitamai.

Bĭlibog, ad. (d. bulbog), morning : bulo, bog.

Bilieli, v., see bile, bilibile, to be quick, &c.

Bilikit ia, v. t., to peel (as a banana). [Cf. Fi. loqa-ta to peel.] E. lahasa to peel.

Bĭlĭmitamai, ad., the morning (lit. awaking) of the morrow ; bĭlĭmitamai ki nia the morrow following it, sera bĭlĭmitamai every recurring morrow : bulo, mitamai.

*B*ilis ia, d. *b*olis ia, uolis ia, v. t., to spread out anything on the ground as a mat ; hence to make a bed ; hence na uol, s., that spread out, a bed, d. na mauol ; and from this latter is mauoli ki make a bed with (something), spread it out for a bed. [Mg. velatra, mivelatra to spread, expand itself (be spread out), mamilatra, v. t.,

to spread.] A. faras'a to spread out anything, as a mat on the ground, spread (a bed for anyone), hence fars" a bed.

*B*iliti, s., the fat in the belly of a pig: connected with *b*ele na, the belly. A. badana to grow fat.

Bĭlĭsai, v., used as ad., together, as i tili bĭlĭsai ki nia he told (two or more things) together : it is really a v. t., and tili bĭlĭsai ki, lit. he told gathering-together it: bila ia, or bilaia, and sai (see saisai).

Bilo, v. i., d bulo, q.v., to awaken, to open the eyes ; bulo nia, d. bulobulo i, v. t., to awaken (from sleep), to cause to open the eyes. [Sa. ala to awake, Ma. ara, v. i., wake up, whaka-ara, v. t., rouse, Fi. yadra, open the eyes, awake, yadrava, watch for, vakayadra-ta, to awaken.] H. 'ur to awake, be awake, cause to awake, Hi. to arouse, awake (from sleep) : to watch, followed by the prep. 'al, to watch over anyone. Ef. bilo has the pref. b'.

Bilo sia, v. t., d. for balo nia, wash.

Bilōra, for bulōra, q.v.

Bilu, or biliu, v. r., to go backwards and forwards between two places or parties: liliu, liu.

Bilu, nilu, uulu (wulu), q.v., to dance (*a woman* or *women* ; *men* dancing are said to sali).

Bilulu, v. r., vie with each other, contend with each other for superiority. A. 'ala' ('alu),

3, vie, compete, contend for superiority : see lulu, or lu.

Bilubaki, v. r., to land cargo from a ship, or to land passengers (land each other): luba-ki.

Bimeta na, v. and s., to be his guide, lit. his eye : bi to be, and meta eye.

Binako, v. t., d. banako, q.v., to steal : bi, or ba, pref.

Binaka, s., mats, cloth: see banu.

Bināta, and dd. bunats, and

Binauta, v. i., to be numb, devoid of feeling, as one's limb from stoppage of circulation of the blood in it : bi to be, nāta a person (as if the limb belonged to some other person). See ata.

Binēn, v. i., d. syn. c. banotu, q.v., and baina, q.v. ; the difference between binēn and banotu is that the former has the final n = there, the latter tu = there ; the difference between binēn and baina is that the latter has elided the n of the prep. and has i = ne = to. For n or na = there (that, sc. place), see uān or uāna that, yon.

Bināts, d. for banotu.

Binoinoi, v. r., be confusedly together (as different kinds of things, people of different districts or languages), tumara noinoi ra :

Binofinoi, a., confused, perplexed, d. bunofunoi : noi, nea.

Binōtĕ, d. for banotu.

Binu na, s., head or first part, as binu nafanua head of the country (the chief and nata-

mole tabu are said to be binu naf.), binu naui head of a yam, syn. bau naui, binu namīt first part of a mat, from which the weaving or plaiting begins ; hence

Binu, v., as binu namit make a beginning of a mat, make the part from which the plaiting begins : connected with bau head, bau sia to weave or plait, bau namīt plait a mat. See bau.

Binu, v. i., to whistle, dd. bin, bōgĕ. [Epi bobo, Am. mofin, Ml. P. and U., puinpuin, winwin, Sa. mapu, To. mabo.] A. fahha, and fahfaha, sibilavit.

Binunu, v., complete, ba binunu ki, to go throughout, complete (a piece of a fence) : nu, num.

Bio-so, v. i., to call or cry out, shout, calling : bio, and so, q.v. The verb bio, or fio (see rafioso), means to cry out, shout. [Sa. piapio an outcry, a shouting, Mg. feo voice, sound, report.] H. pa'ah, to call, to cry out.

Bira gia, d.,

Biri gia, d. firi gia, v. t., to carry on the back, take, bring, lead. [Epi mbario, carry on the back.] A. hamala, to carry on the back, bring, send, impel to do something, S. hmal, collect, carry.

Biri-nāla, s., the plaited or braided (rope) handle of a carrying basket : see āla, and bir ia to plait.

Biri-ofa, s., the cloth in which a child is slung and carried on the back of its mother : biri (gia), and ofa (ia), d. afaia, both of which verbs signify to carry on the back.

Biràgoro, v., d. *boragoro*, q.v., to make, break into a noise near someone : see *bora* ia, and goro.

Biraka, v. r., to give presents to guests at a naleouan (feast after a death), lit. to give presents (or rewards) to each other : raka tia.

Birakāna, s., the giving of such presents.

Biri-raki, v. t., to give presents to guests at a naleouan : biri a (biri nabo ra, *i.e.*, make their hearts void of evil thoughts, *i.e.*, pleased or good), and raki.

Birausi, v. r., to follow each other : rausi.

Bir ia, or biri a, v. t., to make void, bring to nought, as counsel, bisa biri nalo na : the radical notion is *break to pieces*, biri na maietoa break to pieces or put an end to (one's) anger, appease, biri nabo na bring to an end the evil feelings of one's heart, appease. This verb is much used after other verbs, as mitroa, bisa, &c., think void, *i.e.*, despise, &c., and ba biri nafanua means to go all through the land : tale round, tale-firi all round ; re-duplicated it is

Birifiri, nearly the same meaning as biri ia. H parar to break in pieces, Hi. hefer to break, as a covenant, make void, be void, bring to nought : eg. para', and following word.

Biris ia, v. t., to break down, destroy, birisi nakoro break down a wall : the notion of breaking in pieces, asunder, is implied in this word, which is cognate with the preceding. H. paraŝ to break, break down, &c.

Biri, v. i., to warble, whistle (birds). [Epi faru, forfaru.] See *bora* ia, *biragoro*.

Bíri̇̆, d. for bǔra to be full, q.v.

Bir ia, v. t., to plait a string or rope. [Sa. fili to plait ; to be entangled, involved ; filigā to persevere, Ma. whiri twist, plait, Ha. hili braid, plait, twist, fasten, Tah. firi to plait.] A. marra. 4, to firmly twist (a rope) ; to wrestle, to be locked together in wrestling 1, 4), to fasten, 1, 4, to be bitter (lit. and fig.), 10, to persevere, marīrat' a rope firmly twisted together, or a long rope, muʻuarr' firmly twisted together (a rope).

Bir ia, v. t., d., to stick, stab, pierce, as biri naui to stick a knife or fork into a yam while being boiled to know whether it is cooked. See *bur ia*.

Birife, v. r., to seize, pull hither and thither (to take away a man's property as a punishment). See rau.

Birigirigi, v. r., to be moaning, bemoaning oneself. See rigi.

Brigi, d., v. t., bri (*i.e.*, biri), prob. for meri, to do, make : therefore it is bri-gi (biri-gi). See meri.

Birigite na, s., d. for bura na, q.v.

*B*iriki, s., a part, side. A. farik' a part, from faraka to divide, separate, &c. Hence

*B*iriki, s., a "falling" star, a meteor: used also as a name of men.

Biri-sai, v. t., to pierce open, birisai na *b*ago āso pierce open the tunnel (or end of it) of the robber-crab, fig. to lay open some hidden wickedness: biri to pierce, and sai, q.v.

*B*iroa, and biroaroa, v. r., to turn each other (in some work, causing it to be done in some other way), as, when one is doing some piece of work, to make him do it some other way is to biroa : see roa to turn, to change.

Bisa, fisa, or basa, v. i., to speak, na fisān, d. nafsan, the act of speaking, speech, a word; tabisa to speak earnestly (ta, q.v., and bisa), tafisafisa, d. tafisfis, to speak earnestly ; to pray (so used now in Christian sense) ; to utter inarticulate sounds (as those made by a cocoanut on the gravel which a rat is turning about trying to get at its kernel). [My. bacha to read, recite, chant, Tag. basa, Fi. vosa to speak, talk.] A. nabasa and nabaṣa to speak ; to peep or chirp (a bird) ; nabsaʿ a word.

Bisafisa, v. i., redup. of foregoing, to speak rapidly (as one in delirium).

Bisa, or fisa, d. bia, q.v., to be how many? so many, a few; bisa-mau, d. bisi-*b*a to be only a few, few. See mau.

Bisàb, d. for bisif, v. i., or a., surpassing, excelling, as fonu bisab an excelling (big) turtle, i uia bisif it is good, surpassing or excelling. See safe.

Bisai ki, v. t., to show, d. bisā ki. See sai.

Bisakaui, d. for bisaku tia, q.v.

Bisàki (d. biski), d. transposed for bakasa, q.v.

Bisaki a, or busaki a, v. c., to raise up, to place above, fig. to appoint or make one a chief. See saki.

Bisaku tia, v. t., d. bakasau, q.v. See siku tia.

Bisalot (for *b*osa-lot), v. i., to clap the hands, lit. bring (the hands) together, sound, or crack : *b*osa ia, and lot.

Bisau, v. i., dd. futum, busuf, or busofu, bisobu, to sprout forth, spring up. See futum.

Bisaui, d. for bisaku tia, bisakaui.

Bisēka, v. i., d., to sit (as talking with a neighbour) : sēka.

Bisela, v. r., to bear, bring forth, give birth to : sela tia

Bisera, biserasera, v. i., to be not of one size, to be different : sera ia.

Biserĕ a, v. r., to be near : sere a.

*B*is ia (kwis ia), or uis ia, v. t., to take with the hand, grasp, take hold of, accept, receive. H. kabas, Pi., to take with the hand, hold, receive, A. kabasʿa take with the hand, lay hold of, seize, S. ḥbas to compress.

Bisi na, or bŭsi na, s., the posteriors, the backside, the

5

rump. Compare busi a, d. for muri a, q.v. [Mg. vody the posteriors, My. buri the back, the rear, Ma. muri hinder part, Sa. muli the rump.]

Bis ia, or bisi a, v. t., to beget, procreate, make to be born, as a father his child : matis one begotten or born, namafisien the being begotten or born. A. nafisa to bring forth (*a woman*), manfus' one born.

Bisi a, or fisi a, v. t., to rub one stick on another to produce fire, bisi nakabu produce fire by friction. The rubbing stick is pointed and rubs a groove into the other, the rubbed out dust at the end of which gradually is ignited. [Mg. fositra rubbed so as to produce fire by the friction, mifositra to produce fire by friction.] A. fasa'a, 2, to rub (a thing), so that its soft and broken interior may be emitted.

Bis ia, or bisi a, v. t., to uncover or dig up anything buried under ground, to dig up, or uncover, by removing the covering earth, a dead and buried body, or any other thing buried in or covered with earth, as a yam, &c. A. nabas'a to uncover what was covered or hid, as what lies hid under ground ; to dig up again, or uncover by digging (*a corpse*).

Bisíbà, v. i., or a., d. for bisamau (bisa-mau). See mau.

Bisif, v. i., or a., d. for bisab, q.v.

Bisobu, v. i., to sprout forth, spring up. See futum.

Bisua, v. r., to meet together, to meet each other : sua.

Bisuaki, or fisuaki, v. r., or a., order or command (or send) each other ; i bisuaki he commands, that is, he commands some other person, or persons : sua ki.

Bisueri, v. r., scold or vituperate each other : sueri.

Bisuraki, or bisureki, *i.e.*, bisuraki, v., to speak, lit. to speak for, about : although raki is a t. prep. this word is commonly used absolutely, nafisuraki speech, a word or utterance, nafisuraki sa bad talk : bisa, and raki.

Bisuru, v. r., lie (deceive each other), bisuru ki lie to (someone) : suru, d. soresore.

Bitā, v. r., to be joined together, associated (of men) ; bitā ki, t., make to be joined together, or associated : tā, bitā-naki.

Bitabelu, and, d., Bitafetabelu, same as tabelu : belu.

Bitago, v. r., beg (from each other, or one from another), also bitagò sa, t., beg it, *i.e.*, beg (for himself) it : tago fia (q.v.) beg of him.

Bitaki a, v. t., to place or fix the hot stones on the nakoau in the oven, d. uataki a, bitaki nakoau : taki a.

Bital ia, or bitali a, d., v. t., beg, ask him (for something) : preformative bi, and tali. [Sa. fesili to question, ask, sili, ps. silia, to ask, inquire.] A.

sa'ala to question, 5, beg, 6, question, ask each other.

Bitānaki nia, v. t., r., to accompany one, bita-naki : bitā (see tā), and naki, t. prep.

Bitau sa, v. t., to invite, and Bitautau (of many): tau, tautau.

Bitau ria, v. t., to marry her : tau ria.

Bite, v. t., to cut ; bitēsu, d. bitēïu, to cut reeds (see usu). [My. potong to cut.] A. batta (and batta) to cut ; hence

Bitĕ, s., an instrument for cutting, knife.

Bitè lua i. See butè lua i.

Bitefa, v. r., to arrange themselves opposite to each other for battle : tefa.

Bitei a, v. t., to paint, to smear with intei ; tei turmeric, a reddish powder (made from a plant) much used for smearing the body, or wounds, or the nafona (native cloth). A. 'a'da'u crocus, sanguis draconis, a red gum used for healing wounds, a plant with which cloth is coloured or tinged, yadda'a to tinge or colour a *thing* with the thing called 'a'da'u.

Bitelo, d. butol, bitol, v. i., to be hungry. [Fi. vitolo to be hungry.] A. talalha to have an empty belly, tolilha id.

Biteriki, s., an old woman, a matron, opp. to māriki an old man, a senior ; mā-'riki, bite-'riki, see fiteriki ; bite means "woman." The common word for "woman" in one dialect is matu [Ja. wedo], q.v.

Bitia, or fitia, v. i., to put forth bati na (of bananas and taro, *i.e.*, to put forth shoots) ; formed from bati by the a. ending a. See bati na, nabati na. Dialect syn. sulia, from suli na.

Bīto, s., one lame, H. pasalh, to be lame, pisseah, lame.

Bitoli, v. r., to pass (or go before) each other : toli a.

Bitò sia, v. t., to extend, spread out (as cloth, &c.), H. matalh, S. mtalh (or mathalh, mthalh), spread out, extend.

Bituà sa, v. r., give it, place it ; hence bituāna, s., a giving, gift : tua i.

Bitua ki, v. t., place, lay down : tua ki.

Bitubetuba, v. r., lit. to be touching each other (of things in a series, then, to be continual, uninterruptedly, constantly ; not redup. it is

Bitub, to be touching or reaching to each other, as in tālĕ bitub, it is all round (the two ends of that which goes round), meeting or touching each other : tuba ia. [My. tubi-tubi, successively, uninterruptedly.]

Bituma ki, v. r., to point to with the finger : tuma ia.

Bo, conj., particle connecting verbs thus, i tulena bo lotu he arose and worshipped i tili a bo ban he said it and went away : the bo can sometimes be and sometimes is omitted as i tulena lotu: d. syn. kai. A. fa, Wr., A. Gr., II., §140. "One finite verb may be put in opposition to another. In this case *a*) the first is the preparative act, introductory to the second," as in the above Ef. examples: " the older and more elegant form is to insert the conjunction fa," its omission being a later construction. As to the o in bo it seems the same as the o in the following word, q.v., but here denoting the subject, *i.e.* bo = and he or and she, d. syn. kai.

Bō, d., other dd. fō, mō, uō, ō, a particle used after another particle to form the future tense, thus i ga bo ban, dd. i ga uo ban, i g'o ban, k'e fo ban, i ba mo ban (or i mba mo ban) he will go away: without the bo (uo, o, mo, fo) as i ga fan, &c., the meaning is imperative, or permissive, let him go, he must go, should go, may go, lit. that he go, the particles *ga* (or ka) and *ba* being final conjunctions denoting ut, that, to (as in, I told him to go): see *supra* ba, conj., and *infra* ka (ga), conj. In Ml. P., Motu, &c., this ba alone forms the future tense, and in Florida and Vaturanga this k' (ka, ga) alone forms the future, thus k'e fan, *i.e.*, ke fan that he go, Ef., is in these two languages not only equivalent to this, but also equivalent to ke fo ban he will go. It is therefore manifest that the particle bo does not by itself express the future idea, but, in Ef., is a mere adverbial enclitic to a final conjunction which does. It may perhaps in this construction be best rendered by ' then,' iga bo ban he will go, lit. that he then go, k'e fo ban he will go, lit. that he then go. See the following—

Bō, an adverbial particle used to form the present progressive tense, as i bo ban he is going: i ban denotes either he goes or he went. This is the same particle used in the future tense denoting "then." As used in the present progressive tense, it may be best rendered literally by ' now :' i bo ban he now goes, he is now going. H. 'epō, ad., properly here, there, but always in reference to time now, then: according to Ges. composed of 'e demonstrative and pō or pōh (here, there, this latter being for pahu or bahu in this or that (place) (the prep. b' and pron. 3 pers. masculine).

*B*o na, redup. *bobo* na, or bobo na, s., the heart (*i.e.*, the mind, the seat of the intellect and affections). The original meaning is seen in the phrase na kasu na*bo* na the cartilaginous substance on the front of the throat, lit. the stick, or tree, of the *bo* (pectus). [Mg. fo the heart, mind.] A. bahw' the cavity of the chest (pectus).

*B*oa, v. i., to emit odour; na*bo*, d. tamo, to emit odour, *bou* odour. [Ha. po, puia, id., My. bau, Mg. fofona, odour.] A. fāha, fāh'a (fā'a) to emit odour.

Bôb', d., father (voc.) See āb, bābu, &c.

Bobo. See bo na.

Bobo, v., as bobo ki atelagi to hail the new moon by making an exclamation or a series of sounds like bo! bo! bo! [Mg. babababa, cry, &c.] S. yabeb clanxit, H. yabab, Pi. to exclaim, cry out.

Boboi, s., a mask, cover, or disguise; not only a mask for the face, but a cover of the whole body, made of kaka maniu, &c., and painted so as to appear terrific (to children); used at the naleouan after the death of a chief when the nabea was set up. Perhaps so called from covering oneself with the mask or disguise. See bo-fia, &c.

Bobu, s., redup., d. bua, grandfather (voc.), mother's father. See bua, tobu na.

Bo-fia, and reduplicate

Bobo-fia, v. t., to cover, to be upon a thing, or above it, covering it;

Bo-gia, v. t., or bu-gia, to cover, to excel, to be above, over a thing, covering, not implying so close proximity as bo-fia;

Bo-gor ia, v. t., bo-gia, and gor ia, to be covering over—see gor ia;

Bog-kor ia, v. t., to be above, over, to overtop, overshadow, as a tree over a smaller plant, a higher chief over a lower: the g in bog is the g of bo-gia. See kor ia;

Bogi, or bog, s., darkness (from its covering), night, also day in counting as "third day," bog tolu, or mog tolu, &c., te nabog some day, some time, also naubog, i.e., na ubog;

Bogien, s., darkness;

Bog, s., a dark powder, used in painting;

Bog, s., symbol of chieftainship (buried in the grave of a chief), from bo-gia to excel, be over. [Sa. po night, ps. pogia to be benighted, Ma. po night, season, Hades (from being dark), Ha. po night, darkness, v. to be dark, become night, to be out of sight, hence slain, lost, to overshadow (as the foliage of trees), assemble thickly together, a. dark, dark coloured, ignorant, obscure, popoi to cover, poi, id., Ja. bungi night.] A. "amma to cover, 4, to submerge, H. 'amam to shut, close, to hide, conceal, fig. to surpass, excel, also to be hidden, A. "amma to be hidden, covered with clouds (of the sky), "amma' darkness, dust, "āma to be cloudy (of the sky), 2, night came as a cloud, 'āmo day, season or year, 'amiya to be blind, hidden, "umiya to faint, Sa. matapo blind, matapogia to faint, Ef. meta-buta blind (see infra, buta). These words are all egg.; in Ef. the egg. are numerous. See bau (head), &c.; cf. bau-goria with bo-goria, &c.

Bok, redup. bokauok, v. i., onomat., to blow, to pant. [Ma. puka to pant.] H. puah to breathe, to blow, Hi. to pant.

Boka tia, v. t., to strike, bisa

boka tia to reprehend. [My. pukul, Mg. poka, strike.] A. baka‘a to strike with repeated blows; to cut up; 2, reprehend.

Bokas, s., d. for bakas, flesh; Hades.

Bokanoka, redup. of boka tia.

Bokota, v. i., or a., dirty (as water): gota.

Boláf ia, d. for baláf ia: d. bolboláf ia.

Bolà sa, d. for balà sa.

Bolau ki, to steer (a canoe or ship): bouolau.

Bole, d. buele, v. i., to be lost, absent: buele.

Bolo, v. i., or a., to be empty (as a cocoanut): balo.

Bōlo, s., a small basket. [Ma. paro a small basket, To. belu a cup.] H. kpōr, or kēpōr, a cup, E. kapar a basket.

Bolo, v., to do, redup. bolofolo, to do, to act, nafolōn, nafolofolōn, deeds (doing, acting), work, conduct;

Bolo, d., to behave deceitfully; and

Bolo sia, v. t., to do one, to treat him (as in quarrelling), to treat him, bolo sā, bolo uia ki, to behave ill, to behave well to. [Fi. vala, valavala, v. i., valata, v. t., to make or do, vala to fight, valavala. s., work, custom, habit.] H. pa‘al to make, to do, po‘al or poōl deed, act, work, A. ba‘ala move oneself, act, do work, do (something to someone), 8, devise (deceit against someone), fi‘l’ action, work, fa‘ilat custom.

Bolis ia, d. for bilis ia.

Bolboloa, or bolòboloa, d. for balebalia, large.

Bolōf ia, d. for baláf ia.

Bologa, v. i., to turn itself about (as something sinking in water), tafiloga, id. See bulo ki.

Bōlu, v. i., to be blunt (as an edged tool). A. bohira to be blunt (as a sword).

Bon, bono, v. i., to be shut, closed, stopped, bonò sa shut because of it, bon, bonbon to crowd together, crowded together:

Bono tia, or bonu tia (and mono tia, bunu tia, munu tia), v. t., to shut, close, plug, stop, block up, and

Bōn, a., and s., 1,000, d. mānu 1,000, bunuti, bunti, 100. These words denote, lit., a gathering, crowd. [Sa. puni-puni shut in, close in, cover over, punita‘i to stop with, tapuni to shut, momono to plug, monoti to cork, plug, puipui to shut, Ma. pani, papani block up, kopani shut to, close up, close in, Mg. kombona or hombona shut, closed, mikombona to shut, close, coalesce, Ha. pani to close, shut, stop, Sa. mano a myriad, a great number.] H. ‘amam prop. to gather together, to collect, to join together, then to shut, to close, A. ‘‘amma to cover, to obstruct, cover in front (as the mouth and nose of an animal), ‘amn’, or ‘ammon, a great crowd of men. See monotia, munutia, munuai.

Bono-gor ia, to crowd together (gor ia) about him or it.

Bonbon, d., a., redup. of bon, crowded together, namer bonbon people crowded together.

Boōlau. See boūolau.

i. *Bora* ia, or *borai* a, v. t., to rend, split open, split; *borai* nabati na part the teeth, *i.e.*, open the mouth to speak, hence *borai* to make a noise, boraigoro make a noise (as children) about or near (one), boraiuora-goro, id., dd. *borà-goro*, *bira-goro*, id., borōrai, v. t, redup., rend, split open, elo *borōra* the sun (rising) rending or splitting asunder or bursting through (the clouds). ta*bàre* (tabàrre), v. r. (passive), to be split open, burst, hence to be open (as a door), maora, or mauora, redup. maorāora, v. i., to be rent, hence uora a place, especially a landing place for a canoe (perhaps from being an opening or split in the reef), and, therefore, often in names of places, a side (of an island) as nora n tan, uora n lig, lower, upper side (of Efate), bora a basket woven out of the frond of a cocoanut palm whose stalk is *split asunder*, and the frond itself, bora the sides of the head or face, the temples (which women used to cut and tear open with a sharp shell (kai) in mourning for the dead). A. fara' to split, rend, slit, 5, tafarra' to become slit, rent, burst, *i.e.*, open, farya*t* tumult, clamour.

Bora, s., the temples : bora i.

Bora, s., cocoanut leaf, or basket made of it, or plaited for thatching houses : *bora* i.

Borabora, s., cocoanut leaf basket : *bora* i.

ii. *Bora*, v. i., to spring up, sprout, grow (of plants), be born (of men) ; bakauora ki, v. c., make to *bora* (men and plants), nauora na, nauorauora na offshoot, offspring (of plants and men), ōra naui the vine of the yam ; fara a cocoanut (fruit) that begins to shoot. [Motu vara to grow, to be born, Oba *biri* to grow.] H. parah (A. farih'a, 2) to break out, burst forth (of the young as issuing from the womb), to sprout, to flourish (a plant), Hi. to cause to do so, sprout, shoot, H. perah sprout, shoot, A. farh″ offspring, shoot or sprout.

Bora-bau, v. and s., over-head, noon, only in the phrase elo i *bora*-bau the sun is overhead, lit. splits-head : *bora* i., and bau.

Bora-goro, or *borai*-goro, or *borai*-uora-goro, to make a tumult, noise near (one) : *bora* i.

Borai, s., c. art., the sugar cane ;

Borairai, s., a reed like sugar cane growing in streams. A. bara', 4, to find sugar cane.

Bora-kai, v. and s., to tear or rend the kai (a shellfish, or its shell): borai i. Men who were worthless and died poor, and had no pigs killed at their death and burial, *bora*kai in Hades, their jaws being torn and bleeding in doing so.

*B*ora-kese na, s., gills of fish ; *b*ora I., and kesa (dark coloured); dd. moresc na, kurumasc na.

Borau, v. i., to ride or be carried (on a canoe or ship, horse, vehicle, or other thing), to voyage. [Fi. vodo embark, go on board, ride, Sa. folau a voyage, the crew and vessel, To. felau to navigate, make a voyage, a canoe, a fleet of canoes, a voyage, My. prahu, prau a canoe, boat, ship, general name for any kind of vessel, bâr-prau to travel by boat or ship.] A. markab', E. markab a ship, vessel, A. rakib' navigating, voyaging, rakiba to be carried, to ride (A. markab' denotes a vehicle, carrying-beast, chariot, as well as a ship), H. rakab to be carried (on a horse, chariot, the clouds, &c. — so Ef. borau).

NOTE.—A. markab' is an infinitive, and therefore is naturally in Ef. and Fi. a verb, My. and Sa. a substantive, and To. both a verb and a substantive.

*B*orea, s., c. art. na*b*orea, a dream, or vision (in sleep) ;

*B*orea ki na*b*orea, v., to dream a dream, or see a vision (in sleep). [Tah. ria a vision in sleep.] H. mar'eh a vision (in sleep), A. rôya sleep, what is seen in sleep, from ra'a' (H. ra'ah) to see, then to have a vision in sleep, E. id.

Bor ia, or bori a, v. t., to break, bori nakasu break a stick, mauori, mauoriuori to be broken, and

Bori sia, redup.

Boriuori sia, v. t., break to pieces. H. pōr inf. of parar to break, break to pieces (pur to break), Hithpolel to be broken.

*B*orroa, v. i., to grow crooked, for *b*oraroa : *b*ora II., and roa.

Boro-silaia. See buru masila.

Boroaki, v., c. t. ending, to bequeath to, or order to do (by will, when dying) ; to commission (one to do something), give orders to. [My. pásân to commission, enjoin, Sa. poloa'i to leave commands (as on going a journey or dying), to command, Mg. hafatra (hafarana) a will or testament, order, bequeathed, ordered.] A. wa*s*a', 2, to bequeath by will, 4, id., and to give power to, or commission, by will ; to command, to enjoin. H., Pi., sivah to charge, command, delegate, commission.

Borōri sia, contraction of boriuori sia

*B*osa ia, v. t., to compress, manu i tumana *b*osa ia a bird compresses itself (with its closed wings), i *b*osai naniu he compresses a cocoanut (so as to break the shell), press together, squeeze (as a sponge), hence *b*osa, or uosa, v. i., to be compressed, i.e., narrow, and ta*b*osa (sela uosa a narrow track, natamole ta*b*osa a man thin as if pressed together), redup. uosauosa ; *b*osa naru na clap the hands, *b*osa-lot clap the hands with a sound, d. *b*osa ki, i.q. *b*osa ia.   A.

hamaza to press with the fingers or hand, to compress, push, strike, bite, break.

Bosabosa, s., froth (coming from the mouth, as of one in sickness), sputum, d. fut. [Mg. fotafota slaver, spittle, foam, mifotafota to slaver, to foam.] A. bozāk', bosāk', saliva, sputum.

Bota, v. i., and a., to be, or become, different, other, alien ;

Bota ia, v. t., to divide, part, make one remove from the other, botauota (or botōta) redup.; i toko botauota he is in the middle or midst, exactly between two things, lit. he is parting or dividing (the two things), māuota, or māota, to be divided or parted, hence na maota the midst or middle space between two things, i.e., the space by which they are parted, removed, or distant from each other. [My. beda, or bida, distinct, separate, different, beda-kan to separate, to distinguish, to make a difference.] E. b'ud other, alien, different, A. ba'oda, and ba'ida to stand apart, be distant, remote, 2, 4, make to be so, 6, to be apart from each other, also to recede or go apart from someone, 3, make to be apart or distant, also to go apart or be distant, bo'd' distance : cf. banabota diverse, different. Hence

Bota, s., c. art., a person unmarried (apart) ;

Botauota, and

Botōta ia, v. t., redup. of bota ia.

Botu, v. i., to swell (of a girl's breasts). A. nabata, 3), n. a. nobōt', begin to swell (a girl's breasts).

Boua (bowa), v. i., to rain, d. for bū.

Boūa ki (bowa ki), v., d. ua ki, to fruit, to produce fruit. Ch. Pael 'abeb to produce fruit.

Bouolau ki, v. t., to steer (a canoe or ship), then, fig., to steer a country (bouolau ki nafanua), &c., that is, govern it, bouolau ki emeromina govern the world (of God). [Ml. dd. barau, baro, walu, foro, Sa., Ha., uli, Sa., also, muli, My. mud·i in mamud·i-kan, Ef. uolau (wolau) in bouolau-ki.] E. hadafa to steer (a vessel or ship), then, fig., to govern men, to steer, i.e., govern the world (said of Jesus Christ), mahdaf rudder, helm. See uolau, infra.

Note.—Bouolau ki is reduplicate, see bolau ki (d.), id., and uolau ki, and note the pref. b' (for m) in bolau.

Bu, d., verbal pron., 1 pl., excl., dual moa : d. au, dual ara.

Bua, d. bobu (q.v.), voc., maternal grandfather : c. art. tobu na, q.v. [Fut. bua.]

Bu (nalo), v. t., to see (a thing). See bunu, bunu sia. [Santo d. vi to see.] A. ba"a' (final w or u) to look upon, observe.

Bu, s., c. art., a bundle. [Fi. ai vau.] See bau si and afa.

Bua, v., divide, as ta bua i cut, divide it (cut it open), mafua, and tabua, to be rent open, cracked, ti bua i press rend it (press burst it open, as new wine old wine skins), and fai (or fae) in magafai a half, a division (of a thing), and lao fai (see fai). [Sa. vaega a division, vaevae to divide in parts, cut up, mavae to be split, to be cracked open.] A. fa'ā, n. a., fa'w', or fa'y', 1, 4, to split, cleave, 7, to be open, to be separated, rent, cleft.

i. Bua, v. i., to be empty, vacant, having nothing (as an empty cocoanut), tābu, *i.e.*, tā bu, men having nothing, or naked (name applied to the naked people of some neighbouring islands, *i.e.*, people who use no waist cloth). A. bahiya to be empty and bare (as a house).

ii. Bua, and bubu, d. mobu, v. i., and a., to be deep (as the sea, or a pit), i toko bua (said of a yam down in the ground), ebu or ebua in the deep part (of a thing), i toko ebu or ebua, and sofa ni ebu is consumption or phthisis in the deep part (*i.e.*, inside) of the body (deepseated); ebua the abyss, Hades, Malo abua, id., bua-riri abyss, Hades (riri to sink), and bu-gia, or bubu-gia to sink deep, d. na tibu the deep. [Ma. kopua deep, An. ubo deep, Fi. tobu, d. nubu, deep.] A. 'amuka and ma'uka, 1, to be deep, also, to be distant, far off (emai, ufea), 4, make deep, 5, to be deep, H. 'amak to be deep, 'amek, 'amik deep, E. 'amaka to be deep, 'muk deep, mā'mak any depth, a valley, the abyss (Hades).

iii. Bua or fua (in na fua-goro,

d. na mua-goro, a spring on the shore covered by the flood tide), so called because the sea mua gor ia flows over it, and mua v. i., to flow (the tide);

Buafua, v., na tas i buafua, or naroa i buafua the sea or current flows or carries things floating on it :

Bua tia, v. t., to take (make to go) :

Bua a, v. t., make to flow upon (a thing), pour upon, moisten. [Ha. puai to flow, as blood from a vein, or water from a fountain, to cast up; to boil up, as water from a spring, My. buwang eject, expel, cast.] H. naba' to bubble forth, gush out, Ch., S., A. naba‘, naba". "The primary syllable is ba‘, ba", like bak, imitating the sound or murmur of boiling or bubbling." Cf. egg. II. bu'a to swell up, Arm. bē'ā' to boil up, H. ba'ah make to swell and boil, A. ba"a to gurgle out (as blood). The connection between the ideas of *going* or *flowing out* and *taking out* (making to go out) is seen in the eg. Ch. nēpak to go out, caus. to take out, and also in H. yabal to flow, caus. to bring, bear, carry.

Bubu, v. i., to gargle. [Sa. pupu to gargle.] See under preceding word, and cf. A. ba'ba‘, or ba'ba'u gurgling sound of water flowing from a bottle or flask.

Bua na. See bui na.

Bu gia, and

Bubu-gia, v. t., to sink down, to dip (anything), put it down into the water; uta bugi rarua load a canoe *deep* :

Bubu, v. i., to be deep : bua II.

Buele, d. bole, v. i., to be lost, missing. [My. ilang to lose, be lost, missing, Mg. very lost, missed.] A. sʻaʻa to be lost, missing.

Bugafuga, v. i., to be awake, to awake, bugò nia, v. t., to awaken one. [Sa. fagufagu, fafagu to waken, rouse from sleep, ps. fagua, Mg. foha, fohafoha imp., awake, mifoha, v. i., to awake, mamoha, v. t., to awake, fohazina being awakened.] Nm. fāk, v. i., to awake, 2, 4, v. t., awaken.

Bugo nia, v. t., to awaken. See preceding word.

Bui na, or bua na, s., c. art., backbone, tail, rump. [Fi. bui tail, Fut. bua back, To. mui after, the hindermost end, tip, or extremity of anything, Sa. muli the end, the rump, Mg. voho the back.] See muri.

Buigo, or *bigo*, v. i., to lose the way, be at a stand, perplexed, not knowing the way. [Compare Sa. pogia to be benighted.] See bog.

I. Buka, v. i., to be filled, swell out, as the belly when filled with food, or as a sail filled with wind; namarita na i buka his belly is puffed up or swollen, or pants (with rage), mafukafuka to be swollen or puffed up, nafukāna the being swollen or puffed up. [Mg. voky satiated, filled, mimoky, v. i., mamoky, v. t., vokisana, havokisana, My. bakat stuffed, filled, Ma. puku to swell.] A. nafahʻa to inflate, 8, to be inflated, to swell, naphʻatʻ inflation of the belly, manfuhʻ ventrosus; obese.

Buka, s., a swell, as a ground swell. [My. bakat, id.] See buka.

Buk, s., as nabuk natamole a band of men, [H. puu, a gathering or collection, sign of plural number, he puu kanaka a gathering or band of men.] See buka.

NOTE.—This word is used in Ef. also for a gathering or collection of things, thus : nabuk anena i oní au I am in his debt, but lit. his collection of things (which he has given me) remains on me (*i.e.*, I have not yet repaid it).

II. Buka sia, or bukí sia, v. t., to open, as a roll of cloth, buka ūa (ūwa) open the oven. [My. buka to open, unclose, uncover, Mg. voha opened, mimoha, v. i., mamoha, v. t., to open.] A. fakka, v. t., to open.

III. Buka, v. i., to bark (a dog), buka ia bark at it, bukai kusüe bark at a rat, d. syn. oro-maki; also, buka to cough. H. nabah, A. nabaha to bark (a dog). Formed from the sound. A. nabaha is followed by acc. with or without a prep.

IV. Buka ia, v. t., to hit upon, meet, fall in with, find, as i ba bukai uago buele he hit upon, met, fell in with, or found a lost pig. H. paga'id., as in Ex. xxiii. 4.

Bukāru, or bakāru, d. fakāru, v., to joke, jest, bukāru ki, v. t., mock, deride. [My. gurau to joke, and kara, id., bârgurau, mânggurau, joke, jest, mâng-gurau-kan, v. t., mock, deride.] A. kahara, 5), laugh, joke.

Buko na, s., c. art., protuberance or knob, as nabuko nani protuberance or knob of a yam. [Ha. puu.] See buka i.

Bukoro, s., enclosure round a house at its base, name of a tree and its fruit (from its kernel being *enclosed*), a proper name (of men). [Ma. pukoro sheath, case, halo, net.] See koro.

Bukota, v. i., or a., to be dark-coloured, dirty, blackish (as water with dust or earth in it) : gota.

Bukubukura, a., full of little swellings (pimples): ra a. ending. [Ha. puupuu, id.; Sa. po'u pimple, po'upo'ua full of pimples.] See buka i.

Bukutu, s., a rise, hill. [Ha. puu, id., My. bukit a hill.] See buka i.

Bul-meta na, s., eyeball, gleaming, part of eye. See bila.

Bula, mbula, d. for bila, q.v., big, large.

Būlĕ, a., adult, nafera būlĕ a lot of grown up men (adults). A. bala'a to reach mature or full age, bāli'' adult ; and

1. Bule, v. t., complete, used after other verbs adverbially, as i ba bule nafanua he went completely through the land,

le bule nagusu it (a canoe) completely rounded the point, nafisan i soka bule nafanua the word shot (lit. leaped) through the whole land, from end to end, noai i sera fule (or fulefule) nalia the water ran completely throughout the place. Bule is really a verb, in these instances, in apposition to the verb preceding it, as he went — completed (finished) the land, &c. [My. bulah the whole, To. fuli all.] A. bala''a, n. a. bulū'' to complete, go through to the end.

11. Bule, v. t., to strip off leaves, ora nani i bule nakasu the yam vine strips off leaves from the tree, mafule to be stripped of leaves (a tree). [My. bulus stripped of leaves.] A. 'abala 1, 2, to strip off leaves, foliis nudavit *arborem*.

Būle, s., a shell, lit., gleaming, shining, glittering, See bila.

Bulibog, d. for bilībog, for bulobog: bulo.

Būlī, s., a corpulent person ;

Bulia, a., swollen ; and

Bulifulia, a., swollen here and there (the body), a a. ending, and mabulu and fuluara, q.v. [Sa. fula stout, fulafula swelling, fulafula, fufula to be swollen.] H. 'afal, prop. to swell up, be tumid, A. 'afila to have a tumour or hernia. See telatela.

Bulai, s., d. for belaki, and

Bulai, v. t., d. for belaki, to gird.

Bulo, v. i., d. for bilo. Bulo is also thus used: iga uo bulo (bo) mai, he will come by-and-by, lit. he will awake and come (of a ship, man, or thing), hence bulo-bog morning, lit. awaking of day, or night, bulo āsa, bulo metamai, and d. bulbog, &c., and bilebog (for bilo-bog);

Bulõ nia, v. t., to awaken ; bulo nameta na open his eyes ;

Bulobulo i, v. t., awaken him. See bilo.

Bulo ki, v. t., to turn, to twist, also bulo sia, bulu sia, buli sia, tafolo to be turned, twisted, tafulus to be turned, bologa, to turn itself (as a thing in sinking in water), tafiloga, id., bulora, or filora (ending ra), twisted, confused (as a lot of things turned or twisted about). [My. pulâs, Ja. pulir to wring, twist, to turn aside (out of the way), to turn, turn round, Sa. milo to twist, mimilo, milo-milo, ps. milosia, milosi, to be twisted, to be perverse, milo-milosi, Fi. mulo-ca to twist a single thread, Ma. miro to spin, twist, mimiro to move swiftly, miro, s., thread, a whirling current of water.] A. malla, n. a. mallo, to turn, to twist round ; to twist one-self about, malmala, 2, to roll oneself about, malla to hasten, move quickly.

Buloki, v. i., or a., to be sticky, d. bubulu. See bulu tia.

Bulõra, v. i., or a., to be twisted; a. ending ra. See bulo ki.

Bulu sia, or bulo sia, or bilo sia, v. t., to wash. See balo nia.

Bulu sia, bulo sia, or buli sia, v. t., to turn. See bulo ki.

Bulu tia, v. t., to plaster, over-spread with some sticky sub-stance (as lime, paint, pitch), to cover with a plaster or poultice, as a wound, nabulu, s., plaster, &c., bubulu, bulu-bulut, buloki (and mabulu, q.v.), to be sticky, as plaster. [Fi. bulu-ta to bury or cover with earth, to apply an ex-ternal remedy, ai bulu an external application or thing that covers or buries, Sa. puluti to glue, to pitch, pulu glue, gum, resin, pulu-pulu to cover the body with a cloth, pupulu to interpose, to meditate, ps. pulutia, Fi. bulu-ta to repair an injury, lit. to bury it, ai bulubulu a peace offering, or thing offered as a reparation of an injury.] H. kapar, A. "afara to cover, cover over: A. "afara to cover, cover over ; to cover (white hairs, with some dye or tincture, Ef. bulu tia) ; to pardon (sin), 2, to cover with dust, H. kapar to cover, over-spread with anything, as with pitch, to pitch, Gen. vi. 14 (H. koper pitch); to cover (i.e., pardon) sin, Pi. to make expia-tion for an offence.

Bulu, bulufulu, and fulufulu : bule I.

Bulu, v. i., to fall down (as fruit from a tree, &c.), mala bulu faint, fall down (a man), and

Bulu aki, v. t., throw down (as firewood, &c.), (make to fall down). H. napal to fall, S. npal, Ch. něpal, id., Hi. hipíl to throw down (make to fall).

Bulu aki, d. for bulo ki, to turn, twist.

Bulum, or buluma, d. bulim, v. i., to be changed, lit. turned: luma.

Buma, v. i., d. fuga, to flower or blossom, nabuma na, s., its flower or blossom. [Ml.P. pug to blossom, pugan its flower or blossom, Sa. fuga flowers, blossoms, My. bunga flowers, blossoms, Mg. vony flower, mamony to blossom.] S. habeb to produce flowers, hababa', or habobo', flower.

Buna sum ia, v. t., to cork, plug, hence

Bunaso, or funaso, s., c. art., a cork or plug: see bono tia, or bunu tia, and sume lia.

Bunāts, d. for binata.

Bunofunoi, d. binofinoi, v. r., to be confused, perplexed. See binoinoi : noi, no i, no ia, nēa.

Būma, s., an insect that makes a shrill sound in the jungle in the evening, hence būma i gai (the būma makes its sound) is often used for "it is getting dark," "it is evening."

Bunu, d. for fanau, q.v.

Bunu lia, v. t., d. for balo nia, bulu nia,

Bunu sia (bu-nusi a), v. t., to see (a thing) : bu.

Bunu, s., death, destruction, as ru sua bunu ;

Bunu ea, v. t., to kill or destroy (fish, men, &c.), to extinguish or quench (a fire, or lamp), ru sua bunu they met destruction (having fallen into the sea), mafunufunu and mafunei, d. fanci, to be ended, to be anni-

hilated. [My. bunoh to kill, mambunoh, mamunoh to kill, Mg. vono killed, mamono to kill.] Hence

Bunufunu, redup. of preceding word. A. fana', disappear, pass away, vanish, 4, make disappear, destroy, annihilate, 5, destroy and annihilate (wipe out) each other (in war), fani caducus.

Bunu tia, v. t., same as bono tia. Hence

Bunutia, s., hundred, d. bunti (cf. bon) ; and

Bunuta (and bunta), v. i., or a., to be silent, lit. to be shut (the mouth), ba funuta, be silent, exactly equivalent to the vulgar English "shut up," hence nafunuta, s., a silent person, one that says little (a term of praise).

Bur, d. for bila, bula, to be big, large.

Būra, or fūra, v. i., or a., to be empty, to be devoid of, as i bi an fūra it is an empty shadow, a būra ki nalo I am empty of the thing, devoid of it, A. fara"a, 1, 2, to empty. See baro. Hence

Bura, s., rubbish ; nabura naniu the husk of the cocoanut, nabura na the husk or worthless part of a thing : hence the stalk of a fruit (as a worthless thing thrown away as rubbish) is called in different dialects bura-tena, bura-gitena, bara-tuna, biri-gitena, and miri-gitena, i.e., the bura of it.

Būra, d. birī, v. i., or a., to be full, bakafura to fill. [Mg.

feno full, mameno to fill, My.
pânoh full, mâmânohi to fill.]
H. mala' to fill, to be full, Pi.
to fill; with another verb, to do
anything *fully*, *i.e.*, thoroughly,
so Ef. bera-tia, d. bera-katia, as
lo b., look fully or thoroughly
at it, *i.e.*, watch it, rogo b.,
hear fully, *i.e.*, obey, i uia b.
it is good fully, *i.e.*, thoroughly
good, and it can also be said
tea berakati na, *i.e.*, tea anena
berakati a thing fully or
thoroughly his; A. mala', S.
mla', same as H.   Hence

Burafura, furafura, s., the jungle,
forest, vegetation : so called
because it fills the land. A
place covered with any kind
of weeds, &c., is called nalia
bura a full place.

Bura-gitena, and
Bura-tena, see bura, s.
Burasa. See marasa.
Burau, s., a long or tall cloud;
the sky : eg. barau.

Bure ia, furc ia, or burō a,
burei ki, furci ki, v. t., to
wash, rub, as bure naui wash
off the earth from a yam,
furei ki natuo na cleanse his
feet, furei ki lu nasoga, bure
biakik wash, cleanse a child,
bure nabau na ki narora rub his
hair with oil, oil his hair. H.
marak (rub), polish, cleanse
by washing or anointing (egg.
marah, &c.)

Bure ia, or bura ia, v. t., d., to
leave, allow, forsake, abandon.
A. bara', 3, to leave, abandon.
[My. bir, to permit, allow.]

Burei a, d. marag ki, v., to spit
out, to spit, to spit on. A., 4,

mara"a to emit saliva, bar',
mar" saliva.

Bur ia, buri, v. t., to pierce,
stick, buri uago stick a pig :
d. for biri.

Buria, v. i., or a., to be swollen
(of the body), to have the
dropsy. [Ma. kopurua drop-
sical, My. buru elephantiasis,
burut hernia.] The a in buria
is the a. ending. A. nabara to
raise up, heap up, 8, to swell,
nabra*t* a swelling on the body.

Būria (bauria, bouria), v., to
kindle or make a fire (in the
oven), ru būria ua (uwa), and
ru būria, they make a fire in
the oven, or, simply, they
make a fire, kindle up: this is
done every evening about an
hour before sunset. See bara
(H. ba'ar), and compare H.
bo'erah kindled (an oven).

Burog. v. i., or a., offensive,
mouldy, filthy (as food). [Ma.
puru mouldy, and kopuru,
kopurupuru, id.] A. mara"a
to be contaminated.

Buru masila, v. i., to roar (of
thunder), tifai i buru masila,
d. boro silaia, the thunder
roars, or thunders sounding :
for masila and silaia see sila.
[TaSa. biri thunder, and to
thunder, Ml. P. omburumbur,
Ml. A. amburambur, to roar
(of thunder), TaSa. roro to
roar (of thunder), Ml. P.
berver thunder.] H. ra'am
to roar (as thunder), ra'am
thunder, S. r'em to thunder,
ramo' thunder.

Būru, burufūru, v. i., or a., to be
short : d. *m*īto, q.v.

Buruma ki, or bĕruma (or bīruma) ki, v., to be in the relation of son-in-law to parent-in-law, or of parent-in-law to son-in-law, syn. monaki (mo-naki);

Burumà, or birumà, c. art. na buruma, s., one in that relation, son-in-law, mother-in-law, father-in-law : see mo na. E. (hamwa) tahamwa to contract affinity, to be joined in affinity (with someone), to marry the daughter of someone, tahmā affinity, specially the relation between a father-in-law and son-in-law, then (abstract for concrete) son-in-law.

Busa, v. i., or a., redup. busafusa, to be young, springing up (of plants and animals), hence to be inexperienced, foolish, to be spotted (the skin, as with cold, &c.) [My. mud·a young, immature, not deep in colour (light), foolish.] A. wabis'a to be spotted (with white and black spots, as the nails or skin), 4, to germinate, or put forth plants (the soil).

Būsa, s., or a., dumb, mute. A. yabisa to be arid (see bēs), 4, to be silent, mute.

Busa, a., orphaned, meta busa orphan. A. yabisa to be arid, dry. An orphan is called meta busa because deprived of it's mother's milk. See bēs, bēsu.

Busī, v. i., to blow, spout (as a whale). [Sa. pusa to send up a smoke (also applied to spray, dust, and heat), Tah. puha to blow (as a whale), puhepuhi to blow out of the mouth, blow, as with bellows, Ha. puhi to blow or puff, breathe hard, blow a trumpet, &c., Mg. fofotra blowing the bellows, mifofotra to blow the bellows, My. âmbus to blow, make a current of air, âmbusan bellows, âmbusi to blow, drive a current of air.] A. nafatha, i.q.. nafah'a, to blow with the mouth, blow out, puff, eject venom from the mouth (as a serpent), eject spittle (a man).

Busa, s., nabusa a mist. See under preceding word.

Bus ia, v. t., d., to lay down, leave, and bis ia in turu bis ia leave, abandon, allow ;

Busfus ki, d., redup., d. for bure ia, or bura ia, q.v.

Busi a, or fusi a, v. t., d. for muri a, q.v. [Mg. fody returned, sent back.]

Busa ia, or fusa ia, v. t., break or smash to pieces, smash (as a yam), mafusai ps. H. pus, or fus to break in pieces.

Buta, d., in meta-buta blind, lit. eye dark. [Fi. matabuto faint, buto darkness, Sa. matapo blind, matapogia faint, My. buta blind.] See bog, bātu. A. 'amiya to be blind, "umiya' to be faint.

Buta, or futa, v. i., to spring up or out, as water from a spring ; to spring up or out, as smoke from a fire ; to spring out, as a musket ball from a wound—i si buta ia he shot him, the bullet springing out from or glancing off his body, wounding but not fatal ;

Butafuta, d. futfut, redup., to
spring up or out, as water
from a spring ;
Butu-raki, or butĭ-raki, d., v. i.,
to appear, come in sight. [Ma.
puta, v. i., pass through, in or
out, come in sight, My. târbit
to issue, come out, emanate,
spring, arise, appear, escape.]
A. nabata to spring up or out,
as water from a spring, 4, ps.
form, to appear, go or come
forth, come in sight.
Butāki, dd. mitāki, milāi, q.v.
But, d. for bota, unmarried.
Butia, or buti a, or futi a, v. t., to
pluck, as a fowl, pluck out or
up, as weeds, mafuta to be
plucked. [Fi. vuti-a to pluck
feathers, hairs off animals,
hence, to pull up grass or
weeds, Sa. futi to pluck
feathers or hairs, fufuti, ps.
futia, My. bantun to pluck,
pull out.] A. namasa, 1, 2,
to pluck out, as hairs.
Buti a (for ba-uti a), v., d. for
bakauti a, q.v. [Mg. vita completed, finished, mamita to
finish.]
Bute (lua i), v. t., to praise. A.
madalia to praise.
Buti na, biti na, s., a knob or
excrescence growing on a tree,
a joint (from its bulging out).
See botu.
Butili, bitili, fitili, v. r., to speak
of each other, speak of one
behind his back : tili a.
Buto, v. i., to germinate, bud.
A. nabata germinate. Hence
Buto na, s., bud, d. muto na.
Buto na, s., navel, then middle;
malĕbuto (lit. the place of the
middle), the middle (of the
body, a land, anything), d. but,
hence d. tu-but rainbow, lit.
stand in the middle (of the
sky). [TaSa. buto navel, taga
nabute stomach, To. bito, Sa.
pute, Tah. pito navel, Tah.
pitopito a button.] See preceding word and botu : the
navel is the knob, as it were
the bud (bursting or swelling
out). (Compare navel, from
nave, prob. from nabh to
burst.)
Butol, v. i., d. for bitelo, q.v.
Butua, v. t., d. for bitua, to
place, lay down, give ; tā
bituatua to speak (or pray)
while giving (or laying down)
an offering (to the natemate).
Hence
Butut, s., a place where offerings
to the natemate are put : now
used for "altar."
NOTE.—The verb butua or
bitua is the reflexive of tua
ki : ba butua ki go backwards
and forwards between two
things, to halt between two
opinions.
Buturaki. See under buta, supra.

E, article, for a, sometimes i :
a, nĕ, na, in.
E, dem., this, that, as mal e (for
mala uai) that time, then : e
is a contraction for uai ; rag
uai this time, now. See i
(d.), dem. This e, or i, is
used also as a tense particle—
see i.

E, or i, prep., in, on ; t. prep. : anī, nī, a, i. [Sa. i in, at, with, to, from, for, of, on, on account of, concerning, Ma. i of, &c., and t. prep., My. i t. prep., Fi. e, or i, in, with or by (instrumental).] A. li, lī. lĕ, T. nĕ, Gurague ya, or ia.

E, inter. ad., where ? See sĕ.

Ei, ad., yes. [Mg. ey, Sa. e, id.] A. ey, or ei, yes.

Ei à, or ei ia, ad., yes, that's it : preceding word, and dem.

Ei eri, ad., d. syn. ei à : ei, and eri dem.

Ei, ad., here, d. i, q.v.

Ei (ū-i), ad., no. it is not. [Er. ĕyi, Mg. ai, id.] Neg. ad. e, and i, dem. H. 'i, E. 'i, not.

Eba, v. See tali-eba, tali-ofa.

Ebau, ad., at the head (of the island, i.e., the east), opp. to etu at the foot (west) ; e prep. and bau.

Ebago, ad., in the end (of the house), inside : e prep., and bago.

Ebua, or ebu, ad., in the deep : e prep., and bua II.   Also ebua, s., the abyss, Hades.

Ebut d., in the middle ; e prep., and but, d. for buto, q.v.

Egura, s., the stick used for spreading (scraping) out the heated stones of the oven : e art., and gura ia.

Eis, ad., same as ais.

Eka na, s., a relative, family connection.   See aka.

Ekatema, ad., on the outside of the house, outside : e prep., and katema, q.v.

Eksakes, d. for kesakesa, q.v.

Eko, s. See neko.

Ekobu, ad., in the inside, in the house, inside : e prep., and kobu.

Elà, d. for elau.

Elagi, ad., and s., above, heaven : e prep., and lagi, q.v.

Elalo, or elalu, ad., in front, before : e prep., and lalo, or lalu, see alo, or alu na.

Elau, ad., on the sea, by the sea : e prep., and lau

Elo, s., d. ālo, the sun : āli.

Elo, or èl', v. i., to be sweet, pleasant, agreeable, redup. lolo. [Ha. olu to be pleasant, agreeable.] A. halā', halw', id.

Elol, ad., d., in the belly, inside : e prep., alo na, lalo na.

Emai (or emai), ad., in the distance, afar, far away ; d. ufĕa : e prep., and mài. [Sa. mao, mamao to be far off, distant, mamao, ad., far off, distant.] A. ma'oka to be far off, distant, ma'k' distance.

Emalebuto, ad., in the middle, inside : e prep., and malebuto na.

Emate n, s., d. for namatigo na, the grave : matĕ.

Enea, or inia. d., personal pron., 3 sing., he, she, it, dd. nai, nigā, kinini.

Enera, or inira, pl. of preceding word, they, dd. nāra, nigar, kiniara.

En', vulgar pronunciation sometimes heard for nunu to wipe, rub off.

Enī, v., d. for anī, contracted en, an, to abide, be.

Enu, pers. pron., 1 sing., I, dd. anu, kinau, kinu, keino.

Ère na, or èri na, d., mother. See ani na, note.

Erai, dem., d., this : arai.

Eri, dem., this. See arai.

Erik, dem., this, here. See s. arai and ka.

Eru, dem., same as eri, d. nro, nra.

Eru, s., c. art. nīcru, arms, war : āru na.

Esān, ad., here, there, and

Esānien, id., and

Esās, id. : c prep., and the demonstrative particles se, na, q.v. See ais (eis). [My. sini, sika, here, sana, sanan, situ, there, and with prep. disini here, disana, disitu there, Mg. ato, eto, aty, ety, here.]

Esega. See asaga.

Esike, s., a forked stick, that which sike tia grasps, seizes : sike tia, e art.

Esai, or esei, s., the open, open space, d. esai leba a road, lit. big open space : sai.

Eso, or ēsa, d., ad., yes: ei (supra), and so or sa, dem.

Esu, d., ad., outside, away, e prep. and su. [Cf. Fi. esau (e sau) on the outside, sausau outskirts, sausau kei vuravura ends or outsides of the earth.] H. kĕsu, or kṣu only, pl. kaswē, kiswoth ends or extremities (of the earth), A. kasā', n. a. kasw', kasā' to stand apart, be afar off.

Esuma, ad., in the house, at home : e prep., and suma.

Et, v. i., or a., d., to be many. Cf. A. 'āda' to be many.

Etaku, ad., at the back, behind. [Sa. i tua, id.] E prep., and taku na.

Etan, ad., on the ground, down : e prep., and tano the ground.

Etu, ad., at the foot (of the island, i.e., the west, opp. to ebau) : e prep., and tua na the foot.

Eüo (ēwo), ad., no, it is not : e, as in ëi, and uo dem.

Euta, ad., on shore, ashore, on land, opp. to elau : e prep., and uta.

Fa (and fĕ or fī), inter. pron., c. dem. sa or se, safa, sefa, what ? also where ? It is ua in matuna, q.v. A. ma', H. mah what ?

Faa na, s., d. mao na, the thigh : mao. See bua, fai.

Fa, or ba, q.v., to go.

Fafa-sia, v. t., redup. of ba-sia, to tread upon (of many).

Fā, d. for mau, in mal fā nin = male mau ua = this very time, now.

Fafan, for bafano, to wash the hands.

Fafaga, redup. of faga.

Fāfatu, v. r., to trust, confide, fafātu isa to trust or confide in him, or in it. See under fatu.

Fafine, s., d., a woman (i.e., wife-man), and, a., female. Fa-fine (see Note 3, infra) is fa (for which see mera, infra, man in general), and fīne a female, and denotes lit. female-man, as ata-mani denotes lit. male-man. [Sa. fafine, Fut. fine, Mg. vavy, My. pârâmpüan woman,

female, bini a wife.] H.
nkebah, f., a woman, a female
(a genitalium figura dicta) of
persons, and of beasts, S.
nekebta', pl. nekbata'.

Note 1.—The nĭ in fafine,
fine, the same as the nĭ in
kurunĭ and atamanĭ and the
final n of the My. părămpüan,
is a suffixed particle ; fafi-nĭ
is thus the same as vavy, and
the difference between fafi-nĭ
and fi-nĭ is that the former has
fa or va prefixed. In fy (fi,
vy), as also (as it occurs in
various dialects) in fu, ueo,
bio, bo, foya, bayi (Santo d.
nekepai), bai, bua, the ancient
feminine termination, t, or th,
as in the H. form of the word,
is not heard : it is heard, as
in the Aramaic form of the
word, in matu (*infra*), bite
(-riki), or fite (-riki), Ja. wedo,
other dialects but, fid.

Note 2.—In Santo dd.
occur katsai, karai, a woman,
female : with katsai compares
Ysabel gase ; and with karai
Efate kurui, or koroi, kuruni,
nagurui, naguruni, Wango
urao : these belong to another
stem, for which see s. v. lai.

Note 3.—The fa, or va, in
fafini, vavy, is the same (by
elision of the r) as the para in
My. părămpuan, Ja. părăwan
or prăwan (Ta. dd. pilăven,
brăn, New Guinea d. mer-
wine).

Fagan ia, v. c., same as bagan ia,
q.v. Hence

Fagafaga, v., redup., and

Fagafaga, s., a bait, and

Faga, s., that which is given to
eat, food ; a present, a bribe.

Fai (vai), c. art. nĭfai, dd. noai
(n'uai, *i.e.*, n'wai), nai (n'ai), s.,
water. [An. inwai, Er. nu,
Ml. nue, Epi ue, Sa., Fut. vai,
Ma. wai, Bouru dd. wai, waili,
Ceram dd. wai, waeli, arr, My.
ayer, *i.e.*, ay (ai), and er.] H.
ma' unused in sing., pl. maïm
construct, mē' water; Nm. mâi,
E. mai, water.

Fai, v. t., d., divide or cleave, as
lao fai plunge into, cleaving
(with a spear) : bua to divide,
cleave, and see also maga-fai.

Fai, s., a skate (fish). [Cf. My.
pari, Tag. pagi, skate fish.]
Der. unknown.

Fakal ia, same as bakal ia I.
Hence

Fakal, a. (in active sense) kano
fakal a comforting person,
comforter (in passive sense),
uago fakal domestic or tame
animals, lit. pigs cared for, or
taken care of.

Fakalo, or fakal, s., war. [My.
bárkalahi (kâlahi) to fight, to
quarrel, kâlahi fight, quarrel.]
(Mahri ghorat war), H. garah,
Hith., to make war (with anyone).

Fakamatua, s., c. art., an ancient
story : matua, tuai.

Fakamauri, i.q. bakamauri, q.v.

Fakarago, s., c. art., the rough
prickly scab that forms on a
sore : rago.

Fakarogo, i.q. bakarogo

Fakaru, i.q. bakaru. See bukaru.

Fakaruku, s., the under part, as
na fakaruku ki nakasu the

under part of a tree (*i.e.*, shade or shelter under its overhead foliage), ki nauot (fig.) the shelter or protection of a chief: rukua (and the caus. prefix).

Fakasa, s., a festival : bakasa.

Fakataliga, s., an ear pendant : caus. prefix, and taliga.

Fakatokoi, or fakatokei, i.q. bakatokoia.

Fakau, or fakaua, s., d. fikau, fikaua, a messenger, ambassador, agent sent to do something for a chief or community ; and

Fakau, or fakaua, s., a message such as the agent sent by a chief or a community carries to deliver, i oti nafakaua he carries the message (of state). See kau, gau, grasp, take hold of, carry, &c. [Sa. feʻau to send for (v. r.), feʻau a message, To. fekau to bid, command, order ; a message, order ; My. and Ja. pânggawa a grandee, a noble : in Java it is the title of the five chief councillors of state, and the word is derived from gawa to bear or carry, convey, bring, Ef. kau to carry, (as a club), Fi. kau-ta to carry, Sa. ʻau to send, ʻau mai to bring, ʻauʻauna a servant, ʻau a troop, gang, shoal, bunch (of bananas), Ef. makau a bunch or cluster (of fruit), d. umkau many, all (collected).]

Faki, or fiki, transitive particle, connecting the verb with its object, after or suffixed to the verb, consisting of the preps. fa, or fi, and ki.

Fala, s. (see under bala II.), a ship's yards.

Falafala, s., cross sticks fastened on a tree for a ladder to climb it : bala II.

Falea, s., a cave. [Tah. farefare, a., hollow, fare a house, Ma. whare, Sa. fale.] See bala III.

Fam ia, or bam ia, v. t., to eat. [Tah. amu to eat.] H. baʻam, A. faʻama, to have the mouth full, to swallow down.

Fanau sa, v. t., d. bunu to teach, to instruct : to preach (recent use). [Fi. vunau-ca to admonish, harangue, preach to.] H. bin, Hi. to teach, to instruct, A. bāna, 2, 4, make clear, explain, lucidly expound, 5, render lucid.

Fanauen, s., c. art., the teaching, *i.e.*, either the act of teaching or the thing taught, law (as "law" of Moses, recent use).

Fanei, v. i., d., to be extinguished, out (of a fire) : bunu ca, bunue a.

Fānu, s., darkness, shade, only in kot-fānu, evening, lit. time of shade, d. rag mēlu. See mēlu.

Fanua, s., inhabited country, land, My. bânua, id. [Malo vanua house, Santo d. venua house, village.] H. banah, to build, as a house, ps. part. banuʻ built, binyaha building ; A. banaʻ, S. bnaʻ.

Note.—The Santo word has best preserved the primary meaning house, or building ; then a country, district, or land is called bânua, or fanua, because, like a house or village (or building), it is the dwelling-place of men.

Fāra ki nameta na, v. t., to fix the eyes, stare with open and motionless eyes. Nm. fajar, or fagar, 2, fix (the eyes), stare.

Fara, s., c. art., a cocoanut (fruit) that begins to shoot. [Cf. Fi. vara, a cocoanut ready to shoot.] *Bora* 11.

Fara, s., a chafed place on the skin, especially on the thigh (from being rubbed or chafed in walking): baro sia.

Fara, or fera, s., a row, or rank, or band ;

Farafara, or ferafera, s., a row, a lot, a band (as of sores on a limb), lit. a number of rows ;

Bifara ki, or bifera ki, v. c., to put or arrange in rows. [My. baris a line, row, rank, file, troops, mâmbaris, v., and baris kan, v., and bârbaris, v., bari-san parade, place where troops are exercised.] H. ma'arakah (and ma'aroth for ma'arakoth) disposing, ranging in order, a row or pile, battle set in array, army, or band ; from 'arak to arrange in order, or in a row.

Fara-bule, s., c. art., a rank, row, or band, of adults or full-grown men : fara rank, and bule adult.

Fara-kāl, c. art., a row or band of men connected together by relationship, as of brothers : fara, and kal, su bakal ia.

Farāti, s., c. art., sticks fastened above and upon the rafters of a house : a. pr. name (the

name of the chief of Sesake, the chief binding the people together as the nafarāti (lit. that which binds together) do a house.) [My. bâroti rafters, Fi. vorati upper cross beams of a house.] From bara tia, q.v. H. ḥibar (E. aḥabara, v. c.) to bind together, connect or join together.

Fare, farefare. See bare, bare-fare, to move.

Farea, s., the public house of a village, d. fare outside. [Mota varea outside, Ml. P. vere, Ur. vari outside, Mg. ivelany out-side (i-velany).] A. barriyy' outer, external (Ct. barri), Nm. barrâni outer, exterior, (and barra, out).

Farea, d. for bi reko to be poor : reko ; and bi to be.

Farofaro, a., tea farofaro, a thing that rasps, &c. : baro sia.

Fāsi, *i.e.*, fa-si, v. t., tread upon, fasi koro bind together the reeds of the koro-fence (which is done by treading upon them) : basi a.

Fasu (na meta na), s., d., eye-brows, tafasi, v. r., to make a sign with the eye. A. "amaza to make a sign (with the eye, eyebrows), 6, make such signs to each other.

Fasu, fasua na, s., a part, por-tion ; member (of the body). [Sa. fasi a piece, a place, fasifasi to split up in pieces, fasi to split, beat.] H. basa' cut in pieces, A. bas'a'a cut, cleave, bas''at part, a piece, cg. H. badad to divide, bad a part, pl. members of the body, A. badda separate, disjoin, budd' portion, part (of anything), badād' part. See s. v. H. badlad.

Fātā, s., a bench, shelf, stand, platform, dd. uēnr', uērē, uētĕ, kofeta (i.e., ko feta.) [Sa. fata raised house for storing yams in, a shelf, a bier, Tah. fata altar, scaffold, piece of wood to hang baskets of food on, &c., Mg. vatra (and vata) box, shelf for keeping rice, &c.] H. 'omed platform, place, 'emdah a lodging (place). See fatu.

Fatok, same as batok and matok : toko.

Fatu, same as batu and matu: tu.

Fatu (see matu ki), hence fafatu, v., to trust in, rely upon, confide in ; matu ki (na koro) to set up the posts or supports (of a fence), palo fulsit, stabilivit ; na matu na, the column of the back, that is, the backbone or vertebral column ; also, post or stake (of a fence) ; fātu stones or rocks ; na fātu na bones ; fāta (see ante) : uota (wota) a chief (column or support or upholder of the people). [Mg. vato a stone, My. batū a stone, Sa. fatu a stone, core or stone of fruit, faafatufatu to persevere indefatigably, fatu (-amoa) to have a swollen shoulder (from bearing burdens), Tah. fatu the gristly part of an oyster, the core of an abscess, fatu lord, master, owner.] A. 'amada 1, 2, 3, to sustain, prop up, make firm or stable, with a column, post, or stake, (matu ki), 8, to rely upon, trust or confide in (fāfātu) ; also, 1, to have the hump or the back contused with carrying (a camel), H. 'amad to stand (be firmly set), confide in, endure, persist, persevere (cf. Sa.), A. 'imād higher structures, column, stake, 'amōd' prop, column, stones put in the ground for supports for the foundation, column, prop of a family, chief, lord, the back, 'amīd' column and chief or prince (of a people), H. 'amūd column, pillar, platform, scaffold. See fāta (ante).

Fatu, s., c. art. nafatu, the ridge of a house, ridge-pole: see bātu. [TaSa. papatu, id., Malo uobatu, id., Ml. U. uobut, Fut. taufufu, id., My. bubungan, bâbungan, and bumbung, Ja. wuwung, id., Mg. vovonana, id.]

Fatuna, s., and ad., d. for matuna, q.v.

Fau, same as bau, a., new.

Faulu, s., barter, i.q. baulu.

Faum, d. fau, new ; na faumuen : perhaps for fauman, redup.

Faus ia, same as baus ia, ask, question ; hence

Faus, pr. n. (Questioner), a spirit, officer of Saritau at the gates of Hades.

Fe a, and fefe a. same as be a, befe a ; nafeāna, nafefeana, s., the act of reading, or counting.

Fĕ, conj., if, should, for bĕ.

Fe, d., conj., then, but. A. fa, id.

Fēa, same as bē, or bēa, to precede, first.

Fefe, same as befe.

Feï, or fē, d., inter. pron., who? [Sa. o ai, Tah. o vai, Ta. ba, Er. me, id.] II. mī, A. man, men, mun, or min, also often pron. 3 pers added man hu who? (who-he?), contracted manu, menu.

Feifei ki, same as beifei ki; nafeifeien, s., the act of indicating or showing, or the thing by which something is made manifest; a sign, token.

Feko, s., a cockroach, and similar insects.

Felak, s., c. art., d., a tribe, or family clan, dd. syn. metarau, kainaga: bala III.

Felaki, s., c. art., girdle to which the nafon, or loin cloth, was attached: it is about six inches wide: belaki.

Fera, c. art., a row. See fara.

Fera-bule, fera-kāl. See farabule, fara-kāl.

Ferafera, rows. See farafara.

Fera, c. art., s., an omen, also fefera; the natamole tabu having poured out some namaluk (kava) to the natemate drinks off his own cup, and then looking into it sees some blood, or a human hair, or some other thing, which is called fera, an omen, or indication, good or bad, as the case may be: or he perceives the omen, good or bad, by "lo namo," which is another species of divination.

Fefera ki, or fera ki, and bifera ki, v., to show by a fera, as the natemate are supposed to do (see under the preceding

word): to give an omen. [Mg. fambara an omen, presage, My. fal omen (A.)] A. fa'l' omen.

Fera, v. i., fera ki, v. t., ferafera, v. i., ferafera ki, v. t.;

Feroa, c. art., s., a crumb: bera, bera ki.

Fet, s., a bird's nest, made like a platform of woven twigs. [Sa. fataniga a nest.] See fāta.

Feta, c. art., s., a tribe: beta.

Fete, or fite, c. art. nafete, inter. pron., what? Nm. matle what?

Fetta, s., soapstone, a soft stone that can easily be cut: fatu stone, and ta to cut.

Fi, v., to be: bi.

Fi, prep., after verbs, or bi, on, &c. A. bi, fi, id.

Fiàre ki, v., to go into the presence of someone, to be unabashed (opposite of maliàre, or malière). See rairai.

Fiatu, v. r., to smite each other, to fight, war: atu.

Fière, v. r., d., to speak, converse. A. liāra, 6, to converse, talk together.

Fifi, s., anything binding round, as a fillet or turban, &c., then a thing going round, as a ship round a cape or island, then hostile talk (with which one's adversary as it were binds him round);

Fifi ki, v. t., to go round, as a yam vine round a stake, a ship round an island: fifi is for fifisi, redup. of fisi, q.v.

Fifis ia, v. t., to bind round: redup. of fisi.

Fikit, or fikat, v. r., to be savage, given to biting, lit. to bite each other: kat ia. [Fi. veikata, id.]

Fikoba, v. r., lit. to chase, or pursue, each other : koba sia.

Fili, or filā, c. art., same as bīla, lightning : bila. [Sa. uila, My. kilat, Mg. helatra, id.]

Filīfilī, s., a gleaming or flashing shell worn as an ornament : bila.

Filora, same as bulora, and, redup.,

Filifilora. See bulo ki.

Fimeri, v. r., to be doing something to each other, usually in a hostile sense, to be fighting : meri.

Fimuri, v. r., to be returning each other, dismissing with presents, repaying : muri.

Finaga, c. art., s., food: kan ia (in finaga the k is elided after the prefixed fi.) [My. makanan, Mg. fihinana, id.]

Firā nia, v. t., supplicate, or pray, him, and without object, firā to supplicate, pray, also bifirā, bifirā nia. [Tah. pure to pray, pupure to pray frequently.] H. falal, fithp., to supplicate, pray.

Firaka, v. i., to delay. A. 'araka, 5), to delay.

Fisa, v., fisan, c. art., s., to speak, word : bisa.

Fis ia, or fisi a, v. t., to bind round, to bind about, as a fillet, turban, or vine round the head, a string round a parcel, a bandage round a wounded limb; fisi namanuk to bind up a wound ; a yam vine binds round a stake (twines round it), and fisi namē to twist a rope (bind round the one strand on the other—this is usually bulo ki) ; a whip or rod binds round the body to which it is applied, hence tale fisi a to flog (see tale to go round), lit. to go round binding about, d. mafisi a to whip, flog : often the final s is elided hence fi-gote fia to flog him to pieces (for fisi-gote fia), lit. to flog—break him, and see fifi (supra), and tafifi ; the word of an adversary is said to fisi the object of his anger, that is, bind him round ; fisi uago bind round a pig (in order to its being carried slung to a pole, so that it may not be hurt). [Sa. fisi to entwine as a vine, To. fi to twist and fihi entwine, twist, Ma. whiwhi be entangled, whakawhiwhi wind round, fasten, My. pusing to turn round, twist.] H. habas' to bind, bind on, bind about, as a head band, turban, tiara, "the seaweed is bound about (fisi na bau gu) my head," Jon. ii. 6 ; to bind up a wound, to bind fast, shut up.

Fisi, a. used as s., i bi fisi (a boy that is circumcised, ru tefe a i bi fisi they circumcise him, he is fisi). A. 'afsa'u e praeputio apparentem habens glandem puer, fasa'a a glaude praeputium reduxit puer.

Firi na, c. art., s., d. fiti na, q.v.

Firi a, or fir ia, v. t., same as bir

ia, to make void, bring to nought ; hence

Firi, in tale-firi, round bringing to nought, *i.e.*, all round.

Firigia, same as biri gia, to carry.

Fisau na, s., d., as nafisau naui = ora naui, the sprout, shoot, or vine of a yam : bisau.

Fisïkō na, s., flesh. [Cf. Bu. juku, My. daging, id., TaSa. veseko, id.] Cf. E. sïgā flesh.

Fīso, c. art , s., an annual reed-like plant whose top is used for food. [Sa. fiso a species of reed.] Der. unknown.

Fisuaki. Same as bisuaki.

Fisueri. Same as bisueri.

Fisuraki, c. art., s., talk, speech : bisuraki.

Fisurakien, c. art., s., the act of talking : bisuraki.

Fisurua, c. art., s., a lie, or lies ; and

Fisuruen, c. art., s., lying : bisuru.

Fiti na, c. art., s., d. firi na, the rib, or ribs, side. [Er. mperi, Santo d. porera na, Ma. rara, Mafoor raar, rib.] H. sela', Ch. 'ala' rib, side, A. s'il', rib.

Fïtaua, c. art., s., d. syn. with fakaua or fikaua : tau.

Fïti, v. i., d., to run. Cf. A. fadda to run.

Fitèriki, or bitèriki, s , an old woman, matron, lady, as màriki an old man, senior, sir : màriki is mā' man, and riki old, and fitèriki is fite woman, and riki old : for fite see under fafine and matu ; and for riki or 'riki old, what follows. [Ma. ariki *first-born*

male or female in a family of note, hence *chief, priest, leader.*] E. lèhèka to advance in age ; be the first-born, or eldest, in a family ; be senior ; alhaka to grow old, lhïk advanced in age, aged ; contracted lik chief.

Fitefa, same as bitefa.

Fitili, same as butili.

Fitia, same as bitia.

Fito na, s., d., syn. bile-meta na, q.v. : buto, v. i., and buto, s., bud.

Fo, d. for bo, particle used in the formation of the future tense ;

Fōga, s., d. c. art. nãfo, *i.e.*, na afo, whetstone, grinding stone, and (because used as whetstone) pumice stone. [To. fuaga (Ma. hoanga, Sa. foaga) a grindstone, a whetstone, fuafuaga pumice stone.] H. hafaf to rub off, scrape off, A. haffa to rub off.

Fōna, c. art, s., d. syn. tofe, the native cloth, or clothing, made from the bark of a tree. [E. Mai funa, id.] H. hafaf to to cover (kafah to cover, to veil), A. haffa to cover with a garment.

Fōnu, s., the turtle or tortoise. [Fi. vonu, My. pãnu, Mg. fany, To. fonu.] A. 'āwinat, 'ayinat, the tortoise or turtle.

Fu, v. i., d. for mu to hum, buzz, lago fu humming or buzzing fly (blow fly) : mu.

Fua na, or bua na, s., nafua n rarua, the bottom (outside) of a canoe or ship, lit. the back, syn. na matu n rarua : bua na, buï na.

Fuagoro, s. See muagoro.

Fuata, v. i., or a, to have raised stripes on the skin (as from blows with a rod, or as are formed by the veins on the arm). See bua III., and bua tia : the radical notion is *swelling out :* ending ta.

Fua tia, i.q. bua tia.

Fuga, d. buma, q.v.

Fugaga, v. i., to well up, spring, bubble up, welling over or spreading asunder (as a spring) : fua, or bua III., and gaga, for which see maga.

Fugafuga, v. i., or a., i.q. bugafuga. [Sa. fagufagu.]

Fugafuga na, s., as fugafuga nabiau, the whitened or breaking crest of a wave, lit. its blossom : fuga.

Fule, and fulefule, or bulefule. See bule I.

Fulu, and fulufulu : i.q. preceding word.

Fuluara, v. i., or a., to have swellings : bulifulia, q.v., syn.

Fulus, v., to turn : bulu sia.

Fumafuma na, s., d. syn. fugafuga na, q.v.

Funaso, c. art., s., stopper : bunaso.

Fura, same as bura, to be full.

Furei, s. See futei.

Furei ki, v. t. See burei a: rub, cleanse ; furei ki natua na, cleanse his feet, as by rubbing or scraping them on a scraper, &c.

Furei a, same as burei a, or bura ia, to leave.

Furiāna, c. art., s., the being swollen, or having the dropsy : buria.

Fus ia, same as bus ia, d. mur ia.

Fusa ia, same as busa ia.

Fusfus ki, same as busfus ki.

Fut, c. art., s., d. for bosabosa.

Futei, dd. furei, futrei, mitoi or mitei, s., the white ant. See rei, tei. [Sa. loi, Tah. ro, ant, gen. name.]

Futfut, d. for butafuta.

Futum, v. i., dd. bisau, busuf, busofu, bisobu, to sprout forth, spring up, grow. [Fila, Meli, Aniwa, Fut., somo, To. tubu; Sa. tupu, My. tumbuh, Ja. tuwuh, Mg. tombo, id. In Ef. (but not in all dialects) sobu denotes also the first springing forth or beginning of any thing, as i sobu it sprang forth, *i.e.,* began ; ru sobu meri a they began did it, *i.e.,* they were the first who did it, were the first beginners of the doing it.] H. samah, Kal and Piel, to sprout forth, to grow (as plants, trees, the hair), and fig. used of the first beginnings of things which occur in the world, as Is. xliii. 19, " Behold I make a new thing ; now it shall *spring forth,*" Hi. make to sprout forth or grow, and fig. make something spring up or exist, H. semah offspring, Ef. atuma, id.

G (pronounced ng).

Gā (ngā), d., pers. pron., 3 sing., he, she, it (nom. suf., n, or na). [Ma. ngā pl. art., Sa. na he, she, this, that, these, those Ha. na, pl. art., and sign of pl. number, My. iña (inya) he, she, it, they.] Mod. S. ani, 'ni, they, also sometimes he or she, and pl. art. (St., p. 22, and fol.)

Ga, conj., usually go, q.v., and : ka, in kai, conj.

Ga, final conj., that, ut, d. ka, or k', q.v.

Ga, dem., this, here, there, always (in this form) suffixed as in nag, naga, q.v., alaga (alia ga) this place, or place here; i.e., here (d. li ke, see ke) ; but alaga may be a contraction for alia naga : ka.

Gabuer, a., and s., grey-haired, aged, a grey-haired, i.e., aged person : kabuer.

Gāfa, s., a fathom (six feet). [Sa. gafa a fathom.] A. kāmat (Nm. kama) a fathom (six feet).

Gafikafī, s., a small basket ; and

Gafikafī, v., to feel for or take hold of a thing in a basket with the fingers. A. koffat a basket, kaffa to take stealthily between the fingers.

Gaga, v. i., to well out, or bubble up, as water from a spring, in fugaga. See maga.

Gai, or gei, redup. gaigai, v. i., to cry, sing, &c. : kai or kei

Gai (ga, final conj., and i, tense and mood particle of the fut.) See i.

Gaigai, v. i., to pant, be out of breath. [Sa. ga'ega'e to be out of breath, Ha. nae, naenae to be out of breath, to pant.] S. kah to pant.

Gai-tagoto, v. i., to scream (as in pain) : gai, and tagoto, for which see koto to break.

Gakalau ia (gkalau ia), redup. of galau ia.

Gakarafi (gkarafi). See karafi.

Gakasi (gkasi). See kasi.

Gakatak (gkatak). See kati.

Gakau sa, v. t., to grasp (as an oar, in pulling, or a branch of a tree) : usually pronounced gkau. See gau, kau.

Gakua, inter. ad., used with verbal pron., as i gakua how ? lit., let it be as what ? indefinitely, let it be as somewhat, let it be so, thus, yes (assent): ga, final conj., and kua, q.v.

Gala, v. i., or a., small : kala.

Galakala, v. i., to laugh. [My. gálak to laugh loud continuously.] A. karkara to laugh loud and long, karkara to laugh, cf. kalla, 7, to laugh.

Galau ia, v. t., to cross over, d. (transposed) lakau ia, q.v. E. halafa to cross over, ahlafa make to cross over.

Gale-baga, s., d., bowstring : kale-baga.

Gal ia (al ia, kal ia), v. t., to stir round (as water or any liquid). [Ma. ngaru a wave, ngarue shake, move to and fro, Ha. ale well up, aleale make into waves, stir up, as water, ale a wave, Sa. galu a wave, gagalu to be rippled, galu to be rough, break heavily on the reef, &c., My. • alun, Mg. alona, a wave.] H. galal to roll, hence gal fountain, well, pl. waves, S. galo' a wave.

Galu, c. art., s., husks, peel, &c.

(for pig's food), better part of a thing; pudenda; d. the inner bark of trees : see kalu tia. Cf. Ch. gilla', S. gelo', A. gillu, gullu chaff, &c., a covering, better part of a thing.

Galu tia, v. t., galuti nāsu to put the bowstring on a bow, nabela galu covering board on end of a canoe ; and

Galu, c. art., s., bowstring. See kalu tia.

Galugalua, v. i., or a., d. sagalugalu, to be aged, experienced (of persons), to be mature, also to be worn out as with age (of anything), as if to be full of agedness, and mere husk or skin : it has the a. ending a; nagalu matua an aged, full-grown, or full-bearded person, or one not immature. A. galla, 2, to become aged and expert or experienced.

Gan ia, ganikani a, v. t., to eat : kan ia.

Gara, v. i., to be dry : kara.

Garagara, v. i., to be strong, vehement, and garakarai : kara, karakarai.

Garā sa, v., to meet (any person or thing), to come upon, hit, as ru ba gára nata they went, met a person, i ba garā sa it (as a calamity) came upon him, i si garā sa he shot (hit) it or him, i bisa garā sa he spoke met. (or hit) it, i.e., he spoke to the point. H. karah and kara' to meet.

Gara ki, v. See kara ki.

Gara, d., pers. pron., 3 pl., they :

ga and 'ra. [Ma. ngārā they, them.]

Gar ia, v., and, redup.,

Garikari a. See kar ia.

Garo i, v. t. See kar ia.

Garu tia, and redup.,

Garukaru. See karu tia.

Garei ki. See karei ki.

Garaf ia, v. t. See karaf ia.

Gari, a., d. for kasi.

Gasa, inter. ad. See kasa.

Gas ia, v. See kas ia.

Gasua, and gasukasua, a. See kasua.

Gāt. See gaut.

Gat ia, v. See katia.

Gat, v. See kat.

Gatikati. See katia.

Gati, d. for kasi.

Gato na, d. karo na.

Gau, v. t., to grasp : kau.

Gaua, a., barbed (of a spear) : kau, v. t., tagau. It has the a. ending a.

Gaut, d. gāt, in bati-gaut a plant with kook-like thorns, lit. grasping teeth : kau, v. t., 'tagau.

Gel ia, v. t., to clasp (in order to lift or carry), carry away ;

Gele tia, v. t., id. ; and

Gelakela, v., used of many carrying away. See kele tia and kalu tia.

Gel ia, for gal ia.

Gema, d., verb suf., 1 pl., excl. : gami, nami.

Gemi, d. gami, nami, nom. suf. 1 pl., excl.

Geraf ia, for garaf ia.

Gere na, s., in mele-gere na the hollow in the tail of a fish. [Ml. P. kare, tail ; My. ekor, ikur, tail.] H. 'ahōr, A.

'oh'or', hinder part, rear, end ; Nm. ĕkir, end.

Gesa, gesakesa, for kesa, kesakesa.

Gi, prep., and ki, q.v., to, belonging to, of.

Gī, s., porpoise : perhaps so called because of the squeaking noise it makes on rising out of the water. See next word.

Gia, gkī, giki, v. i., creak, squeak, ping, moan. [Fi. gi to squeak, Sa. 'i'i squeak.] A. nakka, nakik' creak, &c.

Gie na, or gia na, s., name, dd. kiha na and gisa na, q.v.

Giè sa, or gie ki, v. (see preceding word), to have or acquire a name for or in connection with something.

Giki. See kiki, small.

Gil ia, or kil ia, or kili a, v. t., to dig. [Sa. 'eli, My. gali, Mg. hady, to dig.] A. kara', n. a. karw', to dig.

Note.—Kili natano dig the ground, kili ki nakasu natano dig a stick into the ground.

Gkiliki (i.e., gikili ki), redup., intensive, as ba gkiliki natuoma dig thy feet (into the ground), i.e., stand firm, or simply ba gkiliki.

Gkita, i.e., gikita, v. redup. See gita, kita.

Ginit ia, v., gini gota fia. See kinit ia.

Girigiri, v. i., or a., to be bright, brilliant, shining, polished. [To. gigila bright, brilliant, polished, My. gilang and gilau to shine, glitter, be bright, brilliant, dazzle.] A. gala' to be clear, shining, &c., galiyy' bright, shining, polished.

Note.—The A. word also denotes to be or appear uncovered : Ef. d. karo to be unclothed, have the clothes removed, naked.

Gis, or gisa, ad., together, lit. as one, with numerals, as rua rua gis two two together, in twos, and so with all the numerals. H. k'ehad as one, i.e., together, Ch. kahăda. See ki as, and sa, s, one.

Gisa. See kisa, or kesa.

Gisa na, s., c. art., name, dd. gie na, kiha na (for kisa na). [TaSa. kitsa, Ml. U. se, Malo isa, Epi (Ba.) sia, (Bi.) kia, Ta. dd. rige (narige), na'ge ('ge), An. da (tha), Fi. yaca (yatha), Am. sa, Paama isa, Ta. d. hge (nahge).] A. 'ism' and sim', H. s'em name.

Note.—The Ef. gisa (kiha, gia) has the dem. k' (or g') prefixed, as Epi kia and TaSa. kitsa. This dem. is not prefixed in Epi sia, Ml. se, Am. sa, Malo and Paama isa : in all these the final m of the original is elided, as it is in trä (q.v.) blood, and nu (for num) ; this final m appears as ng in Ta.

Gis ia, v. t., to feel, touch, and Giskis, redup. See kis ia.

Gita ia, v. t. See kita ia.

Gite troa i, for gita troa i. See kite troa i.

Go, conj., connecting substantives and sentences, and. [Ml. P. ga, ka, Ml. U. ko, Fi. ka, and.] Amb. ka and (with numerals).

Goba (gote fia), v. t., to cut, as a

nakoau with a knife. [Mg.
kafa cut, mikapa, v. t., to cut.]
H. gub, A. gāba, to cut.

Goba sia, v. t.   See koba sia.

Gobera, or gobāra, s., or kobara,
side, as kobara kerua the other
side : ko dem , and bora ı.

Gofu sa, v. t.   See kofu sa.

Gofkofua, a.   See kofkofua.

Gkofita (for gokofita), a., sticky,
gluey. [Mg. fita, fitaka, clay
adhering, wet, sticking to.]
A. 'amada, 2, 5) to be wet so
as to stick (earth or clay).
Note the prefixed ko (or go),
as in Fi. ka, Ja. ka, the
sense of the compound being
passive.

Gogo, v. i., to wade, to wade half
swimming ;

Gogo, s., an aquatic bird. [An.
agag to swim, Sa. 'a'au to
swim, Fila kaukau to bathe,
Ma. kau swim, wade, Ha. au,
auau, swim, bathe, hasten, cf.
Ja. kumbah to wash.]   A.
hamma, 1, hasten, 4, bathe, or
wash oneself in cold water,
10, bathe in hot water ; and,
general term, wash the body.

Goi a, or go ia, v. t., or ko ia, as
goi naniu to rub, scrape, or
grind out by rubbing or scraping the kernel of the cocoanut,
suru-go ia (cover-drain out) to
cover with one's mouth the
the aperture of a drinking
vessel and drain out the contents, koi a mark or boundary,
also koika nafanua ; redup.,

Goko ia, v. t., to scrape (nafona);
to mark paint, or smear
(nafona, i.e., native cloth), koko
the paint used for this, gokoi

(or gokai or gokei) nafona.
[Sa. 'o'ai to mark or paint
native cloth.]   II. hakah, i.q.
hakak cut into, hack, engrave,
carve, draw, paint, delineate,
hok a defined limit, a bound,
A. hakka, 3), grind by rubbing,
1), hack, cut, pierce, 7), drain
out (as milk), hakka scrape,
rub ; hence also

Gko, or goko, v., to cut into, cut,
hack, always followed by
another verb, as gko bora ia,
gko gote fia (used of cutting
up the nakoau or native pudding), na kokoen, s., the cutting
up.

Gokolau, see gakalau (gkalau ia).

Gōlĕ, s., a cripple, one lame.
A. gayala to be lame.

Gkola (gokola).   See kola, kokola, to be dry.

Gkola.   See kola shout.

Gkolau.   See kolau.

Golī na, c. art., s., bird's beak,
lips, mouth. [Sa. gutu mouth
(of animals, wells, bottles),
Ma. ngutu lip, rim, whaka-
ngutungutu grumble at, scold,
Fi. gusu mouth, Fut ragutu
beak.]   A. nakara to peck
with its beak (a bird) ; to
scold, nakrat foramen (gulœ),
mankar bird's beak.

Goloba, v. i., to be filthy, dirty.
Karafa, 3, to be defiled, 4, to
be infected, contaminated,
Nm., 4, to disgust.

Golu tia, v. t.   See kalu tia.

Gon, v. i., to be firm, fast : kon.

Gkon (kokon), redup. of preceding.

Gkon (gokon), v. i., to be bitter :
kon, kokon.

Gonai a, v. t. See konai a.

Gor ia, or kor ia, v. t., to enclose or surround with a fence (nakoro); then to enclose as with a fence a sick person (shutting out and prohibiting evil spirits or evil influences from him)—this is done by the "Sacred Man" (natamole tabu)—hence gorokoro to divine, and nekoro divination, or incantation, with its accompanying rites; redup., gorokor ia (native Christian prayer, Atua O, ba gorokoro gamia uga toko loga namolien anago— O God, enclose us that we may abide in the loga (enclosure) of Thy salvation); gorŏ sa to conceal it (as a crime with which one is charged); gor ia to prohibit, as tuba gor ia prohibit, impede, obstruct, bisa gor ia speak impede, or obstruct him; tu gor ia stand obstruct; gkoro (gokoro), v., and nakokoro, s., a prohibition, also an obstruction or thing put to close up or obstruct the entrance to a house, a door. This verb is much used after other verbs as ba gor ia to go obstructing, i.e. to meet, d. bakor to meet, or rather to come or go before, i.e., appear before (anyone), then to arise, come into sight (as a man, ship, &c.), and take place (as an event); meri gor ia, bati gor ia, like gor ia, simply mean to enclose or surround with a fence, sera gor ia to enclose or encircle (the head) with a fillet, hence seragoro-bau a hat; gore na a brother's sister, or sister's brother, brother and sister being children of the same mother, or of the same nakainaga. A. ḥagara impede, prohibit, interdict, 2, to have a halo surrounding it (the moon), (see koro), 4, to conceal; ḥigr', ḥogr' a fence, a wall, what is prohibited, genitals of a man or a woman, kindredship, relationship, ḥāgir' a fence; H. hagar to gird, ḥagōr a girdle, clad. Nm., 2, to fence round, confine, forbid; E. hagar town, village (Fi. koro, id.)

Gore na, s., brother's sister, sister's brother. See under preceding word.

Goro, v. i., or koro, to snore. [Ma. ngongoro (redup.), My. ngorok, Mg. erotra, id.] H. naḥar, A. (ḥ'arra, ḥ'arḥ'ara) naḥ'ara, S. nḥar snort, breathe hard through the nose, E. nĕḥĕra snore;

Gore na, c. art., s., the nostrils, nose, dd. usu, gusu. [Fi. ucu, Sa. isu, Ma. ihu, My. id·ung, Ja. irung, Mg. orona, nose.] H. nḥīraim, du., the nostrils, S. nḥīro' the nose, A. noḥ'rát aperture of the nose.

Gorot ia, v. t., to cut round, as to cut round a stick in order to break it; hence

Goro gote fia, v. t., cut round, break it (as a stick). Nm. ḥ'arat to shave off in turning, H. ḥarat (q.v.), S. ḥrat cut in, engrave. See karati.

Gota, redup. gogota, v. i., or a.,

black, dirty, bukota dirty (as water with dust or earth in it). [Gilolo kokotu, kitkudu, black.] A. katama to be dusty, 9, black, kātim' dirty, black, katām' black, blackish, &c.

Gota fānu, s., or ad., evening, d. kot' fān, d. syn. rāg mēlu, lit. time of dusk, or sunset : gota, or kot', a time (see kota). A. wakata, 1, 2, to fix a time, wakt' a time, a point or part of time : fānu. [Santo punu to set (the sun), puni dusk.] H. pun (perhaps i.q. A. 'afana = 'afala, cf. II. 'apal, see melu) to set (as the sun), to be darkened.

Got, v., cut. See koto fi.

Gote fi, v. t. See koto fi.

Gotokoto, v. i., to begin (break or cut, as it were, into the doing of something, "break ground" in the matter), as i gotokoto bat ia he began—did it : koto fi.

Gū, d. mu, nom. suf., your, 2 pl. (ku verb. pron., 2 pl.) : separate pron., 2 pl., kumu.

Gū, dd. mu, kama, verb. suf., you. See preceding word.

Gu, d. k (for ku), nom. suf., 1 sing., my, as narugu my hand.

Gua, inter. ad., how ? lit. as what ? It is used with the verbal prons., as i kua it is how ? Indefinitely i kua it is so (assent), lit. it is as somewhat : kua and gua are equally used, d. kasā as what ? how ? The sole difference between kua and kasa is that in the latter the dem. s' is prefixed

to the inter. pron. See ka as, and sā what ? Ch. kĕmah how ? (as what ?), A. kama' as, so.

Gua, v. i. See kua.

Gūku, v. i., to shrink, shrivel, be incurved, maguku to be incurved, guku rumu ki mō na to shrink or incurve the bosom to her son-in-law (of a mother-in-law shrinking together and covering her bosom and face so as not to be seen by her son-in-law), d. kuku ruma [Mg. kainkana aged, kainkona bent, curved, shrivelled.] E. guihkuă (gwihkwă) to be incurved, bent, specially from old age, hence guhuk' one aged, bent, and shrunk together.

Guku-taki, v. t., to make guku. See guku.

Gulu tia, v. t. See kalu tia.

Gulu, v. i. See kulu.

Gum ia, v. t., or kum ia, to absorb in the mouth (as a lolly). H. gama' to absorb, to drink up, to swallow, i.q. Ch.

Gum ia, v. t., dd. um ia, gu ia (gw ia), m ia (mw ia), to seize, grasp, catch, hold, with or in the hand. [Sa. 'u'u to take hold of, to grasp, ps. 'umia, Fi. qumi-a, ququ, id., My. gāngām, Ja. gāgām to clutch, to clench, the fist, the clenched hand.] A. kamkama to collect, to seize or catch with the hand, to take.

Gunut ia, v. t. See kinit ia.

Gura ia, v. t., to scrape off, gura ua to scrape or rake off the heated stones from an oven, magir ia, v. t., scrape, magura,

v. i., or ps. a., diminished,
lean, igura, d. igiri, the stick
for scraping or raking the
stones from an oven, gura biri
ki (d. syn. sera biri ki) to
startle (one) (as by coming
behind one and suddenly laying or sweeping the hand on
him) : kar ia, garu. H. gara'
to scratch, to scrape, scrape
off, then take away, withhold,
to diminish, Ni. to be taken
away, withheld. Note the Ef.
magura denotes lit. taken
away from, i.e., diminished,
lean, with the prep. ki, magura
ki to withhold from (one),
meta magura ki he eyes withholds (something) from (one)
he is stingy ; in one d. i meta
makur ki is said to denote he
eyes withdraws from (one), he
is covetous, lit. he eyes scrapes
off (from someone).

Gure sia, v. t., to gnaw : see
gura ia and kar ia. [Sa. gali,
gnaw, Fi. quru, v. i., quru-ta,
v. t., to eat anything unripe,
to scranch, eat ravenously, to
gnaw, My. greb to gnaw.]
This word seems properly to
denote scranch, scrape off,
absorb, H. gara' scrape off, A.
gara'a to absorb, swallow.

Guru ki, v. t., to gather together,
guru-maki, v. t., id., or kuru
ki, kuru-maki, gkuruk (guku-
ruk) gather together (without object) ; and

Gurua, s., c. art., a field (of
battle, of yams), so called because men or things are
gathered together in it: kuru.
H. gur, 3), to be gathered, to

gather together, 'agar collect,
gather in.

Gurui, and

Guruni, s., c. art. naguruni, a
woman, wife, female. See
fafine, Note 2, and lai.

Gusu, v. i., to stoop. A. nakasa
to stoop.

Gusu na, s., c. art., the nose :
gore na.

Gusugisu ki, v. den., from preceding word, to nose (a thing),
i.e., smell it. [Mg. oroka
(from orona the nose), mioroka
to kiss by touching noses.]

Gusi, v. i., to be crooked, con-
torted, magusi crooked, con-
torted. A. 'akis'a to be
crooked, contorted, 5, id.

Gusu, v. i. See kusu, kosu-mi.

Gusu-mi, v. t. See kosu-mi.

Gut ia, v. t., and gukut ia
(gkut ia). See kut ia.

Gutu ki, v. t. See kutu ki.

I, verb. pron., 3 sing., he, she,
it, sometimes pronounced e ;
also dd. i, e, verb. suf., 3 sing.,
him, her, it. [Epi Ba. o, Epi
Bi. e, him, her, it ; Fut. i,
Ml. P. i, TaSa. i, he, she, it.]
Separate pron. nai, dd. inia
or enea ga, or niga, he, she, it.

I, dem., d., this, here, d. ei, rag
i, for rag uai, this time, now :
like e, q.v., contraction of uai.

I, or e, a tense particle used
after ka (sign of past tense, as
i ka fano he went), and ga,
and ba (final conjs.) thus, i kai
bano he had gone, i gai bano

let him have gone, the notion expressed being that the action (as going) was done or is to be done *before* the doing of something else. Dialect syn. ko, ba i bano = ba ko bano = that thou have gone, lit. that thou *now* (before something else to follow) go. [Cf. e after verbs in Ha. and Tah.] Probably the dem. e this or that (contraction of uai, this, now, that, then), thus i kai (or ka e) bano he went then (that time), ba i bano go *now* (this time), d. kui ban, you now go (as bidding farewell).

I, in ëï, it, or that, not that, no : syn. ëüo.

Ī, no, compare e in ëï. [This neg. ad. is seen in Sa. i (in i'ai no), To. i (in ikai no) ; for the kai, see tika.]

Ia, verb. suf., 3 sing., dd. i, e, him, her, it.

I, prep. (also e), contracted from ni (li), often t. prep. [Ma. i, id.]

NOTE.—The verb. suf., 3 sing., is often combined with this prep. ia, d. i, for iia, ii.

Ia, s., d. for bia, child.

Iak, s., d., mother (vocative). See aka and i art. [Mg. kaky and ikaky, my father (voc.)]

Ibē! iebē! iboï! interj., exclamation of wonder, surprise, and pleasure, d. bai. See bai ; i as in io, iore.

Igam (i, art.), dd. agam, nigami, kigami, kinami.

Igin, d., ad., here ; i prep., and gin (or kin), q.v. [Sa. i 'inei, Fut. ikunei, id.]

Igira, d. for igita.

Igiri, s., and

Igura, s. Same as egura.

Igita, dd. agita, nigita, kigita, nininta : i, art., and gita, for nita.

Ika, s., c. art. naika, fish. [Sa. ia, My. ikan, Santo d. ika.] Cf. H. dag, pl. const. dëgë and dagah, const. dëgath, fish. It is possible that ika is the same by the elision of the d.

Iki, a., small, little; in kariki (kar' iki) little children. See kiki. [To. iki small, little.]

Ikin, or kin, s., c. art. nikin, a bird's nest. [Mg. akany.] H. ken, A. wakn', wukunat, id.

Ilibagoen, s., a basket with closed bottom, a purse, or wallet : ala (basket), *b*ago, uon.

Ili-fiki, v., also lele- or lili-fiki, d. syn. kelu-faki, as rarua i ili-fiki nagusu the canoe rounds the point, or cape. See lele, lili ; fiki or faki is a compound of the two preps. fi (or fu) and ki.

Ilisela, ad., throughout, for lili-sela, lit. all round (throughout) the way : lele (or lili) sela.

Imrum, d. imrau, ad., inside the house : i prep., moru hollow, um house. See katema.

Īn, s., c. art. nīn, the wind, the air : lagi. [My. angin, Mg. anina, the wind.]

In, dem., this, d. na. [Cf. Sa. nei this now, Mg. iny that, this, My. ini this.] S. hana this, Ch. 'ahen, Assy. annu, this.

Inia, inea, or enea, d., pers. pron., 3 sing., he, she, it.

Inin, here : i prep., and nin this.

Inini, d., s., c. art. nainini, spirit, soul. See anu.

Inira, inera, or enera, d., pers. pron., 3 pl., they.

Inira, or nira, or nera, d., verb. suf., 3 pl., them.

Inuma, s., d. for isuma.

Io, ad., yes. [Sa. io, Fi. io or ia yes, Ja. iya.] H. 'ihu', E. 'ewa, yes.

Iorĕ, ad., d. ōrĕ, yes. [Fi. iarai yes.] From io, and ri dem. See eri.

Iru, or eru, or ru, verb. pron., 3 pl., they, d. iu, or u.

Ira, or ĕra, or ra, verb. pron., 3 dual, they two.

Ira (d. ir), or ra, verb. suf., 3 pl., them.

Isi, s., c. art. naïsi na, basis, foundation ; naisi matua na its great foundation, naisi matua nafisan the great foundation of the discourse or speech, its text, naisi namal the foundation of the affair ; and

Isuma, d. inuma (s to n), s., a clearing for a plantation, lit. the foundation of the clearing for cultivation. See uma. A. 'iss', &c., a foundation.

Is, ad., or interj,, no, not so. [Mg. isy, id.] I, neg. ad., and s' dem. See sĕ.

Ita, s., c. art. naita, d. for nāta, a human being, man. See ata.

Ita, interj. of exhortation, come! now then ! come now ! [Ta. ita, id.] A. hi'ta adesdum, adeste.

Itaki, s., dd. otaki, uataki, a

split stick for grasping and lifting hot oven stones, the native tongs : i art., and taki.

Iu, or ĕu, verb pron., 3 pl., d. for iru, or ĕru, they.

Iu, s., c. art. naiu or naiyu, d. for nausu. See usu.

K

K, d., verb. suf., 2 sing., thee, d. ko. A. ka thee.

Ka, kĭ, or kĕ, ad., as tera kĭ māla move (lit. fly) like a hawk (of the dancing of women who move with both arms stretched out like the wings of a hawk); usually prefixed to another particle, as kĭte as, kasā as what ? d. kua (kuwa) as what ? A. ka, H. kĕ as.

K, d. gu (ku), nom. suf., 1 sing., my, as naruk my hand. [My. ku, Mg. ho.]

Ka, k', tense particle, past indefinite, as a ka bano, I went, i ka bano he went, d. ki ban he went (ki is k' tense particle, and i he, the verbal pron. being after the tense part., whereas in i ka it is before it). In one dialect the particle te is added, as a kate ban, ku kate ban, i kate ban, &c. In another dialect the particle te is added thus, kate ban (k' tense part., a verb. pron. I, and te tense part.) I went, kute ban (u represents the verb. pron. you) you went, kite ban (i verb. pron. he or she) he went, tu kute ban (1 pl., incl.), again kute ban (1 pl., excl.), we went, kute ban you (pl.) went, ru kute ban they went: used sometimes for pluperfect. See te. As to ki ban he went, it may also denote the present, " he goes," or what practically is not distinguishable from it. [Fi. ka a sign of the past tense, sometimes of the present.] See the word following the next.

K', d. ga, d. ka, final conj., that, in order that: prefixed to the verbal pron. it loses its vowel: in the d. in which this particle is pronounced ga, the verb. pron. is put before it—i ga he that, i.e., that he, d. ke (k' that, e he) that he, ka (k' that, a I) that I, d. a ga: the order seen in ka that I, ke (or ki) that he, is the older and more correct: examples, ka fan that I go, ke fan that he go, let him go, and so with every verb in the language. This is not a tense but a mood, though the idea of futurity is implied: to make the future tense fo (see bo, mo, uo) is added, thus ka fo ban I shall go, I will go, ke fo ban he will go (he shall go is rather ke ban, i.e., he must go, but also let him go, and he may go, and to go or that he go). As final conj. A. ka', H. ki, that, in order that (with the future), Latin ut (with the subjunctive). It is not surprising that k' in some dialects denotes the future. Thus in Florida it denotes the future, as ke bosa (k particle of tense, e he) he will speak, compare Tigre Mat. xvi. 27 (when the Son of Man) *shall come* (kimatse), for the simple future in Ethiopic: this Tigre ki is k' the particle in question (A. ka') and i, verb. pron. or preformative, 3 sing. [Ef. d. ga, d. k', final conjunction, Ysabel ge, gi, Raratonga ka, usually kia, Ma. kia (the a is a dem. added), To. ke, Mg. h': Raratonga ka, future, in some places past, Florida k', future, Mg. h', future.]

Ka, d., dem. ki, or ke, this, there (near), as nauot ka this chief; ke, and ga in naga. See word after next below. [My. iki, ika, iku, this, that, TaSa. aki, or ake, this.] E. ka dem., seen in zeku, Amh. yeh, or ihe, for ike this, Arm. dek, dak, deka', dake', A. daka. With the Semitic demonstrative ka, Dillmann, Gr. Eth., §§ 62, 65, seen in these words (whence E. kia, prefixed to personal pronouns) compares probably Assy. aga this (Sayce, Assy. Gr.)

Note.—This Semitic dem. ka is seen also in E. 'elku, 'elketu, Ch. 'illek, A. 'olaka, &c., these, those.

Ka, prep., usually ki, rarely ka, as d. i ba ka tafa (commonly i ba ki tafa) he went *to* the hill: ki, or gi (ngi) is to, belonging to, of, for, from, and transitive prep. after verbs; prefixed to the nom. suf. it forms poss. prons., as kagu, kama, kana, &c.; kana his, for him, is syn. c. kakana, kanana. [My. ka to, unto, towards, after, according to, much used in composition in the formation of other preps. and ads., as in kan transitive prep. after verbs, and akan to, &c., and particle of the future tense, Mg. ho to, for, belonging to. and particle of the future tense, Ma. ki to, towards, &c., and, after verbs, transitive prep.] Amh. ka to, of, from, Himyaritic ke or ki after verbs transitive prep.; H. ki is a conj., that; compare 'ad ki until (conj.), or until that, with E. and Amh. 'eska, 'es, for H. 'ad, prep. to, unto. Thus the same particle which is a final conjunction (see above, under k' (ga, ka), final conj.) in A. and H. is a prep. in Himyaritic and Amh.

Ka, or ki, dem., rel. pron., art. (same as word before the preceding, above), prefixed to nouns, as kafika the scented, that which is odorous, kalumi that which lumi, spider; to numerals, as karun second, katolu third, &c. (twoed, &c.); to poss. pron, as kakana, kanana, kinin, kiana; to pers. prons., nom., kinau, kigita. [My. ka, Mg. ha, Ja. ka, Fi. ka, Ma. (katea, kotara, &c.); and see under baka, note]

Kaba sia, d. See koba sia, to follow.

Kabe, s., a small basket. [Ma. kakapu a small basket for cooked food, so called from

being curved (kapu) like the hollow of the hand (kapu).] S. kapo' poculum, H. kaf, or kap, hollow of the hand, pl. a hollow vessel, pan, or bowl, H. kafaf to bend, curve.

Kabĕ, s., a kind of crab.

Kābe, d. kāfinĭ, s., a pigeon, d. kime. [Ma. kukupa, Tah. uupa, Am. um, Epi ama, id.] A. hama' pigeons.

Kabu, s., d. koau, the native "pudding" (tied up in a bundle, and cooked in the oven); the main article of native food: see kofu. [Tah. ohu a bundle of some food tied up and baked in the native oven, Sa. 'ofu'ofu to envelope in leaves (for cooking).] A. kobbat, kabab', "kibby", the national dish of the Arabs, made of pounded or brayed wheat and fish or flesh, gathered into a round mass, and cooked in the oven. See the verb under the word kofu.

Kabu, s., fire; and

Kabu tera gia, v., to burn heating it (cold food), to warm or heat (cold food). [My. api, Sa. afi, Mg. afo fire, Sa. afia, ps., to be burnt accidentally.] S. hab to burn, A. hobahib' (redup.) fire.

Kabu, s., in talekabu na. See kobu.

Kabuer, v. i., or a., to be grey-haired, aged;

Kabuer, d, s., a husband, lit. an aged man;

Kabuera, d., s., a wife, an aged woman, d. abuera, or abura, c. art. nàbuera, nàbura (k elided). A. kabira to be advanced in age, kabīr advanced in age and fully grown, E. 'eber old woman (k elided).

Kaf, v. i., to be bent (as with hunger). See also kai. [Ma. kapu curly, kapu the hollow of the hand.] II. kafaf to be bent, kaf hollow of the hand.

Kafika, s., the rose apple. [Fut. kafika, Fi. kavika, Ml. P. havih, Malo avica, TaSa. kabika (khabika), id.] II. tapuali an apple (so called from its scent, from nafali), A. toffāli' an apple, not only the common one, but also the lemon, citron, &c.

NOTE.—The ka-, in kafika. is not for ta-, but the Oceanic prefix ka, that (that which).

Kafinī, s., d. kabe, q.v.

Kafikafi, v., gafikafi, q.v.

Kafu tia, or gafu tia, v. t., to wrap up (a thing, as a stone, with cloth, so as to cover it all round), same as kofu sa, which is used of thus wrapping up food to be cooked ; hence

Kafukafu na, s., pellicle, as of an egg or fruit (its wrapper or covering), d. kamu.

Kai, v. i., to be bent, for kaf, q.v.

Kai, conj., d. syn. bo, conj., q.v.: ka (see ga, conj.) and i, he, she, it.

Kai, or kae, tense particle (compounded of ka, q.v., sign of past tense, and i or e) of the pluperfect. See i.

Kai (or kei), gai, v. i., to cry, sing (men, birds), sing out,

sound, &c. [Ml. P. keke to sing.] E. nakawa to sound, give forth a sound (of the human voice, songs of birds, &c.), A. naka'a to cry out, sing out.

Kai, s., a sharp shell used for scraping : goi a.

Kaimi sia, v. t., to make to exist, as (the heathen used to say of the sea, &c.,) i tumana kaimi sia it made itself to exist ; and

Kaimis, s., c. art. nakaimis one that does anything hiddenly and wonderfully, as destroying an enemy by changing one's form magically and deceiving, &c. II. kum arise, exist, go forth, grow up, stand (be fixed), Hi. cause to arise, exist, A. kāma, 2, rightly appoint and dispose (a thing), 4, prepare (evil against a person), &c.

Kainaga, s., c. art., a tribe or family clan. [Sa. 'aiga a family, relations, To. kainaga a meal, victuals.] See kan ia.

Kakana (kakagu, kakama, kakagita, &c.), poss. pron., syn. agana, &c., q.v.: kaka (= aga) is ka dem. or rel., and ka prep. [Epi gka, gkana his, &c.]

Kakei, s., c. art. nakakei, a story (traditional). A. liaka' to narrate, Nm. liucèya, narrative, tale.

Kaka, s., kaka naniu. See under aka.

Kakat, s , a bite. See kati a or kat ia.

Kala, v. i., or a., little, small. See under bakal ia II. [Mg. kely, id.]

Kāl, s., a child. See under babal ia I.

Kalai, d., s., a spider's web, and d. nilau, and

Kalau, d., id., lit. that which is woven. [My. labalaba and lawalawa a spider.] II. 'arab to weave. See kolau.

Kalau, gkalau. See galau ia.

Kale-baga, s., d. kalemaga, bow-string (made out of the baga or maga tree): kalu.

Kālī, s., native spade, digging stick: kil ia.

Kal ia, or gal ia, q.v., and redup., Kalikal ia,

Kalu, and galu, s., bowstring, kalu nāsu: kale in kale baga. See kalu tia.

Kalu, s., d. kul, cloth, clothing, lit. a covering; and

Kalu tia (same as galu tia), d. kulu tia, v. t., to cover, as with a mat or rug, i kalu ki nakalu he covers (himself) with cloth or clothing, i kalu, d. i kulu or i gulu, middle sense, he covers (himself), as with bedclothes, i.e., mats or such like, also to put the bow-string on a bow (or galu tia), and to clasp round with the arms (a violent man, to re-strain him, or a pig, &c., stooping to lift it in order to carry it): the vowels of this word are changed in kalu, kulu, kele (galu, gulu, gele), golu. See similar changes of vowels in the My. word under kela, infra. A. galla, 2, to cover, 5, to be covered, clothed, gullu coverings, clothes, &c., as rugs: the idea of covering

arises from that of wrapping round or rolling up—see the eg. H. galal to roll, and its related words in Ges. Dict., and see below, under kela, kelu.

Kalumi, s., the spider, lit. that which lumi. See lumi to swell.

Kama, d. for kabu, in anekama, q.v.

Kama, d., verb. suf., 2 pl., you, d. mu.

Kamam, d. for kinami, q.v.

Kami, d., pers. pron., 2 pl., you.

Kami a, v. t., to seize, grip, take with the fingers, or with nippers, compress or squeeze between two things (like alat ia); same as kamut ia, q.v.

Kamu na, s., pellicle, d. for kafukafu na, q.v.

Kamut ia, or gamut ia, v. t., to take, grasp with the fingers, nip, then (like alat ia) to nip or cut with scissors, to cut the hair; hence

Kam, s., c. art. nikam, native tongs (a split stick for grasping hot oven stones, and lifting them), lit. that which (kami or kamut) nips, seizes, grasps, d. kau, q.v., or gau (agau), and

Kamkam, s., scissors. [My. cubit, or chubit, Ja. juwit, to nip, pinch, My. angkub = agau, tongs, nippers, Ha. umiki to pinch with the fingers, Fi. qamu-ta to take hold of, or hold as with pincers, to shut (the mouth), ai qamu, anything to qamuta with (My. angkub) as pincers, bullet mould, vice.] H. kamas to squeeze together, hence to take with the hand, kamat to hold fast with the hands, to sieze firmly, kafas contract, shut (as the mouth), habas to take, grasp with the hand, A. kabasa to take with the tips of the fingers, kabas'a take, grasp with the hand.

Kana-, pref. to nom. suf., forming poss. pron., kanagu, kanama, kanana, &c. : kanana, d. kinin, is syn. c. kakana, q.v. [Epi kana-, d. kona-, as kanaku, my, &c.] Kana- is ka, dem., and na, prep. See ni.

Kana, v. i., also kin, and ki, d. kano, to shrink from, to be unable ; i kana bat ia he is unable to do it (shrinks from, or is afraid), i sua bo kin, or bo ki, he takes (acquires) a mind shrinking from, afraid, unable (to do something). H. ka'ah to be fearful, faint-hearted, A. kā'a to abstain or decline from fear.

Kan ia, v. t., to eat, redup. kani-kani: tea kanien that which is for eating, nakanieu act of eating, the eating, food, finaga, q.v., food, bagan ia to feed, make to eat, or fagan ia, q.v., and faga, fagafaga, nakabu faga devouring (eating) fire, nalagi kanikani a strong wind, kana a squall ; kainaga a tribe, family clan (from eating together). [Fi. kana to eat, kani-a, to eat, vakani-a feed, cause to eat, used also of the *heat* of the sun, and *violence* of the wind, Sa. ai, My. makan, Mg. (m transposed) homana, hanina, to eat.] A. 'akala to

eat, 3, eat together, 4, to feed, cause to eat, 'akil' one who lives with one, messmate, familiar friend (cf. kainaga, and A. 3), H. 'akal to eat ; A. 'akala, 2), to scratch (the head), 'akila to be itchy, Ef. makini-kini to be itchy.

Kana, s., a squall. See under preceding word.

Kanau, or kanao, s., d. kanoa, kano, child ; nasuma ni kanoa, or kano, the womb, lit. house of the child (or fœtus). In E. Mai this is called kiri fanau the cover (kiri = kuli = skin or covering), or skin of the child. This word is familiarly used by men to each other as a vocative, as kanao, or kano, mate ! (child !), pl. kanŏ magā you people, d. nakanoa, kano ni Efate man of Efate, pl. nakan Efate people of Efate, lit. children of Efate, d. nati ni Efate (see ani, ati, child) : hence kano is sometimes equivalent to "person," as kano sa, kano uia, a bad, a good person ;

Kan, c, art. nakan, children (of a place) ;

Kano, or kanoa, s.—see kanao ;

Kanoa, s., c. art. nakanoa, see kanao. [My. kanak child, related to anak, id., as Ef. kanao to ani, q.v., child : that is, kanak and kanao have the prefix ka, and kanao = that born, that which is born, so Mg. zanaka (anaka), with a different prefix or article, and Sa. fanau has the prefix fa or f', the anau being identical

with the anao in kanao.] A.
walada, H. yalad, E. walada
to bring forth, bear (of a
mother), to beget (of males),
and used in E. also of
the earth bringing forth its
produce.

Kano, or kanoa, d. kanau, or

Kanoka, v. i., or a., to be produced (as it were born, of
yams), naui i kanoa (d. kanau)
the yam is produced, born, or
growing (as if the insat had
brought it forth new born),
naui kano new or growing
yams. See preceding word.

Kara, or gara, redup. garagara,
v. i., or a., strong, hard, and
d. karakarai, or garakarai,
strong, tagaragara strong,
vehement. [My. kras hard,
violent, strong, vehement,
force, Mg. hery power,
strength, force, might, mihery
strong, powerful, mighty, hery
being forced to, compelled,
constrained.] See next word.

Kara, or gara, redup. garagara,
v. i., or a., to be dry, bagara
ia, v. c., to make dry, to dry
(a thing), nakarān the being
dry, also the being (bare and
dry) poor, poverty ; kara dry,
then (see preceding word)
hard, strong, stiff, rigid (as
dry wood). See also kara, s.,
and makarakara, v. i., *infra.*
[My. kring dry, kring kan to
dry (a thing), Mg. haraka
dried up, scorched, parched.]
H. ḥarar to burn, be hot (cf.
A. ḥarra, E. ḥarara); the
primary idea is that of "the
shrivelled roughness of things

that are dried or scorched,"
Ges. ; to be burned, to be
dried up.

Kara, s., c. art. nekara, the
nettle (so called from its
burning ; compare makarakara
to be burning, to be hot, as
the mouth with pepper, or the
skin stung by a nettle). See
preceding word, and compare
H. ḥarul the nettle, so called
from its burning, from the
root ḥaral = ḥarar.

Kara ki, or gara ki, v., to seize,
grasp, and

Kar ia, or gar ia, v. t., to
scratch, scrape, shave, seize,
redup. garikar ia, also karu
tia, or garu tia, v. t., to
scratch, and karo i, or garo i,
v. t., to scratch, scrape, redup.
garokaro, and karokaro, karokaroa, or garokaroa, itchy,
scratchy, scabby, and garu
and tagaru, v. t., to seize,
grasp, garu sera (grasp everything) be grasping, redup.
garukaru, id., karo to scrape,
sweep, to swim (*i.e.*, *sweep*
with the arms—to swim without doing this is āfa, or ofa),
karati, karakarati scratched,
marked, scored ; kārī, s., a
plane (from being moved with
a sweeping or sawing motion,
or shaving); karc sia, or kares
ia, v. t., to scratch, scrape ;
gure sia, v. t., to gnaw,
scranch. [My. garis, Ja.
garit to scratch, score, garu to
rake, &c., garut scratch, scrape,
claw, garok to scrape, gârap
grasp at, gâraji a saw, greb to
gnaw, karat, karot, kârot

grind or gnash the teeth, make a grating noise, karut to scratch, kârok to rub, curry (a horse), kikir to rasp, file, a rasp, file, avaricious, Mg. haratra shaved, manaratra to shave, kory gnaw, scrape, Fi. kari, or karikari, v. i., kari-a, karitaka, v. t., to scrape, karokaro prickly heat, itch, Sa. ʻili a rasp, file, saw.] A. garra to drag, snatch, sweep, seize, H. garar to scrape, sweep, saw (primary meaning), to drag or snatch away, to saw (mēgerah a saw), to gargle, produce rough sounds in the throat (see Ef. karo, throat, *infra*), cognates S. graʻ to shave, H. garaʻ scratch, scrape (see Ef gur ia, magir ia), &c.

Karati, and redup.,

Karakarati, a., see kar ia.

Karaf ia, v. t., to scratch, scrape (the earth or ground) ; hence

Karafi, v. i., to creep on the ground (as it were scratching or scraping on the ground) : see kar ia. Karafi a is kara fi a, fi, q.v., prep.

Karaka, v. i., to move tremulously (creep), as crabs and such like animals do ; karaka ki naburuma (a mother-in-law) creeps or shrinks away from her son-in-law (trembling and afraid) : kara-ka, compare preceding word.

Kare sia, or kares ia, d. karas ia, v. t., to scratch, scrape, and, from the idea of scraping together, being gathered together,

Karesi, or karisi, s., a cluster (as of cocoanuts), and

Karesibum, pr. n., of a person mentioned in a myth, one of the two sons of a woman who came down from heaven, lit. blossoming-cluster. See kar ia.

Karei sa, d. karei ki nia, v. t., to dislike, be averse from, hate. [My. iri to hate, Mg. hala hated, detested, abhorred.] A. kariha to dislike, abhor.

Karei, or garei turi a, to dislike (the thing he is bidden or sent to do) abiding with him (someone). See turi a, and cf. kita roã sa.

Kărĭ, s., a plane. See kar ia.

Kărĭ, v. i., to hasten, takărĭ, id. [Cf. Ma. kari rush along violently.] A. kăra, 1, 8, to hasten.

Kari-iki (kariki), s., little child, little children, and

Kari-kiki (karikiki), s., id. (kiki little), and

Kari-riki (kaririki), s., d., H. ʻeker a shoot, and riki little.

Karo, karoi, garoi, v. i., to swim (sweeping with the arms) : kar ia.

Karokaro, and

Karokaroa, scabby, itchy : kar ia.

Karo na, s., c. art., dd. gato na (garo na), kanro na, the throat, gullet. H. garon the throat from garar (see kar ia), E. guère the throat.

Karo, v. i., d., to be uncovered, have the clothes off, naked. H. galah to be naked. See girigiri.

Karu tia, or karut ia. See kar ia.

Kasã, and kasafa, also kasãna,

inter. ad., as what? how? why? d. kua : ka, ad., as, and sā, or safa, q.v., what?

Kasāna, inter. ad., as what? kasā, with the dem. na suffixed.

Kasau, s.. c. art., small branch, fruit stalk, nakasau na its small branch, d. (transposed) sakau, id., and also a reef. See sakau. [My. gusong a reef of rocks.] A. kas'ib' long and slender branch, H. kisbe', pl. const., "the ends, *i.e.*, the roots *of the mountains* (in the depth of the sea)," Jon. ii. 7; perhaps the branches *of the mountains* (running out into the sea).

Kas ia, or kasi a, gas ia, v. t., to rub, wipe. [My. gosok, gosot, gosoki, gisik, kisil, to rub, Mg. kasoka rubbed, mikasoka to rub.] A. kas's'a, 3), to rub, kas'a' (kas'w') to rub, wipe.

Kas-toru, s., handkerchief, lit. sweat-wiper : kas ia, and toru, q.v.

Kasī, v. i., or a., to be sweet, redup. gkasi (gakasi), dd. gari, gatr, kati. [Cf. Mg. hanitra fragrance, manitra sweet smelling, My. manis sweet, luscious, mild, gentle.] A. nakusa to be sweet, nakīs' sweet, fragrant with sweet odour.

NOTE.—The k elided and initial n retained in My. and Mg., and the final has also been elided in Tah. mona sweet, and Ef. mina sweet, pleasant.

Kāsu, s., an old man, a kind of priest or sacred man. [Fi. qase an old man.] S. kas'is'o

an old man, a priest, from kas' to grow old (Freytag), A. kas's' a Christian Presbyter.

Kasu, or kas, d. kau, s., c. art. nakasu, tree. wood. [Epi. dd. iesi, lakai, Ml. dd. nice, nai, TaSa. tagai (taghai), Futrakau, Sa. laau, My. kayu, Mg. hazo, tree. wood, Mg. hazo hard.] II. 'es tree, wood, Ch. 'a', from H. 'asah, A. 'asa' to be hard, firm.

NOTE.—Kasu has the art. k.

Kasua, or gasua, d. kasu, v. i., or a., hard, strong, redup. kaskasua, id., nakasuāna, s., the being hard or strong, strength. [Ja kakas hard, firm, rigid, stiff, cf. kuwasa strong.] H. kas'ah, A. kasa' to be hard, stiff, H. kas'eh hard, firm, fast, strong, powerful.

NOTE.—In Ef. nabona i gasua his heart is hard, meri gasua ki nia treat him hardly, or with violence.

Kat, or kati, v. i., to thunder, tīfai i kat, or i gat, the thunder thunders. See following word.

Kat ia, or gat ia, v. t., to make fast, as nakasu i gati natua na the log makes fast his foot, *i.e.*, jambs it and holds it firmly fixed against something ; to compress between two things, hence to bite, redup. katikati na kakat, s., a bite, fikit to bite each other, savage, to be pressed together, hence to be inspissated, clotted, curdled, katak, redup. gkatak, gakatak, with the suffixed k as in kanok or kanoka ; nalagi i katikati

the wind becomes fixed (in a
certain direction) ; i tua gat
ia sa he gave him by compact
or computation for it, i mate
gat ia he died by compact or
computation for it, i.e., he died
for it as for sin; i kati, or gati,
to thunder, is said to be the
same word, tifai i gat, and
when a " thunderbolt " rends
a tree it is said tifai i gati
bora ia the thunder bites, rending it (bora I.) The Efatese say
that the thunder has teeth,
and the idea in tifai i gat is
that the tifai is biting i.e.,
grinding its teeth together, or
rending with its teeth. [Ma.
kati block up, closed, kakati a
bundle, sheaf, and, v. t., tie
up in bundles, katikati, v.i.,
champ, move the jaw as in
eating, Fi. kata (vei kata =
fikit) to bite, a., close together,
as boards on a floor, My. gigit
to bite, gigitan a bite, Mg.
hehitra, s., hold, grasp, seizure,
clutch, bite, kaikitra a bite,
bitten, manaikitra, v. t., to
bite, kekerina being bitten.]
A. 'akada to bind, fasten, to
make a compact, to compute,
to coagulate, become clotted,
inspissated.

Katau, s., a kind of crab. [Cf.
My. kâtam a crab; to nip,
snip off.] Cf. A. katama to
bite, cut off. See koto a kind
of crab, infra.

Kati, d. for kasi, sweet, redup.
kakati.

Kate, tense part., d., past, a
kate, ku kate, i kate, au kate,
&c. : ka, and te.

Kate, d. Same as a kate, but
with the a verb. pron. after
the k', or between the k' and
te. See ka.

Kate, s., c. art. nakate, anything, a thing, lit. the that-
that, d. nete (ne te, the that ,.
See ka, and te. [Fi. ka a
thing.]

Kate, s., kate ni rarua the stick
on the outside of the canoe
superstruction on the side opp.
to the sama.

Katema, ad., outside of the
house. H. hus outside, and
ema house. See imrum, suma.
In ekatema, q.v.

Katoro, s., a basket. A. ka'tarat
a basket.

Kau, or gau, redup. kaukau (c.
art. agau, d. ni kam, tongs,
forceps, nippers, for grasping),
v. t., to grasp with the hand, i
kau nabe he grasps a club
(carried on his shoulder), then
to carry anything on the
shoulder, i kau nauos he grasps
the oar (in rowing), i kaukau
narā nakasu (the flying fox)
grasps the branch of a tree
(moving along it as it were
hand over hand, till it finds a
resting place), hence ba kaukau
(of men) go seeking a resting
place. See kam, kamut ia
[My. gawa, Fi. kau ta, to
carry.]

Kau, d. au, a lizard, perhaps
from grasping or clinging.

Kau, v. i., to bend (as with
hunger), also kai, and kaf, q.v.

Kau, s., d. for kasu, tree, wood.

Kau, v. i., or a., d. for kasua,
hard, strong.

Kaua, s., an open worked wicker basket or trap for catching fish : so called because

Kaukaua, a., full of openings or apertures, as if windowed, or apertured : the final a is the a. ending. A. kaww' an opening in a wall, kawwa*t* a window (Nm. couwa dormer window), Ch. kaw a window, from kawah, or kavah.

Kaukau, s., c. art. nakaukau, the upper cross (*i.e.*, above and across the kiat) or binding sticks between a canoe and its outrigger (sama) ; from grasping or holding together, kau, v. t.

Kĕ, or kū (cf. kei), dem., this. See ka, id., and ko id. ; kōrua, kĕtolu, d. kārua, &c.

Ke, d., that he, k', final conj., and e (or i) verb. pron , 3 sing.: ka, k.

Kĕ, keke, interj. See ake ! and ako ! [Florida ke ! keke !]

Ke, d., verb pron., 2 sing., you, dd. k, ma, ko.

Kĕtaku, or kĕĭtaku, s., the hinder end of a canoe, . ad. behind : for ko itaku. See kobĕ.

Keikei, s., c. art. nakeikei, tattoo marks or lines upon the skin. [Fi. qia to tattoo.] See goi a (or koi a, or kei a).

Kei naniu, for koi naniu. See goia or goi a.

Kei, d , dem., this, that (near), for koi, q.v.

Kekel, s., d. for kal, child, infant. See under bakal ia ɪ.

Kĕl, redup. gkĕl (kekel), v. i., to sweep round or wheel in curves (of a bird in flight without moving its wings); and

Kĕla, s., the curved beam or wall-plate that goes round the end of a native house ; and

Kele tia, v. t. (see golu tia, gele tia, gel ia, gulu tia, kalutia), as keleti, kel, or golu nāsu put the bowstring on a bow, nuana i laba i keleti narā nakasu its (a tree's) fruit plentiful *bends* the branch of the tree, i keleti wago (or other heavy thing to be carried) he stoops down and clasps the pig (or other heavy thing) to lift and carry it, hence kelakela, or gelakela (of a people carrying such things, as in going to a nakouan); and

Kelu-faki v. t., to round or double a cape (of a canoe or ship), eg. syn. ili-fiki ; and

Kĕlu, a., going round, as bagana kīlu its (the army's) rear or hinder part (see bago, baga) going round, making a detour (to surprise the enemy). [My. guling, goling, giling, gulung, to turn round, revolve, roll, roll up, igal to whirl, curly, and ikal to whirl, gyration, Mg. kodia a wheel, rolled, mikodia, mikodiadia to roll, and mikodinkodina, &c., also koriana, twirled, mikoriana to twirl, and mitsingerina, mitsingeringerina to turn, wind, roll, revolve.] H. 'agal, i.q. galal, to roll, to revolve, 'agar, hence 'agur revolving, whirling, gyrating (of a bird in flight), A. karkara to turn (a mill) round, 2, to revolve, wheel (as a bird in flight), H. gilgal a wheel, &c.

Ken, for kana, v. i.

Kerikeri, v. i., to be deep, as a pit, the sea. A. ka'ara to be deep.

Kesa, kesakesa, gesa, gesakesa. See kisa.

Ki, ad., see ka, ad., as : also in kite.

Ki, d., that (because) he : k', that, and i, verb. pron., 3 sing.: ka, k'.

Kĭ, d., dem., this, or kĕ, id. : ka, dem.

Ki, v. i. See ken, kana, d. kano.

Ki, prep. (the usual form), c. art. aki the, that which to, or of, also gi, agi. See ka, prep.

Ki, same as ka, art.

Ki, redup. kiki, v. i. See gi, gki (giki), v. i.

Ki, d., verb. pron., 2 pl., you, dual kia: ku.

Kia-, or kie-, pref. to the nom. suf. forming possessive pronouns kiagu, kiama, kiana, kiagita, kiagami, kiamu, kiara or kiata : kiana his (country, plantation, house, vicinity) ; kia (or kie) is ki, dem., the, that (same as the first ka in kakana), that which, and a or e, q.v., prep. The use of kakana is different, his or its (as a weapon to kill him, a door for a house, oar for a boat, &c.) [Epi kiaku, kiamo, kiano, kiandro, kie-memi, kiemiu, kialo, same as Ef. kiagu, kiama, &c.]

Kia, d., verb. pron. 2 dual, you two, d. ko ro. [Epi ko, An. ekau, id.]

Kiag, d. for kiama, thy (vicinity): kia-, and g suf. pron., 2 sing.

Kiat, s., c. art. nakiat, the sticks which cross from the canoe to the outrigger (sama) joining them together. [Sa. Tah. iato, Ta. niciatu, Fut. akiato, Ha. iako, id., Ma. kiato thwart of a canoe.] A. gaiz' pl. gawaiz', 'agwizat, gizau', &c., beam which crosses from one wall to another joining them together, from gaza to cross over, go across.

Kie, s., c. art. nakie, the plant whose leaf is baked, dried, and split into thin threads to be woven into mats, &c. [Sa. 'ie a fine mat, cloth.] See under neko.

Kigami, d. kinami.

Kigita, d. syn. nigita.

Kīkĭ, v. i., or a., and iki in kariki, small. [To. iki id.] See under neko.

Kikita, or gkita, redup. of kita.

Kilakila, a., knowing sagacious, shy, i meta kilakila (of an animal). [Fi. kila wild, suspicious, on the lookout, as an animal.] A. 'akala, 1, 2, to be intelligent, prudent, sagacious, 'akil', a., id.

Kil ia, or kili a, v. t., to dig, hence kāli, s., a digging stick, and nakīli, s., a current (as in the sand, lit. that which digs). [Sa. 'eli to dig, Ma. 'eli to be dug, My. gali to dig, Mg. hady ditch, trench, &c., dug, mihady to dig.] E. karaya, A. kara', H. karah, Ch. kera', to dig.

Kīli, s., c. art. nakīli, d., a current : kili a.

Kilikili, v., redup. of kili a, used of many digging : ru kilikili they (as the people of a district and whose yams are ripe) dig.

Kiliti, s., a sow, a mother-pig. [An. karite, or kerite, an animal that has had young.] Kiliti, lit. that brings forth (young), or the bringer forth, i.e., mother.   See ki or ka, art., and for liti, see ani, note.

Kin, s. See ikin, nest.

Kin, d., dem., this : ki dem., and in dem. [Assy. agannu this, aga dem., and annu dem.]

Kinam, d. kinami.

Kinami, pers. pron., 1 pl., excl., we, they.

Kinau, pers. pron., 1 sing., I, shortened kinu, dd. keino, anu, enu : ki, art., or dem. prefix, and nau (for naku, hence nom. suf. gu, d. k). [An. ainyak, Epi. nagku, TaSa. enau, Sa. o a'u (for ko aku), My. aku, Mg. izaho, aho, I.] H. 'anoki, shortened 'äni, Assy. anaku, Aram. 'äna', 'eno', E. 'ana, I.

Kinit ia, also ginit ia and gunut ia, v. t., nip with the fingers, nakini na the fingers (nippers), kini gote fia nip, breaking it (reeds for thatching), hence nakini-got reeds for thatching. [Fi. kini-ta nip, pinch between finger and thumb, Sa. 'ini to take hold of with the nails, pinch, ps. 'initia, Ma. kini, Ha. iniki, My. gântâs (cf. Ef. d. gint ia, for ginit ia) to break off, nip off, snap off.] A. karasa, to nip (with the fingers), pinch, grasp with the

points of the fingers or hand, snip off.

Kini na, s., c. art., the fingers, or toes, lit. the nippers, or graspers ; also claws, talons.

Kini gote fia, v. t., and

Kinigot, s., c. art., see kinit ia.

Kintu, dem., that (near): kin. dem., and tu.

Kinu, I, see kinau.

Kiri, d., s., c. art. nakiri, d. syn. ori, rubbing stick for producing fire. [Sa. 'ili rasp, file, saw.] See kar ia, magiri a.

Kirikiri, s., gravel, pebble. [Sa. 'ili'ili, Ma. kirikiri, My. krikil, kärikil, karikil, gravel, pebble.] H. garger, A. girgir' a berry, from H. garar, see kar ia, cg. A. garal' gravel.

Kirikiri, a., small, like pebbles, in bia kirikiri little children. See preceding word.

Kis, s., a shell, used for cutting. A. giz'at a shell, from gaza'a to cut.

Kis, d., dem., this, here : ki, dem., and sě, dem.

Kisa, a., in mita kisa blind (the eyes sunk into the head). A. has', id. And

Kisa, or gisa, v. i., or a., redup.,

Kisakisa, v. i., or a., to be putting forth leaves, hence to be green ; hence

Kisa, s., c. art., nakisa, d. takis, a green stone or chalk (used only for painting himself by a a chief), a chief's grave (in the bush, sacred). A. h'awisa to have the eyes sinking into the head, 4, to put forth leaves (a plant), to germinate.

Kihi na, d. kui na, q.v. : kihi na,

i.e., kisi na (h being for s in that d.)

Kis ia, or kisi a, v. t., also gis ia, redup. giskis, to feel, touch, lo giskis to look, exploring (as at a person's body partly uncovered). A. gassa to feel, touch, to explore or grope with the hand or with the eyes, H. gas'as', Pi., E. gasasa to feel, touch, S. gas' to feel, touch, to explore.

Kisau, v. t., d. kisur, to remove, get out, stand apart : i kisau ki nabua he removes from, or stands out, or gets out of the road, ba kisau get out (of the way), remove, stand away. A. kasa', kasww', kusuww', kasā', to stand apart, to be remote.

Kistu, dem., this here : kis dem., and tu.

Kisur (ksur), d. for kisau. See (d.) ēsu.

Kita, a., little, small, li kita small place (name of small boat entrance of Havannah Harbour) opp. to li leba big place (name of large entrance to Havannah Harbour). [Sa. iti, itiiti, small, few, Ma. and Tah. iti, itiiti, small, little, My. kate, kite, diminutive.] E. hasasa, hasa to be small, minute.

Kita (rare), or kite, ad., as, takes the verb. pron., as i kite fatu it is as (or like) a stone, kite or kite uan as, as if, i bisa i kite i maieto he speaks as if he were angry, i marafi kite nifila it is quick as lightning. A. kada like, as this, as that. See ki, as, and te, kite, or

kita, lit., as that, or like that.

Kita, or kite, conj., or, d. ko : rarua kite boat a canoe or boat ; inter. particle at the end of sentences, d. ko, as i bano kite ? has he gone ? fully this is, i bano kite i tika ? has he gone or not ? For kite, disj. conj., see ko, conj., *infra.*

Kita, v., to divine, redup. kikita, gkita, lit. to perceive or feel with the eye or the mind (cf. rogo, rorogo), bati kita ia, or gita ia to try (cf. bati rog ia), lit. make or do feeling or perceiving or knowing or finding out. [Ma. kite to see, know, perceive, find out, discover, matakite to divine, s. one who foresees an event.] A. wagada to find with the eye or the mind (*a thing sought*), to perceive by the feeling of the body (*a thing*), or by the mind, 4, make to find or to perceive.

Kità ia, and gità ia, v. t., to hate, redup. kitakita ia, to be envious of, to hate ; and

Kita roà sa, or kita roà i, to hate turning after him (someone), as a boy sent a message meeting another boy and (hating to do the message) turns after him to play. See roa. H. kut, followed by prep. bĕ, to loathe, also kus and nakat.

Kita, in bakita and bakitakita. See makitakita, id.

Kite. See kita, ad.

Ko, verb. suf., 2 sing., you (pl. for sing.), dd. k, ke, ma.

S

Ko, d., verb. pron., 2 sing., you, d. ku.

Ko, sign of imperative, 2 pl. (sing. ba), lit. that you : k' final conj., and o fragment of pers. pron., 2 pl.

Ko, d., ad. of assent., d. syn. na, and redup.,

Koko, id., d. ko, interj. See ako and kori : ko, dem.

Ko, ad., now, d. syn. uo (wo), as i ko toko (d. i uo toko) he now remains (has not yet gone) ba ko toko remain now, or just now, d. syn. ba i toko (bai toko) ; and i ko toko, d. i uo toko, in another d. is i ta toko. For i, uo, and ta, see these words. H. koh, ko' (from kahu, k' as, and the pers. pron., 3 sing., as a dem., like as this) (so, here), now. [An. ko just now ; in this way].

Ko, dem. See koi, kofeta, kofakal : E. ku (ka dem., and u (o) pron., 3 sing.)

Ko, d., disj. conj., or ; inter. particle at the end of a sentence as, i bano ko ? has he gone ? fully, i bano ko i tika ? has he gone or not ? D. syn., in both uses, kite or kita. [An. ka, id., Er. ku or.] H. ki or, 1 Kings xviii. 27, syn. c. A., S., 'aw, or, in this passage).

Note.—Kite and ko have both a dem. suffixed to ki, the former te, the latter o (the o in the preceding word), and therefore lit. denote or—this.

Ko, s., c. art. nako na (for n ako), the face, a part ; nakona his face (see nako, infra), nakonako ki to face (someone), nako nafakotoen a part of the price, ba tu au nakon give me a part, nakon ru bano nakon ru toko a part (of the whole number of men) go, a part remain ; and, without the article, shortened to ko, as ko-bē ni rarua, or nakobe, the fore part of a canoe, ke-itaku ni rarua, or nako-itaku the after-part of a canoe ; ko-be the part before, the front, i baki kobe he goes to the front, kē-itaku the part behind, behind, i baki kē-itaku he goes behind, or to the rear. A. wagt' (wagto) the face, a part or side, wigāt a band, wagaha, 3, to face (someone).

Koa, a., fibrous, stringy, as a yam when cooked, naui koa : aka, ako, and a a. ending.

Koakoa, redup. of koa, very stringy or fibrous.

Koau, s., c. art. nakoau, d. kabu the native pudding. See kofu sa.

Koba sia, v. t., to follow, to drive away, to pursue : i koba nabona he follows his own heart (does or strives to do what is in his mind) ; v. r., fikoba to follow each other, or to drive away each other ;

Kobausi a, v. t., i.e., koba, and usi to track ; to follow after. A. kafā to follow, to drive away.

Kobara, s., see gobara : ko dem. prefixed.

Kobu, d. See kubu.

Kofa, s., and redup.,

Kofakofa, s., an alcove, temporary house or shed, tent. H. kubah a tent, chamber (so called from its arched form, from kabab to make gibbous and hollow, to arch, to vault). A. kubbat tent, vault, chamber, hence the word *alcove*.

Kofakal, s., a herd of pigs cared for, lit. the or that cared for: ko dem., and fakal.

Kofe na, s., nakofena, his skull, the skull. A. kihf' the skull.

Kofeta, d., s., fata, q.v., with dem. ko prefixed, a bench, platform.

Kofu sa, v. t., to enclose (as fish in a net), wrap up or enclose (as a pudding in leaves, to be put in the oven). See kabu, d. koau, the native pudding; and

Kofukofua, a., redup., and with a. ending a, bent up at the edges, as a shovel, or anything, as it were *rolled up* or turned over. The pudding, koau, is laid on a mass of leaves, very wide and long, which are rolled up or over it all round, completely enclosing it, and then tied up. [Fi. kovuta, kokofu blistered (small balls or pimples), kovu banana leaf in which native puddings are done up, d., a coat, kovuna to do up in a kovu, Sa. 'ofu a garment, 'o'ofu put on a garment, 'ofu'ofu to envelope in leaves (for cooking), 'ofulua twenty leaf dishes of native food; Ma. kohu, kokohu, a.,

somewhat concave, bent or warped so as to become concave (cf. Ef. kofukofua), kohu to cook in a native oven any article contained in a hollow vessel, To. kofu to enclose or wrap up, to clothe, Ha. ohu to roll up (as the sea that does not break) a roller, a swell, ohua a crowd of people, ohui to twist round, ohuohu heavy, burdensome, a wreath worn round the neck, to dress in uniform, Tah. ohu a bank or ridge of earth thrown up, a bundle of native food tied up and baked in the native oven, to bend downwards as the branch of a tree, to stoop, to twirl round as a wheel.] A. kabba to roll up into a ball, to make into balls (food) for cooking, to invert, to stoop, to be heavy, A. kobbat', kabāb' (see under kabu, d. koau, *supra*): kobbat also denotes a mob of horses, crowd or mass of men, herd of camels, a ball of threads rolled up together, a heavy ponderous thing, a hill, kabkaba, 2, to be wrapped up, enveloped, to wrap up or envelope oneself (in one's garment).

Koi, d., dem., this, d. kei: ko dem., and i dem.

Koia (ko-ia, ko-ya), same as preceding.

Koi, s., and

Koika, s., a boundary, from

Koi a, or ko ia, v. t. See goi a.

Koko, s., c. art. nekoko, reddish juice or paint for nafona made from a plant (also called nekoko): goko ia. [To. koka, Sa. 'o'a, id.]

Kokoro, s. See under gor ia.

Kokoti, s., a net for catching fish : koto.

Kola, d., and redup.,

Kokola, v. i., to be bent, kola ki na buruma (a mother-in-law) bends or stoops to the son-in-law. See kele tia (golu tia) &c.

Kola, v. i., and redup.,

Kokola, v. i, or gkola, to be arid, dry ; hence

Kōla, s., a dry stick or log. A. kahala, kohol', to be arid, dry.

Kola, v. i., and gola, and redup. gkola (kokola), to call out, cry out, to speak loud ; hence

Kola oli, s., echo, lit. calling out like. See oli a. [Fi. kaila to shout, Mg. akora, s., shouting.] H. kara' to cry out, call out.

Kolau, redup. gkolau. See galau ia.

Kolau, s. See kalau, spider's web, dd. kalai, nilau (i.e., lau) ; namera kolau web of fat on the inwards of a pig. [An. nilva = kolau, nilvanilva = namera-kolau].

Kolau (see preceding word), pr. n., prob. originally given to a warrior full of stratagems. See also the verb under kalau, to weave, to lie in wait, watch in ambush (as in war). A. 'aruba to be wily or cunning.

Kolobu na, s., its joint (of a bamboo or reed), applied also to the knobs or rivets on a tank. A. karibu joint of a bamboo or reed.

Kolōfa, v. c., to be bent, as

with hunger or famine, redup. gkolōfa. See lofa ia, lōfa. The prefixed ko is the dem. [Fi. kalove bent, from love-ca to bend.]

Komam, dd. kinami, kimam.

Kon, v. i., or a. (with ending n), and redup.,

Kokon, gkon, to be bitter (of anything), kona ki to be bitter towards (someone), namarita na i gkon his belly is bitter (he is angry). [Sa. 'ona, 'o'ona, bitter, sour.] A. ko' and ko'a' very bitter.

Konai na, s., c. art. nakonai na, his gall or bile : kon bitter.

Kona, v. i., gona, to stand firm, to be fixed, firm, then, to have the mind fixed upon, to be occupied with, kona ki. H. kun prop. to stand upright, Hi. to set up, found, then to apply one's mind to, Ni. to stand firm, fixed, steady, firm, constant.

Kona gor ia, v., to stand firm protecting him (as in war). See gor ia.

Konā ia, or konai a, v. t., and gonai a, to pierce (as a board with an instrument like an awl). E. kanawa to pierce.

Konai sai a, v., to pierce through. See sai a.

Kore na, s., see gore na, brother's sister, sister's brother, children of the same mother (actually), or, if not, members of the same nakainaga.

Kor ia. See gor ia.

Korò sa, v. t., conceal it (as misconduct of which one is accused) : gor ia.

Koro, s., c. art. nakoro, a fence, a wall, d. ara, c. art. nára : gor ia.

Koro, s., a fish fence, enclosure for catching fish ; a ring (or halo) round the moon : gor ia.

Koro, s., c. art. nekoro, incantation or rites of divination ; and

Koro, v., to divine : gor ia.

Koroatalagi, d., or nakoroatelagi, the sky, dd. koroinlagi, rikitelagi, lit. the fence, or that which surrounds or encloses the atalagi, q.v.

Koroinlagi, s., d., the sky, lit. the fence, or that which encloses heaven. See lagi, elagi.

Koroki, v., to insist (as in argument), provoke, irritate. S. gareg (Pael) to provoke.

Kori, or koria, also kuri, or kuria, s., a dog: cognate oro, to bark. [Sa. uli, id., Ma. kuri a dog, any quadruped, To. kuli a dog, Fut. kuli, Ta. kuri, Epi kuli, kuliu, TaSa. vuriu, Malo vuria, Ml. kuri, Mg. alikia, id.] A. gorw' a young dog.

Kori, interj., also in akori, kori la ! this now indeed ! here, or there indeed ! : ko dem., ri dem.

Koro, v. i, to snore. See goro.

Koroi, d. kurii a woman ; and

Koruni, kuruni, q.v. See fatine, Note 2, and lai.

Kos ia, kus ia, v. t., to cut or shear off (as the end of the outer covering of a young cocoanut fit for drinking); and

Kosu mia, v. t., to husk a cocoanut, also kusu mia, gusu mia ; i gusu, v. i., said of a ripe cocoanut which separates itself and falls from the tree, kusu mia or gusu mia, v. t., to gather cocoanuts from the tree, kusu, or gusu, v. i., to be ripe, soft, makusukusu to be ripe, soft, kusue na, s., the soft place on the top of a child's head, the last to close up, makus, q.v., s., cutter or knife. A. gazza to cut off, shear: to cut (grass, &c.) in order to gather provender, to cut off the clusters of dates from the tree ; to begin to ripen (dates), 4, to have (sheep) ready for shearing, or ripe grain, to be ready to be gathered from the tree (dates), to be ripe or ready for gathering (fruit of the palm tree), for reaping (grain), for shearing (sheep) ; migazz' a cutting instrument.

Kosu, s., a cutting instrument made of bone: preceding word.

Kosoáfa, s., c. art. nakosoafa, dd. nasoáfa, soáfa, a plant used in ceremonial or ritual purifications: it is swept down the limbs to carry away the uncleanness ; lit. the tree that carries (away) : kosu (see kasu), and afa ia.

Kota, s., a time, in i ta kota ki (a person) he appoints a time to or for (someone); and in

Kotfān, d. for gotafānu, gota fānu, q.v., evening.

Koto bolo, s., a basket (see bolo). [Ml. cat, Malo cete, To. kato,

Sa. 'ato, a basket.] A. ka'ṭaṭ a basket (for carrying dates).

Koto, s., a kind of crab : so called from nipping. See following word.

Koto-fia v. t., kote-fia, kotu-fia, gote-fia, redup. kotokote fia, gotokote fia (intensive), to cut, to cut off, break off ; eni gote fia to lie across it, bala tagoto inclined across, across, ba gote fia go across it, soka gote fia leap across it ; sai gote fia, tuba gote fia pronounce judgment against him, condemn him to death, i gotokoto bat ia he made a beginning, first did it (*broke ground in the doing of it*), makoto broken (a stick, or anything), ceases (as war), a makoto ki I cease from (a thing, as a thing I have sold), have no further connection with, separate from, cease from (a thing or person), kuti nakoau cut up the pudding (cooked), gkuti (gukuti) to make a stealthy invasion or inroad, i gai tagoto, or makotokoto he screams abruptly, cries out in sharp, sudden, broken screams ; kokoti a net (cutting off the fish) ; bagote fia to buy it, make it separate from its former owner) ; i kote fiau isa he breaks me off from it (a thing I possessed) ; bikutu, v. r., decide about (someone), bikutu ki nia decide about him, sera makoto to be startled, surprised, makot a place. [Sa. 'oti to cut (as the hair), 'o'oti, 'oti'oti, Fi. koti-va to clip, or shear, ai koti scissors or shears

(originally a shell or shark's tooth).] A. kata'a cut, cut off, separate, cross (a river) ; cease; decide about (a thing) ; to snap (as a rope, break) : to break off, cease from (a journey, &c. = makoto ki) ; to invade, or make an inroad, stealthily &c. ; makta' a place.

Ku, verb. pron., 2 sing., and pl., you.

Ku, dem., this, as nai ku na, d. gā kin, this (is) he, or it, nai ua naga, nai ua, nai naga, nai kis. [My. iku that.] E. ku, id. See ko, ka, ki'.

Ku, d., kua, or gua, v. i., to cry out, vociferate, cry or call out, low (an ox). H. ga'ah, S. g'o' cry out, vociferate, low (an ox).

Kua, gua, preceding word.

Kua, ad., inter., and indef. : gua.

Kuba na, s, c. art. nakuba na, its or his day ; d. for uba na, or ube na, q.v.

Kubega, s., d., a net (for catching fish). [Sa. upenga, Tah. upea, Ma. kupenga, id.] A. kiffaṭ a net, from kaffa to wrap round, &c.

Kubu, s., inside, the belly, also kobu, and kabu, d. kama (in arekabu, q.v., ānekama), then, inside (a house), and with the prep. e, ekubu, ekobu in the inside, inside : then, ekobu in one d. denotes also a house. [Mg. kibo the belly, kobany its centre or middle, kobony the inside, inner part, entrails.] A. ga'fu the belly, interior cavity of a thing, inside (of a house), from gāfa to be hollow.

Kufagufa, d., v. i., to fly, to flap the wings, flutter. [To. kapakapa to flap the wings, My. kapak to fly, flapping the wings, not gliding.] A. h'afaka 1, 4, to fly, to flap with the wings.

Kui na, d., s., c. art. nakui na, d. kihi na (i.e. kisi na, in that d. h is for s), the back, rump, tail : kui na is for bui na, and kihi na (i.e. kisi na) for bisi na, by the change of b to k.

Kuku, v. i. See guku.

Kuli na (d. uili na), s., the skin, bark. [Ha. ili, Ma. kiri, skin, bark, My. kulit skin, hide, pelt, leather, bark, rind, husk, shell, Mg. hoditra skin, bark.] See mulu sia.

Kulu, v. i., to wrap oneself up, to cover oneself up (as in bed).

Kulu tia, v. t., same as kalu tia ;

Kulu, s., c. art. nakulu, cloth, covering, that which covers ;

Kulekule, or kulukulu, d., id. : kalu.

Kuma na, s., or guma na, c. art. na kumana, inner bark, pellicle or cover, as of an egg, orange, &c. : d. for kamu na.

Kum ia, v. t. (see gum ia), to absorb, redup. kukumi.

Kumu, d., pers. pron., 2 pl., you, dd. akam and akamus, kami, nikam, nimu, nēm or nēĕm, egū. [My. kamu, Tag. kamo, Ml. P. hamdi, Epi. kamiu, Ta. ituma, id.]

Kunuti na, s., c. art. nakunuti na, the kernel of fruits, as the almond; also new yams : kano, kanoa, kanoka. [Cf. To. kano the inmost substance of anything, kernels of fruit, also flesh, kano he mata eye-ball (Mg. anaka in anakandriamaso pupil of the eye).]

Kūra, s., c. art. nakūra, a plant ; so called from its bitterness. Of a stingy man who withholds food from a visitor it is said nalo anena i bi nakūra. See under gura ia.

Kuraf, d. for karafi, q.v.

Kuri, or kuria, s., same as kori, koria, dog.

Kūru, or kūra, a., shrivelled, dried, nāli kuru shrivelled dried leaves (as banana leaves when withered and dry are). See kara, or gara.

Kuru ki, v. t., to gather together ; and

Kuru maki, v. t., to gather together ; and

Kuruk ; and

Kukuruk (gkuruk), v. i., or mid., to gather itself, or to be gathered together : see guru ki ; belonging to this stem are also takāra, crowd (of men), and makara to be gathered together, d. (transposed) maraka, or meraka.

Kuruni, s., a woman. See fafine, Note 2, and lai.

Kurui, s., and

Kuruku na, s., kuruku natua na, the ankle : kuruk. The ankle is so called because the leg gathers itself, as it were, into the knob of the joint.

Kurumase na, s., d. (transposed) for borakese na, q.v.

Kus, d., v. i., to be hidden ; d. gusu (i.e., kusu), q.v., to stoop.

As to connection of these two meanings, see *belu* : a man *stoops* to avoid being seen, or to be hidden.

Kus ia, or kusi a, v. t., to go in the track of, follow, usually usia, q.v. (the k being elided), rafe kus ia to go through following it (as a pig going through a hole in the fence of a garden following another pig), hence the proverb, uago iskai i *bora* bua nakoro, uago laba i rafe kus ia one pig bursts open the fence, many pigs go through the opening following (or after) it: in takus ia, rukus ia (nrukus ia) the k also is not elided. See usi a.

Kusu na, d., s., dd. kui na, kibi na, bui na, q.v.

Kusu, v. i., and

Kusue na, s. See kosu mia.

Kusue, or kusuiie (pronounced kusuwe), d. kusu, s., rat (or mouse). [Ta. yasuk, Ml. dd. khasup, akasu, Pa. asua, Santo dd. karibi, keriu, Ma. kiore, Sa. iore, My. tikus, Mysol kelof, Gilolo luf, lupu, id.] A. kutrub' rat.

Kut ia, v. t., to cut, and

Kukut ia (gkut ia), redup.: i gkuti ban he goes to make an inroad stealthily (as in time of war); also si kut ia (si to shoot) to shoot not killing, but only *cutting* or wounding: and

Kutu ki, bikutu ki, to decide about (someone). See koto fia.

Kutu, s., louse : the back of the head. Sa. 'utu louse, an in-sect which eats the skin of the hands and feet, My. kutu louse, To., Fut., kutu, Ta. kiget, An. cet, Ml. P. cut, Malo utu, louse.] A. kuddla*t*, pl. kiddan, flea (and kiddan flea, an animal biting like a flea), kudad' the back of the head between the ears, pl. fleas, Ef. *bala* kutu na the hollow of the back of his head (*bala* III.), from kadda to cut.

NOTE.—There is no other word for flea in Ef., but to distinguish a flea from a louse the former is called kutu n koria the kutu of the dog, so Fut. kutu kuli, My. kutu anjing (anjing dog), TaSa. utu vuriu, but Malo utu (simply). The Efatese say there were no fleas in the island before Europeans brought them. In Sa. flea is 'utufiti, and in Fi. kutu ni manumanu.

La, d. le, ad., indeed, certainly, surely, particle of emphasis, as uisi la yes indeed, i la masikina he indeed is one, or one only, i le sa he is indeed bad, i ga fano la let him go indeed. [Sa. la, My. lah, id.] A. la certainly, surely, indeed.

La ia, or lai a, v. t., to put out, or eject from, the mouth, as food, froth, the tongue (see lē): lua.

Lāba, v. i., to be much, many ; laba or leba, labalaba or lebaleba, to be or become big, grow up, d. lafulafu to be or become (grow) big, lalaba, or leleba big, great, leba elder; tea laba or leba plenty, enough (no more), it is enough, milāba last, nameligu milāba i en lu ua my last footprint is in this place, *i.e.*, I will come no more here, tea milāba the last (person or thing), i libi milābā sa he looked upon it for the last time, d. leb, indeed, very; barab (barau, &c.) long. [Sa. lava to be enough, indeed, very, loa long (and leva long, of time), Mg. lava long, tall, continuing long (= Ef. barab, baraf), My. luwas, luas wide extensive, large, ample, Fi. levu great, or large; in great numbers, all, as era sa lako levu they are all, or many, gone (= Ef. ru lāba bano), vakalevu-taka to increase; cause to be great or many, balavu long.] H. rabab to become much or many, to be increased, to be much or many, inf. rob a being much or many. abundance, multitude; poetically multitude is almost used for "all" (so in Fi. and Ef. levu, lāba), a being great (of might), a being *long* (of a way), rab much, many; enough, (it is) enough (no more, cease, leave off, so Ef.); big (great, large, vast), applied to a *wide* space, to a *long* way, and to things generally in the sense of great, big; elder. The cognate and supplementary verb is rabah, to be multiplied,

increased, often to be many; to become great, to grow up, to be great.

Labalaba, or lebaleba, v. i., and a., redup. of laba, or leba, v. i., and a., to be great, big, as natasē leba the great sea. See lāba.

Labo, s. See leba: leba boa.

Laf ia, or lafi a, v. t., to take, take up, carry (a thing), take up (a song). [Ha. lawe (ps. lawea) to take, carry.] A. rafa'a, to take up, carry.

Lāfi na, s., c. art., the cover, sheath, or envelope of the flowers or buds of the cocoanut palm; the hard substance (of same shape) of the cuttle-fish (d. namagi rofarofa = little canoe of the cuttle-fish). A. "ilāf" a cover, sheath, or envelope, H. 'alaf to cover, to wrap up, A. "alafa to enclose in a sheath or vessel.

Lafuis, dd. rifālu, libuis, lifāru, q.v.

Lafulafu, d., v. i., and a., to grow up, big: lāba.

Lāga, v. t., to seek, search for, lāgā sa seek it, bilāgā sa, id., and redup.,

Lāgālāgā sa, v. t., id. (frequentative). A. rāma to seek, search for, n. a. marām'.

Laga tia, v. t., to raise, lift up (as a thing from the ground), and

Lāga, s., that which raises: lāga laga ti (the planks of a boat).

Laga ia, or lagai a, v. t., to raise, lift up (as the wind raises thatch from a roof); then to raise (a thing, so as to make it conspicuous), as i mirama laga tia it (the moon, &c.) shines raising it (into view, making it conspicuous) ; hence Laga (without object) to shine (to raise into view, make conspicuous), bisa laga tia to speak raising it (into view), laga tia to speak with a loud voice, laga, v. i., to sing, and

Lagalaga, v., redup. (in all these senses) : nalagalaga na, s., a thing raised from or off something (as a scale from the eyes, husk from grain, &c.) ; malaga, malagalaga, to be raised (so as to be conspicuous, as a ship on the sea); balaga tia, v. c., to make raised (a thing), balaga-saki nia, v. c., balaga na (see under these words), tabalaga, v. r., to raise itself, be raised (from above, or off, anything) ;

Lagi, s., with prep. elagi, ad. (used also as a prep.) and s., the sky, heaven, above : ulua, lua, lulu. [Sa. laga to rise up, to raise up, redup. lagalaga, s., a stick for raising up flat coral, v., to raise up (as a heavy weight), lagalagaola to raise the finger nails from the flesh, lagi the sky, heaven, v., to call out with a loud voice, to sing, Ha. lana to float (on water), float (i.e., be lifted up, raised) in the air, lani sky, heaven, luna the upper side of anything, the upper, the above, a., upper, higher, above, and, with a prep., ad., or prep., above, Sa. iluga, id., My. langit sky, firmament, lalangit

the palate, an awning, canopy, Mg. lanitra sky, heaven.] A. 'alā' to be high, to be above or upon (a thing), 2, to raise, lift up, 3, to manifest, to call with a loud (high) voice, 4, to raise, 6, to stand out high, &c., hence prep. 'ala' above, 'ilian' and 'iliyyan' tall (high), high voice, and 'illiyyuna the seventh heaven, paradise, Assy. ad. (used as a prep.) elānu, elān, above, also ellaon, and elien, elinitu high, a being high, which has u the a. ending, and suffixed to it the abstract ending t in the usual way).

Lagāraf, v. i., or mid., to mourn (as for the dead) : laga tia, to raise, and teraf ia to scratch, from raising the hands and tearing or scratching the cheeks in mourning (see bora I., bora na the temples).

Lagāfaru na, v. and s. compounded, to raise its wings (a bird) : laga tia, and afaru na.

Lagafasu ki, v., make a sign to : laga tia, and fasu na.

Lagilagi, v. i., to be proud, uplifted. [Ha. lanilani to be high-minded, proud, show haughtiness.] See laga tia. A. 'ala', 5), to be proud.

Laga ki, v. t., to have, to possess. See laka.

Lagi, s., c. art. nalagi, the wind : other forms of this word are in and redup. agiēgi, with article nīn, nàgiēgi, the air, the breeze. [Ml. nien, Paama lag, Am. lig, yig, Fi. cagi (thangi), My. angin, Mg. anina the wind, Sa. matagi to blow, be windy, ps. matagia, s., the wind, Ma. matangi the wind, kotengitengi gentle wind, kohengi or kohengihengi wind.] A. nasama to blow gently (the wind), nasam' a light wind, na'sam' and nasim' a light wind, breeze, air.

Lago, s., fly; lago fū buzzing fly, blow-fly. [Sa. lago, a fly, My. langau a large fly, a blue-bottle.] A. lakka'u a fly, from laka'a prehendit extremo rostro rem.

Lago, s., the wooden pins whose sharpened ends are driven into the sama (outrigger), and whose upper ends (crossed) hold and bear up the nakiat of a canoe. [Sa. lago props of a canoe.] See preceding word.

Lagor, or lagora, or lagorō, ad., d. lakor, q.v.

Lai a. See la ia : redup.,

Lailai, v. t., frequentative or in-tensive.

Lai, or lei, contracted to le, li, s., woman, as le kiki little woman (in addressing a female child or girl), le or li meroan women, ladies (in addressing an as-sembly of women) : this word is used before names of fe-males, as ma, q.v., is before names of males, as lei, le, or li māko madam, mistress, miss, or lady, mako. [Fi. adi, con-tracted di, id., Mota iro, ro, id.] H. 'is's'ah, Ch. 'ita', S. 'atto', A. 'untha, woman, Ch. emph. 'itta', 'intta', id.

NOTE.—For other forms of

this word see koroi, kurui, kuruni. See under fafine, Note 2. Koroi, &c., have the dem. or art. k' prefixed.

Lai, s., c. art. nalai, or inlai, or nilai, sail (of a canoe or ship). [Sa. la, Ma. ra, Mg. lai, My. layar, id. ; My. layar, to sail, to navigate, also bārlayar and malayar.] A. killā'at sail of a ship, kala'a, 4, to make sail, to sail, to navigate.

Lailai, v. i., to be delighted, re-joice. [Mg. laolao play, play-things, milaolao to play.] A. laha', n. a. lahw', to play ; to be delighted.

Lai a, or lei a, or la ia, v. t., to pluck, to gather (fruit), lai nua nakasu to pluck or gather the fruits of trees. See bila ia, or bilai a. [My. lāli to pluck, to gather.] E. 'araya, H. 'arah, to pluck, to gather (as fruits).

Lai a, or lei a, v. t., to tie up, as lei namanuk to tie up a wound. A. 'ara' to tie up ; fasten.

Lak, d. for lako, q.v.

Laka, s., laka leo, foundation or cause of a matter or affair ; and

Laka, or lake, c. art. nalake na, its foundation, then, its cause, as nalake na tafa the founda-tion of the hill or mountain, Atua i bi nalakegita God is our foundation, i.e., our upholder, te uane i bi nalake nafakal that is the cause of the war, then nalakena because, lit. its cause ; and

Lake, or laki, v. i., to marry (of a woman) : lake ki nanoi marry

a husband, lit. betake herself
to a husband ; and lake kiena
betake herself to his house,
and then generally of anyone,
i lake he betakes himself (to
dwell somewhere), i lake en
lu ua he has betaken himself
to dwell here ; laga ki, v. t.,
to have, to possess, d. lakea ki,
telakie na its possessor, or
telake na, c. art. atelakie na
or atelakea na, or atelake na,
id., Atua i bi atelakea gita God
is our possessor, possesses us.
[Ma. taketake, a., well founded,
take, s., root, stump, post of a
pa, cause, putake, s., base,
root, reason, cause.] A.
rakaha to lean upon (something) ; to betake oneself (to
someone) ; to place upon,
found, as to found (his house
upon a rock), 4, to support
(prop up), 5, to abide (in some
place ; to use free power (in a
matter) ; rukah' the firm side
of a mountain, by which it is
upheld, pl. 'arkāh' a foundation.

Note.—The expression tu-
lake is composed of tu to give
(or tua), and lake, and means
to give in trust to (to give
relying upon or trusting in)—i
tulake is he gave in trust it, i
tulak irà sa he gave in trust
to them it (as a present or
money to be taken charge of
and conveyed by them to the
person for whom it is in-
tended).

Lakau, v. t., d. (transposed) for
galau ia, q.v., to cross over.
[Sa. la'a to step, to pass

over, ps. la'asia, redup. lala'a,
la'ala'a ; la'ai to pass over,
break over (as a wave over a
canoe from one side over to
the other), la'aga, la'asaga a
step, a stepping over.] Hence

Lakau, s., a crossing place in a
fence ; a stile.

Lako, s., d. lak, a small enclosure
(like a hole, for putting or
confining a pig in). See following word.

Lako, v. i., dd. laku, loku, loko,
roko, nrok, to stoop, be curved,
then stoop or crouch, concealing herself (as a mother-in-
law from her son-in-law), to be
concealed (as one stoops in
order to be concealed, see
belu, kusu), redup. lakolako, c.
prep. ki lakolako ki to be
crouching and stooping and
concealed from (someone), toko
lōku to abide concealed or in
concealment, luku, id., luku-
taki nia, or loko taki nia, to
place him in concealment (as a
wounded warrior for surgical
treatment), ba lako-saki nia to
creep upon it stealthily (as a
hunter upon a bird), hence ba
lako to hunt (birds), lit. to go
concealed, luku or luk a hole
or pit, luku noai a well, lako,
or lak (see preceding word),
baluku (i.e., ba luku) a curved
ba (concavity). [Fi. roko a
bowing form or posture, a.,
bent like a bow, ad., sa lako
roko goes stooping or bowing,
ai roko bowstring, roko-ta
bend a bow, roko-va bow to,
pay respect to, rokoroko, rev-
erence, respect, bakaroko bow

down with weakness, or go stooping, Sa. lolo'u to bend, bend down, bend round.] A. raka'a, n. a. roko', or ruku', to stoop, or be curved or bent, to bow or be bent down (as in prayer), ruk'at a hole, pit.

Lakolako ki, redup. of preceding word ; and

Lako saki, the same, c. compound prep. saki.

Lakor, ad., *i.e.*, la-kor, indeed now : lakor is sometimes practically syn. with la as i fi la mai matol, or i fi lakor mai matol he may indeed come to-morrow, or the latter may be rendered, he may indeed now come to-morrow. This is the lit. translation, but it might be expressed, he may perhaps, or possibly, come to-morrow, hence i lakor sa ko māki it indeed now is bad, or don't-know, and simply i lakor sa expresses that the thing very probably is bad in the speaker's opinion, who, however, does not state, as a positive, ascertained fact that it is so : la ad., and the dem. particles ko and r' (ra, ri, ro, ru).

Lākōrě, s., a kind of flute. A. nākōr' cornu, tuba, Nm. naqour clarion, A. nakara, 3, to make hollow, hollow out (as wood).

Lala, s., an idiot, one demented, a fool. [Fi. lialia, s., an idiot, a., foolish, out of one's mind, Mg. adala, s., an idiot, one destitute of reason, a lunatic, a fool, a., foolish, infatuated.] See alialia.

Lālā gor ia, v. t., to conceal, deny : gor ia, and lālā for laulau, redup. of lau.

Lalo na, or lalu na, s., c. art. inlalo na, the belly, then the front (see elalo), and the under side (as of cloth) : alo na.

Lam ia, d., v. t., to eat, hence

Lamien, s., c. art. nalamien, act of eating, food. H. laham to eat.

Lao. See lau.

Lāsa, or lās, s., a bowl (as a kava bowl), a dish, a cup. [Ml. P. ras, Malo lasa, Santo las, id.] A. tās' vasculum, Ct. tāss, a bowl, Nm. saucer, flat cup.

Laso na, s., c. art. inlaso na, the testicles. [Pa. asi, Am. luho, Ml. dd. lisi, erasi, Fut. raso, id., Sa. laso scrotum.] A. h'isy', and h'usy', and h'usya/, pl. h'usa', the testicles.

Lasoa, v. i., or a., to have swollen testicles : preceding word and a. ending a.

Las, or lasi, v. i., or a., big, large, great, sufficient ; and redup.,

Lasilasi, id. ; and

Las ia, or lasi a, v. t., to meet, *i.e.*, to suffice, be sufficient for, as nafinaga i lasigita the food is sufficient for (meets) us and you, tilasi a, id., also to meet, come upon, come across (a person) i tilasinami nabua he met us—them on the way, bakatilasi a to suffice, redup. tilatilasi a, id. A. 'aras'a to meet, 'arus'a to be wide, large, 5, ta'arrasa, for which is used also ta'arras'a to meet, 2, to make wide, large.

Lau, s., the sea; usually with the prep. e, elau, or a, alau, q.v.

Lau, s., c. art. nilau, dd. kalau, kolau, q.v. [Bisaya lawa a spider's web, Fi. lawa a net; an ambush; to lie in ambush.]

Lau ia, v. t., to plant (a yam or other plant); to plant anything upright, as a post or stake; to plant (a spear in anyone); laulua i to plant (words in anyone), putting him out, or exposing him in his true colours; lau suru ca to plant (words, in anyone) tempting him; and

Lau, v. i., to stand upright (to be planted), lau tu lit. to stand planted, i.e., to stand upright; to fall down (planting itself), as rain, &c.; and

Lau gor ia, v. t., to plant, surrounding or concealing him or it; redup. lālā gor ia (for laulau gor ia), id., intensive; and

Lau fai ia, v. t., d. lau bua i, to plant (as a spear, in anyone) piercing him. See fai, bua. [Sa. to, to plant, to build, to fall (as rain), &c., To. tau to implant, to plant, to drop, to fall, &c.] H. nataʻ, fut. itaʻ, inf. ntoaʻ to set (anything) upright, to plant (any plant); to plant (anything, as a people); to fix, fasten in; set up (as a tent, an image).

Launa, s., c. art. nalauna, redup. nalalauna, a community, as the people of a village or district: rau. [Ha. launa, v., "probably, a spreading out," to associate, be on friendly terms with, a., friendly, social.]

Lausa. See lousa.

Lausu na, s., the nose, d. for nagusu na; la art. (usually na), and usu, for gusu, q.v., nose.

Le, s. See lai woman.

Lē, v. t., for lai a, or la ia: i lē mina he puts out the tongue.

Le, ad., d. for la.

Le, also leo, and lo, v., to see, as lo nasān see evil, lo nafanua see the land, to look, lĕbi or lībi (li bi) look upon, libisia (d. limsi) look upon him, libi nata look upon, see a person, d. le ba nata look upon a person, le ba ia, or le ba i, look upon him, see him, d. lekā nata look at a person, lekā look at him, see him;

Lele is, redup., to look for it, d. leoleō sa, rai, q.v., aspect, look, forehead, rairai to be in countenance, unabashed, unashamed, leo, or lo, to watch, i.e., to look, ba lo behold. [Sa. leo to watch, redup. leleo: leoleoga a watching, leoleosaʻi to watch, My. liat to see, to look, liati, liatkan, &c., Mg. hiratra sight, seeing, Fi. rai, a., seeing, rai, rairai to look, rai-ca to look at, rairai a prophet (a seer), vakarai-taka to show.] H. raʻah to see, raʻah bĕ look upon, see, raʻah ʻeth look at, Hi. to show, roʻeh a prophet, seer, A. raʻaʻ to see, 4, show, E. reʻya to see. See also borea, naborea.

Le, leo, lu (in lu rik, d.), lo, s., c. art. nale na, naleo na, nalo na, his voice, speech, word, rogi nalō na hear his voice, i.e., obey him, or rogi berakati nalōna, or naleōna, d. nalēn ; without the nom. suf. and with or without the art. it signifies a thing, something, as nalo sikai one thing, nalo lāba many things ; nalo nagiena on account of, for the sake of, his name, lit. the thing of his name ; lo-soko true, lit. true thing, lō-soko, lo *b*alo empty, worthless thing, lo sa bad thing, lo uia good thing, d. lo amau true, lit. true thing, hence the expressions sera-loamau, or sera-lēsoko to believe, sera-lo*b*alo to deem worthless, despise. [Sa. leo the voice, a sound, leoleoā, a., loud talking, To. lea speech, voice, language.] A. la'*a*' to speak, n. a. la''w' sound, voice, lo''*a*t word, language, dialect (see misleo, *infra*).

Lea ki (or le-aki), v. t., to throw away, throw down (anything), to throw down (as the wind trees), and redup.,

Leleaki, v. t., intensive. [To. li to toss (anything light), liagi (liaki) to throw away, lei and leilei to throw away, leina a throwing away.] E. warawa to throw away, throw down.

Leana, v. i., or a., d. lēna, d. lēg, to be straight (not crooked), then to be right, upright, righteous, bisa lēna speak straight, *i.e.*, right, natamole lēna a straight, *i.e.*, upright or righteous man ; tu lena to stand straight, stand up. [Fi. donu straight, then righteous,

vakadodonu-taka to make straight. Sa. tonu, a., right, straight, correct, To. tonu straight, direct, clear, faka-tonu to make evident, manifest, tonuia righteous, tu tonu (stand) upright.] II. thakan to be or become straight, Pi. to make straight, to dispose rightly (proverbs).

Lē *b*a i, le ba i, or le be ia, d., v. t., d. syn. lē ka, to look upon it : le to look, and prep. ba.

Leba, redup. leleba, lebaleba (intensive), v. i., or a., to be or become big, great : nalebale-bān, greatness, the being great : laba.

Leba, s., c. art. naleba, s., a species of earth, clay, mud, dirt, lebalebara, a., dirty, soiled (a. ending ra), d. leba-lebā, a., id. (a. ending a), d. la*b*o (*i.e.*, leba *b*o, or *b*oa) stinking leba slush, mud. [Ha. lepo to be dirty, defiled, soiled, s., dirt, ground, clay, lepolepo dirty (intensive).] A. tabi'a to be dirty, ta*b*e', taba' dirt, mud, taba'a to impress or seal, 4), to make a water vessel from clay, tub'an clay.

Lebaleba, v. i., or a. See leba, laba.

Lebalebā, a. See leba, s.

Lebalebara, a. See leba, s.

Lebule, v., *i.e.*, le (lele) to go round, and bule, q.v., to complete, to go completely round (of a canoe, as round a point or headland) : lele, ili-fiki.

Lēg, v. i., or a., d. for lēna, leana.

Lei. See lai, s., woman.

Lĕka, v. t., d. lĕ to look, and prep. ka to, at, lĕkā look at him, lĕkă nata look at, see a person : le.

Lele, or lili (lle, or le, lli, or ili, l') to wind, to go round, turn, curve, as raru i sefa, soko, or ba lele ki nafanua the ship runs, moves swiftly, or goes curving round the land (island), nafisan i soka lele nafanua the word moves swiftly round (*i.e.*, all through) the land, le-bule, q.v., le, or li-taku na, or lele taku na to turn behind his back, lele takunā sa to turn behind one's back with it (*i.e.*, to do, say something, concealing it from someone), ili-fiki, or lili-fiki nagusu, to round the point or cape (a canoe), ilisela or lili-sela as i surata ilisela he walked all the way, lit. round the way (see sela), i talele (or talle or tàle) he turned aside, i talele ki he turned or turns aside from (a person or thing), malele to be bent or curved (as a branch of a tree heavy with fruit), bilele, v. r., to turn hither and thither, lūsi a, or lŭlūsi a (*i.e.*, lele usi a) lit. to go round following or tracking it, as lulusi noai sera he follows the stream, walking in the water, lusi nakasu goes along a stick, lili maroa lit. to go round turning itself. [Fi. lele-ca to bend.] H. lul to wind, twist about, cg. to galal, 'ul, &c., hence lul, pl., winding stairs, lula' loops.

NOTE.—See the cognate liu, liliu.

Lele, s., tortoiseshell, the cover of the turtle ; a tortoiseshell bracelet. The shell of the turtle is called lele from its round or curved form. See preceding word. [Mg. rere the largest kind of tortoise.]

Lĕna, d. leana, q.v.

Lĕmina : le, v. t., to put out, and mina, s., the tongue, to put out the tongue, syn. lua mina. See lĕ, v. t.

Leo, to look, see le ; le or leo goro gita to watch, look for, expect us.

Leo, s., c. art. naleo, thing, affair; hence

Leouān, s., c. art. naleouān (*i.e.*, naleo uān that thing, or affair), a feast (in heathenism), or heathen gathering, in which offerings or sacrifices are made to the natemate, and presents given to the guests.

Lĕr, v. i., d. for liliu, q.v., to return, go or come back, also i mer lĕr brigi he did it again, lit. he mer (q.v.) returned did it.

Lesilesi, for lasilasi.

Les, s., c. art. nales, a plant with thick dark leaf ; and

Lès, a., dark or dusky, as in fal'lès (falc les) dark or dusky cave (name of a big cave at the entrance of Havannah Harbour) ; ra lès Dark-rā or Dusky-rā, a name of Hades. See rā. A. la'isa n. a. la'as' to become dark, or blackish, 'al'asu of a dark colour, dusky ; multus et densus, *de planta*.

Les, s., coral rock, or stone. Cf. A. radhat a rock in water; radat rocky, stony, a place like a rugged hill.

Let, v. i., or a., to be stiff, rigid; redup.,

Lelet, id., intensive; and

Let, s., spasm, rigidity, as in tetanus; and

Letilet, or

Letilot, v. i., to crackle, as the bubbles of boiling water; and

Letilot, s., c. art. naletilot, d. naltelta, froth, *i.e.*, lit., bursting bubbles. See lita.

Let ia, for alat ia;

Leti bati ore, same as alaterabati;

Leti lua i, v. t., to grasp, or seize, taking it away, leti lua i kiana grasp it away from him;

Letileti, a.: natamole letileti, a grasping man: alati a.

Li, s., place: for alia.

Li sia, v. t., to lay down, put down, and

Li-saki, v. t., to throw down, throw away: leaki.

Lia, s. Same as li, or alia, a place.

Li, transitive prep. See ni, id.

Li, s. See lai, woman

Li, v., d. See lulu.

Liba, s., an arrow with a broad point (about the size of a shilling) for shooting birds, or the arrow head of such an arrow; and

Liba ia, v. t., to shoot birds with the liba (which does not *pierce* them, but kills them by a violent blow or shock). A. lagafa to strike violently;

lagif' an arrow with a broad head.

Libi sia (li-bisia), d. leba i, or leba ia (le-ba ia), v. t., look upon him, see him: le to see, look, and prep. bi.

Note.—In two other dd. this compound occurs (the prep. b changed to m) as lim si or limi si, and lumia, or lumia (lu-mi a), look upon him.

Libo, v. i., hide, to vanish, disappear, be hidden, talibo, id.; hence libo, s., a vanishing demon, a demon that assumes the aspect of someone to deceive, and appears to one in the forest, and then vanishes after the evil deed is committed, leaving the victim to return home to die; liboki, c. art. naliboki, a name of Hades (the invisible world, or hidden refuge or home of the dead);

Libo, s., an evil demon. See libo, v. i.,

Liboki, s., c. art. naliboki, the invisible world, or hiding place where departed souls dwell, Hades. [Sa. lafi to hide oneself, lalafi (of many), lafita'i to conceal, lafitaga a hiding place, Mg. levina buried, interred.] A. s'aba', n. a. s'ab'a and s'ubu', to hide (in the earth), 8, to hide, be hidden (hide one's self), cf. s'āba to lie hid in wait for the enemy, mas'ba' hiding place.

Libu, v. i., to be covered or dirty with ashes, ash-coloured;

Libu, s., an oven stone, the stones that are heated red hot for

9

cooking in the oven (so called because covered with ashes, or ash coloured) ; hence

Lilibu ki, v., to put the libu on the oven fire to be heated. See abuobu.

Libu, or lebu, s., d., the middle of the lower part of the body at the upper part of the back of the pelvis. [Ml. Ur. livu, TaSa. libuka, the middle.] H. leb the middle, heart, lubbu cor et medulla *rei*, &c.

Libuis, d. lifāru, q.v.

Lifa ia, v. t., to bend, and redup.,

Lifalifa ia, id., intensive; malibai, to be bent, see also lofa, malofa, and lufa. [Sa. lavalava wrapper round the loins, lavasï to tie round and round, entwine (as a serpent), lavelave, lave, to entangle, be intertwined, intricate, My. lipat (lampis, lapis, lâmpit, lâpit), Ja. lâpit, to fold, lap, lay in plaits, Mg. lefitra folded, bent, plaited.] A. laffa to be intricate, involved, intertwined ; to wrap up, wrap round, to fold : Nm. wrap up, roll up, loffa coil of turban, winding of road, lifafa wrapper, envelope, bandage, S, to be wrapt, &c.

Li-fiki, for ili-fiki, q.v.

Lifalifa, v. i., to blaze, nakabu i sor lifalifa the fire burns blazing, or putting forth flames. [Ha. lalafa, lafalafa, to blaze (of a fire).] A. lahiba, n. a. lahb', to blaze, put forth flames.

Lifāru, s., and a., dd. libuis, rāfālu, rifālu, a part, some, as

natamole lifāru some men, lifāru ru bano lifaru ru toko some went, some remained. [Fut. cfaru some, many, Niue (Savage Island) falu some.] A. ba's'u a part, some, and c. art. alba's'u some (= lifāru, dd. libŭïs, rifālu, rāfālu).

Lifu, s., d. for rifu, q.v.

Lifu, v. i., and redup.,

Lifulifu, v. i. (intensive), to be covered, dirty, with ashes, as in mourning, d. for libu, id.

Liga, s., d. taliga, ear, the ears : taliga.

Liga, v. i., to sing, and redup.,

Ligaliga, id. (of many), and

Ligana, s., c. art. naligana a song, d. nalag : laga.

Liglig, v. i., to be proud : lagilagi.

Lìgï sia, v. t., to pour out, maligi, or maligsi, to spill, be poured down. [Sa. ligi, liligi, ligiligi to pour, maligi to spill, to be poured down, maligi, s., a pouring (of rain), Ma. ringi, riringi to pour out, An. aijagjig to pour out.] H. nathak, Ni. to be poured out (of water, rain), Hi. hitik to pour out.

Liko tia, v. t., to tie, fasten (with a rope, as a boat to a ship, an animal to a stake, &c.), and

Liko, v. i., to be fastened to, affixed to, adhere to : i likò sa it is fastened to it, as a leech to the body, &c. ;

Liko, s., c. art. naliko, a rope for fastening or suspending ;

Likoliko, redup. of liko tia (used of fastening or suspending the yams to a horizontal pole).

[My. lákat to adhere, lákatkan to fasten, Ja. rakât to adhere, Mg. raikitra, stuck, adhered to, miraikitra to adhere, rekitra, id., mandrekitra to fasten.] A. 'alika to adhere, be affixed, be fastened to, 2, to suspend, 4, make to adhere, fasten, 'alako a rope.

Likau, for lakau, v. t.

Lilia, d. for liliu, q.v.

Lili-maroa, v. i., to go round turning itself : lele, or lili, and maroa.

Liliu, v. i., to return, go or come back : liu.

Lima, num., five ; d. c. art. nalima na his hand ; bakalima, q.v. [Sa. lima five, the hand, My. lima, Mg. dimy five, Epi jimo (and limo) five, juma hand ; d. lima, yima, or sima hand ; d. lima five, ma hand ; An. nijman, or nikman (= Ef. nalimana) his hand, five.] A. h'amsat, h'ams' five, alh'ams digiti ; Mahri khomo, Sokotra khemah, five.

Lim si, d. for libi sia, q.v.

Lina, s., the light. [Mota dina, My. dina, Er. dan, day.] As i en lina it is in the light (not concealed), d. i en ali : aliati ali.

Lirea, v. i., or a., for litea, q.v.

Lira, redup. liralira, dd. nrirmrir (i.e., tirtir), litralitra, litalita, v. i., or a., to be bright, shining, gleaming, brilliant. A. nas'ara, 2) and b), nas'ira, 4, to be bright, shining, gleaming, brilliant.

Lisoa, v. i., dd. tiso, toto : toto.

Lita, v. i., and liti, to crackle, to burst, explode, as wood, or a stone in the fire, see letelot, also lot to crackle (as a fire), explode (as a gun), to sound (as a crack or explosion), and melita to crack or crackle (as wood in the fire, &c.), and then nagiena i melita his name resounds ; and

Lita ia, or litai a, or litai ia, v. t., lita i lita ia a spark, or fragment of something, bursting or crackling or exploding in the fire, leaps or explodes on to him ; also, a wasp stings him ;

Lita, s., a spark, fully lita nakabu (see preceding word); also a red wasp (because it is red like a spark, or because its sting burns like fire) : d. (transposed) tila ;

Lita-kuruma na, v., to have the breast (kuruma, see ruma) thrust forward or out (bulging or swollen out), in a spasm (the opisthotonic) of tetanus, then, to be bulging or swollen stiffly out (of the face of a log or board that should be level) : see let spasm, or rigidity, as in tetanus ; let, lelet to be stiff, rigid (of anything, as of a dead body, &c.) [Fi. lidi, lidilidi, to burst, or explode, s., report of an explosion, as of thunder, or a stone in a heated oven, lidi-ka to strike in flying off, lidi ni buka a spark, lidi-ka to crack between the finger and thumb nails, as a louse, My. látok to crackle, to decrepitate, látup, and látub, id., látum to boom,

or give out a booming noise.]
A. s'at'iya to burst, break (be
broken), 5, to burst, exploding
into fragments; and, 1, to swell
out, stiffening, so that the
hands and feet stand out stiff
and rigid (of a dead body),
s'asa' to become rigid and
fixed ; to swell out, becoming
stiff and rigid, so that the
hands and feet stick up (of a
dead body), 4, to make rigid
or stiff and fixed, s'ata' id.,
s'at'iyyat fragment of anything
burst or exploded off or out
from it.

Litea, a., or v. i., dirty, to be
dirty, d. lirea : used of anything, as cloth, &c. Also, as
in English we speak of a
" dirty-looking " sky or night,
so tokalau meta lirea dirty-
looking tokalau (tokalau is an
easterly wind). [My. látah,
Ja. latup, turbid, foul, muddy,
Mg. loto dirtiness, filth, dirty,
soiled, maloto dirty, filthy,
foul.]   A. latah'a, n. a. lath',
to be dirty.

Liu sa, v. t., to go before, to
precede him, to be greater
than him, d. tōli a, *i.e.*, to, to
abide, to be, and 'li a to go
before, precede (this to may
be prefixed to any verb, and
is to liu and d. toliu sa =
toli a = liu sa, with the added
sense of continuance) ;

Liu uaki (waki), or liu áki (see
also lu-aki), v. t., to turn, as
to turn a stick end for end, d.
lia ki, and lilia ki ;

Liliu, d. lilia, d. lēr, v. i., redup.,
to turn back, return, go or

come back : liliu, luaki, q.v.
[Sa. liu to turn, to turn over,
to turn into, to change, redup.
liliu, liuliu, faaliliu to turn
round, maliuliu to be able to
turn, Fi. liu, v. i., to precede,
go before, be greater than,
v. t., liu-taka to precede, go
before, ai liuliu the first : liu
e. preps. e, mai, ki, eliu,
mailiu, kiliu, ad., before, afore-
time, preceding in time or
space, Mg. aloha (ha formative), a., first, before, previous,
ahead, mialoha to precede, go
before, taloha before, My.
dáulu first, to precede, Ja.
talu beginning.]   A. 'ala to return, to rule; b), to precede, go
before; 2, to order to return;
to interpret (in Mod. A., especially in malicious sense), to declare, institute, direct, define ;
hence tawil' interpretation of
the hidden sense, allegorical
interpretation, 'awwalu first,
before, the first thing, the
beginning, 'awwaliyyu first,
before.

Lo, s., d. li, alia, as lo koi, or
koia, d. li ke, this place, here.

Lo, s., thing, and c. art. nalo : le.

Loamau (lo thing, and amau
true), s., a true thing, truth,
a., true, d. syn. losoko or lesoko (lo, or le, thing, and soko
true).

Lo, v. i. and t., to look, to see:
leo, le, id.

Loa, s., c. art. naloa, dirt (on
anything).

Loa, redup., loaloa, a., and v. i.,
to be black, to be blackish.
See also malolo, or milo, mi-

lolo. [Fi. loa a black cloud, black paint for the face, loa-loa, a., black, loanimata the black part of the eye which surrounds the pupil, Ml. U. aro, P. roro, dirty.] This be-longs to the word following, loa i, loa sia, loa ria, to smear with lolo (the face), or with intei (the body, cloth), hence the body, &c., so smeared soon becomes milo dirty, covered with dirt, yellowish from the intei (milolo), black from lolo, nikis, loaloa. So H. hel'ah rust (i.e., dirt covering) of a pot.

Loa i, v. t., to rub, smear; and

Lo-fia, v. t., same as alo-fia, q.v., to rub on, to smear; also

Loa sia, v. t., and redup.,

Loloa sia (d. loloa ria), v. t., to rub, also to flatter; hence

Lolo, s., paint (for the face). [My. lulut, and lulur, to cleanse the skin by friction and cos-metics, to rub the skin with cosmetics, to smear.] H. hala' to rub, strip, A. hala' to rub and to smear the eyes with collyrium, halō' oil or paint (used by women for their faces), H. hala' (A. hala', see člo, lolo, sweet, pleasant), Piel to stroke, to soothe anyone, from the primary idea of the roots hala', halah, i.e., that of rubbing, hence to stroke any-one's face, i.e., to soothe, flatter.

Lobu (l', art.), s., bamboo (the plant); also bamboo water vessel and bamboo knife. [Santo lumuo, Ml. nambu (n, art.), New Guinea dd. bau,

ifa, inba, diem (d', art.), kem (k', art.), Sa. 'ofe, To. kofe (k', art.), bamboo, Ha. ohe bam-boo, a reed generally, bamboo knife, a kind of flute.] H. 'ebeh a reed, A. 'aba'at' a reed, 'abau reeds.

Lofa na, s., c. art. nalofa na, his track (so called because his track is marked by bent grass, &c.) : lofa, lifa ia.

Lofa ia, v. t., to bend; same as lifa ia. [Sa. lofa to cower down, crouch, Fi. love-ca to bend, kalove bent.]

Lōfa, s., hunger or famine (be-cause it bends one); a sword (because it is flexible) : lōfa lofa ia hunger or famine bends him : lofa ia.

Lo-fia, redup. lolo-fia. See loa i, loa sia.

Lōga (ending ga), s., an enclosure, the inside of an enclosure; given as d. syn. for elol (in the sense of enclosure, that is, the inside of an enclosure). See alo.

Lokoloko ki, same as lakolako ki; lako, v. i.

Loko-taki, v. t., same as luku-taki : lako, v. i.

Loku, a., concealed, i toko loku he remains concealed : lako, v. i.

Lokuloku ki, same as lokoloko ki.

Lolo, s., voc., uncle, redup. of alo ana, q.v.

Lolo, s., and c. art., a black paint for the face (under the eyes) : loa i, loa sia.

Lolo, s., c. art. nalolo, thread : the native thread was made by rubbing the fibre between

the hand and the thigh : loloa
sia,

Lolo, a., or v. i., redup. of elo,
q.v., sweet, pleasant.

Lolo-fia, redup. of lo-fia, and

Loloa sia, or

Loloa ria, redup. of loa sia, q.v.

Lolo-mina, a., lolo sweet, pleasant,
and mina, q.v., gentle and
pleasant.

Lolofa, a., or v. i., d. lulum, lumu
to be wet, moistened : see tiu,
d. luma. [Fi. luvu to sink in
the water, luma to kill by
putting the head under water,
Ma. rumaki to dip in water,
Mg. roboka plunged, dipped,
soaked.] Ch. seba' to dip into
(H., A., id.) Ithpael 'istaba'
to be wet, moistened.

Lor, s., d. roro, the oily milk
expressed from the grated
kernel of the cocoanut for
puddings. See ror, roro ia.

Los, or loso, redup. lolos, or
loloso, v. i., or mid., to bathe,
to wash (oneself). [TaSa. lalos,
Ml. roso, Malo loloso, id.,
Ml. roso-vi to wash (clothes,
&c.)] A. rahas'a, n. a. rahs', to
wash (clothes, the body), H.
rahas to wash (the body), to
wash oneself.

Losia, v. i. See lusia.

Lot, v. i., to crackle, as a fire ;
explode, as a gun, &c. ;

Lotelot, v. i., redup., to crackle
frequently and rapidly, as the
bubbles in a boiling pot ;

Lotelot, s., c. art. nalotelot, same
as naletilot, froth ; also,

Lot, s., c. art. nalot, froth (i.e., a
mass of bursting or crackling
bubbles). See lita.

Louua, d. for loamau (lo a night,
and uua, i.e., uwa, for amau,
true).

Lousa, redup. lolousa, v. i., to be
wet, or losa, lolosa. See lūsa.

Lu, s., d. for lo a thing, in lurik,
a thing, lit. little thing.

Lu, s., a place, for li, alia, as lu
ua, this place, here, lu uān
that place, there.

Lu, v. i., to rise up, as intano i
lu the ground rises up (as when
the swelling yams below heave
it up), redup. lulu, nabiau i
lulu the waves rise up ; also
lu, d. lua, to take up, then to
take out, away, also to throw
up (lua i and lua ki nia), i.e.,
to vomit, to put up, also to
put out, as to put out the
tongue, lua mina (also lai
mina and le mina) : lua, lualua to take out, or put out
(anything, as yams from the
ground or a plantation, or
demons from a man possessed),
lua nafunaso take out the cork
or stopper (take it up) ; lulu
to be uplifted, proud (see lagilagi, liglig) bau lulu a proud
person (lit. high head), also
lulu, d. lī, to vie with, contend
for superiority, bilulu, v. r., to
vie or contend with each other
for superiority, bilulu ki vie
or contend with each other
for superiority about (something) ; lu ē a take it up (used
of water taking up a solid, as
a medicine, dissolving in it,
because the medicine, as a
preparation of iron, lies at the
bottom of the water, and, as
it dissolves, rises in it) ; na-

kabu i lua nāsu the fire puts out, or sends up, smoke : to this stem belong also ulua to grow up, ulī, ālī, and ula, a leaf, and lulu the hair (of the head, face, or other part of the body), redup. uluulua to be growing up, putting forth leaves, also to be hairy, to be woolly (as a sheep) to be covered with down (a plant) : to this stem also belong (the -ga, or -gi, being formative) laga tia, laga ia, lagi, elag, elagi, lagilagi, malaga, &c. See *supra* under the word lagi. [Fi. lua, lua-ra, lua-raka, to vomit, Sa. luai to spit out, Ha. luai to vomit, lualuai to ruminate, chew the cud, to raise the food again from the stomach to the mouth, as ruminating animals, Ma. ruaki, Tah. ruai to vomit, My. luwat, or luat, to vomit, luwar, or luar, out, away, luwari and luwarkan to put out, expel, Mg. loa, s., vomit, mandoa to vomit, loatra, ad., over and above, loatra taken up, put out, mandoatra to take out or up, loarana being taken up.] See A. 'alu, H. 'alah under the word lagi. A. 'ala', n. a. 'uluw', to ascend, go up, be above it, over it, overlay it, become supernatant upon it ; overcome, become superior ; exalt (himself) ; recoil (from), remove, or go away (from), 2, to take up or off, 3, to vie, contend, or compete for superiority, 4, take up, take out, &c. H. 'alah to go up : inanimate

things are also said to go up, as smoke, a rising ground, a plant which sprouts forth and grows, whence the participle 'oleh (a plant) sprouting forth (Ef. ulua, ulu), and 'aleh a leaf (Ef. ulī, ālī) : used also of things which are *taken up*, carried away, Hi. (causative) to take out or up (as out of a pit), to take up, or away, to put up (*the cud*, from the stomach into the mouth, Ha. lualuai), of ruminating animals, generally, to make to go up (out or away), E. redup. la'ala, 'al'ala to make to go up, lift up, take up, le'lena height, highness, &c.

Lua, v. t., see under preceding word. This verb is much used after other verbs, as sela lua i bear or carry (taking) out, or away, bā lua i, &c. ; miroa lua i think (taking or putting) out or up (discover it by thought), &c.

Lualua, v. t., redup. of preceding. See lu.

Lua, s., c. art. nalua, a land slip: lua, lu.

Lualua, s., c. art. nalualua, an old plantation (out of which the yams have been taken) ; the hair or grass-like growth on rocks under the sea : lua, lu.

Luaki, s., an allegorical utterance, a proverb or parable ;

Luaki, v. t., i luaki nafisan he makes his speech allegorical (*turns* it from the obvious sense), i tili luaki lau erā sa he utters a proverb (parable, or allegory) planting it on them

(lit. planting, piercing, or fix-
ing them with it) : liu uaki,
or liu àki.

Luba ki, v. t., to pour out (as
water, grain, &c.), luba, mid.,
to pour (itself) as rain ; also
used of pouring out anything
(as men) from a ship, luba
kira pour them out, or land
them, hence bilubaki, v. r., to
pour each other out, to land
(men) ; malubaki to be spilt,
poured out (water or fluid),
talubaki to be spilt or poured
out (as water or fluid). [My.
tumpah to spill, shed, pour
out, mânumpah, id., Fi. livi-a
to pour gently, or in a small
stream, talivi to be poured
out, spilt. A. sabba to pour
out (of all things, and of things
dry) ; to pour, be poured out,
5, 7, 8, to be poured out, and
sâba, n. a. sa'b', to pour out.

Lûfa, s., loin wrapper, *girdle*
round the loins. See lifa ia.

Lug ia, v. t., to bend, make
curved, and redup.,

Luglug ia, id., d. nugnug ia;
hence

Lug, s., c. art. nalug, d., the
native pudding (see nakoau,
kabu), so called because
wrapped in leaves which are
bent or curved round it.
[My. lengkok bent, crooked.]
A. lâga, n. a. la'g', 2, to make
curved, to bend.

Luk, or luku, s., a hole or pit, a
well : luku noai well (pit or
hole) of water : lako.

Luku, a., same as loku.

Luku-taki, v. t., same as loko-
taki. See lako, v. i.

Luluk, s., a thing rolled up (as
cloth). See lulu ki (luluki).

Luko, v. i., same as liko, v. i.

Luku tia, v. t., same as liko tia.

Luko, s., c. art. naluko, same as
liko, s. ; takes the nom. suf.
nalukona, or nalikona, its
rope, *i.e.*, the rope for tying or
fastening it.

Lukuluku, same as likoliko.

Lukoluko, and

Lukuluku ki, same as lokoloko
ki : lako.

Lulu, v. i., redup. ; and

Lulu, v. t., l'lu, d. lĩ, vie, contend with for superiority, dispute with : lu, and see bau
lulu and bilulu.

Lulu, s., c. art. nalulu, as nalulu
nabau na the hair of his head,
nalulu na his hair : lu, and
see uluulua.

Lulu, v. i., to roll : i lulu ban, it
rolls away ;

Lulu ki, v. t., to roll up (as cloth
into a bale) ; hence

Lulu, s., c. art. nalulu, a roll, a
bale ; and talulu, and talu or
tal'lu, s., a roll (of cloth), a
crowd (of men), a herd (of
pigs), a heap (of stones) : see
also malilu to roll. H 'alal
to roll, hence to be round,
thick, *eg*. galal, lul, &c.

Lulu, v. i., to sink, d. tutu, q.v.

Lulia, and

Luluia, v. i., for ululia : alialia.

Lumi a, *i.e.*, lu mi a, to look
upon it, see it : d. for libi sia,
d. lim si, d. le ba i or le ba ia.
See le, leo, lo.

Luma, or lum, v. i., and redup.,

Lumlum, to be wet. See lolofa,
d. ;

Lūma, s., the wet, as luma iga luma the wet is about to wet, or will wet ("it will rain," or " is going to rain ") ;

Lume a, v. t., lume nafanua to wash (immerse) or cleanse the land by a religious service or ceremony performed by the natamole tabu, or priest: so if a man has been poisoned, natamole tabu i lume a ki the poison, cleanses or washes him from the poison by a religious service or ceremony. When the land is suffering from drought, natamole tabu i lume a, or lumi a, and the hard-baked and therefore barren earth becomes soft and moist (lum, lulum), clothed with verdure, and fruitful, yielding abundance of food ; redup.,

Lulume a, id. The radical meaning of the word is to dip, to immerse (see under lolofa). [Fi. lomo-ca to dip, to dye, luvu to sink in water, to be flooded (as the land).] H. saba', A. sab''a, to dip into, to immerse, then to dye, to tinge, S. sba' to tinge, saba' to wash, E. tam'a to tinge, to immerse (in water). See also riu, tiu, tutu, tuma.

Lumĕ sia, v. t., to turn, d. lume to wrap up, buluma, or bulima, to be turned, to be changed (in form or appearance). [Tah. rumi to wring, turn over, upset, Ha. limu to turn, to change, to have various appearances, limulimu twisting, turning.] E. tawim to roll up, fold up.

Lumi, v. i., to swell up, d. lugi. A wārama to swell (cg. H. 'aram, rum).

Lūsa, v. i., to be wet, also lousa, lolousa. E. rehsa to be wet.

Lusi a, redup. lulusia. See lele (and usi a).

Lusia, v. i., to be dirty, faded, i bi namau lusia (of a lazy, languid husband). [My. lāsu languid, feeble, Mg. lazo fading, withering, faded.] A. lātha to dirty, to be slow, 5, to be dirty, lūtha langour, laziness, 'alwathu languid, faded, withered. See milesu.

M'

(ma, mí, or mĕ), a formative prefix or preformative particle : the m' is sometimes changed to b and f, as toko, or to, mato, bato, or fato ; in the causative prefix it is b' or f', being the initial consonant of baka or faka, rarely ba or fa ; in the reflexive prefix it is b' or f', being the initial consonant of bi or fi. In bi, or fi, q.v., the i is a fragment of the ancient reflexive prefix, as the a in ba or fa, q.v., is the ancient causative prefix. In many cases ma- (often mi-) is found prefixed to verbs having a passive sense, the same verbs being without the ma- active : in these cases we may regard the word as representing the ancient ps. part. The preformative m (originally ma) in H. and Arm. mĕ or m', A. mo,

or mu, E. ma, Amh. uia, was
attached to infinitives and
participles (active and passive).
Sometimes ma- in Ef., or m'
(b', f') is to be regarded as
originally prefixed to the sim-
plest form of the verb. See
mago (*bago*), borau (A. markab, an infinitive), &c.

M, ad., contraction of mo, q.v.

Ma, s., day; in mās, maisa, mes,
masus (nanum, nanu, nanofa,
nanoasa, nāsa, nāsa, āsa) to-day,
lit. this day. H. yom, A. ya'm',
S. yom, Ch. emphatic yoma',
and sa, dem.

Ma, prep., for, contraction of
magi or of manĕ (d. mini), as
i manai (or maginai) bat ia, d.
i manena bat ia, d. i māsa bat
ia. See magi. [Ma., Fut.,
&c., ma, id.]

Ma, s., contraction for maga, in
names of places. [Ma. ma,
id.] Maga.

Ma, d. me, prep., with (of
accompaniment), and. [Ha.
me, Ma. me, with, and, Mg.
amana with, and, Mota ma,
me.] H. 'im, A. ma' with,
together with: may, like me,
&c., sometimes be translated
by and.

Mā, v. i., for mānī: anī, v., q.v.,
c. preformative m'.

Mā nīa, v. t., to rub, grind, or
grate (as yams);

Mā, s., c. art. nimā, a fern tree;
the rough bark of it (used as
a grater): nimā that which
mā, *i.e.*, grates. See fōga, afo.
[Mg. fafa swept, cleared off,
wiped, cleansed, mifafa, mafafa,
to sweep, wipe, clear away.]

11. ħataf 11. to rub off, scrape
off, A. ħaflĭ to rub off.

Mā, s., a man, a male, opp. to
lai (lei, le, li) a female, a
woman; used also before
names of men, as lai before
names of women; as ma
tuele, Mr. tuele; ma-riki lit.
old. man, senior, sir, often
used also before names of
men, like ma: mā is a contraction of mare, q.v. [Ysabel
(Gao) mae male, and used also
before masculine names.]

NOTE.—This ma (contrac-
tion of mare) occurs also in d.
ma'anĭ, manĭ (sometimes pronounced mwanĕ, or moan),
and denotes male (the nĭ in
manĭ, like the nĭ in kurunĭ, is
non-radical, being a suffixed
particle), thus nata-manĭ, or
ta-manĭ, a male, male, lit. a
male human being, and in
another d. the initial m is
elided and for manĭ we have
ānoĭ, q.v., a male, male.

Ma'anĭ, or maanĭ, or manĭ (or
mwanĭ, or moan), a., male, d.
ānoi, s. and a., male: see preceding word. [Malo muera,
Oba amera, Celebes burani
(husband, Wallace), Ambrym
milig, Bali muwani, Epi d.
man, and Ef. ta-, or ata-mane,
Epi dd. sumano, atamani (su-
mano, ata-mani), Ta. yeru-
man, TaSa. la-mani, Fi. tangane, To. ta-ane, Fut. and
Sa. tane (ta-ane), id.]

Mbā, v. i., for bā, or mā, v. i.: a
mere euphonic change.

Mbăt, s., d. nābe, a club. [To.
mata a kind of club.] Nm.

nabboud a club ; also nabbout a staff, club.

Mabe, s., c. art. namabe, the chestnut tree and its fruit. [Tah. mape, id. ; also the kidneys of any animal ; An. mop(o) the chestnut, also the inside (*i.c.*, belly) of a box, inside (*i.e.*, belly) of an animal, the pluck, the heart, liver, and lungs, Malo mabue chestnut.] See under amo, amoamo.

Mabelu, mabelubelu, v. i., d. ; refl. of belu ; to be bent, doubled, folded : belu.

Mabor, d. mäuora, q.v.

Mabulu, v. i., or a., d. mafulu, fat : bulia.

Mabulu, s., a large kind of pigeon.

Mabulu, v. i., or a., sticky ; waxy, as a yam when cooked : bubulu, bulu tia.

Mafa, a., swollen, in las mafa, d. las mäu, swollen testicles (mäu for mafu). H. bua‘, ba‘ah, A. ba“a’ to swell. See fuata, bua III.

Mäfa, v. i., as i maf ban he goes hiddenly or unobserved = i bi bei ban ;

Mäfa na, s., his being hid or unseen (in going) : see bei, and afa.

Mäfa, d., v. i., or a., to be broken, cracked, d. mafua, q.v. [To. mafä crack, rent, split.]

Mafa ia, or mafai a, v. t., to cover : bo-fia.

Mafaifai, v. i., or a., to be smashed to pieces : fai. See bua to divide, cleave.

Mafaku, v. i., to be plucked up, or out : baku sa.

Matiritiri, v. i., to be loosed, to be made void : bir ia, v. t.

Mafasu, v. i., to be broken off, snapt off. [To. mafachi, id.) Base a.

Matis, s., a knife, d. for makus, q.v.

Matisi, s., a child, one begotten or born, and

Matisi, v. i., or a., to be begotten, born, brought forth ;

Mafisien, s., c. art. namafisien the being born or brought forth : bis ia, v. t., to beget.

Matisi a, v. t., to beat : tisi a.

Mafu, s., c. art. namafu (d. namam), a mist; ceremonial uncleanness : abu, abuobu.

Mafua, v. i., to be split, cracked : bua to divide, cleave. [Sa. mavae to be split, cracked.]

Mafukafuka, v. i., to be swollen out, puffed up : buka i.

Mafule, v. i., to be stripped of leaves : bule.

Mafunai, or mafunei, v. i., to be consumed, annihilated, as wood in the fire ; and

Mafunufunu, v. i., to be brought to an end, to be ended, finished, annihilated : bunu ea.

Mafusai, v. i., to be smashed to pieces, as a yam : busa ia.

Mafuti, v. i., to be plucked : but ia.

Mäga, v. i., to gape (see maka, gaga, fugaga), open out, then to wonder, then to gape or open the mouth (to speak), to speak, maga asi is to speak about it, lit. to open the jaws, part asunder the jaws (asi), maga lua i speak it up or out, lit. gape outing it, maga lo saki, d. maka lo saki, to gape looking up ; hence

Maga, s., a small canoe, namaga ; and

Maga, s., c. art. namaga, d. nabaga, the banyan ; and

Māgān, s., c. art. namāgān, the art of gaping, wonder; and

Magamaga, v. i., redup., to gape often and rapidly, to pant; and

Maga-fai, s., a division, a part (see fai, bua) ; and

Maga, s., the first part in names of places, as gorges or valleys, and especially of places in the depths of the abyss of Hades ; sometimes, but rarely, contracted to ma, as maga-tika, or ma-tika, the lowest abyss in Hades. [Ma. maga brook, watercourse, ditch, and contracted ma in names of streams, Sa. faamaga to open the mouth, to gape (To. fakamaga) ; maga a branch (as of a tree, road, or stream, or anything having a branch, or forked), Tah. maa cloven, divided, My. nganga to gape, mangu wonder, amazement, mangah to pant, palpitate, mânga open.] E. naka'a to gape, to yawn, to be rent, parted or sundered, and of water gushing forth (see fugaga), A. manka' a place where water remains (i.e., a hollow, fissure in the earth, or valley), naka'a to rend asunder, E. nka'at an opening, gap, fissure ;

Maga, s., see above, in names of the following places in Hades, signifies chasm, yawning chasm, gulf, or abyss, of which there are several, some say six, one below the other, viz.—

Maga-boaboa, evil-smelling abyss —see boa ;

Maga-bua, profound abyss—see bua ;

Maga-lulululu, sinking sinking abyss : lulu ;

Maga-nabonabo, evil smelling abyss : nabo ;

Maga-seasea, abyss of oblivion : seasea ;

Maga-tika, or ma-tika, abyss of annihilation (this is the lowest abyss) : tika ;

Maga-tiro, sinking abyss. See tiro.

NOTE.— Magatiro in one dialect is magalulululu in another ; and magaboaboa and maganabonabo denote the same. Thus there are five abysses yawning one below the other in succession. All these are below abokas, which is the uppermost, and the first to which departed souls go, and also the general name of Hades.

Magaliu, s., name of a place in Efate, lit. the turning gap. See liu.

Magāli, v. i., to be turned round : elo i magāli the sun is turned round (it is late in the afternoon). See kelu.

Magāsi, v. i., to speak about, lit. to open or part the jaws : maga, asi.

Māga, prep. and pron. of 3 person, denoting with-them, thus —(1) kihe māga? who they!

d. se māni? d. se mai? d. fei mānag? (2) John māga, d. John mānag, d. John mera uan (or meroan), John and his companions ; (3) natamole māga, d. mānag, d. mera uan a man with them (*i.e.*, a man with those beside him), some men, indefinite plural. The literal meaning of māga in (1), (2), (3), is with-them there : kihe māga? who he with-them there (beside him), or together with them there (beside him); John māga John together with them there beside him ; natamole māga the man together with them there (beside him). It is probable that māga is a contraction of which mānag is the fuller form ; and the -ga (for naga) is the dem. there (see ga, dem.) This mānag = with them there : in address a number the speaker says tāgu māga, or mānag, or mera uan, my friends, lit. my friend with them there (beside you); so tai mānag, &c., brother with them there (beside you), brothers. The expression mera uan is me with, together with, ra them or those, and uan, dem., (that) there, and mānag and māga differ in having the r elided (as it is in ëu, u, for eru, ru, they, verb. pron.) and the suffixed dem. nag or naga, q.v., instead of uan, q.v. Mani (and mai) are not used as in (2) and (3), but only as in (1) in the above example. [Ma. ma,

Ha. ma, Fut. ma, Ta. min, d. mi (meh) pl., mī, dual.]

Magasaga, v. t., to make a saga (crotch, fork) : maga, and saga.

Magau, pr. n., c. art. namagau, for nabagau. See bagau.

Magi (d. syn. mini), comp. prep., for, contracted ma, q.v. : magi is agi, q.v., and m' on account of, in, to, and thus aginai = what is his, his, maginai on his (account), in his (interest), *i.e.*, for him ; in one d. the genitive prep. nig, q.v., of, denotes also for, nigā = his, and also = for him. Both magi and nig, when = for, are placed between the verbal pronoun and its verb, thus, i maginai, or i nigā matī, he for him died. The prep. m' or mi is, except in this case, mostly used before the object of a verb—see le bai limī sia, lu mia, li bi sia, in which it occurs as mi, bi, and ba, and see also bai, or bei. [Mota mun for, An. imi to, for, Ma. ma for, &c.]

Magie na, prep. and s., for his name, i magiena bat ia he for his name did it, tuga magie-gita bat ia let us for our names (*i.e.*, for each of us) do it, &c. : ma, *i.e.* magi, for, and gie name.

Magīri a, v. t., to scratch, scrape : giri a.

Mago na, s., c. art. namago na : bago na, q.v. for meaning and origin, is the same word by change of m (the preformative) to b.

Magoago (m' prep.), d., ad., dawn, early morning, lit. at dawn. [Cf. Arag vaigogo to-morrow.] E. goha to dawn, goh dawn.

Magoro, s. See muagoro.

Magura ki, v., to withhold from, d. makur ki : gura ia.

Magura, v. i., or a., to be lean, d. makur : gura ia.

Magura, s., c. art. namagora, contraction of muagoro.

Maguku, v. i., to be bent, &c. : guku. [An. mecuc old, wrinkled, makaka bent, crooked.]

Magusi, v. i., to be crooked, con-torted, cross-grained, as wood ; also, nabona i magusi his heart is crooked.

Mai, ad., here, as bano-mai to come here, lo mai look here, &c., and v. i., d. for the full expression bano-mai, d. umai, to come here. See banotu, note, and bai, bei, be.

Mai, s., c. art. namai, a rope, a string. See d. mē.

Mai a, or ma ia, v. t., to chew (softening food for an infant). [Sa. mama to chew, ps. maia.] A. ma"ma"a to chew (meat), but not wholly.

Mai, d. for mani, as sei? who (is) he ? se mai ? who (are) they ? See māga.

Maia, s., a species of banana.

Mai, distance, only in emai, ad., q.v.

Maita, or maieta, d., and

Maito, or maieto, d., v. i., or a., to be black, black. [My. itam, Mg. mainty, Bisaya maitum, Tagala itim, black.] A.

'adhamo' ('ahtamo, 'athamo, &c., id.) black, 'idhamma, and 'ithamma (i.e., dahama, tahama, 9), to be black.

Maieto, maito, v. i., to be angry, maitō sa to be angry on account or because of it, maito ki nia to be angry at him, maito ki niā sa to be angry at him on account of it. A. ma'it'a to be angry, ma'it'o, and mā'it o angry.

Maietoa, and

Maietoan, s., c. art. namaietoa anger, namaietoan the being angry, anger.

Mailoa (ma-, prep.), s., ad., d., dawn, early morning, lit. at dawn. [An. imraig to-morrow, Mg. maraina morning.] See aliati.

Mailua. See malua.

Mailum, mailumlum. See malum.

Maimai, v. i., to be in a tumult (of haste or passion), namarite na i maimai his inside (heart, feelings) is in a tumult. [Mg. maika, and maimay, a., hasty, in a hurry.] A. ma'ma'a to do a thing hastily, to be in a tumult, ma'ma'at crackling (of burning reeds or such like).

Mairī, v. i., to live : dd. maurī, mōlī.

Maisa, ad., to-day, dd. mās, mēs, masusa. See ma, day.

Mak, v. i., d., to fall, become mild, gentle, die away, as the wind : eg. mäo. S. mak to be cast down, prostrated, humble, mild.

Maka. See mako.

Maka, v. i., or maga, q.v., to gape, to wonder, to be amazed, i makā sa, or magā sa, he is amazed or gapes at (because of) it; and maka lo saki, or maga lo saki, he gapes looking upwards. See maga.

Makaka, v. i., or a., to be ragged or fissured, as cloth. See aka.

Makāl, s., an ant (so called from its smallness, or quick and light movements): kala, and bakal ia II.

Makāl, s., shame, pudenda. See under bakal ia II.

Makāl, v. i., or a., and redup., Makalkal, to be sharp: bakal ia II. [To. machila, sharp.]

Makalakala, v. i., or a., to be itchy: connected with makal, ant, thus, makal i makamakala ki nau an ant moves about on (is creeping or running on) me, and therefore a makalakala I am itchy: bakal ia II.

Makamakala ki, v., to move about or creep on (one), of an ant (makāl), hence makalakala itchy.

Makara, v. i., to be assembled, to be a crowd or many together, dd. maraka (transposed), and merā, or marā (k elided): kuru, guru.

Makarakara, v. i., or a., to be burning, as the throat from eating currie with too much pepper: kara.

Makas ia, v. t., to pluck out or off, as a scab or anything from the skin, loose bark from a tree, husk from a cocoanut. A. nakas'a, 3), to pluck out. See bakasa ki.

Māki, v. t., to be ignorant of, not to know; redup.,

Makimaki, as i makimaki isa he is ignorant of, does not know, it;

Māki, don't know (in answer to a question);

Māki, pr. n. of a demon or spirit, one of the officers of Saritau at the gate or entrance of Hādes. When the spirit of a deceased person presents himself after death for admission to Hades, Faus (another spirit) asks "Who is it?" If Māki says, "Māki" (i.e., don't know) a dreadful punishment is inflicted by Saritau; if he says "He is one of our people" admission without punishment is given. [My. mukir, Ja. mangkir (mungkir), to deny, disavow.] A. nakira, 1, 4, 6, 10, to be ignorant of, not to know, 4, to deny, to disavow, Munkar' name of the angel who together with Nakir is said to have the office of examining deceased persons in the grave.

Mākinikini, v. i., to be itchy: kan ia. [Sa. ma'ini, ma'ini'ini, to tingle, to smart.]

Makit ia, v. t., to seize or take with the uatàki (native tongs) the hot oven stones, ru sela uataki makiti fatu isa, or maki fatu isa. H. hatah to take, take hold of, seize. It is once applied to a man, elsewhere always to fire or burning coals.

Makita, redup. makitakita, v. i., or a., to be bent, curved, only in the expression lo makita to look bent, i.e., to look round

or back, lo makitakita, id., d.
bakita, bakitakita. A. ka‘at a
to bend, to curve) mak‘ut”
bent, curved.

Mako, and maka, s., offspring;
in pr. names, as maka fŏlu, lai
or li mako, &c.: aka (ako).
[TəSa. maka pi grandchild
(offspring, or offshoot, of grandfather, pi), Fi. makubu, or
mokubu, grandchild.]

Makota, or makoto, v.i., to be
broken, and redup.,

Makotakota, to be much broken:
and

Makota ki, to be broken from,
i.e., to cease from (some person
or thing): and

Makota, s., a part (of a plantation), a place, makot i milate
the place is cold, i.e., there
is no one about the place
(on calling at a house and finding no one at home), makota
ua this place, lit. this part:
koto-fi a.

Makus, s., a wooden knife (used
for cutting up puddings), d.
mafis.

Makuskus, or

Makusukusu, v. i., to be soft
(ripe): kosu mia.

1. Mala bulu, v. i., to faint, falling down (of men), to become
weak and falling down (of
breadfruit)—see bulu; and

Māla, s., faint, as mate ki māla
to faint, lit. to die in a faint:
a species of hawk (of a
faded colour);

Malamala, v. i., to be foolish
(My. bábal, silly, doltish), c.
art. namalamala, a fool, one
foolish; and

Mala, s., c. art. namala, a fool,
one stupid, foolish, senseless;
and

Mala nono, v. i., to abide senseless, deprived of sense or
motion (as by terror): no to
abide. H. nabal to be or
become faded (used of leaves
and flowers falling off from
being faded), to fall down, to
faint, to lose one's strength (of
men: bulu, q.v., to fall down,
H. nafal, is eg. to mala, and
the two verbs occur together
(cf. mala bulu) in Job xiv. 18,
(of a mountain falling and
lying prostrate, like a dead
man); to be foolish (the mind
faded), flaccid, devoid of vigour,
stupid, nabal foolish, senseless.

II. Malamala, v. i., or a., to be
naked, naked; and

Mala, s., or malala (intensive), the
cleared place at each village, in
the midst of which the nabeas
are set up, and in which are
performed the sacrifices, singing, and dancing of the intamate; often in the names of
places (because cleared or bare,
because having a mala, or
cleared place). [Ma. marae
enclosed space in front of a
house, yard, Tah. marae, a.,
cleared, as a garden, or a place
of worship, s., the sacred place
formerly used for worship,
where stones were piled up,
altars erected, sacrifices offered,
prayers made, and sometimes
the dead deposited, Sa. malae
the open space where public
meetings are held.] And also

Mala, s. (also malo) a place or

part (as of a garden), a part
of time, and

Malmal, s., a small place, or part.
See under ali or alia.

III. Mala, v. i., or a., d. malala, to
be loose, and redup. malamala,
id. A. ḥalla to loosen, maḥlul'
loosened, loose, Ct. maḥlūl
loose.

Malamala ia, or malamalai a, d.,
redup. of (malai a) mīlai a, or
milei a, q.v.

Malāñāfi, v. i., or a., to be thin.
[Ha. lahi, lahilahi, thin, My.
ramping thin.] A. raffa, n. a.
rafaf', to be thin.

Malārĭ, d. for mīlātĭ, q.v.

Malasilus, redup. of milesu, q.v.

Malat, s. See melat.

Malatiga, d. malandigi, ad., and
prep., near, malatiga ki near
to : mala place, and tiga, tigi.

Malau, v. i., to be bad tasted (as
stale food), to be corrupt (as
bilge water), faded (as a fallen
leaf). [Tah. marau old, worn
out, fading.] A. malaḥ'a to be
bad tasted, have a corrupt
taste (food), maluḥ'a to be insipid (meat), maliḥ" corrupt,
insipid (food).

Malei a, or male ia, v. t., to requite, maloi au isa requite me
for it. [My. balâs, malâs, to
reply, requite, Mg. valy, ma-
maly, to reply, requite.] See
liu, liliu : the idea is "make
return."

Maleoleo, d. malolo, v. i., to
become tame, gentle (i.e., intelligent), as an animal does
when domesticated. A. ra'a',
4, 'ar'ā', n. a. 'irā', to become
prudent, intelligent.

Malebuto, ad. and s., middle
part; inside, heart: mal (mala)
place, part, e prep., and buto
the middle.

Malele, v. i., or a., to be bent,
curved : lele.

Malēra, v. i., to be thin, running,
of a fluid, as paint. See lōr,
roro, ro ia, roro ia.

Malēr, d. malĕru or malīru, v. i.,
to be transparent, shining (as
smooth water or glass re-
flecting the light : lira.

Maletiletĭ, v. i., to be stiff (as the
back, in some disease): let, lēt.

Malĭ, and redup. malĭmalĭ, v. i.,
to be drooping, as the countenance in shame ; and

Malĭ, s., c. art. namalĭ, a plant
(which when eaten is said to
make one so) ; and

Malĭĕrĭ, i.e., malĭ-eri, v. i., to be
ashamed, lit. to be drooping
or abashed in the face or
countenance : see rai face,
forehead. [My. malu to be
ashamed, abashed, malumalu
bashfully, Mg. malo, malomalo, bashfulness, mimalo, mi
malomalo bashful, meek-eyed,
shamefaced.] H. 'amal, 'amel
to languish, to droop, prop. to
hang down the head.

Maliblib, v. i., weak, limber, d.
maliflif : lifa ia. A. laflafa
weak.

Malibu, s., widow (also widower),
i.e., one mourning, lit. covered
with ashes : libu.

Maliflif, d. maliblib, q.v.

Malifus, dd. malus, mäus, v. i.,
or a., bent : lifa ia.

Maligo, v. i., to be dark ; and
redup.,

10

130

Maligoligo, id., intensive ; and

Maligo, s., c. art. namaligo, darkness, d. malik, q.v.

Malik, v. i., redup. malikoliko ; namalik, s., to be dark, darkness, d. maligo. [Epi mikoleko, Vanua Lava malegleg, meliglig, black.] A. halika to be very black (holakliko very black), part. mahluk'.

Malilu, v. i., to roll away, to roll, malilu ki, v. t., to make to roll, to roll (a thing) away : lele.

Malilua, v. i. See malua.

Malio ki, v. t., to forget (a thing): lailai. [My. lalai, Ja. lali, to forget.] A. laha, n. a. lohiyy' being diverted to forget (a thing).

Malis, d. for malūs : malifus.

Malitiga, dd. maririgi, multig : malatiga.

Malo, s., a place, part ; a part of time ; mal or malo tageli a crooked part (either a place difficult of access. or crooked conduct) : c. art. na malo na the trunk (of a tree or the body) : mala. See ali, alia.

Malo, s., a kind of rock in the sea. [Santo malo a rock.] Cf. A. marw' very hard stones.

Malo, v. i., to be weary, unwilling, averse ; malo ki, v. t., to dislike (a thing). [My. malâs averse, &c.] A. malla to dislike, to be tired, weary ; mallo disgusted, wearied.

Malöï, s., a mask. [To. bulo to mask, to veil, buloa and bulobulo a mask ; veil for the head. Ha. pulou to cover the head, veil the eyes, s., a veil.]

A. barka'a to cover the face, to veil, 2, to be covered with a veil, veiled, burka'o a veil, burkū' id.

Malöïlöï, v. i., to be feeble, tottering from weakness. [Ha. loeloe, maloeloe, feeble.] A. la'la'a, 2, to be twisted and moved (from hunger), to be infirm and weak from disease or languor.

Malolo. See maleoleo.

Malosu, d. milesu, q.v.

Malu, v. i., or a, to be bare, cleared ; redup.,

Malumalu, id. See ali, alia, mala.

Malua, v. i., to do anything gently and quietly, not to be in a hurry, to do after a time, by-and-by, d. mailua, malilua, d. malulu. [Fi. malua go gently, not to hurry, by-and-by, vakamalua gently.] A. mahala mahlu, to do anything gently and quietly, not in a hurry, 2, to grant that a thing may be done by-and-by.

Malubaki, v. i, to be spilt : luba ki.

Malum, v. i., to be weak, faint, soft ; to do anything weakly, i.e., gently, not in a hurry.

Malumlum, redup., also mailum, mailumlum. [Fi. malumu, malumulumu, weak, faint, sick, My. lâmah, Ja. lâmas, soft, flexible, weak, feeble, faint, Mg. lemy softness, meekness, gentleness, malemy soft, meek, gentle, TaSa., nalum, Ml. malum, id.] A. s'a'afa, n. a. s'a'f', s'u'f' to be weak, infirm, s'a'uf', id.; also to fold, double,

mas′′uf′ (part.) weak, debili-
tated.

Malūs, d. for malifus.

Mal-tageli. See malo, s., and
tageli.

Mam, v. i., or a., to be soft (as
ripe fruit), ripe. A. ma‘w′
ripe or ripening dates, mā‘a,
to have such dates (a palm),
mā‘ soft, mild (of food).

Mam, s., c. art. namam, d. for
mafu.

Māma, s., voc., father, dd. āb,
abāb.

Mamau, redup. of mau, q.v.

Mānĭ, v. i., or mān, contracted
mā, to abide, to be : anĭ.

Manamana, s., c. art. namana-
mana, a pudding mixed with
pig's fat wrapped up (munu
tia) in leaves to be cooked in
the oven ; a captive taken in
war (because such were cooked
in the oven and eaten). See
munu tia, bunu tia, &c.

Mānag, d. māga, q.v. : mānag,
i.e., mā with them or those,
nag (dem.) there.

Manāki, v. i., to stay for the
night, to rest, as a guest ;

Manaki, s., c. art. namanāki, one
who does so, a guest. [My.
mânâng to rest.] Mod. S.
manch to rest, Mafel, i.e., the
causative with the preformative m ; H. nuah to rest, A.
nah′a to kneel down, as a
camel, monah′ a place where
camels lie down (to rest or
sleep).

Mandu, d. for matru.

Maneinei, v. i., to be weak. A.
na′na′a to be weak.

Măni, as sei who (is) he ? se

mănĭ who (are) they ? d. kihe
māga ? See māgā.

Manifenife, v. i., or a., to be
thin. [Sa. manifi, manifiniti,
My. mimpis, mipis, nipis, tipis,
Mg. manify, thin, hanifisina
being made thin.] A. nahifa
and nahufa, n. a. nahafat,
nahif′, manhuf′ thin, slender.
Ct. nahif thin, nahafat thin-
ness.

Manru, d. for matru.

Mānu, s., a multitude ; d. a
thousand (d. bon a thousand),
mānumānu (d. bonbon) a very
great number, or multitude ;
see bon, bono tia, bunu tia,
munu tia. [Sa. mano a great
number, manomano innumer-
able.]

Manu, s., a bird, birds. [Ja.
manuk,   Ta.   manug,   Er.
menok, Vanua Lava mon,
Tag. ibon, Poggi umah, Sa.
manu, id.] H. ‘of birds, fowl
(feathered creatures), ‘uf to
fly ; E. ‘awif to fly, ‘ef a
bird.

Manumanu, s., a streamer or flag
of a native canoe sail : preceding word. [Fi. manumanu, id.,
also a bird.]

Manu na, s., the palate and
upper part of the throat. A.
hanaku the palate and lower
part of the mouth answering
to it (eg. nanoa na, q.v.), A.
hanaka to rub food with the
palate, 2, to rub the palate.

Manua, v. i., to be finished,
ended ; and

Manunu, id., d. manubu. See nu.

Manubu, v. i., to be finished,
ended ; and

Manubunnbu, id., redup.: nubu, num, nu.

Manubunubu, d. matumutumu, to be soft, sleek, as the skin of a newly born pig, or of an infant. See nubu, tumu, noba. [Ha. nopunopu to spring or swell up, a., soft, spongy, thoroughly cooked, plump, fat, swelled out, nopue plump, round, as a well fed, fat hog.]

Manugnug, d., v. i., to be bent: luglug ia.

Manuka, s., c. art. namanuk, wound. [Sa. manu'a to be wounded, s., a wound.] A. naka' to wound.

Mao na, s., d. faa, thigh. [My. päah, id., also the limbs or quarters of a slaughtered animal, Mg. fe the thigh: cf. Sa. vae the leg, vaega a division, vaevae to divide in parts, cut up a slaughtered animal, mavae = Ef. mafa, d. mafua, and see Ef. fai.] See bua (also fai, maga-fai).

Mao, and redup.,

Maomao, v. i., to be gentle, mild. A. mahiba to be mild, cg. mak.

Maoni, v. i., d. mānī: anī, v. i.

Maole, or mauolĕ, s., c. art. namaole, a bed; hence

Maolĕ ki, v., to make a bed with (something): d. uol, see bilis ia (bolis ia, and uolis ia).

Maon, s., d., c. art. namaon, sweat: der. uncertain.

Maora, v. i., to be rent, redup. maoraora (intensive): bora ia.

Maosa, d. taos, v. i., to be fatigued, tired. [Fi. oca (otha) weary, tired.] A.

fatha', 4, to be fatigued, weary, 'aftha' fatigued, worn out.

Maota, or mauota (mawota), v. i., to be parted asunder; redup.,

Maotaota, id., and

Maota na, s., c. art. namaota, interval: bota ia.

Mara uoka, a., having the hands chapped with hard work, as with digging with the kālī, or with using an axe, naruna i bi mara uoka: maras, and boka tia (or uoka tia).

Mara, v. i., to rest, stop, mara tu stand still;

Mara bakarogo, v. i., or a., to be quiet, rest quiet, peaceable: mara, i.e., maro, q.v., and bakarogo.

Marag ki, v. t., d., to spit out, to loathe. See burei a, burog.

Mārafī, v. i., to hasten, be quick; redup.,

Mārafīrafī, id. See sarafī. S. rhab whence sarhab, Pael, to hasten, mĕsarhība sudden, mĕsarhībat hastily, quickly. Uhlemann (Syr. Gr., §25, A, b) gives sarheb (Saphel, similar to Aphel) to permit to hasten, and to hasten = arheb (H. rahab to urge on, press, &c.)

Maraka, v. i., or a., to be willing, desirous,

Marakaraka, id., redup. See raka.

Maraka, or meraka, v. i., d. for makara, q.v.

Marasĕ, v. i., to be softened or excoriated (as the hands with work), to be peeled off, excoriated, tamaras peeled off (of the skin of a body softened

or macerated in water). A.
maras'a, maratha, to macerate
in water, rub), scratch with
the nails ; and

Maraserase, redup., to be peeled
or excoriated here and there,
as the skin. Compare marate.

Marasa, or murasa, d. burasa,
v. i., used as an ad., gently,
slowly, by-and-by, as ba
marasa mer ia do it gently,
not in a hurry, slowly, or by-
and-by. A. ratha to delay,
to be slow, 2, soften ; be
fatigued, murayyath' slow.

Marate, v. i., or mareti, to be
excoriated, peeled, as the hand
with hard work. See marase.
H. marat, to make smooth ;
to polish ; to make bald,
pluck out the hair ; marut
to be peeled (as the shoulder
with carrying burdens). Ch.
to pluck (wings), to be
plucked, A. marata to pluck
from the body (hairs), 3,
pluck out hair and wound
with the nails.

Marate, or marete, a., in fatu
marete oven stones (hard,
smooth or *bare* stones, worn
smooth by the sea): preceding
word).

Mare, v. i., to be turned, lo mare
to look turned (round), look
back. See roa, rea.

Mare, s., a man (male, not fe-
male), Sir, Mr., as Mare uota
Sir or Mr. uota : see ma,
maani, or mani, and mariki.
[Tah. maroa a boy, a male
(tamaroa boy, tamahine girl),
Motu mero a boy (not a girl),
Malo muera, Oba amera, a

male, vir.] Ch. mare' lord,
S. mar, A. mar' (also homo,
see *infra* mera), mor', mir', id.,
mara'a, 2) to be virile, masculine, and brave, as becomes a
man.

Mariki, s., lit. senior, sir, old
man, Mr., opposite to tite riki
matron, old woman, Mrs. : mā,
for mare, and riki.

Marita na, or marite na, s., the
belly, bowels, also a rope or
string; hence

Maritausa, v. i., to be angry, or
marita sa, or marita na i sa :
and marita uia to be well or
kindly disposed. See sa, uia.
A. muryita' the belly. See
the verb under marate.

Maritau, v. i., to wither, be
withered. A. sālia, 2, v. t., to
wither or dry plants (as the
sun, wind), 5, tasawwalia to be
withered.

Maro, v. i., to breathe, to rest,
be quiet, to be glad, restful,
contented, satisfied ; maro ki,
v. t., to perceive the odour of
(to breathe or inhale the odour
of), to smell ; redup.,

Maromaro, v. i., to breathe ; to
rest ; hence

Maromaroan, s., c. art., the act
of breathing or resting, rest ;
and

Maro na, s., c. art, breath. A.
rālia, n. p. maroli, to rest (*i.e.*,
respire) ; to be glad ; to perceive the odour of : to blow
(wind), 2, to be quiet, to rest,
4, to breathe, H. ruali to
breathe, blow, Hi. to smell ;
to be pleased, glad (smell with
pleasure).

Maroa, v. i , to turn round: roa.

Marobaroba, v. i., to fall down, as the smoke of a fire signal. See taruba.

Marou, and marourou, s., d. (transposed) for rūma.

Māru, v. i., or a., d. mēru, to be limpid, clear, pure (of water). A. namiru, namīru, id.

Maru, d. for matru, q.v.

Maru sa, v. t., to rub ; masturbate ; to joke. A. marah'a, n. a. marh'u, to joke, to anoint, to soften (the body with oil), H. marah to rub.

Maruen, s., c. art. namaruen, joking, &c.

Mārua, v. i., to cease, leave off, marua ki to cease from ; and

Maruāna, s., c. art., cessation: baro, v. i., bārua.

Mas, s. See maso.

Mās, ad., d. for maisa, mēsa, masusa.

Mas, and sam, ad., alone, only : ma for mau (as in sikei mau), and 's, sa, one.

Masa, d., v. i., to go, to walk. A. mas'a, id.

Masāna, s., c. art. namasāna, the going, walking.

Masa ia, v. t., to rub, rub off, masa ia nāfo rub it on the nāfo (to rub the rust off it) ;

Masamasa ki, redup., rub (as the rust off a needle, on a stone) ; and

Masamasoa ki, v. t., end. 'a, to stroke, smooth, flatter ; and

Masa, v. i., at ease (as wild animals in their lair, as if smoothed into gentleness) ;

Masamasa(n)ta, d., v. i., or a., end. ta, smooth, as a board :

dd. musi ki, mus ia, to stroke, smooth, rub. H. mas'ah to stroke, anoint, A. masaha to stroke, to flatter, wipe off, ma'asa to rub strongly, ma"as'a to rub gently, masīh' smooth, S. ms'ah to anoint ; to measure; A. masaha to measure (land), H. mis'hah, mas'hah a part, a portion (Ef. mas, maso, mis, id.)

Mas, s., also maso, masé, and mis, a part, a portion, a place (part of the land), as bau-maso na, q.v., masleo a portion of speech or words, as of a song, masleo naligana, a portion of human speech, dialect (see leo), maso ua this part, or place. See preceding word.

Mas', or masu, v. i., d., to come ; hence

Masuen, s., c. art. namasuen, the act of coming. E. mas'a to come (H. masa' means to come to, i.e., to attain to, to arrive at, anything).

Mas ia, v. t., to shave, as masi nasina to shave the chin or part of the face covered with the beard : masi noai shave off the surface of water, bail out : hence, redup.,

Masimasi, v., to bail out (a canoe or boat), and

Māsi, s., a knife, and

Masimasi, s., id., d. mismis. A. māsa to shave, mūsa' pl. mawasi a knife.

Masaki. See misaki.

Masei, s. See masoi.

Masere, s., c. art. See miseri.

Masere, v. i., to be treated kindly : sere a, bakasere a, te masere, one treated kindly, as a beloved child.

Masere, v. i., to be torn : sere. [Fi. kasere, id.]

Masiba, v. i., to be broken, done into fragments ; and redup., Masibasiba, id., intensive: siba ia.

Masi-balo, s., wilderness, lit. empty part (of land). See mas, maso.

Masīka, v., in sera masīkā sa to desire, covet (a person or thing). A. s'aka, 5, to be desirous of.

Masiki na, d. mihi (for misi), v. i., taking the nom. suf. agreeing in number and person with its subject as, a masikigu I alone, ku masikima thou alone, i masikina, or masikinia, he alone : siki, and pref. ma.

Masila, or masilī, v. i., to be thin ; and

Masilasila, d., redup. ; and

Masila na, s., c. art. namasila na, chip, shaving. See sila ia.

Masila, in buru-masila, q.v. See sila.

Masirsir, d., v. i., to sob (as after crying). A. zahara to utter the voice, to give forth a sound, to pant or gasp with vehemence and groaning.

Mas-leo, s. See mas, s., part or portion, and leo voice, speech.

Maso, s. See mas, s., a part, portion, place.

Māso, v. i., or a., to be cooked, done, d. mahi. [My. masak, Mg. masaka, Ma. maoa, and maoka, and maonga, cooked, also ripe, Bugis motasok ripe, Tah. maoa cooked, ripe, Fut.

moa, Santo, d., mäa, cooked, To. momoho ripe.] A. sawa' 2, to finish off (see infra su, si), 8, to be finished ; and (of food) to be cooked, done ; Nm. (Part.) mostewi cooked (meat), ripe (fruit).

Masoi, masoei, or masei, s., star, stars, d. mohoi, c. art. namohoi. [Epi d. mohoei, Fila masoi, Fut. fatu, Sa. fetū, Santo dd. vitu, matsoi, vitui, vitiu, My. bintang, wintang, and lintang, Mg. kintana and vasiana, Tag. bitoin, Sumbawa bintoing, Sulu bitohon, Tobo tói, Matabello toin, Menado bituy, Sanguir bituin, Cajili tūlin, Mayapo tūlu, Gani betól, id.] A. dara'a, 7), n. a. duruw', to glitter and twinkle (a star), durriy' glittering and twinkling (star), and dar'ariy' glittering and twinkling stars.

Masoi, or masei, star, is used in pr. n., as Masei, Mare Masei, &c.

Masok, v. i., to be violently agitated or enraged, as namari-tama i masok, lit. his belly or his bowels leaped up : soka to leap.

Masoko, a., true, exact, to the point, as nafisan masoko a word or speech true, exact, or to the point ; as an adverb, bisa masoko to speak truly, exactly, or to the point, bā masoko to go exactly, ba masokō sa go exactly upon it, &c. : soko.

Masol, v. i., to turn aside, decline. A. zāla, n. a. zuwul', to decline (as the sun) ; cease to be in place, remove ; start on a journey and change one's mind.

Masu, s., c. art. namasu, the time of harvest, or of plenty of food, opposite to sukei, q.v., lit. the coming, namasu nafinaga the coming of food, as yams, taro, bread-fruit, &c. : mas' (or masu), v. i., to come.

Masua na, s., c. art. namasua na, the top, crown, or summit (of anything) : sua, su.

Masua, v. i., or a., to be bald. A. nazi'a to be bald about the temples, manzu".

　　　NOTE.—Sa. tula, My. sulah, Mg. sola bald, A. sali'a to be bald on the fore part of the head, sul'at place of baldness.

Masuku-taki. See musuku-taki.

Masula ki, v. t., to scorch (as the skin of a pig in order to its being scraped and prepared for cooking) : sulu.

Masusa, ad., for mas, maisa, to-day.

Māt', v. i., to ebb; to be low water ; hence

Māt', s., c. art., namāt, the ebb; low water; the shore left bare at low water. [Sa. masa to be low tide ; to be sour ; to have an offensive smell; To. maha, mamaha, to ebb, Fi. māti, to ebb, and s., namati the ebb.] A. mātha to macerate and dissolve (a thing in water), H. masas, eg., to melt, flow down, to waste away.

Māta (or mwāta), a snake. [Sa, Fut., Fi. gata, id., Malo moata, Santo del. mata, maura, My. ular, id. (Ma. ngata snail, slug, leech).] A. h'āta to creep

along like a thread (a serpent), mah'īt' place of a serpent, through which it creeps.

Mata, s., the eyes, usually mita, or meta, q.v.

Mataisau, s., a carpenter. [Sa. mataisau, id.];

Matakseu, d., id. Mataisau is lit. the eye (or director or master) of cutting. See (mata), meta, and sau.

Mataku. See mitaku.

Mataloa, s., a pig with crooked tusks, one on each side, that is, a mature, full-grown pig. A. sala"a and sala"a to have or acquire a tooth or tusk on each side.

Matāta, s., a phosphorescent worm (which gleams brilliantly). [Fi. matata to clear up, as the weather, the sky.] A. s'ā'a to shine ; Nm. mos'ui phosphorescent.

Matau, s.,d. na mitau, an anchor: tau.

Matautau, v. i., to utter sounds as one in sickness or pain, to groan, moan. A. 'aha, n. a. 'awh', to say ah ! alas ! oh ! to be in pain, (2), 5, id. With matautau cf. A. part. of 5.

Matĕ, v. i., to die ; and redup.,

Matĕmatĕ, v. i., to be quiet, soft, gentle ; and

Matien, s., c. art. namatien, act of dying, death :

Matigo na, s., c. art., the grave, d. emate n ; tamate, v. i., to become calm (wind, wave), s., peace, a calm ; also a series of feasts or festivals held every fifth day (see d. syn. belaki). [Sa. mate, My. mati to die,

Mg. maty, a., dead, matimaty
lukewarm.] A. māta to die ;
to become calm (the wind), 4,
to soften by cooking. This
word occurs in all the Semitic
languages.
Matiratira, v. i., or a., to be
shining, bright (as any polished
surface). See tare.
Matiu, d., v. i., to sink. See tin sa.
Mato, and
Matoko, v. i., to remain, abide,
to sit : to, toko. [Mg. mito-
atra, mitoetra, mitoitra, mito-
moetra, to reside, dwell, abide,
sit, rest.]
Matōl, ad., to-morrow : tola.
Matoltol. See matultul.
Matu, v. i., to abide, to abide
standing : tu.
Matu, s., c. art. namatu, d.,
woman : fafine. [Ja. wedo,
Sula nifata, Tidore foya, id.]
Matu ki, v. t., to strengthen or
support with posts (a fence),
matu ki nakoro ; and
Matu na, s., c. art. namatu na,
post or stake (of a fence) ; the
backbone, vertebral column,
the back : fatu.
Matru, v. i., to be thirsty, to
thirst, dd. manru, mandu,
maru. [Sa. gālala to have
intense thirst, Ml. P. meruh,
Epi mereu, TaSa. maroku,
Malo madoce, Bugis madoka,
Santo (Pelia) marara, Marshall
Islands maru, New Caledonia
malu, to thirst.] A. "alla, 1,
b), and 8, to thirst, "alall'
thirst, "āll' thirsty, ma"lul'
intensely thirsty, &c.
Matua, v. i., or a., to be old, mature, elder, then (full-grown)

large, great ; also wise, opposite to busa, as meta matua
wise, lit. old or mature, i.e.,
experienced eye, bo matua,
wise, lit. old, mature, i.e., experienced heart; te matua the
aged, or the ancients ; meta
matua ki to withhold from (a
person, something);
Matuatua, redup. of preceding
word, very old ;
Matua, s., or ad., the right hand,
or side : tuai. [Sa. matua
aged, elder, mature (matuatua,
dim.), a parent, Fi. matua
mature, My. māntuwah a
father or mother-in-law, Mg.
matoa eldest son or daughter,
matoatoa a ghost, apparition,
Malo matua right hand.]
Matūki, a. used as s., one trusted
in, confident, brave, as a
warrior : tuki. [Mg. matoky
confident, brave, trusting.]
Matulu, v. i., or a., to be swollen,
thick ; and redup.,
Matultul, id.: telatela, telatelana.
Matumutumu, d. manubunubu,
q.v.
Matuna, s., and ad., c. art. namatuna, d. fatuna, something,
anything, somewhere, any-
where, somehow ; also a ghost
or apparition, lit. something :
ma, or fa (the inter. pron.
used indefinitely), q.v., and
tuna, dem., te (or tu) with the
dem. na added to it. See safa,
or sefa. H. mah anything,
something, whatever, Ch. mah
di whatever, what that, that
which, A. ma' that which,
whatever.
Maturu, d. matur, v. i., to sleep,

bakamaturu ki to put or make to sleep. [My. tidor, Ja. turu, to sleep, Mg. tory, s., sleep, mitory to sleep, Bugis matinro to sleep, Ml. P. metur, Malo maturu, TaSa. tsuruve, Santo dd. chinaru (tshinaru), chinaro, chiranu, noro, rontui, An. umjeg (umjeng), Fi. moce (mothe), Sa. moe, ps. moea, to sleep.] H. yas'en, A. wasina to sleep, sina*t*', H. s'enath, and s'enah, sleep.

Mau, v. i., to recover from sickness, be well : abu.

Mau, v. i., a., and·ad., to be together or all together (as a number of men), to be whole (of a thing) redup. mamau, id.: nai mau it wholly, or only (of a substance), nara mau they wholly or only (of a number of persons) ; and

Mau na, s., c. art. namau na, d. nabai na covering of it (a bird), *i.e.*, its feathers ; na mau the bunch of feathers worn as an ornament on the top of the head : na mau nasuma (d. na bau nasuma), nakasu, the top of the house, of a tree ; mau naliati (d. bau naliati) mid-day :

Maumau, s., redup., the surface of the land or sea. See bau, bai. [Epi momou the whole, Ha. pau, a., all, ad., wholly, Mg. aby all, every one, the whole, Ma. hou a feather (see under bau sia).] H. 'amam, A. 'amma, to gather together (see bau sia), to be or become universal, to include or affect all, to cover wholly (see derivatives, Lane's Dict.), complete

perfect, universal, whole, numerous, all.

Mau, or amau, a., true, lo-amau, or lo-mau, a true thing, d. maurí, or mōrï. [Tah. mau true, Fut. mari, To. mooni, Ma. pono, Sa. moni true]; and

Mau, a., used as s., one firm, intrepid, brave, *i.e.*, warrior of such a character, also, in Mautukituki, pr. n. of a mythological hero. [Sa. mau to be firm, to be decided, unwavering] ; and

Mau sa, v. t., to come upon, obtain, find, bamau ria reach to. See bamau. [Sa. maua to obtain, reach to, Tah. mau to seize, take hold of] ; and

Mau āsa, d. mau is, v. t. (to trust in), to desire, tea maumauen, a thing trusted in, or desired, te namauena, id. [Ma. pono to covet] ; and

Sera lo-amau āsa, v. t., to believe on or in (him or it). [Ma. whakapono, Fi. vakabau]; and

Mau, ad., very, indeed, continually, as bisa mau to speak continually, toko mau abide continually, constantly, &c. [Ha. mau continually]; elagi mau above indeed, in the highest place, toga mau very far away, malitiga mau very near, etaku mau, or maumau (intensive) behind indeed, the last (as the last *day*), malĕ mau ua naga this very time, d. mal fā nin (fā for mau), bïsa mau few indeed, very few, d. bisiba (ba for mau), sikei mau one only.

[Fi. dua bau, Sa. tasi pe, one only] ; mas (for mau sa only one), and sam (for sa mau one only), are like sikei mau (but without the kei suffixed to the numeral sa or së) ; ti bano mau did not go indeed [Aniwa, Fut., sī fano ma, sī fano mana, id.] ; this mau after a verb preceded by the negative is very commonly used, but may be omitted, and ti bano, ti bano mau, are both used, though the latter is the more common. H. 'aman to prop, stay, sustain, support ; to carry (sustain) a child ; 'amen to be firm, unshaken, faithful, A. 'amuna to be faithful, 'amana to confide in, trust, 'amina to trust, be secure ; H. Niphal to bear in the arms, to be firm, to be of long continuance, continual ; to be sure, certain ; Hi. to lean upon, trust, confide in, believe; stand firm, still, A. 'amana generally the same ; S. 'eman to persevere, be constant, and, contrarily, to cease, A ph. to believe, 'amen, &c., verily, truly, certainly, E. 'aman id., also truly, and 'amanawi, id., 'amana to believe ;

Mau-tia, v. t., to save, to protect : mū-tia.

Maua ki, v. t., to give food to (people, as to those who have been doing something for one); and

Maua, s., c. art. namaua, food, or provisions. A. māna to give food, mawunat provisions.

Mäu, d. for mafa, swollen.

Maūaūa (mawawa), v. i., to be separated. See mafa, bua.

Maūori (mauori), v. i., to be broken, and redup.,

Maūoriūori, intensive : bori a.

Mauri, s., as mauri nalagi the place where the wind ends at, to leeward ; the left hand or side, opposite to matua. [Sa. muli matagi, To. mui matangi, the place where the wind ends at, Ma. maui, Malo marao, Ta. maul, Epi dd. mali, mau, left, on the left hand.] See muri. Mahri manghūra behind.

Mauri, v. i., to live, dd. mairi, mōle, bakamauri make to live;

Maurien, s., c. art. namaurien, life. [Fi. bula, Sa. ola, Fut. mauri, My. idup, Ja. urip, Ta. murif, Mg. velona, to live, Epi d. meouli, mauli.] A. 'ās'a, n. a. 'ais", ma'as", ma'īs" to live, 4, make to live.

Mauri, a., true, tili mauri speak true ;

Mauri, s., c. art. namauri, a prayer or incantation, lit. what is true : mau true.

Mäus (mawus), d. for malus (malifus).

Mauta, d. mautu, s., a rising ground ; one's native land : so called because (i tu mau tu) it remains firm or continuing. See mau. [Sa. mauga a hill ; a residing at a place (from mau).]

Me, prep., d. ma, q.v.

Me, or mea, v. i., to make water ; also, redup.,

Meme, id., and

Me, s., urine, me-rikĭ dysuria, lit. small or scanty me ; and

Me, or mea, v. i., to flow, wet,
us i mea the rain pours out, i
me nakoau it (a fluid, as water)
flows upon or moistens the
pudding : nai me a flood or
freshet, lit. flowing water, d.
naum a stream, lit. flowing
water; na bisi me semen genitale. [Mg. mamany to urine,
amany urine, IIa. mi, mia, mimi,
to make water.] A. māha
to have water (a well), leak (a
ship), 2, to pour water; to wet
with water ; emit water (the
ground), mā' juice (of anything), semen genitale (H. me),
H. me (of the feet) euphemism
for urine. See Ges., Dict.,
s. v. ma', who gives a root mo'
to flow.

Mē, s., c. art. namē, d. namai, a
rope, or string. [Sa. maea,
To. maia, id., Mg. fehy tied,
mifehy, mafehy to tie, kofehy
a cord or string, i.e., that
which ties.] E. mawakha,
contr. mokha to tie, bind,
mokh a bond, band, rope,
vinculum.

Me, and

Meamea, long ; as tali me tuturu
(see tuturu), a rope long,
hanging down, i barau meamea
it is long, like a long streak of
water running down a tree, or
the face of a cliff. See me,
mea to flow.

Memi, d., v. i., to be gentle,
tame : mao, maomao.

Mela, melamela, for mala, malamala, fool, foolish.

Melat, s., c. art. namelat, or
malat, flower (of a plant),
then flower (of anything), that

is, crown or most excellent
part, as namelat natamole the
flower of men, the most excellent of men. A. warada
2, to flower, ward' a flower.

Mele na, s., c. art. namele na,
the hollow ; as namelēru na
the hollow (palm) of the hand,
d. nal'nāru na (see alo, aru,
belly, hand), namele natuo na
the hollow (sole) of the foot
or feet, namele gere na the
hollow of the tail of a fish.
[Mg. faladia, i.e., fala dia, sole
of the feet.] A form of the
word bele na belly, hollow.

Melesia, d. melesira. See milesia.

Meliboi, or melibai, v. i., to be
bent, as grass by the wind, &c. :
lifa ia.

Mēliki, d., v. i., to be dilatory,
slow : malua, and suffixed ki.

Melita, v. i., to crackle, resound
(as one's name) : (lot) lita.

Mēlu, v. i., d. meliki : malua.

Mēlu, s., shade, rag mēlu time of
shade, evening, melu na its
shade, or his shade (protection);

Melu, v. i., to be shady (as the
day), and redup.,

Melumelu, id. [Sa. malu to be
shaded, to be protected, malumalu to be overcast, cloudy,
Mg. malomaloka shady, cool,
gloomy.] H. 'afel obscure,
dark (of the day), 'afal to be
obscure, dark : eg. 'amal or
'amel. See mali.

Mēlu, s., that which, or what
milu departs or removes (from),
separates (from) : milu.

Men, a. See mina.

Mena na, s., the tongue (of
animal) ; of fire (flame) ; of

knife (blade or edge); of breaker (edge of the wave); to be the namena, or tongue, of anyone is to be his spokesman; hence

Mena ia, or

Menamena ia, v. t., to lick it with the tongue, tongue it. [Epi mena, TaSa. me, Santo (P.) meme, Guebe mamalo, the tongue.] A. manmul' the tongue, from namala to be a detractor; to creep, climbing up (a tree), &c.

Mer, ad., d. mero.

Mera (for mara), s., c. art. namera, man in general, people, as namera ni Efate, the people of Efate: mera is contracted to fa in fa-fine, q.v., and especially Note 3. A. mar', mir', a male, or, in general, man, Ct. mir'a man in general.

Merai, a, used as s., pertaining to a male, the male organs of generation, virilia: merai gara (gara bare) addressed to young boys not yet wearing a waist cloth, or naked; a man is sometimes jocularly or disrespectfully spoken of as merai tamana the merai of his father: mare, q.v., with the a. end. i. A. mar'yy' virilis, pertaining to a male.

Mera, s., d. mara, a rippling (of water): meromero.

Mera, conj., lit. with them, or with those: me with, and 'ra them or those, as John mera Peter John and Peter; this can also be expressed John me Peter, and John nara Peter (John they Peter); with dem. uan,

Mera uan, dd. syn. manag, māga, as John mera uan John and his companions, lit. John with those there (beside him); mera uan can also be used of inanimate things, as fatu mera uan a stone with those (stones) there (beside it), stones.

Merā, d. contraction for meraka, maraka, for makara, q.v.

Merā, ad., again, d. for mero, q.v.

Merafālu, some, as koria merafālu some dogs: me with, and rafālu, see lifāru.

Merafālu, s., c. art. namerafalu, contraction of namera rafālu, some people.

Merà gi, d. for

Merà kia, v. t., to go before, leading, to lead.

Merakien, s., c. art. namerakien act of leading, also meramera, redup., leading, and nameramera, s., act of leading or ruling, kingdom, that led or ruled, natamole meraki, or meramera, leading or ruling men. E. marha to lead; to go before.

Merakolau, s., web-like fat on the intestines (of a pig): mera fat (see merei), and kolau, q.v., a web (spider's). In An. this is called nilvanilva (redup. of nilva spider's web).

Meràroa, v. i., to turn round: roa i.

Mer ia, v. t., to do, to make to work, act, namerien, s., act of doing, what is done, conduct; fimeri to be doing something to each other, fighting;

Merimeri, v., to keep on doing.

5555555555555555

A. 'amila to work, Nm. to work, act, be active, practise, 4, cause to work.

Merei, s., marrow; eel: caterpillar; medulla of banana fruit. H. merī' fat.

Mero, ad., again, dd. merā, mer, moro, mrō, ro, and mo, m, contraction of mero, as i mero bano he again went, lit. he turned went, d. i mer lēr ban he again went, lit. he turned returned went: roa i.

Meromero, v. i., hoarse, gruff, as i bisa meromero he speaks hoarse, gruff. [Mg. barabara hoarse, having a rough voice, bara-feo a coarse, gruff voice, farina hoarse.] A. "ar"ara, 1, 2, to make rough sounds in the throat (whether with the voice, or liquor, or the breath), "ar"arat hoarse sound; sound of boiling water.

Emeromina, ad., and s., in the world, the world, lit. in the light, opposite to abokas in the under-world, Hades (which is dark and gloomy): e prep., and meromina, s., formed from mirama, or merama, to shine.

Meru, v. i., d. for māru, q.v.

Mes, ad., d. for maisa, to-day.

Mesa, ad., perhaps, expletive used at the beginning of a clause. E. 'emsa but if, quodsi.

Mesau na, v. t., to desire, and redup.,

Mesausau, desire much, be lustful;

Mesauen, s., c. art., desire, will, what one wills: sau.

Meta, v. i., or a., to be raw, then, unripe, crude, green. [Sa. mata, raw, unripe, Mg. manta raw, unripe, crude, green, My. mantah raw, unripe.] A. 'anut'a to be raw.

Meta, s., the eye, the eyes: mita.

Metita, v. i., or a., to be rotten, to be falling to pieces from rottenness. A. tha'ita to be rotten; to be falling to pieces from rottenness.

Mi, v., to be, d. for bi, q.v.

Mi a, redup. mimi a: for gumi a, q.v.

Miel, v. i., or a., to be red, and redup.,

Mimiel, id. [Sa. melomelo, memelo, red, My. merah, red; the ruby; bay colour in a horse.] A. ma"ir' reddish, 'am"aru of the colour of red clay.

Mihi, d., masiki, q.v.

Mikit ia, v. t., d. for makit ia, q.v.

Mila, v. i., or a., to be shy, skittish, to be wild, opposite to malolo. [My. liyar wild, untamed, shy.] A. hali'a to be uneasy, timid, impatient, shy. Hence

Mila, s., a wild animal; a warrior sleeping out in the bush and watching to cut off stragglers.

Milau, for malau, q.v.

Milaba. See laba.

Milag, s., a part, or half, c. art. namilag. Ch. pelag a half, A. filag' a part, a half.

Milago, v. i., d., to be sick, to be ill, have a disease. A. s'aniya, 2), n. a. s'ana' to be ill, to be sick with a latent disease, Nm. mos'na' faint, languid, moribund.

Milagoen, s., c. art., the being ill, disease.

Milākesa, or milākisa, v. i., or a., to be darkish green : milo, kisa.

M'lame, d., s., c. art. nam'lame, dew : mala. clear (rainless), and mea.

Milātĕ, dd. malārĕ, mīlānr, v. i., or a., to be cold, cold. [Sa. maalili, Tah. māriri, Ma. makariri, Fut. makiligi, id.] A. makrur' cold, from karra to be cold.

Milāte, s., c. art. namilātĕ, cold, the being cold, also namilatea; and redup.,

Milamilati, v., to be coldish : milāte. [New Hebrides, TaSa. makariri, Ml. U. milas, Malo macariri, Ml. P. mereus, Epi meneni, cold.]

Mile na, s., place, its place, d. for alia na, q.v., and see malo a place.

Mile ki, mile raki, v. t., to seek for (as for a pig in the bush), milemile ki, id., also mole ki, mole raki, molemole ki. A. 'āla, 2), to go through a place, 4, to seek for; to desire eagerly.

Mile, or milei, v. i., or a., used adverbially, to be good, good, as noa milei a tell good (well) it, bati milei a make good (well) it, syn. noa uia ki, bati uia ki (uia good), dd. mitā ki, butā ki, as noa mitā ki nia, bati butā ki nia, id. [Raratonga meitaki, Tah. maitai, Niue mitaki, Fila, Meli, Ma. marie, Ha. maikai, to be

handsome, good.] A. malih' beautiful, good, Nm. melieh elegant, good.

Milĕsia, v. i., or a., d., and Milĕsira, id., to be faded, dirty, mouldy : endings a and ra : and

Milĕs, v. i., or a., to be faded, drooping, withered : lusia. [Mg. malazo withered.]

Miles, s., c. art. namiles, the forest, the jungle, the bush. [My. alas a forest, alasan a forest country ; a foundation, alas-kaki footstool, Mg. ala a forest, a wood, Bugis alok, id., Fi. ra below.] A. 'aras'a and 'arus'a to abound in grasses and herbs (of the land) ; 'ars" the earth, soil, region, whatever is below, H. 'eres the earth, land, country, region, soil, Ch. 'āra' earth ; below.

Miles, s., a plant with dark leaves : les.

Milo, or miloa, redup. milolo, or miloaloa, d. malolo, d. mīlo, v. i., or a., to be dirty, to be darkish, of a dark, dirty colour : loa.

Milu, v. i., to depart, go away (from), remove, namiluen, s., the removing, departure. See s. v. lu. A. 'ala' ('alw) to remove, or go away (from).

Mim, or mam, q.v.

Mīmi, s., voc., aunt (paternal) See simam. [Fut. moma, id.]

Mimita, s., a sign, a showing of something. See mita, mimita, v.

Mina, a., sweet, pleasant, nice. See kasi. [Tah. mona, monamona, momona, My. manis, Mg. manitra.]

Minranin, d., ad., now; mi nra nin, mi time, nra nin this here; as to mi compare ma day. E. yom to-day, now, this time.

Mina, tongue. See mena.

Mini gia, d. minu gia, munu gia, d. munuma (munu-ma), v. t., to drink, also minu, munu; hence namunuen and namunugien, s., drinking, drink. [Fi. gunuva, unuma, Ml. min, Malo inu, Epi muni, Sa. inu, ps. inumia, s., inumaga, Santo o'o-mia, ulu-mia, My. minum, Mg. minona.] Ch. s'tha', 'is'tho', S. s'tho, H. s'atha, E. sataya; and with the th changed to k H. s'akah, A. saka', E. sakaya, to drink.

Mirá gi, d. for mera kia.

Mirama, v. i., to be light, to shine; namirama, s., light; emeromina in the light, the world;

Mirama ni a, to shine upon or on it, or him. [Sa. malama to be light, malamalama, v., to be light, s., light, malama, s., the moon, a lamp, torch, Ha. lama a torch.] A. lama'a to shine, &c.

Mirārā, v. i., or a., to be light (not heavy), slender, small. A. rakka to be thin, slender, slight, rakaraka to pour out not much (water or other thing).

Mirati, redup. miratirati, d. minrat, minratinrat, v. i., or a., to be loosed, untied: rat ia. [Ma. matara, Sa. matala, matalatala, Tah. matara, mataratara, to be untied.]

Misafe, misafesafe, v. i., to be separated (as a cocoanut from its branch): safe.

Misaki, d. masaki, v. i., to be sick, to have fever, to be ill. [My. sakit, Sa. ma'i, Fut. maki, Ml. P. mesek, Epi dd. msaki, mici, id.] And

Misaki, or misakia, s., c. art., sickness. [Fut. makiga sickness.] A. s'aka', 2), to afflict (someone, a disease), s'akat disease, mas'kuww' afflicted with a disease.

Misal, v. i., or a., to be removed, separate (from others). A. 'azala to remove (one). 5, 6, 7, 8, to be removed, 8, separate (from others), manzul', separated, removed.

Misal, misalsal, or misalĭ, mĭsalĭsalĭ, v. i., or a., to be light (not heavy). See salĭ.

Misaru, v. i., to hang down, prostrated: saru.

Misci, or misai, miscisei, v. i., or a., to be open, cracked: sai.

Misera, v. i., or a., to be parted, disjoined (as joints), separated: sera.

Miseroà sa, v. t., to desire, covet: soroà sa.

Miseroana, s., c. art., coveting, covetousness.

Misèrĭ, s., c. art., part of a woman's dress, consisting of a little mat, terminating in a bulky fringe, attached to the waist cincture and hanging down like an apron. See seri A. 'azzara to cover the body with the covering or garment called 'izār', mizar', a garment, covering, Nm. an apron.

Misimis, s., d. masimasi.
Misimis, v., d. masimasi.
Misa, or *misa*, v. i., to be stinking, rotten, decayed, wasted away; and redup.,
Misimisi, v. i., to be wasted away (of a very old man). Ch. mĕsa, S. msa to be decayed, putrefy.
Mit, s., c. art. na*m*īt, a mat; so called because plaited—see bau sia, Ml. vij, Epi mbie, to plait (a mat). [Ml. devij, Epi yembi, a mat.]
Mita, v. t. (also meta), to look at, watch, observe, view, as i mita natai-inlagi he watches or observes the cloud (to see if it will rain) mitā sa, or mimitā sa, look at, watch it (anything); and mita gita, or bakamita gita = leo goro gita (see leo) watch, look for, look out for (expecting) us: bakamita, v. t., same as mita. [Sa. mata to look at, matamata to look, to view, mamata, id. (of many), Ha. makai, makaikai, to look at closely, inspect, search out, spy, act the part of a spy, to look on, look at, to examine secretly for evil purposes, To. mamata to look, look at, behold, discern.] A. 'āna 1, to emanate (water), to be a spy, 2, to flourish, produce flowers (a plant), to show, make conspicuous, 3, to see, look at or on, 5, to look at malevolently, to look at well, accurately, to be manifest, conspicuous, 8, to look at malevolently, to become a spy, to view or watch, to look out for.

Note.—Mita is probably mu'tan' Mod. A. mu'tān, the n. ag. (Participle) of 8.
Mita na, s., c. art. namita na, the eye, that which sees, looks at, watches, or observes; mita noai a fountain; mita the beginning; mita bud, shoot, "eye" (as of a potato), bud, germ, offshoot (of men); mita nalagi eye of the wind; mita bagona eye of its end, point of its end, end; mita a window, door, or other opening, as the eye (of a needle); i bi mita na to be the eye (i.e., guide) of someone; namita nalo the eye (price) of something; mita kita a spy (in war), see kita; mita ni elo (or al) the sun (eye of light, or fountain or source of light), lit. eye of the sun. [My. mata, Mg. maso, Sa. mata, the eye, &c., Fi. mata eye, source, opening, point.] See mita, v.
Mitā, v. i., to bleed, mitā ni a bleeds on it, as i tumana mitā ni a, redup. mitāmitā ni a, he bleeds on himself (covers himself with blood), used also of rust—it rusts (covers itself with rust): rā blood. [My. bárdarah, Bu. madara, to bleed.]
Mita-*bago* na, s., end, lit. point of its end: mita, s.
Mita-busa, s., orphan child: mita s. (bud, shoot), and busa, q.v.
Mitaga, and mitagataga, v. i., to be heavy: d. miten, q.v.
Mitailau (mita-i-lau), s., d. syn. bilĕ-mita, q.v., lit. germ or

11

source of the tribe or community. See launa.

Mitāki, v. i., to be inclined to one side : taki, tā.

Mitaki, *i.e.*, mita ki, d. milei, q.v.

Mitakisa, s., blind, the eyes re-receding into the head : mita eye, and kisa.

Mitakitïk, d. matakitakï, a., last or first of a row (as of men); from closing up, or, as it were, binding together the series : taki a.

Mitaku, or mataku, v. i., to fear, be afraid ; mitaku or mataku ki, usually contr. to mitau ki, or matau ki, v. t., to be afraid of, to fear ; baka-mataku ki, to frighten (one) ; hence

Mitakua, s., c. art. fear ; and

Mitakuen, s., c. art., act of fearing, fear. [Sa. mata'u, ps. mata'utia, My. takut, Mg. tahotra, s., fear, matahotra, v. i., to be afraid, to fear.] A. taka', v. t, to fear (derived from waka', 8), takiyya*t* fear, caution, taking heed, takwa, fear of God, takiyy' fearing God. See *infra*, mita-taku.

Mitamai, or matamai, or miti-mai, ad., to-morrow. [Mota matava morning, Sa. tafa to dawn.] A. sabaha, 4, to be morning, to be early, to dawn, E. sabha to become light, or day, to dawn, A. sabāh' morning, masbah' and musbah' morning, dawn.

Mitanielo, s.. the sun, lit. eye of the sun : mita ni clo. [My. mata-ari, Mg. maso-andro.]

Mitäo, d., v. i., d. mitefe, q.v. : tao, roa.

Mitarau, s., c. art. tribe, lit. the bud, or germ, spreading out into many branches : mita, s., and rau.

Mitariki, s., the seven stars, lit. little eyes : mita, s , and riki. [Sa. matalii, Ma. matariki, id.]

Mitariki, s., as, lo mitariki to look with little (*i.e.* contracted) eyes. Same word as preceding.

Mitaru, v. i., to sink down : tiro.

Mitasabo, s., a stranger, lit. eye not knowing : mita, sabo.

Mitataku, v. t., as, i tumana mitataku na he heedfully watches himself, he being afraid watches himself : mita, v. t., and see mitaku.

Mitau, or matau, v. i., to abide, continue : tau.

Mitau ki, v. t., to fear : contraction for mitaku ki.

Mitaukien, a., dreadful, to be feared.

Mitausi a, v. t., to look after : mita, v. t., and usi, v. t.

Mitefe, d., v. i., to fall down, as a portion of a precipice : tibe. See roua, roa.

Mitefe-risu, v. i., to fall down (see preceding word), rushing or slipping to a distance : risu.

Mitoftef, v. i., and

Mitefŭtefŭ, id., to twitter, chirp, peep (of a bird or fowl), to make a whispering noise (of men). H. sifsaf to twitter, peep, chirp (of birds), to make a whispering, peeping sound (of the voice of a wizard).

Mitei, or mutrei, s., c. art.,
breadfruit cheese (salt and
sour), that is, breadfruit fer-
mented and preserved. [Sa.
masi, id., My. masin, salt (as
water), Mg. masimasina saltish,
rano-masina the sea (salt
water).] A. māsi' salt (of
water).

Mitela, v. i., or a., to be broken
(as crockery, or pottery). A.
thala'a to break (the head),
muthalla' broken.

Mitela, s., c. art. namitela, a
fragment, lit. that which is
broken, the broken.

Mitèn, v. i., d. mitàga, to be
heavy, to be burdened : tien,
or tiena, q.v., as also tago,
tagie. [Mg. entana, s., burden, voa entana lifted up,
mientana to set out, taingina
placed upon (a horse), tongoa
placed upon, My. tunggang
to ride, be conveyed by any
vehicle, tanggung to bear,
carry.] S. t'an to carry,
Aph. to burden, load, ta'no' a
burden, H. ta'an, Ch. tě'en to
be laden, A. t'a'ana, 8, to sit
on a camel, H. sa'an to move
tents, go forward (as a no-
madic tribe), A. t'a'ana, id.,
E. sa'na, sa'ana, to put on a
horse, &c., and consequently of
other things where one sits, is
placed, upon another, sĕun
burden.

Miti, v. i., to move rapidly, to
strive, quarrel, to jump backwards and forwards excitedly
in a quarrel or a rage, to land
or remove from a canoe; miti
goto depart or go rapidly

across (as an arm of the sea) ;
and redup.,

Mitimiti, v. i., to throb, flutter
(as the pulse). H. nasah to
fly, Hi. hissah to quarrel,
massah strife : cf. tiri.

Mitiri a, v. t., to write, to carve,
cut or make figures ;

Mitimitiri, a., figured, as cloth
(" print ") ;

Mitiri, d. mautsiri, s., c. art.,
writing, figures ; and

Mitirien, s., c. art., act of writing,
what is written. [Santo d.
turi, My. tulis to draw,
delineate, paint, picture,
figure, write, Mg. soratra
colour, writing, written,
misoratra to be spotted,
printed, of different colours,
and soritra, misoritra to mark,
engrave.] E. sa'ala to paint,
figure, A. sāra, 2, to figure,
paint, 5, to be formed, musaw-
wir sculptor, painter, Nm. 2,
to form, draw, trace, paint.
The radical idea is that of
cutting.

Mitiri, s., a kind of locust or
grasshopper (so called from its
mode of moving) ;

Mitiri, v. i., to leap flying (as a
grasshopper) : tiri.

Mitroa, v., to think, mitroa ki,
v. t., to think of or about,
dd. miroa, mitoa, mintoa,
minroa; redup.,

Mititroa, d. minintoa, v. i., to
be thoughtful, sensible ;

Mitroān, s., c. art., act of
thinking, thought : ro, roro,
trotro, rara or trara, romi or
rumi. [Mg. eritra, eritraritra
cogitation, mieritra, mieritre-

ritra, Fut. mentua, To. manatu (Sa. manatu), to think.]
S. 'etra'i to think, Ethpa. of
r'o', Ch. rĕ'ah to think, H.
ra'ah, (3), to delight in, rea' a
friend,   lover,   one   loved,
thought,   will,   Ch.   ra'yon
thought.

Mito (mwīto), v. i. or a., to be
short, redup.,

Mite*mīto*, id., d. būru, burufūru.
[Tah. mure. muremure, Ma.
poto.] H. kaṣar to cut, kaṣer
to be cut off, to be short, short,
A kaṣara to be short, 3), to cut
(hair), to make short, maksur'
short.

Miu, v. i., to be wet : cg. mea.
A. mai' fluid, ma'a to flow
gently on the surface, 4, to be
dissolved in liquid.

Miura, s., c. art., dew : miu, and
ura, q.v.

Mo, ad., contraction of mero.

Mo, d. for bo, dd. fo, uo, o.

Mō na, s., father or mother-in-
law, son-in-law. See buruma,
s.; hence,

Mo-naki, v. t., to be related to
(one) in this relationship :
buruma ki. E. ham father-in-
law, son-in-law, A. ham', hamō,
ham'o, &c., father-in-law or
kinsman of the husband or
the wife, Nm. hamou father-
in law, hamaya mother-in-law,
H. ham, Assy. emu, father-in-
law, Samaritan, a son-in-law,
also, one espoused. "The
proper signification of the
word lies in the idea of
affinity."

    NOTE.—E. Mai ma = Ef.
mo, Fila ma, brother-in-law,

vugōna (vungōna, nearly pronounced like vumōna = (in
meaning) Ef. buruma ; in
Tah. momoa to espouse, to
contract marriage.

Moa, d., verbal pron., 1 dual,
excl., pl. bu.

Moàs, d. for mafàsu.

Mobu, d. m'bua, v. i., to sink :
bua II.

Mofa, s., when the blood of men
or animals has been shed, and
forms a pool on the ground,
one feeling the smell of it, or
of any similar thing, says i
na*b*o mofa it smells mofa ;
taumofa (tau mofa) to make a
sacrifice or offering to the
natemate. See taumofa. A.
ma'haba*t* a small pool.

Mok, s., water flowing from the
eye ;

Mokemok, v. i., to flow from the
eye (of water), to water (of
the eye) : cg. miu, mou. H.
mug to flow, flow down, dissolve.

Mokot, d., s., tongs : mikit ia.

*Mo*la, v. i., to yawn. [Ma. ko-
whera to open, gape.] H.
pa'ar to open the mouth with
a wide gape, S. f'ar, A.
fa"ara.

Mole, d. *b*alo, v. i., q.v.

Mole a, or mole ki, molemole ki,
d. mile a, mile ki, q.v.

Moli na, s., d. batoko na, q.v.

Moli, v. i., d. mauri, to live ;

Molien, s., c. art., d. maurien,
life.

Momoă, or momo, d., v. i., to
yawn. [Tah. mama to open
the mouth, Sa. mavava, Fut.
mava, to yawn, Mg. vava the

mouth, vavana talkative, vava opened, mivava, v. i., mavava, v. t., to open, vavatra spoken.] H. peh mouth, A. fah' mouth, faha to speak, fawiha to have a wide mouth.

Momoa, v. i., d. for amoamo, amo'mo.

Monamona, v. i., or a., to be yellow. [Ma. pungapunga yellow colour, Mg. vony, s., yellow, Amboyna poko, d. apoo, Ceram poko, yellow, d. uninim, My. kūning, id.] A. faka'a, n. a. fuku', to be yellow.

Monam, d. monau, s., c. art., grass (of any kind). A. nama' to grow, namāya vegetation, manma', place of (a tree's) growth. The word "grass" is connected with "grow."

Mono ti a. See munu ti a.

Mori, d., a., true, tili mori speak true: mori true, used like loamau, lesoko, also amori: mauri, mau, true.

Morese na, s., d. borakese na, q.v.

Moro, ad., d. mero, q.v.

Moru, v. i., to sink, or be covered with water, as a canoe in the waves;

Moru aki, v. t., to sink, overwhelm (a canoe), as, nabeau i sera moru aki rarua the waves rush, sinking, or covering, or overwhelming the canoe;

Morua, s., c. art., the deep, i.e., the deep sea;

Mōru, s., any deep place, as a hole, pit, grave; hence imrum (d. imrau) inside of a house, i.e., moru nasuma, or moru uma, the hole, i.e., the inside, of a house. A. "amara to cover (a thing with water), "amar' much water, deep (of the sea), Nm. to overwhelm, drown, "amra deep water, abyss.

Mos ia, for amos ia, q.v.

Mōso, s., the entrance to a harbour; a space or tract of country, as that between two mountains; pr. n. of the village and district on the northern end of Deception Island, at the boat entrance to Havannah Harbour, and in Ro-Moso, name of an inland village and district. H. mahōz a seaport, coast, Ch. id., also a region, A. ha'z' border, side, region, hence also a port.

Mota, s., c. art., and redup., Motamota, id., rubbish, refuse, as leaves of trees fallen on the ground, &c. [Sa. ota rubbish, Ma., Tah., ota, Ha. oka.] And Mota, v. i., or a., to be covered with rubbish, dirty. [Sa. otaotā full of rubbish: a. ending a.] A. "otā' rubbish, refuse, husks, leaves, and scum mixed together, "ata' to have rubbish mixed with scum (as a river).

Mot ia. See mut ia.

Mot, s. See mut, s.

Mot, or motŭ, s., c. art. namot, as nataku namot back of the land, or island; lit. what is broken off, hence a district or place. [Sa. motu islet, district, motu to be broken off, ps. motusia, v. t. motusi, s. motusaga, v. i. motumotu, s.

motumotuga, My. putus to break, Mg. maito broken asunder, snapped, maitoito broken in pieces, otosana being cut, broken, snapped.] A. makta' a place. See the verb under koto-fia.

Mou, moumou. Same as miu, q.v.

Mu, verbal suf. pron., 2 pl., you, d. kama.

Mu, v. i., to coo (as a dove), to hum—see fu. [Tah. mu, a buzz, mumu to make a confused noise, as of a multitude of persons talking together, Ha. mumu, id., Sa. muimui, to murmur, Fut. mu to buzz, Mg. moimoy hum, murmur.] H. hamah coo, hum (as a multitude), A. hamhamah to murmur, &c., Nm. to whoop, drone, sing lullaby.

Mū nia, v. t., to take out (a thing, as out of a basket). [Mg. voaka, mivoaka, to go out, mamoaka to drive out, take out.] See under bua III.

Mua, v. i., to flow out, flow (of the tide) ; hence

Muāna, s., c. art., the flood tide, as opposite to the ebb ; and

Mua-goro, s., c. art., dd. fuagoro, màgoro, a spring of fresh water on the shore that is covered (goro) by the sea at high water : bua III.

Mubu. See mobu.

Muku ti a, v. t., to cover or enclose in leaves (as bananas, to ripen them) ; to rub, wipe off; and

Mukumukuen, s., c. art., the doing so. [Fi. moko-ta, to embrace, to clasp round with the arms, Ma. mukumuku, muku, to wipe, rub.] A. haka to sweep, cleanse by sweeping ; to rub ; to surround, embrace, enclose.

Muli a (mwuli a), v. t., to work into a round mass, as dough or clay ; to gather rubbish into a heap ; to clasp a pig (or man) round with the arms ; and

Mulimul, v. i., or a., round. [TaSa. molmol, Ml. P. moromor, Fi. momoqiliqili, My. bulat, Mg. boribory, round.] This word radically means to *roll* as to *roll* dough into a mass ; to roll rubbish or pebbles into a heap ; to roll or clasp the arms round one. H. 'agal i.q. galal to roll, revolve, 'agol round, and is eg. to gulu tia, &c.

Mulu sia, v. t., to strip off the skin, and

Mulu, v. i., and tamulu, to cast the skin (as a snake, a crab, a scab, men in myths), redup. mulumulu ; and

Mulu na, s., c. art., the skin which is cast ; then, the lower rank which a chief casts off on his being promoted to a higher. [Fi. kuli skin, kulu-caka to strip off the skin, Mg. hoditra skin, manoditra to strip off the skin, hedirana being flayed, skinned, Ef. kuli, d. uili (wili) and uli, skin, mulu si a to skin, mulu, also tamulu, to cast the skin, *i.e.*, to be skinned, or to skin oneself or itself.] A. gild' skin, galada, 1, 2, to skin, to strip off the skin.

Muluen, s., c. art., act of casting the skin ; namulusien, s., the act of stripping off the skin.

Mulua, s., a grove or clump of trees : ulua.

Mūmū, a., saving, protecting, preserving : mū-ti a, or mau-ti a.

Munu gi a. See minu gi a.

Munu-mia, d. munu-gi.

Munu ti a, v. t., to close up (as a wound, a hole in cloth, &c.) ; hence

Munuai, or munue, s., a sacred man (natamole tab) who by his natabuen, or magical power, closes up, or heals, wounds received by men in battle : bunu tia.

Mūrĭ n, v. t., d. for mesau na ;

Mūrĭen, s., c. art., d. for mesauen.

Muri a, v. t. (d. busi a), to return (as a thing borrowed), to repay, recompense, requite (for work done), to return (an injury), repay (a person, for an injury), redup. murimuri; hence

Murien, s., c. art., the act of returning, repaying, pay, re-quital, recompense, retribution.

Muri na, s., c. art., the after part of a thing (as of a stream, that is, the place to which it flows and where it ends), opposite to namita na the fore part of a thing (eye), beginning, source. [Fi. muri-a to follow, also to imitate, Ma. muri rear, hinder part, Sa. muli end, back or hinder part, rump, mulimuli to follow after, To. muli, mui, Ja. buri, the back, rear, behind, after, My. burit the fundament,

Mg. vody the posteriors, stern (of a ship), voho the back, fody returned, sent back, namody to return the thing bought, verina returned, sent back, mamerina to return, send back.] See also mauri, busi a, bisi na, bui na, kui na, kusu na, kihi na, fua na, bua na, gere na, uri na. A. 'ah'h'ara to be be-hind, after, Nm. mo'weh'h'ar placed at the end, mouh'ir stern, hinder part, 'eh'ir, end, 'uh'ur' behind, after part, H. 'ahar to be after, behind, 'ahar after, behind, hinder part, ex-tremity, 'ahōr hinder part, rear, meahōr from behind, behind ; also in Arm. and E.

Murasa, d. marasa.

Muru, v. i., to laugh, muru ki to laugh at (one). See bukaru. [Motu kiri to laugh.] A. kahara to laugh.

Murubua, s., a bat : moru, bua ; from its dwelling in deep holes.

Musa gi a, v. t., to take on board a canoe or ship (men or things) ; redup.,

Musamusa ; and

Musagien, s., c. art., and

Musamusoen, s., c. art., the act of doing so ; and

Musī a, v. t., to put or drag immersed in the water (a thing, as a log) ; and

Musu, v. i., to dive (as a man), to set (the sun) ; elo i musu the sun sets, or has set. A. "amasa dip, submerge, to set (as a star), and kamasa dip, plunge, dive, and makasa im-merse in water.

Musi a, v. t., to remove a child (from the breast), wean it; and

Mus (ki susu), v. i., to be removed (from the breast). H. mus' remove, take away.

Mus ia, v. t., rub, smooth, flatter; Musamus ia, id., redup. : mos ia.

Musuku taki, v. t., to abhor : siki naki.

Mut, v. i., to slip or fall out, as a rope out of a block. A. ma'ata to take a sword out (of its sheath), 8, 'amma'ta, id., also, to fall out (as hairs).

Mū-ti a, v. t., d. for mau-tia, to save, keep, preserve, protect. A. 'amana, 4, render secure, protect, give security to (some-one). Hence

Mūtien, s., c. art., act of saving, salvation.

Mut ia, and mot ia, v. t., to bind : ut ia, ot ia ; and

Mut, s., c. art., a bond, rope. A. makata, 6), bind, mukt' bond, rope.

Mutni, v. i., to sneeze. [Sa. mafatua, to sneeze.] A. nafata (cf. 'afata, 2) to sneeze.

Na, ad. of assent, and interj., d. syn. ko : dem. na. H. na indeed, &c.

Na, d., dem., this, as mal na this time : in.

Na, sometimes a, also in, ni, n, la (in lausu), the article. [Mg. ny, Epi na, Fi. na, a., Sa. le, the article.] A. al, hal, H. ha, A. a (the l being

assimilated to certain letters). In Mod. A. al is pronounced al or el, and l'. In South Arabia am was (and even still is) used for al. A. al (and H. ha) is sometimes used as a relative pronoun ; so in Efate : see nig, agi.

N', a particle expressive of past time, in nanum, nāsa, nanoasa. [Mg. n', Sa. na, sign of past tense.]

Na, d. n, and na or nia (in si-kina, or sikinia), nom. suf. pron., 3 sing., his, her, its. [Sam. na, sing., Mg. ny, pl. and sing., My. nia or ña, pl., and sing.] See nai, note.

Na, d. n, verbal suf., pron , 3 sing., him, her, it. See nia and nai, note.

Nabatí na, s., tooth, teeth; seed, also the shoots from the roots of a banana, and the shoots or roots of taro. [Ml. ribo, Epi livo, Sa. nifo (whence nifoa), Fut. nifo, Mg. nify teeth.] See also bati, beti, bitia or titia. A. nāb', pl. nubūb', &c., tooth, teeth, nāba, 2, 4, to put forth roots (a plant).

Nabe, s., d. mbat, club. Nm. nabboud and nabbout, id.

Nābe, or nābea (nakbe, or nakbea), d. nakima, s., a hol-lowed log, set up in the middle of the malala or mala, used as a drum or musical instrument in the dances of the intamate, and on which the face or other symbol of the natemate (the deceased) is carved. [Sa. nafa, To. natfa, Fut. kafa, a drum, Ml. U. nambwi, id.] H.

nekeb a hollowed thing, that which is hollowed, used as a musical instrument (Ezekiel xxviii. 13), English Version, "pipes:" "thy tabrets and thy pipes;" from nakab to hollow out.

Nabis, s., end, the last, d. nakis: bisi na.

Nabo, or naboa, d. tamo, v. i., to smell ; and

Nabon, s., smell. [Sa. namu to have a bad smell, To. namu odour, either good or bad, Fut. namu.] See boa. A. fāha, 6, to emit odour.

Nabua, s., a road, path. A. nabiyy' and nabiy', id.

Nafete, d. sefete, d. nefeha, d (te)uase (wase), inter. pron., what? which? M.S. mudi, A. mada, Nm. made, what? Nafete is na art., and fete, and sefete, se dem., and fete.

Naga, or nag, dem., this, that: na, dem., and ka dem., changed to ga.

Nāg, or nāga, s., dd. lāg, rāg, nrāk, rān, time. A. 'ān time, and art. al, l'.

Nagasa, inter. ad., when? i.e., naga sa? lit. what time? also indefinitely, when, whatever time. Ml. U. seve-lig = Ef. d. sefe-nag = what time? = naga-sa?

Nago, pers. pron., 2 sing., you, dd. ago, ag, nigo, keiga, keina, nego.

Nagore na, s., nostrils, nose. See gore na.

Nai n, d. for nani n, child. See nei n and ani.

Nai, pers. pron., 3 sing., he,

she, dd. enea, or inia, gā, niga, kinini. [My. inya, or inia (Ef. inia, sing.), pl. and sing., they, he, she.] M.S. ani (also enehe, anyaha), 'ni, na they, those (also enya these), also ignorantly used for sing. sometimes, S. hanun (hanen), anun (anen), they, these, verb. suf. enun (enen), nom. suf. hun (hen).

NOTE.—Nai is na dem., and i (for ni); nigā is ni dem., and ga (for na); ga is for na, which is nia in inia, and na in nom. suf.

Nai, s., water, d. for noai, nifai.

Nai, i.e., n art., and ai s., side board of a canoe to keep the waves out, a protector or defence of a place (a warrior who keeps out the enemy); d. a fence. [Sa. āi a fence, a railing, āi to fence in, To. a fence, Ha. pa, v. and s.] See under baka, s.

Naita natuo, s., d. for ua-natenatuo the calf of the leg, hence nalake naita natuo n the ankle, lit. the base of the calf of the leg.

Nakate, s., d. syn. nete, q.v., lit. the that that.

Nakima, s., d. nabea.

Nakis, s., d. nabis: kusu na, kihi (or kisi) na.

Nakis, or nakisa, or nakes, s., green or blue paint: kesakesa.

Nāko na, s., the face. See ko : n. art., and ako ; hence

Nakonakoa ki, v. (formed by a, a. ending, from preceding word) to assume the face, or appearance of (ki) someone ;

Nakonako ki, v., to face (someone), *i.e.*, front (him). A.
wagaha, 5, id., to front or
face each other.

Nālu, or nālua, an arrow. A.
nabl' arrow.

Namu, s., d., mosquito, d. na
mamamami (d. batirik =
small tooth). [Sa. mamu,
Tah. namu, ramu, Fut. namo,
My. ñamok, Bu. namok, Mg.
moka, Ml. U. num, TaSa.
moke, Malo mohe, Ta. kumug,
An. inyum, Motu namo, id.]
See mu, v. The n in namu is
the art., and namu is the
buzzer or pinger.

Nanoa na, s., the neck, *i.e.*, n'
art., and anoa neck, cg. manu
na, q.v. [Santo d. alo, d.
ralo, Bu. olong.] A. 'unk',
'unuk', 'anik', neck.

Nānua, s., necklace, beads, *i.e.*,
n' art., and anua. H. 'anak
necklace.

Nanofa, ad., d., yesterday, and

Nanoasa, ad., d. nāsa, the day
before yesterday, and

Nanu, ad., d. nanofa, and

Nanum, ad., d. nanu, yesterday.
[Fi. e na noa, Santo nonovi
(pwanovi to-morrow), Epi
niobo (bani = maisa = to-day).]
Nan-ofa, nan-u, nan-um, consist of ofa, u, um, day (see
ma, s., day), and (Fi. e na
noa, e in or on, na the ; noa
past day = nu, num, nofa)
nan', *i.e.*, na the art., and n'
particle expressive of past
time, as in nāsa, *infra*.
Nanōasa (for nanofasa) has sa
(for rua, sometimes ra, 2):
hence na nofa, lit. the past

day, and na noasa the second
past day. Nanoasa, nāsa.
[Epi nua, d. niaha, Ta. d. neis,
id.]

Nāo, s., d. noa, q.v.

Naob, s., lime, d. noba, q.v.

Nāra, pers. pron., 3 pl., they (for
nai 'ra), d. gara, or nigara
(ga 'ra), d. inira (inia and 'ra).
See ra, ru, and nai.

Naro, d. for nalo. See lo a
thing.

Naroa, s., na, art., a current
(of water, especially in the
sea): so called because i roa
turns (itself). See roa.

Nāsa, ad., the day before yesterday, d. nanoasa: nāsa is
without the article and for
noasa (in nanoasa).

Nasafa, inter. pron., also nasefa,
and nesefa : na, art., and safa,
or sefa, q.v.

Nasaga, s., na, art., a stretch of
sea between two places. See
saga.

Nasu na, na art., s., juice, what
flows out, or exudes. [Sa. su
to be wet, sua juice.] A.
nazza to exude, nizu flow,
water.

Nāta, a person. See ata. Nāta
na, or nāte na, soul, spirit ;

Natamole, a living person,

Natamate, or natemate, a dead
person, a ghost, a demon, an
object of worship. See ata,
moli, mate, atamole, atamate.

Natara, s., n art., and atara a.,
a virgin, young woman; naguruni atara a young woman ;
and naturiai a young man, bia
aturiai young men. [My.
dara, Ja. rara, a maid, virgin.]

A. 'aḍara to be a virgin ('aḍera' a virgin), 2, to circumcise ; to begin to have a beard (young man), 'idār' a beard, hence with a. ending aturiai bearded, or beginning to be bearded, a young man.

Nātĕ, or nātsĕ, s., the banana, or plantain, plant and fruit : n art., and ātĕ, or ātsĕ. [Ml. P. nevij, Ml. U. navits, Ero. nobos, Epi vihi, Am. nohos, Ml. dd. navis, abus, Paama ahisi, Fi. vudi, Ulawa huti, Fut. vuji, Fila butsh', Aniwa hutshĭ, Niue futi, My. pisang, Ceram fudi, phitim, Sanguir busa, Mg. ontsy, d. hotsy, id.] A. muz', Amh. muz, id.

Nātĭ-kuru, s., dried, withered banana leaves. See kuru, a.

Natemate, for natamate. See atamate.

Natoara, s., n art., a kind of grass (sword grass). H. hasir grass, A. h'as'ira to be green.

Naturiai, s., aturiai, a., young man. See under natara.

Näu, s., reeds ; Pan's pipes ; for nausu : na art., and usu, q.v.

Nau, v. i., usually nu, q.v.

Nau ia, v. t., to rub, wipe off. See nu ea.

Näüa (nāwa), n art., and äüa (äwa), q.v.

Nĕ a, for noi a, v., to dwell, or be, beside (someone) : the verb no is intransitive, and i is the t. prep. [Fi. no to lie (of things, not persons), Sa. nofo to sit, dwell, remain, Ma., Tah., Ha., noho.] H. navah and naah, to sit down, to rest, to dwell.

Ne, dem., here, there, this, that, uane, kine, netu. See in, na. [Sa. nei this.]

Nei n, or nai n, s., his child, d. for nani n. The n of ani, q.v., is elided : nai for nani.

Nĕgo, pers. pron., d. for nago, q.v.

Nĕko (for naiko), s., n art., and eko the wooden mallet for beating native cloth (in making it). [Sa. i'e, To. igi, id., Ha. ku, kuku, to beat native cloth.] A. waka'a to beat, 7), to sharpen, make thin a knife, 8), make slender, &c., waki' sharp, thin, slender. To. igi means also small, Ef. iki, kiki, id. ; and kie also belongs here, the leaf being rubbed and split into slender threads.

Neinei a, v., as boka neinei a beat it soft, beat making it soft (or weak). See maneinei.

Nĕru, nāru, and nieru, war, lit. arms : art., and aru, q.v.

Nĕt, d. for binĕt, banotu, q.v.

Nete, s., a thing, anything, something, d. syn. nakate : art., and te, dem., lit. the that. Nete ra their thing, also āra te, id., āgu te my thing, āma te thy thing.

Netu, dem., this, that: ne, dem., and tu, v., lit. this or that standing out or up.

Netua, d. nerua, s., twins, art. and tua, or rua, 2, lit. the two. [Fi. drua, id. ; also double, a., as a double canoe, a double fruit.]

Neta ki, v. t., to throw, net ia to throw upon, hit with a thing thrown. A. nada' to throw, H. nadah, Pi., to cast out.

Ni, prep., of (genitive), to, belonging to, also i, in, on, at, with art. ani, q.v., t. prep. after verbs, as mesau ni au desire me (also mesau au, d.), ri, as soka ri join on to, and li, as taka li, d. taka ni, thrust on to, also ra in raki, q.v., as toko raki remain, or abide for, i.e., wait for, or wait upon, and i, as in no i, &c. [Fi. ni, i, or e, of, in, t. prep. na, ra, raka, laka, Ma. i of, belonging to, &c., and t. prep., Battak ni, Bu. ri, Holontalo li, Tag. ni, Mg. ny, n', any, of, belonging to.] A. li, H., Arm. lĕ, E. la, T. nĕ, id.

Ni, art., also na, in, n. [Mg. ny, id.]

Ni, same as na, ad., and interj;

Ni, verb. suf., 3 sing., d. nia, q.v.

Nia, verb. suf., 3 sing., same as na, q.v., once (in sikinia, and sikina, his one, he alone) nom. suf. (which usually is na). See nai, inia.

Niba ki, v. t., to throw away, make to go away. A. nafa' drive away, expel, hurl away (as a torrent, rubbish, the wind, dust).

Nifai, s., water, dd. nai, noai : ni art., and fai water.

Nife ni, a., v. t., to fan, t. prep. ni, lit. to wave, or brandish, on or to ;

Nifenife, v. i., to fan, to wave or brandish, as the branches of a tree in the wind ;

Nife, s., a fan. H. nuf to wave

up and down, Hi. henif to wave, to shake.

Nig, d., prep., of (gen.) for (dative), ni art., and g (for gi), i.e., ki, q.v.), dd. nag, nagi, nagki, and, art. without its n, agi, d. agki (gk for k).

Niga, d., pers. pron., 3 sing. : ni art., and ga.

Nigara, d., pers. pron., 3 pl.: niga, and ra.

Nigita, pers. pron., 1 pl., incl. : ninita.

Nikenika, v. i., to be silent, quiet, or noiseless, or stealthy ; also to move quickly along a sharp ridge (of a mountain), or along a log across a stream. [Ha. nihi to walk very softly and quietly, as on tiptoe, to do a thing quietly or secretly, nihinihi standing up on edge, narrow ridged, or edged, Ma. ninihi to move stealthily.] A. naga' to hasten ; communicate a secret, 3, act, or speak, secretly (with someone), naga' branch of a tree, higher part of land, nagwat higher part of land, a secret.

Niko na, s., the spine (ridge) of a cocoanut leaf. See preceding word.

Nin, dem., d., this : n art., and in dem. [My. nun that.]

Ninita, or nininta, d., obsolete, for nigita, niginta, pers. pron., 1 pl., incl., we (and) thou, dd. keigita, igira, akit, nikit : art. ni, and nita (ni we, ta thou). [An. inta, verb. pron., id., Santo d. niti, or inti, separate pron., id., Ml. d. ante, id.,

My. kita, Mg. isika, Sa. 'o i ta (tou), id.]

Niti a, or nit ia, v. t., to plane, shave (wood). A. naḥata, n. a. naḥt', id.

Niu, s., c. art. naniu, the cocoanut palm. [Fi. niu, Er. noki, An. ncaig, My. nior, Ceram niula, Ml. kula, Mg. nihio, Sa. niu, id. ; niu piu fan palm (therefore niu is a general name for a palm); niui to sprinkle with the juice of the cocoanut, Ha. niu to whirl about.] A. naḥ'lu palm (gen. name), naḥ'īlu (coll. name), naḥ'ala to sift, to pour out or sprinkle (snow, as the clouds), Nm., 7, to drizzle.

No, contr. n, in bano, ban, banotu, &c. [Fi. yani, Sa. ane, To. angi, directive ad., Mg. any there, in that place.] Prep. n (ni), and dem. o.

No i a, or noi a, d. nē a, noi, d. ne : hence redup. noinoi, and r. binoinoi, d. binofinoi. See nē a.

Nono, v. i., no (in no ia) redup., to abide, as mala nono abide senseless. See also binoinoi to abide with each other, and binofinoi, or bunofunoi.

Noa ki, v. t., tell, lit. say to, dd. ni ki, ti ki, nofa, q.v. ; noa i, v. t., say or tell it ; binoa to speak about each other.

Noai, s., d. nifai water; for na uai.

Noa, s. (for na ua), d. näo, a swell, or wave. See uaua.

Noba, s., c. art. nanoba, d. naob, lime (ashes of coral) ; and

Nobanoba, v. i., or a., to be dusty, become dust, fly in the air (dust). See abuobu. [Sa. navu lime, Ma. nehu dust, nehunchu dusky, whakanchu reduce to powder.]

Noba nia, v. t., to wrap in leaves with hot stones and cook, to cook, d. tuma nia; and

Nobanoba, v. i., to be cooked, soft. See also manubunubu, and d. tomo or tumu, tumutumua, matumutumu. [Ha. nopu thoroughly cooked, soft, plump, fat, swelled out, and nopunopu spring or swell up (in the mind), swell, be large, round, spring up.] A. tabaḥa, n. a. tabḥ', to cook, roast, to ripen, 2, to grow up, 7, 8, to be cooked, tubbaḥ' pl. of tābīḥ' fatness, tabīḥ' cooked.

Nobu, s., flood, d. tōbu. A. tāf to flood (Ct.), tawwafu a flood.

Nof, d. for num, v. i., q.v.

Nofa i, v. t., d. noa i, q.v., to tell. A. nabā', 6), 2, show, declare, announce, tell.

Nono. See ante, no, nono.

Notīnotī, v. i., or a., to be spotted (as an animal). H. nakod spotted (as an animal), Nm. nokta a spot, monakkat spotted, H. nakad, A. nakata, to mark with points.

Nōtu, d., contraction for banotu, q.v.

Nu, v. i., d. num, q.v., hence manua, manunu.

Nu ē a, v. t., to wipe, rub off ; redup.,

Nunu ēa, id., and

Nūnu, s., a wiper, rubber, and

Nunu-tafe, s., the wrist, lit. snot-

wiper. [Sa. nunu to grate
down, nuaga a grating down.]
A. thamma, 4), to sweep (a
house, or place), 5), to rub,
wipe off. Cf. nu, A. tamma.
See num.

Nuanua, v. i., to wave about, or
to and fro (as the branches of
a tree) ; nuanua ki, v. t., to
wave, make to wave, or shake
(anything). H. nu'a to move
to and fro, wave to and fro,
Hi. move to and fro, shake.

Nua na, s., n art., and ua, q.v.,
fruit.

Nub, s., d. rub, q.v.

Nubu na, d. tumu na, s., c. art.,
the soft swelling protuberance
of anything (as of a yam)
growing. See nobanoba.

Nubu, v. i., d. num.

Nuf, v. i., d. num.

Nugnug ia, v. t., d. luglug ia,
q.v. : hence manugnug, q.v.

Numnum ia, v. t., d. for nugnug
ia.

Nugnug, v. i., to be careless,
heedless, maturu nugnug to
sleep and be devoid of all care
or thought, be utterly heedless.
A. nūmat heedless, careless,
nāma to sleep, doze, be quiet,
tranquil, 2, deaden (as pain).

Num, v. i., to be finished, completed, dd. nu, nau, nubu, nuf,
nof; ru nau, nu, num, nuf ban
they all have gone, a bat ia i
nu I have done it, it is finished.
See manua, manunu, binunu,
manubu, manubunubu.   A.
tamma, n. a. tum', &c., to be
all, whole, finished, completed,
at an end, and, transitive, to
complete, &c.

Nūra, s., syn. miura, q.v., for
ne ūra : ura.

O, sign of vocative, interj., as
temanami o, O our father.
[Ml., Santo, Malo, o, id.]   E.
o, id.

O, dem., io, äo, ore, or iore, q.v.,
and in otaki, q.v., also in ko
dem., and in bo (mo, fo, uo,
o), q.v.   [Fi. o in oqo, Tah. o,
Mare o, Motu o, dem.]   See
ua.   M.S. hau, pronounced ō,
dem., and egg., that is, the
Semitic pers. pron. 3 sing.
used as a dem., and as a verb
substantive.

O, verbal suf., 1 sing., me, d.
for au.

O, v. i., contr. for onï, q.v. ; also
in bäo.

Ob, s., d., c. art. naob, d. nōba,
lime (ashes of coral) : noba.

Of, s., dd. um, ubu, ūa, cooking
oven : ban ia.

Ofa, in taliofa, dd. taliaba, tali-
eba.   See tali.   Ofa to whirl
round.   [Tah. ohu (also =
kofu, q.v., supra) to whirl
round, Ma. koumuumu, My.
ubâng, mubâng.]   E. kabab
to whirl round.

Ofa, i.q., afa to swim, be above,
float on ; and

Ofa ia, i.q. afa ia, q.v.

Of ia, or ōfi a, v. t., to be near
to, alongside of, d. āfi a ;

Ofiofi, v., a., near to. [To. ofi
near to, at hand.]   A. wahafa
n. a. wahf', to draw near to,
approach near.

Ofa ki, v. t., i.q. afa ki ; nalia ofakien a place of burial, to be buried in, naofakien act of burying, burial.

Ofa, a., high, tall, as a tree. [Mg. avo high, lofty, eminent, proud.] H. gabah to be high, as a tree, gobah height (as of trees), pride, gaboah, high, lofty, proud.

Ola, s., a spear. [Ulawa ilula, New Ireland lelu, Maklay Küste (N.G.) iur, id.] A. 'allat', pl. 'alal', 'elal', id.

Oli a, d. uli a, q.v.

On, s., sand, d. aran, q.v.

Oni contr. o, d. ani, q.v., to abide, be.

Ore, d. ör, ad., yes, that's it : o dem., and re, or ri, dem., cf. iore.

Or, d., s., c. art. naor, or na uor. See uora.

Ora na, s., sprout, shoot, or vine (as of a yam) ;

Oraora na, id. : bora, uora.

Orän, and orain, d., s., sand : arän.

Oraorana, a., na a. ending, variegated. [Tah. purepure spotted, chequered, of diverse colours.] E. hubur variegated, of various colours, Ch. habarbar spotted.

Ore, i.q. aure, q.v.

Ori a, v. t., to rub, grate, ori, v. i., to make a creaking, grating noise (as the branches of trees rubbing against each other) ;

Ori, s., d. kiri, the rubbing stick in producing fire by the friction of two sticks. [Tah. oro, Sa. olo, to rub, olo a plane, My. urut, to rub, kukur to rasp, Mg. otra rubbed, orina being rubbed.] H. garar to scrape, sweep, saw. Cf. the cognates.

Oro, v. i., to grunt (a pig), to growl, snarl (a dog), and with transitive prep. oro-maki to bark at (a person or thing), bioro, v. r., to make a confused murmuring noise (as a crowd of men all speaking at once) ; and

Orooro, id., redup., cf. uru, uru-uru. [Ma. nguru, to sigh, grunt, rumble, ngengere to growl, ngeri to chaunt (in launching a canoe, &c.), ngengeri to grunt, My. kurkur to grunt (a pig), Mg. erotra to snore, erona, mierona, to growl, snarl, roar.] A. nah'ara Nm. to grunt, h'ara to low, h'arh'ara snort, snore, harra to growl, snarl (a dog), to creak, harharat murmur or sound of copiously flowing water.

Oro, d., v. i., or a., to be barren : d. for bara, q.v.

Oroa, v. i., or a. Same as oraorana, to be coloured, variegated : a. ending 'a, d. contr. oro ; hence

Oroa, d. oro, s., a species of grasshopper, so called from its colours.

Otaki, d. uataki, s., native tongs : o dem., and taki a.

Oti a, i.q. moti a, uti a, muti a, q.v.

Ra, d. nra, dem., this, that. See arai.

Rä, s., a depressed place, damp or watery : ruku.

Rā na, s., branch. [Sa. la, Ma. ra, My. daan, Mg. rahana, rahaka.] A. s'agnat, s'agan', id.

Rā, or trā (tā), dd. tā, nrā, s., blood, mitā to bleed. [Er. de, TaSa. rai, Malo dai, Motu rara, Sa. toto (redup.), Ja. ra, My. darah, Mg. ra blood.] H., E. dam, S. dem, A. dam', blood ; damiya to bleed.

Ra, v. i., vociferate, in rasoso, ratioso. H. ru'a, Hi. vociferate.

Ra, verb. and nom. suf., 3 pl. : nara, they.

Ra, num., two : rua.

Ra tan ia, rara tan ia, trara tan ia, tara tan ia, v. t., to forget, lit. to think burying or covering it. See mitroa and tun ia.

Rabā na, s., side (of a river or valley). A. s'affat' id.

Rabaraba, v. i., to flap the wings. A. rafrafa, id.

Rabaraba kaf (or kai), v. i., to be bent with hunger or famine ; and

Rāba, s., hunger or famine, in li rāba goddess, or she demon of hunger (a "sacred stone "). H. ra'eb, E. rehaba, to hunger, H. ra'ab hunger, famine.

Rabag, see tabag,

Rafālu, d. lifāru, q.v.

Raf ēa, v. t., to weave a reed fence ; hence

Rafēna, s., a reed (woven) fence, d. rofe ; and

Rafeen, s., c. art., the act of weaving a reed fence. H. 'arab to weave, intertwine, A. 'araba a knot, H. 'arubah interwoven work, or network.

Raf ea, v. t., to go through (as through a hole in a fence, the eye of a needle); and, c. t. prep., Rafe aki, v. t., to make to go through. A. thakaba, n. a. thakb', to perforate, bore through, to go through (as through the eye of a needle).

Ratioso, v. i., to call out as when in terror or danger : ra v. i., and bioso.

Rafite na, s., wall or side of a house. E. arafete partition, wall.

Raga-ēlo, d., v. i., to warm or dry oneself in the sun (ēlo) : raga is transposed for gara, as baragai for bagarai.

Rāg, s., time, c. nom. suf. ragi na its time : d. rān, rāni na, dd. lag, nag. A. 'ān' time, c. art. al, l'.

Rago, s., c. art., thorns, prickles, a mass of thorny or prickly, or rough and spiky, or jagged matter (as twigs, &c.) ;

Ragoa, and ragorogoa, v. i., or a., to be full of rago, as a reef full of jagged, sharp rocks. H. sinnah a thorn, sĕninim thorns, prickles, from sanan, i.q. s'anan, to be sharp, to prick.

Rāgo, s., rollers on which a canoe or boat is hauled up. Der. uncertain. [Ma. rango, id., also a fly, Ef. lāngo.]

Rai, d. re, s., forehead, aspect, face. [To. lae, My. dai, Ja. rai, id.] E. rey sight, aspect ;

Rairai, d. tairai, v. i., to be in good countenance. See baka-rairai, and lo, leo.

Raite na, or reite na, d., s., mother. See ani na.

Raka, v. i., to be willing, and maraka ; also, redup.,

Rakaraka, id., and marakaraka, id. ; also,

Rakana, s., the willingness, readiness, tuga fat ia rakana sikeimau let us do it, the readiness or willingness for it one only, *i.e.*, with one mind or will. S. rĕgag to desire, to will, Ethpael id., rega desire, will.

Rakaf ia, and rakof ia, v. t., to cleave to, and

Rarako, d. tarako, as toa i rarako sits on, cleaves close to (her eggs). [My. lâkap to adhere.] S. nkaf, etnakaf, to cleave to, cg. E. lakaf.

Raka ia, v. t., to lift, raise up, and

Raka tia, id. A. rakiya, 2, raise up, make to go up.

Rakei a, v. t., to adorn, dress ; tumana rakei a adorn or dress himself ; and

Rakei, d. rakī, s., c. art., dress, adornment. E. sargawa to adorn, dress ; this sa- is not radical, and the original root begins with *rag*, or raq (Dillmann, E. Gr., §72).

Raki, double t. prep., ra and ki, raki na ; or

Raki nia, also d. raki te na [Fi. raka, Maiwo lagi, Mota rag.]

Raku sa, v. t., redup. raraku sa, and taraku sa, and d. taku tia, to remove anyone's things, as in a flitting ; i raraku he is doing so, or is removing to another district, or flitting. H. 'athak and Hi., to remove

away, take away, break up a camp.

Rakua, and, dd.,

Rakum, rakoma, s., a crab : art. ra. [Epi lakum, Fi. qumuqumu.] A. h'umh'um' a crab.

Rāles, a place in Hades, lit. dark pit, swamp, or depressed place: ra, and les.

Rāna, dem. and num., those two : ra, 2, and na dem.

Rāna, and redup. rarāna, v. i., or a., to branch out : rā, and a. ending na.

Rān, rāni na. See rāg, ragi na.

Ran, d., s., water : r' art., and an. [Fi. drano, Sa. lanu, My. danu, J. ranu, Mg. ranu.] A. 'a'n' fons, and art. al, l'.

Rarua, d. raru, s., a canoe, boat, or ship : r' art. [My. prahu, Ml. ndrav, Segaar rai, Ta. laou (laau), An. elcau, Er. lo.] A. markab. See borau, *supra*.

Rās, d. nras, dem. and num., these two : ra, 2, and s, dem.

Ras ia, v. t., d. tas ia, to shave (the beard or chin), shave (or strip) off (as fruit from a tree, shave or strip the tree). E. las'aya to shave.

Ras, or res, d. tas, redup. reres, or teres, v. i., to rustle, crash (as the foliage of plants, or waves of the sea, moved by the wind, or men in a tumult). H. ra'as' the primary notion lies in noise and crashing : used of the rustling of grain moved by the wind, ra'as' noise, tumult.

Rasoso, v. i., see rafioso ; rasoso

12

to vociferate, calling (for help):
ra, and soso.

Rat ia, v. t., d. tat ia, d. nrat, to
loose, untie. See mirati. [Sa.
tala, tatala, Tah., Ma., tara.]
H. nathar, Hi. hitīr, to loose.

Rau', and ndau', v. i., d., to go.
Ct , rawāh to go.

Rau, redup. rarau, v., to grope
for with the hand, seize, snatch
out or away. See birife, rifu.
[Ma. harau grope for with the
hand, Ha. lalau extend out as
the hand, Ma. rau catch, lay
hold of, gather, Ha. lau seize,
take out of a place, To. lau
nip, pinch]; and

Rau, s., leaves (for food to be
cooked, and for putting food
on, as on a plate, when cooked).
[Mg. ravina, My. dawun, Sa.,
Ma, lau, rau, Fi. drau]; and

Rau, s., as rau nasuma eaves of
a house, rau mita lashes of the
eyes, eye-lashes; a tribe, group,
bi rau in parties, rau a fruit
that grows in clusters. [Ma.
rau 100, Ha. lau 400]; and

Rau, in bakarau to divide, distribute ; and

Raua, rauraua, a., hairy, as a
rope, nakasu rauraua a tree
full of branches. [Mg. ravi-
ravy hanging over, suspended];
and

Rau, in bārau, i.e., ba to go, and
rau speak violently and re-
proachfully. [Sa. lau speak,
abuse indecently]; and

Lau, in launa, a community of
people living together. [Ha.
launa friendly, social; lau to
spread out, be broad, as a leaf.]
H. 'araf to pluck, to seize, to
pull ; A. "araf' leaves, "arafa
to pull out (as hairs), "arf'
mane of a horse, "urfat' part
of collected hair, braid of
hair, rafu herd or flock,
warafa to be extended, broad,
rafa' to sew (from the plucking
motion), to make peace, concord, warafa, 2, to part,
distribute, H. haraf, 3, to
carp at, scorn, A. rafraf'
sides of a rope, branches of
trees hanging down, skirt,
vallance. These words are
all cognates, the radical part
being raf, which has the sense
of "seizing and plucking."

Rēa, s., d. for rēko, bisa ki rea
ki nau speak as a pauper to
me : reko.

Rea ki, d. nre a, d. roa i, roi a,
to twist, wring, strain out
juice by wringing, rei a, rerei a, or terei a, d. roroi a, to
moisten the pudding (nakoau)
with lor (the rich oily juice
of grated cocoanut). A. rā‘a,
2, to moisten bread with fat,
rā‘‘a, 2, id., 1, to bend, turn,
3, wrestle, 5, roll itself (an
animal), 6, wrestle.

Rei, s., c. art. nerei, a band of
men ; a clump of trees. A.
rā‘a to grow, luxuriate, 2, be
congregated, rī‘at' a band, a
crowd.

Rei, d. rea, d. reko, q.v.

Rei, d. tei, v., rei natano burrow,
or cover itself with earth, as
the white ant (futei, furei)
does. A. damma, 2), to cover
its hole with earth, dimmat'
ant.

Rĕko (see rei, rea, farea), s., a

pauper, poor. II. rĕk empty, vain, impoverished, poor.

Reluko (or raluko). See taluko.

Rere, rerea, v. i., to break rushing upon the sand or shore (of waves), also tarere. Ch. rĕ'a' to break in pieces, H. ra'a', id. S. etra're', id.

Res, reres, teres. See ras.

Ri, trans. prep., ra in raki. See ni.

Ri, verb. pron., 3 pl., dd. ru (eru) eu.

Ria, verb. pron., 3 dual, d. ra.

Rī a. See tī a.

Rĭ, or rĕ, dem., eri, &c. : arai.

Riu sa, d. tuma ia, to point out. See tiu.

Riu sa, riuriu sa, also tiu, or tū sa, q.v.

Ribu, riribu, to sound (with a trumpet), ribu aki baigo sound a trumpet, taribu to sound trumpets alternately (of two men). See rubua.

Rifālu, d. lifāru, q.v.

Rifu, d. rife, d. lifu mita, s., eyelashes, and see birife or birifu to snatch, pluck away, plunder. [Cf. My. rambiya, rambu, rambut, Mg. rombo, rombotra, rombitra, rombaka, My. rampas, rabat.] See rau.

Rigi, ririgi, or tirigi, v. i., to make a tremulous groaning noise in suffering pain, birigirigi. A. ranna vociferate, utter the voice with weeping, make a noise, twang, tinkle.

Riki, a., small, kari-riki, uarik, batik ;

Riki, s., c. art. neriki, child, little one. [Ha. lii, Tah. rii, Ma. riki.] E. dawik to be small.

Riki, s., triki, nriki (d.), pud. mul. A. rika', id.

Rikit, v. i., to be small : kita.

Rikitelag, d. for koroatelagi : koro, atelagi.

Riri, in buariri (Hades), for tiro to sink.

Riri, v. i., to fly, d. for tiri.

Riri, s., a spark : tiri.

Riri-mita, s., tears : tuau, tuturu. [To. tulu he mata.]

Risu, v. i., to move, shift : rosa.

Ro, ad., again, d. mero.

Roa i, v. t., to turn. See rea ki, rĕ a, mero, ro, meraroa ; and

Roa-leo, and roaroa-leo, s., echo.

Roa, or roua (rowa), or troua, v. i., to fall, dd. ro, rŏuo, tŏuo, tibe (ndibe), täo, mitäo, mitefe. [An. erop, My. rubuh, mârubuh, râbah, mârâbah, ribah, mâribah.] H. rafah, S. rĕfo', etrafi, to cast down, to sink, or fall down.

Rŏ na, roro na, s., thought, mind, also trotroa na, and d. nro n ; and

Roro, or trotro, v., to think, rara (&c.) tan ia, d. totu ; and

Ro-mi a, roro-mi a, v. t., to think upon, delight in, love. See mitroa.

Rŏuo (rowo), i.q. rau', to go.

Ro, v. i., to fall, c. prep. ro bei a fall upon it.

Roba, s., affluence ; and

Roba-leba, s., great affluence, a rich man. A. raf" affluence.

Roba gi a. See toba gi a.

Roba, roroba, or toroba, d. nrob, v. i., or a., to be insane, senseless. A. râba, 2), to be insane, stupefied.

Robei a, d. oro-bei a, v. t., to snarl, snap, bark at or on : ro for oro, and t. prep. bei.

Rōfa, s., a red or purple dye or colour. A. sohba*t* a red or reddish colour.

Rofarofa, or tofarofa, v. mid., to cover oneself with cloth, clothe oneself, be clothed. H. 'ataf to cover, be covered, be clothed. S. 'taf, id.

Rofe, s., d. for rafēna.

Rogo, rog ia, v. t., d. togi (ndogi), d. nrog, also trog ia, to hear, obey, to feel, know (as grief or pleasure), rogo na*bon* to perceive or feel or smell the odour (of anything), rorogo, or torogo, v. i., to be still, s., a species of divination (in order to know what is to be done) by a certain movement in the muscles of the arms or legs, rogorogo ki to make heard, report, rogoan, rogorogoan, s., c. art., report, tāki rogo-saki bend or incline oneself hearing (a person), saki t. prep. ; bakarogo, q.v. ; marogo, or matrogo, or maurog, v. i., to be idle, amuse oneself, marogo ki to amuse oneself at the expense of (someone). [Sa. logo, My. dângâr, Mg. reny and rea.] A. 'adina to hear, to know, to feel the smell of, 2, cause to hear, make known, proclaim, H. 'azan, Hi. he'zin to hear, listen, to obey.

Rogo, trogo, in sera-trogo, s., anything : rogo is r, art., and A. hano a thing. [Santo sonu, TaSa. kinao, Ml. nanu, a thing.]

Roko, v. i., d. lako, d. nrok, to stoop.

Ror, s., oil, also same as lor, the oily or fatty expressed juice of grated cocoanut used to moisten or fatten puddings : ro ia, roro ia, rei a.

Roro na. See ro na.

Roro ia. See ro ia, rei a.

Roroa, v. i. See toroa.

Roro-fi a. See toro-fi a.

Rosa gi a, v. t., to drag, haul, make to move, shift, t. prep. gi ; and

Rosa, v. i., to move, shift, trosa, dd. nros, nrus, tosa, also rusa, risu ; and

Ros, s., c. art., a breaker or wave that sweeps up upon the sand of the shore. [Sa. toso, tosotoso, to drag.] A. ra'asa to move, shake, drag, 4, id., ra'asa, ra'as'a, to tremble.

Rot ia, or trot ia, v. i., to embrace clasping to the breast, to embrace or encircle. [Mg. trotro to embrace, to embosom.] A. sadara, 2, to girth (a camel), sadr', Nm. sadr, the breast (bosom), My. d·ad·a, Mg. tratra, An. riti, Fi. sere. Hence

Rot, s., anything going round another as a band or girdle (as an ulcer round one's leg, &c.) ; and

Rot ia, as ta rot ia, ta rotirot ia, or rutirut ia, cut a band or girdle round (as in barking a tree).

Ru, verb. pron., 3 pl., they : eru, d. ri. E. 'ellu those.

Rū sa. See riu sa, tū sa, tiu sa.

Rua, num., two. See also tua, ra (and sa, in uasa), d. nru.

[Sa. lua, My. dua, Ja. roro, Mg. roa.] H. s'ne, &c., Mahri tharo, Soc. tarawah, M.S. trai.

Rub, s., d. roba, d. nub, d. raba, s., q.v.

Ruba, s., additional wife taken by a man already married. [TaSa. narau a wife, Mg. rafy one of two or more wives of the same husband ; adversary, opponent ; rafitra joining together, contention, strife.] See rau. A. rafā' to join, sew together, make peace, 2, to utter a formula of blessing or prayer to a new spouse, rafa', 2, id. ("Mayest thou live with concord and with children").

Rubaki, s., a big flat nakoau. A. ra''if', round thin cake baked on the hearth.

Rubua, d. rufua, s., clamour ; noise, tumult (as of mourners in wailing). S. rhab make a noise, uproar, tumult, utter lamentations (Mark v. 38, 39), cg. H. ra'am, v., to make a noise, thunder, s., uproar, clamour, tumult.

Ruku, s., a hole, cf. rā ; edible clay found in holes, syn. tano rā ; a bribe secretly given, or given *underhand* to procure the death of one hated, nafaka-ruku hollow or hole under anything, as a cellar under a house, si ruku to go under (through the hole or hollow under) anything ; and

Rukua, d., s., a hole, pit, a hole or hollow with water in it, cf. rā. A. raka' to dig (the

ground) ; to revile (someone), rakiyyat a pit, rika' pud. mul.

Ruma na, s., c. art. nāruma na ; n art., and ruma, or aruma, and kuruma (in lita-kuruma, q.v., the breast, bosom.) [Sa., Ha., uma, Motu geme, id.] A. lla'zūm' the breast, bosom.

Ruma, dd. bara, oro, v. i., or a., to be barren. H. 'arab, E. 'abara.

Rūma, and tūma, s., a pool of water, d. transposed marou. A. 'arīm' a hole, trench, or hollow in which water is collected.

Ru-mi a, ruru-mi a, v. t., same as ro-mi a, also trutru-mi, tru-mi : mitroa. Hence

Rumien, s., c. art., and ruru-mien, thought about, love.

Rūrū, redup. of rū, riu sa. See tiu, tū sa.

Ruru, v. i., to tremble.

Ruru, s., c. art., an earthquake. [Tah. ruru, to tremble.] S. r'el to tremble.

Ruru, s., a cluster. [Tah. ruru to congregate.] See rei.

Rusa, see rosa; rusa gi, see rosa gi;

Rusarusa gi, redup., d. nrus, nrusa gi.

Rutirut ia. See rot ia.

Rūmo, d. rūma, pool.

S̬ā, interrogative, contr. of safa, sefa : s. dem., and a (fa).

Sā, or se, or s, dem., this, here. H. zeh, E. zĕ.

Sa, d. for ta, neg. ad., only in prohibitive clauses.

Sa, sĭ, s. num., one, in gis (or gisa), sam, mas, latesa, sikei, sikatika.

Sa, s' (and see si), verbal suf., 3 sing., with particle s, as in si, q.v., him, her, it, d. a, as ti ki niǎ sa say to him it, d. ti ki niǎ a, id. : sa is s, t. prep., and a, verb. suf., 3 sing.

Sa, s., d. ta, d. sëat, q.v.

Sa, caus. pref. See sarafi, sabera, sagalugalu, sagara, sigiri. [My. sa, Tah. ta.] II. sha, Arm. sa (Shaphel, Saphel).

Sa, v. i., or a., to be bad, evil, sasa, intensive. [Fut. sa, My. jahat, Fi. ca, Malo sat, Ta. ra, Mg. ratsy.] A. sā' to be bad, evil. Hence

San, s., c. art., the being evil ; also the being ill, sickness, misfortune, misery ; and

Sāsānǎ, v. i., or a., to be ill, have a disease : -na, a. ending, and sa redup.

Sābĕ, inter. ad., where ? sa, and be.

Sabe li a, v. t., to bind, tie, d. tami sia. H. samam, cg. A. zamma, &c., to bind.

Sabe li a, v. t., to beat, slap. [My. tampar, Ja. tampel, Fi. saba-laka.] A. safa'a to beat, slap.

Saberi-ki, v. t., to scatter, break asunder or to pieces, scattering, d. sabura ki.

Saberik, v. i., to be broken to pieces, fallen or parted asunder. [My. sibarkan, sâbar.] See bera, tabera. II. s'abar to break to pieces : Gesenius compares parar.

Sabo, v. i., or a., ignorant, to be ignorant, sasabo to be ignorant, to not know (his way), sabonaki, v. t., to be ignorant of or about, dd. sub nĕki, sbunĭ ; see also tasabo ; nàsàbo (for nata sabo) a stranger (not knowing the place), meta-sabo, id. A. safoha to be ignorant, 6, id.

Sāfa, sefa, or sofa, v. i., to pant, redup. sofasofa to hasten, to run ;

Sōfa, s., consumption, hard breathing. [Mg. sefosefo, sevosevo, sevoka, in haste, bustling, to hasten.] H. s'a'af to breathe hard, pant ; to hasten.

Safa, sefa, sefe, inter. pron., what ? c. art. insefa, nasafa, what ? Without the art. it is used adjectively as sefe nakasu what tree or wood? With the art. it is used substantively, as i tili nasafa what does he say? Safa, is sa, dem., and fa, inter. pron. what ? Compare nefe-te. H. mah, A. ma, Himyaritic ba, id.

Safana, c. art. nasafana, what that, what (is) there ; safa, and na, dem. : contr. sāna. [My. apa, mana, Sa. o le ā (ā as in Ef. sā), se ā, le fea, se fea, Fut. taha, tefe, tehe ; rufe (dual), takafe (trial), efa (plural), Ta. nufe, nufena, &c., Epi ava-kai, vai, Malo sava, savana, An. inhe, Santo nine, Mg. ino, inona.]

Safaki, pr. n. Ma safaki, name given to a man who had buried a relative ; a sea animal, so called from burying itself in the sand : afa ki.

Saf ia, or safi a, v. t., to pluck or gather fruit ; to scrape, safi-safi natano (with a hoe), safi-safi-raki scrape, pluck off the husk from (reeds), safi-nauot to excel ; the chief ; safisafi big, so bisab ; bisif excelling ; misafe to be separated (as fruit from a tree). See also sifa, sifī. [Fi. sivi-a, uasivi, excel.] H. 'asaf gather (as fruits), assemble, draw back, take, take away (as breath) ; radical meaning to scrape, yasaf to add, to increase, to surpass.

Saga, or sega, s., a crotch, fork (as made by two branches). [Fi. saga] ; and see nasaga ;

Saga-fi, v. t., to take hold of with a crotch or forked stick. [Fi. saga-va take hold of with with tongs.] See sega. A. s'akka, 2, 5, to be sundered, split (wood), s'ikkat half of a thing, part, distance.

Sāg, ad., d., there. [My. sana.] Sa, and g, dem.

Sagalugalu, d. syn. galugalua : sa-.

Sagarà sa, v. t., to rub, grate, ground on, as a canoe or ship on a reef. [Ha. ili.] Gar ia, and sa-.

Sago, s., a trumpet (conch). H. thaka‘, E. takwa to blow a trumpet.

Sai, v. i., to come forth, go forth into the open (as men), saisai to assemble, sai to shoot forth (of a plant), buka sai (of a blossom expanding into a

flower), sesai shoot forth (as a serpent), misai to be opened, cracked ;

Sai ki, v. t., make to go forth or out (as the tongue, hand, anything) ;

Sai a, v. t., to cleave, split, open it (as a secret, &c.), tili sai a tell it out, &c. ;

Saisai, v. i., assemble (come forth of many) ; also to be associated together, or have in common, ru saisai isa, saisai ki make to assemble ; so or soǎ a follower, companion, associate ; sī to blow (with the breath), to shoot (with a gun), sī to blow (the wind), d. sui, or sī a to rest, or spell (one), to help ; esei in the open, an open space ; bisai ki to put forth, to show ;

Sai, s., c. art. nesai, a scented, white-leaved plant. A. s'ā‘a (y) to become open, be divulged ; c. prep. bi to make open, divulge ; to leave undivided ; to follow, 2, to roast ; to blow (with the breath), 3, follow each other ; to aid, 4, make open, s'ai‘ associate, follower, s'aya‘ common (to many, see saisai), s'āi‘ common (to many), not distributed ; made open, open ; s'ī‘at a band, assembly, s'ayu‘ a fire-stick.

Saka-fē, s., first ripe fruits or yams. [Ha. oo mua.] See māso, and bea.

Sakau, s., a reef ; d. a branch. See kasau. [Fi. cakau, Sa. aau.]

Sakí, v. i., to ascend, go up,

bisaki a, v. c., to put up, to appoint (raise up) a chief; sakesake to be up, to sit upon, tasaki, id., sakei ki to shout a person's name, attributing something (to him). [Sa. a'i, Ha. ae, To. hake, Ma. eke, whakaeke.] H. nasak, Arm. nsak, imp., sak, id.

Saki, t. prep. sa, and ki. [Sa. sa'i, Fi. caka, My. skan.]

Sala, s. See sela.

Sali, v. i., to move lightly, easily, to dance, to float, drift; sali aki, v. t., to send afloat (a canoe, or anything), to send adrift, misal, misalsal, d. salsal, light (not heavy), moving easily, lightly. H. 'azal to go quickly (spin along), A. 'azala.

Sali a, v. t., to weave. [My. sâring,] H. 'azal, S. 'zal, A. "azala to spin, weave.

Sali a, v. t., to deceive; and re-dup.,

Salisali, to deceive. H. s'alah, Hi. to deceive.

Salube, d. saluke, v. i., to be ignorant, not to know. A. sarafa, 3), to be ignorant, not to know.

Sam, a., or ad., one alone, only: sa 1, and m for mau.

Samben, d., ad., there: sān (sāg), and bēn, v. i.

Sama ia, v. t., to rasp, scranch (sugar cane, in sucking its juice). [Ml. U. tsumwi, Ml. P. jimue, Malo samai]; hence

Sama na, s., dregs, shreds, as of sugar cane with the juice extracted, sawdust, &c.; hence

Samā, v. i., or a., dreggy, shreddy: -a ending. H. s'afah to scratch, scrape, scrape off, S. s'fa' to file, s'ofitha a filing, paring: H. Pual to become bald, bare, naked, exposed (as one's bones). See infra, sema, sesema.

Samit ia, also samat ia, d. sumat ia, v. t., to beat, chastise. [Fi. samu-ta, My. chamiti, chamati, a whip or scourge.] H. s'amas to thrust, to hasten (see infra, sumati), s'amat to smite, strike, A. s'amasa to impel, thrust, s'amisa to hasten, speak hastily, s'amat, Nm., to whip.

Samura, s., a thing or word of no consequence, that falls to pieces, as it were: for sabura, saberi-ki

Sān, ad., there, here, esān, also esanien. [My. sana.] Esanien is esan there or here, and ien it is. See anī, v. i.

Sante, s., d. sëate na, q.v.

Sao fi, v. t., to look upon, see, d. sā fi, sao kiana look about (in) his place or plantation. H. s'a'ah, and s'a'ah to look, to look about.

Sar ia, or sari a, v. t., to saw, also seri a to cut with a sawing motion, sāra a saw. [Malo sarosaro to saw, isaro a saw, Fut. scria to saw.] H. nas'ar, Arm. nsar to saw, A. nas'ara, was'ara', as'ara, E. was'ar, wasar, H. sur, to saw, rub, sweep, &c.

Sara gote fi, to saw asunder. See sera, seru, seri, sore, soro, sar ia.

Sarafi, used as ad.; bat sarafi a did it hastily, i.e., badly, confusedly, incompletely. See marafi, and cf. tere ti, sumati.

Saria, v. i., to look around ; saria kiana look about, or go about, (in) his plantation. [Fi. sarasara, v. i., to survey, sara-va, v. t.] II. s'ur (2) to look around or about, (1) to go about.

Saru, v. i., to hang down prostrated (as the broken branch of a tree, or a broken arm), misaru, id. A. sara'a to prostrate, sarī' prostrated.

Saru, v. i., to be loud, noisy, speak aloud, saru goro speak aloud or be noisy, drowning the voice (of someone) ; and redup.,

Saruru, v. i., to roar, resound (as the sea, or a waterfall.) [My. dâru, Ja. sâru, sru.] A. sarra, sarīr' to make a noise ; to sound, to cry out vehemently, make a great clamour.

Sās, esās, ad., here : sa, dem.

Sasāna. See sa.

Sati na, s., the shrivelled and worthless seed yam when the new yam has sucked all the substance out of it : sa.

Sau-fi, v. t., to scoop, or shave, the surface off water ; to cut or shave off the surface of wood, sau-baba, an adze, lit. plank shaver or cutter—see mataisau a master cutter, carpenter ; to strip off, peel off (as clothes) sau lua i. [Sa. mataisau, sâufono, Ma. hau, Tah., Ha., hauhau.] H. s'a'ab to draw water. The primary idea lies in *taking off*

the surface, eg. sahaf to sweep, scrape off, hasaf to strip off, A. sahafa to scrape, peel, or rub off, to shave.

Sau, v. i., to blow (wind) ;

Sau, s., c. art. insau, gentle breeze, cold air, as in the morning and evening, dew. [Ha., Ma., Tah., hau, Sa. sau.] II. nas'af to blow, nes'ef the evening twilight, when a colder gale blows; the morning twilight.

Sau, v., to desire, mesau na, v. t., desire, tumana sau ki nia to boast, speak well of himself, praise himself (lit. desires himself), sau roa i to mock such a one by pretending maliciously to join with him in such boasting, insau a gift, sautoga, id., a free gift, hence, as ad., for nothing ; sau uia [Fi. sau vinaka] liberal in giving, sau sa [Fi. sau ca] stingy, sau mitaki, d., syn. sau uia ; sau sera greedy (desiring everything). A. s'aha' to desire, 2, to say I will give what you desire, 3, to be like (someone), 4, to give to one what he desires, 5, 8, to desire (a thing).

Sautoga, s. See preceding word.

Sau-taki, v. t., to place upon, as food upon food already in the oven, or as a speech upon a speech by another previously spoken ;

Sau roa ki, or sau rouo ki, v. t., to place (their voices) with accuracy together, as giving a shout all together : sau, and rouo or roa ki to cast down, or make to fall. H. sum (sam) to put, to set, to place.

Sāua ia, v. t., to fix (as upon a shelf, in a fork of a tree, &c.) See soa ki (for saua ki) ;

Sāuā ia, v. t., to shoot with an arrow called saua ;

Sāua (sawa), s., a pronged arrow (which adheres tenaciously). A. nas'aba to stick, inhere, be fixed tenaciously, 2, make a thing be so, 4, id., nos's'ābat an arrow, Nm. nas'ab, 2, to shoot, squirt, *fie*, into.

Sĕ, or s, dem., this, here. See sa. Sĕ is the common form.

Sĕ, inter. ad., where? See sā, safa.

Sĕ a. See so ia.

Sea, sesea, or seasea (redup.), v., to forget, be forgetful, sesea gor ia forget him. See maga-seasea. A. saha to forget, be forgetful.

Seara, d., some, a few. S. z'ura small, pl. z'ure' a few (Gen. xxix. 20.)

Sĕatĕ, s., a firestick (by which the fire can be rekindled), dd. santĕ, tā, sa. See sai.

Sefa, sefe, or sīfi. See safa what? This inter. is sometimes used indefinitely in the sense of whatever, however, as a belake namanuka sifi naga I have received, or I carry, a wound however now (or here), fatu sefa a stone however, or what-soever. A. ma qualiscunque.

Sega, s., or saga, q.v., a crotch, fork.

Sega, s., a part; it takes the nominal suf., as segamu a part of you, segara a part of them

or some of them, any part of them, one or more of them. See saga.

Sei, d. fei, inter. pron., sing., who? pl. se mai, d. se mani, d. kihe (for kise) māga. [Sa. 'o ai, Tah. o vai. Ma. a wai (pl. a wai ma), To. ko hai, a hai, Er. me, Ta. ba (pl. niba min), Epi kei, d. sie, Malo isei, My. siapa, siyapa, sapa, mana, Mg. zovy, iza.] H. mi who? Note.—Sei is for sefei : se dem.

Sĕka, v. i., to sit ; sĕka ki to sit about, or on (someone, or thing, consult about it or him) ; biseka, v. r., to sit with some-one, or with each other. H. s'akan (A. sakana, H. sakan), s'aken to set oneself down, to lie down, to rest, to abide, dwell.

Sĕk ē a, skē a, v. t., to raise up, set upright : saki.

Sĕke-mau, v. i., to swear, sĕke, and mau true : a man who swore, as in denying a charge, often tore off his loin cloth, and imprecated all kinds of calamities upon himself if he were not speaking the truth. A. sahaga to peel, scratch, comb the hair, sahug' fre-quently and rapidly swearing.

Sekof ia, v. t., to catch rapidly with the hand (a thing thrown). A. zakafa to take rapidly, snatch, 8, to take with the hand, snatch quickly.

Sela ti, v. t., to bear, carry ; d. sola ti ; selasela (of many) ; sela bear (a child), bisela v. r., to bear, bring forth, nafiselan child-bearing, childbirth, d. bisol. [Fi. cola-ta.] E. sawar to bear, carry.

Sela gisa na, v. t., to call his name (so and so); selà ki, v. t., attribute to (one, something); sela go, as sela tera ki go after (one), sela butuaki go between two points, be of two minds;

Sela, s., road, path; landing-place of canoe; a portion of time (cf. mal place, time). [My. salekan to call, saleh proceed, saleh a road.] A. s'ala' to proceed, 4, to call.

Sel ia, v. t., to bind. [Fi. soli-a.] H. 'asar to bind, S. 'sar.

Sel sa, to be unable, selu bia be able, sele atai nabo na be able to know his mind, d. for sili atai nabo na, lit. to know (how) to enter his mind, i.e., to understand his secret views: sili.

Seloa, s., a flat wooden dish. [Mg. soliaka, flat, as a dish.] H. selaha, pl., pans, such as were flat and broad, not deep, A. zuluh' large pans, E. salil, platter.

Sema, sesema, v. i., to be bare, sticking out (as one's bones), or as the point of an auger or piercing instrument: sama ia.

Semasema, v. i., to rejoice. H. samah to rejoice.

Sema ni, v. t., to praise, glorify. S. s'abah, Pa., to praise, glorify,

Semanien, s., c. art., praise, glory, also act of praising.

Samasamana, or semasemana, v. i., or a., disgusting: -na, a. ending. A. zahuma, H. zaham,

to stink, become rancid, filthy, disgusting.

Semam, s., paternal aunt, ana semam his aunt: susu, mam.

Semen, or saman, s., the outrigger of a canoe, or, more accurately, the part of the outrigger, shaped exactly like a canoe, which floats in the water. [An. jmaig, i.e. jimaig, Ta. timen, TaSa. tsama, Fi. cama, cama kau a canoe whose outrigger is only a stick (kau), in distinction from a double canoe; To. hama the smaller canoe of a double canoe, My. sampan a small boat, Mg. sambo a ship.] A. safina', safin', H., S., sefina, ship, vessel.

NOTE.—The Tongan hama suggests that the semen or saman was originally not a mere log fashioned into the shape of a canoe, but a real canoe, and that the outrigger canoe of Oceania is a degenerate form of the "double canoe."

Semani, s., the rudder, or steering oar of a canoe, d. uosemān. [Paama seman, TaSa. lamani.] Se in semani is contr. for uose, q.v., oar, and mani is manu, a bird, a figure of which (a bird) was carved on the stern of the canoe where the steering oar is held firmly in steering: hence the rudder was called uose-man the oar of the bird.

Sera ia, v. t., to bind, fasten on, as the handle of a basket on a hook, serā ki, id., sera-goro-bau a hat, lit. fasten upon the head. H. s'arar to twist, be firm; S. s'rar to be firm, s'arar to make firm, stable, Aph. 'as'ar to firmly believe. Hence Sera loaman, seralesoko, believe true ;

Sera lobalo, sera teamole, believe worthless, despise ;

Sera tea sa, sera tea uia, believe bad, believe good ;

Sera masika, make firm desire ;

Sera sog, make firm sog, q.v. ;

Sera gor ia, make firm upon, or covering.

Sera ia, v. t., to sweep (as a house), tea sesera, a sweeper, broom ;

Sera, v. i., to run (water, stream, which *sweeps* its bed). See under sar ia, saw, rub, sweep, &c. Hence

Sera guru-maki, v. t., sweep gathering together ; and

Sera kuruk, v. mid., id. ; and

Sera taua ki, v. t., sweep into heaps ; and

Sera lo tua, v. t., sweep things giving (them) to (someone), used of men telling an evil doer of his misconduct and its consequences. Hence

Seralotu, v. mid., to repent ; and

Sera tua, v. t., to sweep (together things) giving (them) to (someone), as a peace offering ; and

Sera biri ki, syn. gura biri ki, to startle ; and

Sera makoto ki, id. See sar ia.

Sera gisa na, d. for sela gisa na ;

Sera usi, v. t., to call (pronounce) after (one, as in learning to read) : sela, and usi.

Sera lua, v. t., to remove (clothing, &c., from one ; also ceremonial uncleanness, sera lua namam), make to go out, or away. A. sāra, 2, remove, make to go ; sār', and sāir', the whole, every, part, some, any. Hence

Sera, any, some ; sera-rogo, sera malo, something, anything ; every, sera natamole every man ; the whole, all (with nom. suf.) sera ra, serasera ra, the whole, all, of them, every of them, sera bakauti era every of them all ; every (kind), sau-sera greedy, bā sera going every (where), a vagabond ; also, d., i nuf sera it is finished all [Fi. sara, ad.] ; bisera, biserasera of every kind (i bisera, i.e., i bi sera it is (in) every (kind, or sort).

Sera ia, v. t., to rend asunder, as the two branches of a forked stick ; misera rent asunder. A. sāra, 3), wrench asunder.

Sera, or sere ia, or serei a, v. t., to importune, entreat. A. nazara to ask importunately, to entreat pressingly.

Serab, v. i., to flow out (as of a vessel, run over). A. sariba to flow (of water), sarab' flowing out.

Sere ra, v. t., dwell among, near them, bisere to be among, near, bakasere a, and masere, q.v. A. 'aṣara, 3, to be near, 6, to be near to each other, 'isr' love, &c.

Seri, v., to be unable to do a thing (from old age and infirmity) ; seri nalo forsake, leave, abandon a thing, bakaseri a, to loose (a prohibition, or tabu). [Fi. sere-ka untie, unloose.] II. s'arah, Ch. sera, to loose, Pi. s'ereh to loose, to desert, leave.

Seri a, v. t., to speak of, decide, consult about ; make a sign, show. A. s'ára, 2, 3, &c., make a sign, show, consult.

Seri a, v. t., to strain ; sāri is strain with it, nakalu sāri straining cloth. S. slal (sal) to strain.

Seri a, v. t., to hollow out (as a canoe). H. sur to hollow out. See sar ia.

Seri, v., as seri taku-ra, to cover their back, seri namaseri, or namiseri, put on the miseri, q.v.

Seri a, seri goto. See sar ia.

Scritau, s., the cutter-up of a human body for the oven, Scritau, or Saritau, or Sāra, pr. n. of a demon who is lord over the entrance to Hades, and whose helpers are Maseasi, Faus, and Māki. See sar ia, and tau.

Sere, as nakasu i tuba sere nakalu the stick thrust tearing the cloth, masere torn : sar ia.

Sereserea, or scriseria, v. i., or a., to be hairy, hirsute ; a. ending a. A. s'a'ira to be hairy.

Sesere, d., rub, grate. Same as sesera.

Sera *mimi*, d., syn. sera bakauti ; and

Serume (sera 'me): sera, and me, or *mimi*, contr. of mau, mamau.

Scru ea, v. t., to rub, wash (clothes,

&c.), seseru, rub (as oil on the head). Same as sesere, sesera : sar ia.

Sēru, s., a comb. [Fi. seru, Sa. selu, My. sisir, syn. garu.] Sar ia.

Sès, d., to be small : sos.

Si, v. See su finished off.

Si a, v. t., scrape, cut (si nabora na scrape the checks with a shell removing the skin) ; sisi a, redup. A. salha', n. a. sahy', scrape off, with the notion of cutting. Nm. also to harrow (the ground).

Si, sisi, to blow (wind, breath) ; si a, v. t., to blow (a thing, as the fire), to shoot (with a gun) ; si-ruku : sai.

Si a, d. sui a, to help : sai.

Si, particle after verbs (t. prep.), as libi si ; sa in saki, as rogosaki. [Sa. si, Fi. ca, My. s, Mg. zi.] Assy. sa, prep., originally dem., Mahri sh', prep.

Siba ia, d. suba ia, v. t., to break (as a yam), redup. sisiba and sibasiba ia ; masiba, masibasiba to be broken, na masiba a fragment. [Fi. sove, kasove, Mg. somba, simba.] Ch. s'ibeb to break in pieces, s'iba a fragment.

Sibu na, s., feathers (short) on a bird's back. A. ziffu small feathers (of a bird).

Sieg, v.i., to hang on the waist cloth (of a woman) ; and

Sieg, s., c. art. nasieg, a woman's waist cloth. A. was's'aha, v., id., wus'ah', s., id.

Siel, a., red. [My. serah.] A. s'ahila to be of a dark reddish (&c.) colour.

Sifa, v. i., to depart, withdraw ; sifa ki, v. t., make to depart, toss, throw away, sifesife, redup. ; sifa, v. i., to assemble. See safi.

Sifanua, s., a cannon, lit. shoot the land : sī fanua.

Sifili, and sifili ki, d., transposed for sili fi, sili fiki.

Sifiri, s., parrot. A. safara to sibilate.

Sig, v., redup. sigsig, v., to be rebellious, disobedient; sigsigleo (leo thing, or voice) to be disobedient, to sin, sigsigleo ki to be disobedient to (one), nasigsigleoen disobedience, sin, bisig, v. r., to be disobedient to someone or to each other. [Mg. odina rebellious, miodina to rebel.] A. 'aṣa' to be rebellious, disobedient, 'isyan' rebellion, disobedience.

Sigir ia, v. t., or c., to strengthen : gara, and caus. pref. si. [Cf. syn. My. mangkras kan, My. mampahery.]

Sikara, v. i., or a., prickly, spiny, and of hair standing on end : ending -ra. A. s'āka, 2, to be spiny, hirsute, s'ākat' spiny.

Sik ē a, v. t., d. siko e, to avenge : soka ria.

Sik ē a, or sek e a, to raise: saki; hence

Sike-rau, d. sī-rau ki, or sīe-rau ki, to raise or lift up a leaf (rau), presenting cooked food to one to be eaten.

Sike, to be swearing, and

Sike-mau (see sĕke-mau), to swear true ; and

Sike, v. t., to comb (the hair) : sĕke-mau.

Sike ti, v. t., redup. sikisiki, to grasp with tongs, or with a forked stick ; hence

Esike, s., tongs, syn. uataki. H. ḥazak to hold fast, stick fast (A. ḥazaḳa), Hi. to take hold of, seize.

Sikitau, s., only child : sikai, sikei, totau.

Sikai, or sikei, num., one, d. sikitika (redup.) : tesa (in la-tesa, q.v., d. la-tcha), also in masiki, d. mihi, also in gisa, mas, sam ; and

Siki, with nom. suf. (translated in this case as nominative, as in H. and A.), as sikīna (his one) he alone, sikīra (their one) they alone, &c. In i sikīna uia (and similar expressions) the meaning is he alone is good, i.e., he is incomparably good ; and

Sikiskei, one (by) one ; sikiski gisa one by one together, and see bakasikei. H. 'aḥad, Mod. S. ḥda, &c.

NOTE.—The ki or kei in siki, sikei is non-radical, as ka in Mg. isaka, iraika. [Mg. isa, iray, also isaka, iraika, My. asa, sa, Sa. tasi.]

Siko e, v. t., to avenge, d. sik ē a : soka ria.

Siko sa, v. t., to gaze at ; siko mau isa to gaze continually (see mau) at, redup. sikosiko ; hence

Sīko, s., kingfisher, lit. gazer (because it sits gazing into the water for fish). H. sakah, Ch. seka', to look at, to contemplate.

Siko ti, or siku ti, v. t., to

adhere to (someone), continue
or dwell with. A. 'as'ika to
adhere to (someone).
Siki-naki, v. t., to abhor, loathe,
abominate, d. masuku-taki, or
musuku-taki. A. zahak, Nm.,
to take disgust for, loathe.
Sila ia, v. t., as ta sila ia chop,
peeling or shaving off, chop or
cut a thin shaving off; hence
Masilā na, s., a shaving, chip;
and masila, masilasila, to be
thin. [Mg. silaka and silatra
to peel, bark, skin, chip off.]
A. saḥala to peel, bark, shave,
or scale off, masḥul' small.
Sila, v., to crack, as thunder,
boro silai a, buru masila, id.,
silasila, redup., ta silasila, id.
[Sa. faitilitili, Ma. whatiri,
Ha. hekili.] A. salla, salsala,
to sound, to crack (thunder),
musalsil' braying (an ass).
Sila ia, v. t., to help, aid, support,
strengthen, tasila (dd. tasiga,
ahika) helper, supporter, sīl
wall plate (supporter of roof),
tua-sīl givers of support (to a
chief, as giving food or other
aid when he is making a feast,
&c.) A. 'azara, 2, to aid, help,
strengthen, support, make firm,
H. 'azar to help, aid. Hence
Sīl, s., wall plate (supporter) of a
house, help (tua sīl give aid or
help).
Sila ia, or sela ia, d. sol ia, silasila ia, v. t., to rub, as to rub
(oneself with oil, &c.) [Fi.
sola-ta rub, Sa. soloi wipe, Ma.
horoi wash, Ha. holoi wash,
wipe, brush, Mg. soroka
sweep.] Cg. sera, seru, &c. See
sar ia.

Sili ki, or sila ki, v. t., make
to shake (anything; if water,
to sprinkle), silisili ki, id., to
pour out, shake out, throw
away, throw down, ru sili ki
fisera they flee in different
directions (those overcome in
battle), lit. they throw (themselves, shake out, or scatter
themselves) in different (or
every, or all) directions. H.
zalal to shake, make tremble,
pour out, shake out, A. zalzala
to shake, make to tremble.
Sili, v. t., to enter, sila isa enter
it (a house), enter him, that is
enter under his protection;
sili fi a enter into him (as a
spirit or demon into a man);
sili-faki, or sili-fiki make to
enter into, also thrust or throw
into (anything into anything).
[Sa. sulu thrust into, take
refuge, sulu-fa'i, and sulu-ma'i,
My. julok thrust into, Mg.
joloka enter, Fi. curu, curu-
curu, curu-ma, curu-maka,
enter, push, or thrust into.]
A. daḥala, n. a. duḥ'ul', to
enter (a house); take refuge
with, 2, make to enter, 4,
make to enter, thrust, &c., in.
This word is used much with
t. prep. bi or fi, as in sili-fi, &c.,
and to denote among other
things the *entering into* a man
of a spirit or demon. See
alialia.
Simi-ki-leo, or sima-leo, d. suma-
ki-leo, s., echo, lit. sound of
the voice. A. zāmat vehement
sound, and leo.
Simbolo, s., d., a basket. Cf. A.
zibbil', zimbil', id.

Sina, or sinĕ, v. i., to shine, be clear, us i sinc the rain clears up, Fi. uca sa siga. [Fi. siga sun, day, My. siyang day, clear.] A. saha', E. sahawa, H. sahah, to shine, be clear ; sun, day, in derivatives.

Sīnu, sisīnu, v. i., to be hot, burn (of the grass on the hills, yearly), to be inflamed (of one's face) nako na i sīnu his face is inflamed (with passion); hence

Sīnu, s., c. art., the burning of the grass on the hills ; a place on which the grass has been burned : see also tunu, bitunu, d. bitsīn. [Sa. sunu.] A. sah'ana, n. a. suh'un', to be hot, sah'una and sah'ina to be hot, 2, to heat, suh'n' and suh'n' hot, H. s'ahan, S. s'hen, to be hot, inflamed (sore), heat oneself at the fire.

Siora, s., a pipe for drawing off water from one place and pouring it out at another ; said to be for sie rau (for sike rau, lit. lift up, distribute).

Sī-rau, or sīerau, contr. of sikerau.

Sīrak, a., used as s., for sītaki, i.e., si tāki blow, heeling over (a canoe), a squall or high wind : si to blow, and tāki to incline over.

Siri ki, v. t., to scatter, sprinkle, of seeds, water, siri kīa ki, i.e., siri ki uia ki scatter or sow well (seeds) ; and

Sirisir ia, v. t., to scatter (or sprinkle) on him (as water or blood spirting on one) ;

Siri, v. i., to sprout, shoot (of a plant) ; and

Siria, d., v. i. (-a, ending), to sprout, shoot ; and

Siri na, s., c. art., a shoot, sprout ; and used of men, offspring ; hence in proper names of children and men, siri (seed, offspring) as siri fakal, &c. H. zara' scatter, disperse, especially to scatter seed, sow, bear seed (of a plant), zere' seed, offspring, A. zara'a scatter seed, to produce plants.

Sisi a, si a, redup. ; hence

Sīs, s., a shell used for scraping.

Sīsī, v. i., redup. of sī to blow ; hence

Sīsī, s., a gun ; si fanua a cannon.

Sito, v. i., cacavit, A. s'ahata 8), cacavit.

Sïu, s., a pricker, or awl (a sharpened bone). [To. hui, needle or pin (of bone).] A. s'i'a' a prick, spike. See sui.

Siua (siwa), v. i., to hunt for fish, or shellfish (on the reef), siuē a (siua ia) v. t., hunt (fish, or shellfish, on the reef). A. sāfa (u) to examine or explore the ground by the smell, hence to hunt.

Siuer (siwer), dd. suuara, surata, v. i., to walk, proceed, go away, sisiuer, redup., walk about. [Sa. savali, savalivali, savaliga.] A. safara, 3, n. a. sifār', to make a journey, go away.

Siua, or sua, d. siuo (siwo), v. i., to descend. [Sa. ifo, To. hifo.] S. s'bab, s'ab, part. s'o'eb (Acts xi. 5) to be let down, to descend.

So e, d. sē a (for so ia), v. t., to call (one) ;

Soso, v. t., redup., to call, sos ia (for soso ia) call him : also in bioso, rasoso, rafioso. E. saw'a to call, H. s'ua', Pi.

Soa, s., c. art. asoa na, companion, follower, or neso (art. ne), especially of the opposite sex, hence tauso, q.v. : sai. [Fi. sa.]

Soi, d., v. t. See si a, to scrape. [Fi. so-ya, soi.] Hence

Soi, or soia, s., the hole scraped out for the yam to be planted in.

Soa ki, soüa ki. See sāua ki.

Soà ni, or soè ni, v. t., to mock. A. haza' to mock.

Soàr ia, or souar ia, v. t., to abrade, scrape, scratch, as rago i souari rarua the roller scrapes, scratches, or tears by scraping, or abrades (the bottom of) the canoe, souasouar ia, redup., and soàra, or souara, v. i, to split open (as a ripe seed, pod, or banana), i.e., to be abraded, or uncover or abrade itself. S. safar to shave, to abrade, H. safar (to scratch, polish), to write, A. safara to sweep, uncover the face (a woman), to shine (the dawn), H. s'afar (scratch, polish), be bright, beautiful, Ch. s'éfarpara, S. s'afra the dawn. See ante, asouara, or asoara the rainbow, i.e., the beautiful, or brilliant.

Soata, v. i., to slip.   A. dahas'a to slip, E. dĕhas'a.

Solbu, v. i., to spring up; also to spring up, arise (of the first

beginning of anything), and to begin, or be the first to do something.   See futum (bisobu, &c.)

Sobē na, s., c. art., the nape or back of the neck. E. zaban id., A. zabbunat neck.

Sofa, sofasofa, v. i., sōfa, s.   See sefa.

Sog ia, or sogi a, v. t., d. sug ia.

Sogo ni a, v. t., to press upon, compress (one, as by crowding upon him), to straiten, sogosogo ni, redup. ;

Sōg, or sōgĭ, s., what straitens, compulsion, force, constraint, &c., as i meri sogĭ au makes or uses constraint or force upon me (to compel me to do something), i tili sōg soko ia he declares force or compulsion upon him (to make him pay a fine, or to suffer death, as the case may be). [My. sâsak straitened, sâsakkan to straiten.] H. suk, Hi. (A. s'aka, 2), to straiten, compress, press, urge upon, force, compel, H. sōk distress.

Soga, s., c. art., d. nasok, dust, rubbish, a lot of things (belonging to one) ;

Sogasoga, id. ; hence

Soga-leba, s., a rich man, lit. big lot of things ; and, d.,

Sogoa, v. i., or a. (ending, 'a), rich ;

Sok, d. soga, s. ;

Soksok, d. sogasoga, s. ;

Sok-leb, d, soga-leba ; also

Sok, s., d., c. art., a cloud.   H. s'ahak dust, a cloud, A. sah'k' ; the verb signifies to rub, hence dust (from being rubbed small).

13

NOTE.—Sogoa lit. signifies full of dust, dusty, dust being taken in the sense which is given it in the vulgar English phrase "to come down with the dust."

Soka, v. i., to leap, jump, go swiftly; to be violently excited, inflamed with anger (of the belly); soka ia, v. t., to spear; inivit mulierem; soka-ba, v. i., to go swiftly away, hence, s., what goes swiftly away, a worthless or lost thing or person; soka-ba ki, v. t., throw away, make to be soka-ba; soka ki, v. t., make to soka, throw. A. zak'k'a, 4), leap, 2), inivit mulierem, 5), go with vehemence, 6), to be angry, burn with rage.

Sōk, s., c. art., what stops or blocks, as a dam : suk ia.

Soka ri, v. t., to join on to (one thing on to another), then to repay (one thing by another, the one thing being regarded as joining on to, or touching, the other), to avenge (one slain, by slaying another, also sĭkō a, d. sĭko e); soka-soka ri, redup. ;

Sokarien, s., c. art., a joining, as a splice; repayment, retribution, vengeance ;

Soka-taki, v. t., to join on to, to meet, tumara soka-taki ra meet together. H. nas'ak (A. nasaka), to join, 2), kiss (join mouth to mouth), join on to each other, meet (of two things), Hi. to join on to (one thing on to another).

Soko, v. i., or a., to be true,

true, as naleoua i sokō sa his voice (prediction) is true as to or about it (thing predicted, as is known when it takes place as foretold), le- or lo-soki, a true thing, truth, tili lesoko to speak truth, d. tili mori speak true, d. tili lo-amau speak truth. See also masoko. [Sa. sa'o straight, correct, right, My. sungguh true.] A. sadaka, n. a. sadk', to be true, H. sadak to be straight, right, just.

Soli a, v. t, rub. See sila ia, id.

Sōlĭ, sosolĭ, v. i., to creep (i.e., to rub or scrape along the ground, cf. karafi) ;

Asolat, s., a worm : a, art. [Sa. totolo, ps. tolofia, Fut. toro, Ha. kolo, TaSa. tari, Malo nsalansala, to creep, sulati a worm.] H. zahal to creep, crawl.

Sore, v. i., to lie, be untruthful, d. bisuru ;

Soresore, id. H. zur to turn aside, A. zāra tell lies.

Sor ia, or sori a, v. t., to give (a thing). [Fi. soli a give, My. sârah and srah to submit, sârah kan to give.] A. s'ara'a, 1, to submit, 4, to give.

Soro, v. i., to burn, flame, soro fi, v. t., send a flame on to, also to treat with violence, to rush violently and with savage rage upon (as a wild pig charging a man), bakasoro-soro fi, v. c., make the fire to burn up. [Mg. doro, sa, tolo, matoro.] A. sa'ara to kindle (a fire, war), 2, to rage (of a camel), 3, to treat with cruelty and rage, so'r' blaze of fire, rage, insanity, sa'ir' flame of fire, fire bursting into flame.

Soroa sa, v. t., to covet, desire;

Sōro, a. used as s., a covetous person, and see miseroa. A. s'arihu to covet.

Soroa, d., v. i., to be sick, syn. sasāna. A. s'arro fever, and a. ending, from s'arra to be bad, as sasāna from sa.

Soroa, s., c. art., d. tiroa.

Sore a, v. t., to saw (one, of the breakers sawing one on the reef); and

Soro aki, v. t., to make a man's body saw on the reef (of the waves or breakers): sar ia.

Sos, v. i., to shrink, become contracted, as cloth when wet, india rubber, &c., to be small (syn. mito), d. sēs small, little. A. 'azā', 4), to be contracted, made small, also 'aziya, 3), to be contracted, 2), to contract, 4, to diminish.

Su, sua, v. i., to rise up (tobu i tubu sua swells up) as ground in which the growing yams are swelling (cf. lua); another form of this word is tu to stand up;

Su raka ti, v. t. (to take up, lift up), to startle;

Sua i, v. t., to take up, lift up, then to take, receive, obtain, acquire, as i su naleo he obtained something; and to bear, as i su nafolofolou sa anena he bore his sin, i.e., he received its punishment; and to meet, as i sua nata he met a person, bisua, v. r.; su-naki to carry on the

head (of women), su-ni to put on (clothes), hence susu clothed (having clothes upon or carried or borne by one); to meet or take up the (odour of a thing) su rogi nabou. The notion of meeting is in that of lifting oneself or rising up against (one); and a swelling in the skin is said to sua, i.e., raise itself up, it rises up; su (nasuma), s., the upper part (ridge-pole) of a house, and masua, s., the highest part or top of anything. Su or sua is also used in proper names of children, as Sua ragoa, &c. H. nasa' to take up, lift up, E. nasa' take, receive, A. nas'a' be exalted, grow, to bear, carry, to bear one's sin, that is, to receive its punishment. H. si', sc'eth height, a raising or lifting up, a rising up in the skin, A. nas'a' to grow up, to be raised, high, 4, to produce, 10, perceive or feel the odour (of a thing), nasā' sprout or shoot (of a plant)—sua (in pr. names), young people.

Su, d. si, v., finished off, as i nu su, it is ended or completed, finished off, i bati su ē a he has finished off doing it; i bano su he has gone, he has finished off going, completed going. The word thus forms with any other verb a completed tense denoting that what is expressed by the first verb is finished off. See under maso to be done.

Su na, s., c. art., highest part (as ridge of a house, or top of the head), cf. masua na top (of anything) : su, or sua.

Sū na, s., c. art. nasū na, q.v., juice.

Sua, for suua (suwa), siua, siuo.

Sua, s., brother. See tai.

Suasua, v. i., to be willing ; and Sua ki, v. t., to impel, order, send. See bisuaki. A. s'ayaya, 1, to be willing, to will, 2, to impel.

Suara, or suuara (suwara), susuara, d. siuer, q.v.

Suāra, v. t., to meet (as a head wind, any obstruction in one's way) : sua, and ara, v. t.

Suer, v. i., d. suerai.

Suerai, v. i., to put out rai, i.e., tai, q.v., dung, cacavit : sui, see si, v.t., and tai.

Suer ia, v. t., to vituperate, d. sur. A. zara to vituperate.

Suba ia. See siba ia.

Sube, v. t., to place, determine, appoint, constitute, syn. tō-naki, as i sube biri a he appoints it over again (and differently), syn. tō-naki biri a, as to appoint a day of meeting, &c., and afterwards to alter the day, appointing another ; i sube roa au he appoints me, changing, changes or alters (roa to turn round, to alter) the appointment he made with me, as having first appointed me a certain day, he afterwards changes the appointment to another day ; hence

Sube, s., what is placed, fixed, redup. susube, as upright stones firmly planted in the ground, nafera susube a row of such stones, sube such a stone, a statue, an idol, or sacred stone; a thing fixed firmly, as a plank firmly nailed, a stone firmly fixed, a wind continuing firmly in one quarter, nalagi i be sube the wind is firmly fixed (in some quarter) ; also, custom, as a thing fixed, sube nafanua custom of the country, sube na its or his custom, also the fixed nature, custom, or disposition, sube nig Atua i lēg the nature, custom, or disposition, or fixed character of God is righteous ; sube i tō-naki nafanua the fixed, or constituted, or established— fixed, established, or constituted the country. In this last sense it is a general term used to denote either the first or early or ancient inhabitants of a place (the original settlers of a district), or, which is the same thing in another form, the persons who figure in Efatese myths, or the spirits of such, now being natemate. Sube is also used as a proper name of men, as Mariki Sube, or Ma Sube, Mr. Sube (the present Christian chief of the village of Moso, in Havannah Harbour), and of women, as Li Sube, Mrs. or Madam Sube. (See ma, and li.) [Ma. tupu firmly fixed, Sa. tupua a stone supposed to have been a man petrified, an image, Fi. tovo habit, nature, practice.] II. nasab, i. q. yasab to set, put, place, Hi. hissib to make to stand, place, erect, set up (as a column), fix, establish (as bounds), Ho. to be fixed, planted, yassib firm ; A. nasaba to place, fix, set up, declare, appoint, constitute ; nasb' a thing set up, a statue, what is worshipped besides God, i.e., an idol ; nasib erecting, setting up ; nasibat stones placed or fixed round a water-hole.

Subu. See sobu, v. i., and d., s., child, offspring.

Su-bua, v. t., to lift up, or ascend, bursting or breaking through (the ground, hence subua (natano) a demon or demons who do so), syn. subora ia, and sua-sai a : su or sua to rise, or lift up, and bua.

Sub-neki. See sabo-naki.

Sug ia, v. t., to kiss, d. sum ia.

Sug ia, v. t., to block up, d. suk ia.

Sui a, v. t., d. sī a, q.v., to help ; to blow upon ; also (see sai a) to make holes in (as a moth in cloth); also to burn with heat, as elo i sui a the sun burns him ; and redup., elo i tera suisui, the sun shines burning (hot); and

Sui, s., heat; sui ni elo heat of the sun. See sai.

Suk ia, v. t., d. sug i, to block up, obstruct. A. s'akka, 2), 3), block up, obstruct ;

Suk ia, v. t., to cause to stoop, suki lifa ia (a burden) makes him stoop, bending him ; to still, as suki namaritana still the commotion (of passion)

within him, suki namaieto stills the anger ; and

Suki, v. i., to be patient, firm, quiet, still, sink (subside). H. s'akak to stoop (A. s'akka), subside, be appeased, Hi. to still ;

Suki a, v. t., make fast, firm, seli suki a, bisa, tili (&c.) suki a tie firm, speak making it firm and sure, meri sukisuki a make firm, turi suki a nail firm. A. s'akka, 3), adhere, cohere firmly ;

Suki a, v. t., to stick, stab. A. s'akka, 7), transfix (with a spear).

Suka, v. i., to draw back, recede, sukasuk, redup. ; hence

Sukei, or sukai, s., c. art., the receding (of food), the annual time of scarcity of food, opp. to namasu. [Fi. suka, cf. cuqa.] H. nasag, sug, to draw back, retreat.

Suku ti. See siko ti.

Suku ti. See sike ti.

Sula, v. i., to rise up (as a rising ground) ;

Sūla, s., a rising ground. H. salal to lift up, cast up a bank.

Suli na, s., shoot (as of a banana), offspring (of man) ; hence

Sulia, v. i., to have shoots (as a banana). [Sa. suli a young banana, son of a chief.] H. neser a sprout, shoot; offspring.

Su-lua i, v. t., to bring up (a child) : su, or sua, and lua.

Sulu ĉa, v. t., to scorch with flame, illuminate with a torch (ne sulu), and see masula ki ; hence

Sulu, s., c. art. nasulu, a torch.

[Sa. sulu, v. and s., Ja. suluh.] A. s'a'ala, 1, 2, 4, to kindle (a fire), 8, be kindled, 10, light or kindle (a torch), s'u'ulu flame of fire, mas''al' a torch.

Suma, s., c. art. nasuma, house, d. uma, see also katema, imrum : the s' in suma is a dem. or art. [My. rumah, Ja. umah, Ml. im, TaSa. ima, Motu ruma.] A. h'a'mat, pl. h'im' &c., house.

Sum ia, v. t., to kiss, dd. sug i, sog ia. [An. aijumnyi, to kiss, Sa. sogi rub noses, salute, sogisogi to smell, My. chyum to smell, to kiss.] A. s'amma to smell. There is no trace of this meaning in sum ia. In E. sa'ama is to kiss.

Sum ia, v. t., to suck, as fat. My. isap, An. admoi to kiss, lick, suck, as fat. A. sahab, Nm., suck in (liquid or air).

Sume li, v. t., to make a sucking noise to (to attract one's attention). See preceding word.

Sumi li, v. t., d. sumo li, to shut, close (as a door), to patch up, repair (as a hole in a mat) ; hence

Sumili, s., a thing like india-rubber in a clam shell which, when touched, causes the shell to close ; an ornament (shell) which stops up a hole pierced in the septum of the nose. A. samma, 4), to stop (as a bottle), 6), to patch up, repair (a thing).

Sumat ia, v. t., to beat, d. samit ia ; d. sumanr i to beat, also used as an ad., hastily, confusedly, ineffectively, as lo sumanr i, brig sumanr i, &c.,

see, do hastily, confusedly, ineffectively (cf. sarati, tere ti). See samit ia.

Sur, v. i., to go (of a departed spirit going to Hades), to writhe and twist with pain. H. sir to go in a circle (cg. s'ur to go, journey), sir hinge, writhing pain.

Sur i, v. t., d. suer ia, q.v.

Sura ia, v. t., to root up, extirpate (as the things growing in one's plantation). E. sarawa to root up, extirpate.

Surata, sursurata, v. i., d. for suara, to walk, go on a journey.

Suru ki, v. t., make to suru, i.e., to be covered, as by inserting an arrow head into the (reed) shaft ; and

Suru faki, v. t., make to be covered, as by thrusting a thing into the dust or earth ; and

Suru goi a, v. t., to cover drain out (as the milk of a cocoanut) by covering the aperture of the nut with the mouth and draining out the contents. For goi see go ia. Tasuru ki to conceal, suruoli, dd. suruili, suruauli (see uli, auli), to take the place, or assume the form of, hiddenly or stealthily, and, s., a demon, or demons, who do this to destroy men. [My. suruk to conceal, Mg. sarona to cover.] E. sawara to cover, tasawara to be hidden, secret, to hide.

Su-rua, s., upper of the two ridge-poles of a house : su na, and rua two.

Suru ēa, v. t., to allure, tempt (deceiving), lit. to deceive ;

Surusuru ēa, id., redup. See sore, bisuru.

Suruk, *i.e.*, su-ruk, also si-ruk, and sai-ruk (see sai, and ruku) to go into the ruku (of anything).

Surut ia, v. t., to scarify, make fissures on the surface of anything. A. s'arata to scarify.

Susu, s., the breast or breasts; a calabash (round like a breast): susu na, d., his mother, lit. his breast, or mamma ; hence

Susu, v., to suck the breast. [Sa. susu the breast, to suck the breast, Fi. sucu the breasts, to suck the breast, My. susu, Mg. nono, the breasts.] H. s'od, A. thidy', pl. thudiyy', breast, breasts.

T
a, passive or reflexive passive prefix to many verbs. [Fi., Sa., My., Ja., Mg., id.] A., E., ta, reflexive or reflexive passive prefix to verbs.

Ta, nom. and verb. suf., 3 pl. (very common), for ra.

Ta, s., for ata man, person.

Ta, neg. ad., not, dd. ti, tu, and see sa. [Sa. le, My. ta, Mg. tsy.] H. lo, le, li, Ch. la, A. la.

Ta ia, v. t., to chop, cut, also to speak or utter (as it were making a chopping noise), redup. tata. [Fi. ta-ya, My. tatah, Sa. ta, Mg. tatana.] A. haḍḍa to cut quickly ; utter speech quickly.

T', conj., that (because), ta that I, te that he, tĕ ku that you : tĕ.

Ta, ad., now, dd. syn. uo, ko, i, as i ta toko, i uo toko, i ko toko, he yet (now) remains : ta, dem.

Ta, verb. pron., 1 dual incl. [An. intau, Sa. ta, for taua.] The ta of nigita, or ninita, and -a, for rua two.

Ta, tra, or ra, d. nra, q.v., blood. Originally tā, as in mitā to bleed.

Ta, s., d. sa, d. sĕätĕ, q.v.

Tā na, s., friend, companion. [Cf. Fi. tau, to, Ma. ta.] A. sāhi, contraction of sahib', friend, companion, ya sahi (cf. Ma. e ta !) O friend, comrade! sahaba to be a friend or companion, to take with one as a companion, 3, to accompany (someone), 8, to be companions to each other. Hence bitā, and bitā-naki, q.v.

Ta-atuta, v. and s. : ta cut, speak, utter, and atuta, s., a fixed or appointed time ; ta-atuta ki appoint a time and place (of meeting) to (someone). H. 'adad, A. 'adda, to number, especially days, time, hence S. 'ad'da, same as H. mo'ad, a set time, appointed time, eg. H. ya'ad, A. wa'ada, 3, to appoint a time and place (of meeting).

Ta-bau, s., syn. tagoto-bau, a cap, or hat, lit. cut-head.

Ta, v., to bend, bow, incline, extend, as ta bau bend the head, bow, ta tuba strike, turning aside, deflecting (a spear, &c.), ta gor ia extend

TAB]   184   [TABE

over it (of time, so many days), ta gor ia extend over (or cover) it (the day in the past named). H. natah, fut. yitteh, to extend, to incline, to bow, to turn.

Tab, d. tiba, neg. ad., not : ta not, and ba for ma as in Assy. aama not, i.e., H. mah, A. ma, used indefinitely.

Taba na, d. tauba na, s., side, or shore (as a side). [Ma. tapa.] A. taff' side, shore.

Taba ia, d. tama ia.

Taba, v. t., to be like, tabale to be like that thing (taba le), so, also tabalai, tabalān, tabalas, tabalo uai (taba, lo or l' (thing), and uai, n, s, i, dem.) to be like that or this thing, tabalo uanaga, id. ; also tabale sā? tabale safa? to be like what thing? to be how? [My. dama-kiyan so, Mg. mitovy.] H. damah to be like.

Tāba, s., property given away in payment of a fine for misconduct : tā to cut, and ba (away) as in soka-ba.

Taba, v. i., to turn, bend, taba lo sua, or lo saki, bend looking down, or up, taba kai bend contracting the stomach (as to avoid a spear), bitelo tababa to be bent with hunger, also tama, as tamā-lu, d. tumalu, to bend rising (in setting forth or out), taba soka to bend, leaping (as in climbing a tree), d. tama or tuma soka, also, to leap aside.   A. dafa', 6, to turn hither and thither, dafa' bending, 'adfa' bent, curved (of men).

Tabaraba, for rabaraba.

Tabag, v. t., to slap.   [My. tapuk, Ja. tabuk).   A. safaka to slap.

Tabalaga, v. r. (see balaga ti), to raise itself off, as a scab, &c. Reflexive causative.

Tabalās', or tabalāsoa, v. i., tabale, and aso to burn, to peel itself off after a burn (of the skin) : tabal' is the reflexive of bale si, or bala si ; and

Tabales, v. i., reflexive of bale si, to peel itself off, as the skin of one's lips ; and

Tabales, s., husk (as of cocoanut, chestnut), finger nails.

Tabara, v. i., to be burned.

Tabara ki, v. t., to burn : bara.

Tabare, tabarebare, v. i., reflexive of bora ia, to be split, split open, to be open.

Tabàre, s., a male animal. Compare E. tabā't mas, a male.

Tabaro, tabarobaro, v. i., to be heedless, careless, disobedient : reflexive of baro ; and

Tabaro, d., s., senselessness, sin.

Tabasuli, v. i., to be detached, broken off : reflexive of basu li.

Tabau sa, v. t., to cover, to be over (surpass, be above another) : bau.

Tabelu, v. i., reflexive of belu, q.v.

Tab ea, v. t., to take ; and

Tabe, s., c. art. natabe, a freshet, lit. that which takes, or carries. [Fi. tabe-a, Mg. taba.] S. nsab to take.

Tabe, v., to lean or incline, tabe to osa lean abiding on it, tabe ki lean upon, trust in (a thing) ;

Tabitab, s., a thing leaned upon, or trusted in. [Fi. ravi, My. arapi.] A. s'afa, 4, to make to lean or incline (a thing towards a thing), 1, be the guest of someone.

Tabei a, v. t., to desire or purpose setting the mind on. A. bayya, 5, id.

Tabeti, v. i., to adorn oneself. Ch. sabet to adorn, Ethpa. adorn oneself.

Tabera ki, v. t., to make to be tabera scattered, taberafera, or taferafera, to be scattered, taberafera ki make to be so : bera, berafera.

Tabes, s., axe: ta to cut, and bes.

Tabisa, v. i., to speak ;

Tatisafisa, v. i., to pray : bisa.

Tabilakigon, d. tabilagon, v. i., to stumble, d. tabila kon, id. lit. to strike, or knock (the foot) by mistake (hastily) fast (that is, the foot caught fast) : ta, bila, or bile, gon, or kon.

Tabora ia, v. t., to cut, splitting (a thing) ;

Taborai na, s., c. art., the body where it forks off or is divided into the two legs : ta, bora ia.

Tabos, v. i., compressed, narrow : bosa.

Tabu, s., naked people, people of other islands of the New Hebrides, so called by the Efatese : ta men, and bua i.

Tabu, tab, v. i., or a., to be forbidden, prohibited ; to be sacred ;

Tabua, s., c. art., sacredness ; and

Tabuen, s., id. A. dabba, n. a. dabbu, to prohibit.

Tabua, v. i., to be split open, cracked, also mafua : bua.

Tafa, s., c. art. natafa, a hill, lit. that which goes up or is high ; and

Tafa (d.), ad., high, above. [Fi. cabe.] T. dayaba to go up. E. diba above.

Tafagka, tafakaka. See baku.

Tafakarua ki, i.e., ta utter, and bakarua ; to repeat a thing, as a slanderer's words to the person slandered.

Tafar. See taiar.

Tafasi, v. See fasu, eyebrows.

Tafe, s., c. art., d. tabe, freshet.

Tati na, s., and c. art. a, atati, follower, successor of a chief (next in rank), that is, his present helper and right hand man, and who is his recognized successor. A. tabi' follower, helper.

Tafea, d. for tofe, q.v.

Tafera, s., c. art., breaker, breakers ; and

Taferafera, v. i., to break, as waves, Ch. tebar, H. s'abar, to break, mis'bar breakers. See bera.

Tati a, v. t., to be near. A. taffa to be near.

Tafifi, v. i., to be involved, entwisted : fifi, fisi.

Tafiloga. See bulo ki, and bologa.

Tafilo, tafolo, taifolo, and

Tafulus. See bulo ki, bulu si.

Tafirofiro, to be twisted (crooked) : biri a.

Taga, s., basket, d. toga, q.v.; d. stomach. [Sa. taga, taga 'ai.]

Tagāl, s., a hook for hanging things on : tageli.

Tagaragara, v. i., or a., strong : gara, garagara.

Tagaru, v. t., to grasp : kar ia.

Tagau, s., a hook, so called from seizing ;

Tagau, tagaugau, v., to grasp, seize ;

Tagau lua, select, lit. grasp or seize, lifting up or out : gau, kau.

Tagatag, s., a mist, or mass of clouds : tagotago.

Tageli, tageligeli. See takel.

Tagi, v. i., to wail, cry, ring, sing, clank, hum, &c. (as a drum, &c.) ; tagi si, v. t., to bewail, tagitagi, redup., natagien wailing, sounding (in various ways). [Sa. tagi, My. tangis, Mg. tany, a cry, tomany, mitomany to cry.] A. tanna to tinkle, &c., Nm. to clank, ring, hum, tanien din, tantun to tinkle, jingle.

Tagia, v., d. tine (ndine), to hoist the sail on a canoe, tagi aki rarua. See under miten and tago.

Note.—The idea is that of making the sail mount on the canoe as a horseman mounts a horse, or a burden mounts, or is placed upon, the back.

Tagiegi, v. i., to be slow, dilatory. A. 'āka, 5, to be averse, to delay.

Tagotago, v., to be placed one thing above or upon another, as the stories of a house, banks of clouds (see tagatag), generations of men ; and

Tago na, s., such a thing, or things, as the story of a house, a generation of men, leaves of a book (which lie one upon the other). See under miten (and cf. tiena, tagi aki, mitaga).

Tāgo fi, v. t., to beg, ask (a person for a thing), tatago sa beg, ask for (a thing) ; bitago, v. r., to be asking, begging, earnestly (from others). [Mg. hataka.] E. tayaka (so Amh., T., Luke ix. 45) to ask, tatayaka to ask earnestly.

Tagōto, s., tomahawk, axe : ta, goto ; and

Tagote fi, v. t., to cut with an axe.

Tagura, s., a heap (of stones) : guru, kuru.

Tai or tae a, v. t., d. for ata ia, or atai a, to know. II. yada' to know.

Tai, s., excrement, filth. [Sa. tae, My. tai, Mg. tay.] H. seah excrement, filth, from yasa' to go out.

Tai na, s., d. ke sua, brother's brother, or sister's sister. [Fi. taci, Malo tasi, Ml. tesi, Bauro asi, Epi tahi, Motu tadi, My. ad·ik, Bu. anri, Mg. zandry.] A. sinw', or sunw', brother, and art. ta.

Taiār, a., d. tafar ; fatu taiar, or tafar, crumbling stone : bera, taferafera.

Taifolo, d. tafolo.

Tairai, d. rairai.

Taka, a., such as, like, such like : S. da'k, id. ('a'k, and d') talis ;

Takani (takan uan, takana uai, &c., putting any dem. after it) like this, that, &c. ; so, in this way, in that way, thus, &c. ; also, interrogatively, how ? S. da'k hana (for da'k see preceding word), such as this, like this. This S. word is composed of d' (dem. or relative pron.), a', or ai (inter.), k', as, like (ad.), and hana, or 'na this ; without the d', S. 'akana how ?

Taka ni, v. t., to thrust on, or into (a thing), to thrust (a thing), taka sila ki thrust making to shake or fall. H. dahah, A. daha, &c., to thrust.

Takal ia, or tikal ia, d., v. t., to carry ; hence

Tak'amo, or takaamo, to carry on a stick across the shoulder: takal and amo. S. s'kal to carry.

Takāra, s., the crowd, lit. men (ta) gathered together (kāra) : ta, kuru, guru.

Takara, s., c. art. natakara, that which seizes, or grasps, or lays hold (of one), as the consequence of some act, &c. See kar ia, tagaru.

Takāri, v. i., to hasten, go swiftly, sail swiftly (as a canoe): kāri.

Takel, takelkel, v. i., or a., to be crooked, then unrighteous, d. tagelī, tagelīgelī. H. 'akal, 'akalkal, A. 'akila, 5, &c., id.

Takes, d. for nakes, or nakisa : kisa.

Tak ia, or taki a, v. t., to fasten (as thatch on a roof, a rope on a log, anything on anything), and see mitakitaki : to fasten the tongs on an oven stone (to lift it), bitaki a, uataki, otaki ; and matuki trusted in, confident, brave ; and taki, s., a mass of anything, as of yams growing together, as it were firmly bound together. A. wathiha to trust in, be firm, steadfast, confident, resolute, +, to fasten, to bind.

Taki, s. See under preceding word.

Tā-ki, v. t., to incline, to pour out (anything by inclining a vessel); taki to incline (oneself), taki mita incline watch, taki torogo-saki incline, hearken to, lo tāki look inclined, look round or back, mitaki to be inclined, lean over (as if ready to fall) ; see si-rāk, i.e., si-taki a squall, lit. blow, incline (a canoe, or cause it to heel over on its side). H. sa'ah (A. sa"a') to incline (as a vessel which is to be emptied) ; to be inclined, bent, stoop.

Taku, v. i., to be after, behind, d. nruk ; or itaku, inruk ;

Taku na, s., the back ; etaku or itaku at the back, behind (d. inruk), also outside (the village), also the (time) behind, or after (as opposite to the time before, the past), as te naliati etaku some day after, as he died, sela itaku ru afa ki nia some time after they buried him, generally tau itaku, naliati itaku, the years, or days after (i.e., hereafter), naliati itaku man the last day, day of judgment. [Sa. tua, Malo tura, Epi taka, Motu dolu, the back.] A. t'ahr' the back, E. dahr posterior part, dahari the last, dehara after, behind, dahara to be after, behind.

Takutaku, v. i., to speak in an unknown or foreign tongue. A. thakthaka to speak with foolish or senseless words.

Taku, s., brothers-in-law, sisters-in-law, syn. tauïeu. A. 'ah'a, 5, to treat or act as a brother, 6, to be brothers and friends to each other. E. ta'ha aguatio, or cognatio, also aguati who are as brothers to each other.

Takuer, or takuwer, s., a big man, a strong man : ta man, and kuwer. A. kabura to be great, of big body.

Takus ia, or takusi a, v. t., to be like, similar to, also, with k elided tausi a, id., and to follow, also rausi a (t to r), v. t., to follow, from usi a, v. t., to follow, and also (in rafe-kusi a) kusi a, id. See usi a, and bausi a. A. kassa to follow ; to narrate, and 5, 8, to follow ; 1, to be near, 10, to ask.

Taku ti, d. raku sa, q.v.

Talakolako, v. i., to whisper, i.e., to conceal what is being said (from someone) : ta utter speech, and lakolako.

Talekabu na, d. arekabu, q.v.

Tale is, v. t., d. tele is, to search for. [Mg. tady.] A. dāra, 2, Nm., to rummage (vulgar), lit. to turn over (things, in search of something) ;

Tale, s., c. art., a belt, also a rope, string ; and

Tale ki, v. t., to make to go round (as a yam vine round a

stake), tale is to coil round something (as a snake), tale ki māro (see roa) to whirl round (as the eyes in dizziness), tale ki to twist round one (crooked dealing, to injure), tālo round, around, taltāl round. [Mg. tady, mitady, to twist, tady a rope, My. tali a rope, string, bandage, &c.] A. dāra to go round, whirl, turn ; be dizzy, 2, make round, 4, turn round, da'ro orb, around, dairo round ; circuit, &c.

Tale, s., c. art., the taro (so called because round.) [Sa. talo, My. talâs, id.] See preceding word.

Taleàba, and taltaleàba, v. i., to whirl round (as a wheel), taleaba ki, v. t., to make to whirl round, to turn round (as a grindstone) : tale and àba.

Talebaga, s., d. syn. kalebaga, bow-string : tale, and baga, s. (the tree from which the string is made).

Talefa, s., a side region, circuit : tale, and fa (ba) to go.

Talefan, s., the circuit of the horizon : tale, and fan to go.

Tale-firi, a., all round (as round an island, &c.) : tale, and firi or biri.

Talle, or tal'le, v. i., to turn aside (as from a path) ; and

Talele, id., talele ki to turn aside or away from (a person or thing.) See lele.

Taleuor, s., a side, circuit : tale, and uor, or uora. See bora ia.

Talemāt, s., plantation, enclosed

and cultivated field. Cf. H. s′ŏdemôth and s′ŏremôth id.

Taliāli, v. i., to be slow, delay : aliāli. [Cf. Sa. tali, tatali.]

Talibo (see libo), to hide, be hid, hide oneself.

Tali-si, v. t., to prize up, wrench up (as the side of a flat stone). See tila ia, or til ĕa.

Tàlĭga na, s., c. art. nataliga na, d. liga na, and nàlĭga na, the ear or ears : ta, art. [Ml. P. ririga, Epi dd. tiline, seligo, An. tikga, Motu taia, Sa. taliga, Fut. tariga, My. talinga, Mg. tadiny.] II. 'ozen, du., used also as pl., 'azĕnaim, 'azĕne, S. 'adna, Ch. 'uden, 'udĕna, A. 'udn', pl. 'adān', and 'udun'. For the verb, see rogo.

Tālo, taloālo. See alo-fi.

Tālo, a., round, and ad., round about : talc.

Talokuloku ki. See taluko.

Taltal, a., round : tale.

Taltalūraĭ, s., a sea snake covered with round strips or bands.

Tàlu, or talŭlu, s , a crowd, herd : lulu.

Taluko, or taluku, and taluko-luko ki, v., to conceal oneself from ; atu taluko baki nia turn away from, or conceal oneself from : lako.

Talubaki, v. i., to be spilt, poured out, to pour itself out : lubaki.

Talug ia, d., and

Talum ia, d. See tulum ia.

Tam ia, v. t., to add to, dd. tàm ia, tàum ia. A. s′amma to add.

Tama ia, d. taba ia, v. t., to cover (as fruit, &c., covering the ground, being abundant),

and see atama that which rubs, syn. orc. A. tamma to cover with abundance (Nm. smother, overwhelm), 2), to scrape or shave.

Tama na. See tema na.

Tamaliām', v. i., to delay. A. mahala, 5, to delay, and H. mahah to delay, linger (prop. to refuse, turn back).

Tamàlu, v. i., to bend, rise (to set out), to go or come forth, set out : taba, lu.

Tamate, v. i., to fall calm, be calm (as the sea, the wind), hence

Tamate, s., c. art., peace (opposite to war), a calm, silence ; also, the festivals in honour and worship of the dead, at which the people of different villages assembled : mate.

Tāmisal, or tāmusal, s., an unmarried person : ta a person, and misal.

Tamaras, reflexive of maras, q.v.

Tami sa, d. sabe li, q.v., to tie.

Tamo, v. i., d. nabo, to smell. see nabo.

Tamon, s., smell, d. nabon.

Tamole, s., man : ta man, and mole to live, living. [Fi. tamata, Sa. tangata, My. orang-idup, Mg. olombelona, id.]

Tamtam, a., dusky ; ragi tamtam (syn. rag melu), evening, lit. time dusky, or of dusk. A. ′atama to be evening, dusky, ′atamat dusk of evening.

Tamulu, v i., syn. c. mulu, q.v.

Tanekabu, s., d. arekabu.

Tan ia, v. t., to earth it, to cover with earth, then with anything (tun ia) ;

Tanu mi, v. t., to cover with earth, put into the ground; and

Tanu maki, id. ; hence

Tano, s., d. tan, earth of any kind, soil, clay, ground, and etan, ad. and prep., on the ground, below. (Sa. tanu, ps. tanua, and tanumia, My. tanâm, tanamkan, tanuman, Sa. tanuma'i, tanuga, tanu-maga.] A. tāna to cover with clay; to cover, tino, dialect tāno, earth, clay.

Tanoabu, d. tanoafu, d. tanoau. s., ashes, lit. earth or dust of the fire : tano, kabu ;

Tanonōn, or tanoonōn, s., level ground, d. tĕn : tano, and onĕ reduplicated.

Tanotanoa, a., soiled with earth : tano, and ending a.

Tanu ea, tanua, v. t., to spit, dd. tani, taniu ; and

Tanua, d. taniu, s., c. art., spittle. [Sa. anu, ps. anusia, Motu kanudi, ps. kanudia, Fi. kanusi.] A. 'antha'a to vomit (tha''a, 7, to come out and be ejected from the mouth).

Tao, v. i., to fall, d. for roa (rouo, tŏuo).

Tao s, d., v. t., to lay down, leave, permit, &c. A. wada'a not used in perfect, fut. yada'o imp. da', to lay down, leave, permit.

Taosi, d. tausi a. See takusi a.

Taos, v. i., d. maosa, q.v.

Taoti na, s., bone, bones, weapons made of dead men's bones. [My. tulang, Mg. taolana.] A. 'at'm', Mahri (m elided) 'atait (Von Maltzan), athâth (Carter), H. 'esem, pl. 'ăsă-mŏth, id., often of bones of the dead.

Tari a, or tar ia, v. t., to rub, wipe (it), tari isa rub, wipe with (it). d. tara ia rub or scrape off (it), baka tar ia gather. [Sa. tele.] See terafi, karafi.

Tara, taratara. See tera to be quick.

Tārĕ, v. i., or a., to be pure, clean, white, tartāre whitish, matiratira polished, bright, shining. A. tahara, to be clean, pure, H. taher to shine, be bright, clean, pure.

Tare, v. i., to cry, call out (of men) ; to call out, i.e., crow (cock). A. saraha and sarā' to cry, call out, sarīh' a crying or calling out, a cock.

Tarere, v. i., to break on the shore with noise (of breakers) : rere.

Taroa, s., a pigeon. [My. dara.] A. tair' id.

Taru si, or taro si, v. t., to pray to (the natemate), tarotaro, redup. [Sa. talalo, talotalo, ps. talosia, Ha. kalokalo, Tah. tarotaro.] A. sala', E. salaya, Ch. sela to pray.

Taruba, v. i., to be thrown down, to fall ; taruba ki, v. t., throw down, make to fall, d. tarubik, v. i., and

Taruba, s., c. art., sticks thrown on or laid across the rafters of a house. H. ramah to cast, to throw, S. remo', id., etremi to cast itself or oneself. See under cg. roa.

Tas, s., c. art., the sea. [My.

tasik, To. tahi, Sa. tai.] A. ta's' the sea.

Tas ia, or tasi a, v. t., to shave : ras ia.

Tas, v. i., for ras, teres.

Tasabo, v. i. See sabo.

Tasiga, s., d. for tasila.

Tasike, v. i., to lift, raise (the head) : saki.

Tasila, s., helper, assistant : sila ia.

Tasmen, s., salt : tas the sea or salt, and men or mena, pleasant (so called because it makes food pleasant tasted).

Tasuru ki, v. t., to conceal : suru.

Tasuki, v. i., to bow : suki.

Tata, s., voc., maternal grandmother. [TaSa., Ml., tata, father, Ml. and Malo tata paternal uncle.] See ani na (atene na, &c.)

Tata, redup. of ta to chop, cut.

Tatau fi, v. t., as bisa tatau fi to speak, diverting or taking the attention : tau.

Tatā-gasi, v. t., tatā same as tatau (in preceding word) redup. of tau, and gasi to (wipe) stroke, smooth, flatter.

Tatalai, redup. of talai, also tilai, titilai, v. i., to warm oneself (at the fire). [Fi. tatalai, Mg. mitolo (boho).] H. dalak to burn, Hi. to heat, Ch. dělak.

Tatamares, tamares with ta-, doubled.

Tatia or tati a, d. for rati a. [Sa. tala, Tah. tara.]

Tatok, or atatok (or natatok, s.), a., resident, native : ta man, and toko.

Tatu, s. (see tui), a stake, post (of a fence), then tatu nafanua lord or chief of the land. A. watada to fix, stake, make firm, watadu stake, post, H. yated pin, nail, then prince.

Tasilasila, v. i., to make a clear startling sound (of men), to crack (of thunder) : ta chop, &c., and silasila. See sila.

Tau, tautau, v. i., or a., to be pure, clean, white. [Ma. tea.] A. nasa'a to be pure, white.

Tau, v. i., also mitau to be fixed, abide, as i tau suma he abides (in) the house, i tau narā nakasu it is fixed or abides (on) the branch of the tree (as a bird or fruit), nabona i tau isa his heart is fixed on (the person or thing), i tau isa it is fixed, abides, or (as fruit) hangs on it (the branch) i tau ki nuana makes to tau, as a tree makes fruit to tau, yields (fruit), nakasu i tau the tree yields (fruit), tau isa to hold firmly (with the hand), tau gi to grasp firmly with the hand, to pluck off (as a fruit), tau nata take hold firmly of a person (taking him to one's house as a guest), tau ē a ; mamitau, matau, d., an anchor (what holds firmly), tau ri to take hold of firmly, or be fixed firmly to, to marry (a woman), tau lua to attach or be fixed firmly (to one), bringing out one (as from bondage, or from her relations), to redeem ; to marry ; tau raki to attach firmly to, as a boat to a ship to be towed, bitauri, v. r., to be attached firmly to each other, to be married; tau asa, to measure (it), toū gi and toū ni to measure, to weigh, and to-naki (for tau naki) to place, set, fix firmly, appoint, determine, establish, tau, s., a measure, also to, toto, and (t to r) boroaki to give commands to one's family, to make one's will, to commission (anyone to do something), tau, redup. tautau, v. t., to commission (one to do something), hence fitaua, c. art. na-fitaua one commissioned, a messenger, also a commission or message (syn. fakaua, q.v.), also tau, tautau to divert or amuse the mind (of one), to *fix* his attention (as of a child to make him stop crying), then to deceive, to take up a man's attention deceitfully concealing your real aim, belaki tautau sa to lead one, diverting his attention or soothing his mind (with a view, when he is off his guard, and in a suitable place, to tomahawk or otherwise kill him); bitau, bitautau, v. r., to invite (as to a feast), taua a heap, also a crowd (of men or a herd of animals), from the things or people being firmly compacted together or attached to each other; tau a season, a year, from tau in the sense of to bear fruit (of a tree—see above); tau to be fixed, to abide firmly, is also used and may be used before any verb, like toko or to, anī, tu, to denote continuous action as i tau bat ia he continues fixedly doing it. (So Fi. tau, or dau, Sa. tau.) [Ma. tau to light, rest, be anchored, be suitable, &c.; Sa. tau fixed, to fit in, be anchored, pluck fruit with the hand, buy (see tau lua), taula'i to anchor with, hang up with, hang on to (tau-raki), taula an anchor; Fi. tau-ra take hold of, seize, tau-vata equal (tau, or to, equal), Ma. taua army, Tah. taura a herd or flock, also a rope, Sa. tau a season, a year, Mg. taona a year, season, also gathered, collected (cf. taua); also enticed, allured, attracted (tau, tautau), mitaona to gather in, collect, entice, draw, My. taun a season, year.] H. sawah to set up, place (S. sŏ'), Pi. sivah (A. wassa', see boroaki) to constitute, appoint, to decree, to charge, to command, to commission (delegate *anyone* with commands), to give last commands to one's family, to make one's will (Rabb. sava'ah a will), eg. s'awah to be even, level; equal in value, equivalent, be fit, suitable, be like, resemble, Pi. to make level, then to compose, calm the mind; to put, set, s'ivah pĕri to yield fruit (frucht ansetzen); followed by acc. and k', to make one like anything. Hi. to liken, compare (to-naki, *infra*).

Taua, s., a heap, a crowd, a herd: preceding word.

Tau, tautau, v. t., to commission. [Fi. tatau-naka, id., My. titah, to command, order, decree (to-naki, *infra*.)] See tau.

Tāü ni, or tāö ni, v. t., to cook, to bake (in the oven). [Sa. tao, ps. taoa, taoina; taona'i to bake food the day before giving it; To., Ma., tao.] A. taha, n. a. tahw', to cook. Hence

Tāö, s., c. art., leaves for cooking which are put into the oven along with the food to be cooked. [To. tau the cooking leaves, Tah. tao leaves and stones put into the inside of a pig to be cooked.]

Tauĕru isa, v. t., to haul, drag, tau place, fix, and eru, *i.e.* aru, the hand, lit. fix the hand on (to drag) as to drag a man to punishment.

Tauī a, v. t., to twist, wring (as to wring clothes after washing them), to milk (as a goat) squeeze, or wring (the milk out). A. tawa' (E. tawiy, H. tawah) to wring, twist.

Tauïen, or towien, s., a sister's husband, a wife's brother, that is, brother-in-law : but, d., a general name for reliable friend, brother, or sister, and in another d. the word is applied to father-in-law and son-in-law. [Fut. safe, Aniwa nosafe, Ta yafuni, d., c. art. nevun.] A. safiyy' a friend of a pure and sincere mind, *i.e.*, a real friend, safa', 3, to be of sincere and pure affection (towards someone), 4, to show sincere love, 6, to live in mutual sincerity of friendship.

Taubora, s., an ornament that hangs or is fixed on the side of the head : tau, bora.

Taulalo, v. or s., to hang, or be fixed or what hangs or is fixed in front of the belly, nasieg i taulalo : tau, lalo.

Taunako, s., a thing (like the peak of a cap) worn or fixed over the forehead. [Cf. syn. Sa. taumata]: tau, and nako.

Taumako, s., the wild (edible) yam that grows on the hills : tau, and mako for which see aka, ako.

Taumafa, d. taumofa, v. i., to give an offering (to the natemate), taumafā sa give an offering of or with it (something), taumafa ki nia offer it (something), taumafa tua i make an offering, giving to him (a natemate). [Ml. P. tomav, Ha. kaumaha to offer in sacrifice, to offer a gift upon an altar, s., a sacrifice, Tah. taumaha a portion of food offered to the gods or spirits of the dead.] Tau (to place) and mafa, or mofa (q.v.), a gift or offering. A. ma'haba*t* a gift H. habhabim (Hos. viii. 13) offerings (to God), A. wahaba, H. yahab, to give.

Taumi a. See tami a.

Tauruuru, v. i., to grumble, murmur, mutter : ta, and uruuru.

Tausi a, v. t. See takusi a.

Tauso, or tausoa, v. i., to commit adultery or fornication (of either sex) : tau, and so, or soa. [Fi. dauca.]

14

Te, dem., rel. pron., conj., as
agute mine this, ana te his
this or that ; te uia what (is)
good, that which is good, or he
or she who is good, te sa that
which is bad. or he or she who
is bad ; in this sense d. tea, as
tea uia, tea sa ; te nata what,
or whatever person, any person, someone ; te, redup. tete,
may be used substantively, as
te ru ban, or tete ru ban, some
went ; te dem. is found in tite
(nafite, sefete, what this, that,
or it? or simply, what?) also
in matuna, banotu, binote ;
with art. nete, s., the that,
anything, something, and d.
with dem. ka prefixed nakate,
id. ; te is also found with ka,
dem. prefixed in one d. as a
tense particle (see kate, tense
particle, *supra*) ; te, or t', is
also used as a conj. and before
the verbal pron. of the 1st
person sing., a, and of the 3rd
sing., i or e, loses its vowel, as
ta ban that I go, or be gone,
tē ban that he has gone, or
because he has gone. In one
dialect for i kate, ku kate, a
kate ban, he, you, I went,
there is ka te ban, ku te ban,
ki te ban, I went, you went,
he went, in which the verbal
pronouns are suffixed to the k.
A. da, dem., du, rel., S. d', Ch.
di, rel. and conj., that, because.

Tea. See te.

Teba, or taba, v. i., to dry up
(of liquid or moisture), to become dry ; and mun teba ki
to drink, making it dry (liquid).
E. nasepa to become dry (as
a river) ; to dry up (as a
spring), nĕsup dry, dried up.

Teel, s., shellfish, &c., got on the
reef, lit. te el', that which is
pleasant, sweet, or tasty : te,
elo.

Tefa, tetefa, v. i., to draw up in
order of battle ; and

Tefa ki, v. t., to put in a series,
to range (troops, in order of
battle) ; bitefa range themselves in order of battle, face
to face ; tefa gi, d. tefa ni,
v. t., to put things in a series,
either one before or one
above another; rogo tefā sa
hear paying no attention, dis-
obeying, lit. hear putting
down, d. syn. rogo tao sa (see
tao). [Fi. tuva, v. i., tuvā,
v. t., to place in regular order,
to range in close compact, or
place one upon another, tuvai
nai valu, tuvai valu to put in
the attitude of war, put in
battle array, tuva na lawa ni
valu arrange or put in ranks
the lawa ni valu.] A. safla,
1, 2, 6, 8, to set or place in
order in a series ; to arrange
the line of battle, draw up in
order of battle ; Nm. to
arrange (troops), 2, id., to
range themselves mutually
face to face.

Tef ia, or tefi a, redup. teteti,
v. t., to cut ; tefi, to circumcise. [Fi. teve, tava, Sa. tefe,
To. tefe, Sa., To. tafa.] A.
'as'aba to cut.

Tefarafara, v. i., to break (of
the sea) ; and

Tefara, s., c. art., breakers :
tafera, taferafera.

Tefarere (*i.e.*, tefarrere), v. i., to break rushing up on the shore (of the breakers) : tefarafara, tefara, and rere.

Tei, s., c. art. intei, a reddish powder made from a plant, turmeric : bitei a.

Tei. See rei.

Telake na, d. telakea na, s., c. art. a, lord, owner, possessor : lake.

Telatela, v. i., or a., to be large, wide ; and

Telatelana, id., c. ending -na, and see matulu, matultul, matoltol, swollen, large. [Epi toru large, Sa. tetele, telatela, latele, vatele, Ma. tetere, large, swollen.] H. 'adīr large, great, 'adar to be wide, A. 'adira to have hernia (to swell out).

Tele, v. t. See tāle is, to search for.

Teluko. See taluko.

Telei, or talai, s., the ancient axe, or adze-like axe (a shell). [Sa. talai to adze, Ma., Tah. tarai chop with an adze, Ha. kalai to chop, hew, pare, carve.] A. s'araha to cut, slice, carve, dissect.

Tema na, or tama na, s., father : t', art., and ama for afa, as mama for abab (q.v.) [Sa. tamā, My. rama, id.]

Temabalu, s., brothers, lit. te (he who) ma (with) balu (brother) : balu ; and

Temabalu ta, for temabalu ra, who (or those who) with their brother, *i.e.*, brothers. So tema in the following words is lit. he or she who or those

who, or that (person) or those (persons) with.

Temabau ra, s., d., uncle and nephew : bau.

Temabele ta, s., mother and child : bele na.

Temagore ta, s., brother and sister : gore na ; d. mera gore na. (See mera).

Temaloa ta, s., d. syn. temabau ra : aloa na.

Temamō ta, s., mother-in-law and son-in-law : mō na.

Tematrāfa, for temarāfa, s., father and child, lit. that (*i.e.*, the child) with the father. See afa.

Tematema ta, s., father and child : tema na.

Temataku ta, s., a man and his brother-in-law (his wife's gore na) : taku na.

Temaratauīen, s., *i.e.*, te māra tauīen that with (his) tauīen, d. syn. temataku ta : tauīen.

Temarauota, s., *i.e.*, te māra uota, that with (her) uota (husband), wife and husband : uota, d. me nimariki.

Temasere, s., a beloved one, especially a child much cared for ; te that, masere loved, cared for. See also sere a, bakasere a.

Tematete ta, s., maternal grandmother, and her grandchild : tena na.

Tematia ta, s., paternal grandfather (&c.) and his grandchild : tia na.

Tematobu ta, s., maternal grandfather and his grandchild : tobu na

Tematua ta, s., paternal grandmother and her grandchild : tua na.

T'te na, s., juice : toto.

Tēn, d. for tanonon.

Tena na, s. See atena na ; d. atia, or tia na.

Tēr, v. i., to be slow, tardy. A. 'ah'h'ara, 5, to be slow, tardy.

Terā sa, v. t., be ignorant of, forget, not to know (it), d. rera, d. tenr. A. s'alla to not know, be ignorant of ; forget.

Tera, v. i., to shine (of the sun), tera ia, v. t., shine upon it (of the sun). [My. tārang, tārang kan, Fi. cila, Malo sarasara.] H. sahar (cf. zahar, &c.) to shine.

Tera ia, tetera ia, v. t., to go after, to do anything after (or in the track of) another, baka-tera ia to answer (make one's word to go after another's), ba, and sela tera ia go after, gua tera ia shout after, bisa tera ia speak after ; also to rehearse, recount, tera usi to recount following, tera uti na to go after following. [My. turut follow, go after.] A. 'athar' track, 'athara, 4, make something follow another, 5, 8, follow the track of someone, go after, 1, recount, rehearse.

Tera, v. i., to be quick, swift, tera ki māla wheel, swoop, shoot, or glide swiftly like a hawk, tera gulu ti swoop (upon one) clasping (him, as in war), tera tukituki run rapidly beating the ground with one's feet, tera belbel to be exceedingly swift or quick, tera mau to be quick indeed

or truly, to be instant, do instantly, tera bile to be very quick, teratera, redup. ; tera lo saki to turn quickly, looking up, tera tabo (d.) to turn quickly bending the head down. [Ma. tere, Sa. tele-tele.] A. darra, 10), to run vehemently, or swiftly, 4, to turn or whirl a spindle very swiftly, H. darar (also) to fly in a circle, wheel in flight ; and like A. darra to spout, to pour out (as rain, &c.) Hence

Ter ea, v. t., to pour into ; and

Tera, s., c. art., a pouring out : natera ni us, a rain squall, an outpouring of rain.

Terā, a., having (lit. that has) branches, as tera rua, tolu, &c., having two, three, &c., branches (of a tree) : te, and ra.

Terati, v. t., to scratch (as the ground) : cf. H. sarab, and see tari a, tara ia ; d. syn. garati, or karati. See kar ia.

Terāgi, v. t., in kabu teragi, to heat cooked food over again teragi is for reragi, as in bau-ragi a, bau-terag ia (see bau sia, baraga i, raga-elo).

Teratera, v. i., to be delirious, insane ; A. hatara, 1, 4, to make, or to be delirious, insane ; also torotoro.

Tere, teretere (a, ra). v. t., to feast, to entertain (especially visitors at a festival), also to make a feast or banquet for a friend who visits one. The radical idea lies in that of gathering folks together for a festival, or enclosing them as it were in one's house and hospitality. II. 'asarah an assembly of people for keeping a festival, 'asar (primary idea is that of surrounding, enclosing), Ni., 3), to be gathered together, especially for a festival, A. a'asir breakfast and dinner, or supper.

Teratär, v. i., to stagger, totter (as a man drunk). A. tartara to stagger (as a man drunk).

Tere, s., c. art., the mast (of a canoe or ship), calf (column) of the leg. A. sariyat, Nm. sari, the mast (of a ship), a column.

Tere, s., and teretere, s., the comb (of a cock); the eaves of a house. [Sa. tala, Tah., Ma. tara, Ha. kala.] Nm. torra crest, comb of bird, A. torrat extremity, side of anything, forelock, pointed, from tarra to cut, to sharpen, to snatch, to shoot (as plants), to propel vehemently, irritate, stir up.

Terei a, v. t., for rerei a, for roroia : rei a.

Trea ki, for rea ki.

Trei a, for toitoi a.

Terina, s., enclosure. H. tur fence, enclosure.

Teres, for reres : res.

Tere ti, v., used as ad., as boka tere ti to smite or strike hastily (and therefore ineffectively, confusedly), syn. sarafi and sumati, and bile, or bilebile : tera to be quick.

Tete, s., voc., mother. See under ani na.

Tete, and teten. See te.

Ti, and d. tsi, neg. ad., not : d.

ta. [Sa. lē, Ma. te, Fut. si, My. ta, Mg. tsy.]

Ti, v. t., to say; ti ki niä say to him, tell him, ti ki niä sa tell him it : dd. ni, noa, nofa, q.v.

Tī, s., chief, as ti Tongoa chief of Tongoa : for tui, q.v.

Tī a, and rī a. v. t., to push, thrust, propel, or drive. A. daya to propel, thrust.

T'tie na, or t'tia na, s., saliva, water of the mouth, nat'tia na i serä sa his mouth waters because of it, lit. the water (of his mouth) runs at it : titia.

Tia na, or tie na, s. See atia na.

Tiamia, v. i. or a., to be first, d. bea or tobea (for toko bea) : tia to abide or be, and mia, d. bea, q.v. [Oba tomua, Sa. mua and tomua.]

Tiele, v. i., to finish a laugh with shrill cries, in a whinnying manner (of women). H. sahal to utter shrill cries; to neigh (of a horse), A. sahala, n. a. sahil', to whinny.

Tiena, v. i., to be with child. See mitēn. S. t'yina laden, gravid.

Tiba, neg. ad., not. See d. tab : ti ad., and ba for ma, as in Assy. aama not.

Tib ĕa, or tuba ia, v. t., to shoot with an arrow;

Tiba, or tuba, s., c. art., an arrow, i.e., what is cast : tuba. [Mg. tsipika.] E. nadafa, (2) to shoot with an arrow, (1) to strike, (3) to prick, H. nadaf to drive away. The radical idea is thrusting, pushing.

Tiba, s., the post in a house that

supports the ridge-pole : so called because i tuba ia. See tuba, which is the same as tiba.

Tibi li, v. t., to burn, to scar. A. s'ahaba to roast, to broil.

Tifai, s., thunder ; ti art., and fai. [Sa. fai-tilitili, Fila tefachiri, Aniwa tefachiri.] A. bahh'(used of thunder) hoarse, cf. Sa. fa hoarse.

Tibu (pronounced timbu), d., s., c. art. natimbu, the deep (sea) : bua.

Tikal ia. See takal ia.

Tigi na, or tiki na, s., side, edge ;

Tigi elo, v., to bask in the sun, warm oneself in the sun. A. s'aha to bask or warm oneself in the sun, s'ahiyal side, outside or edge. Hence

Tigi (side) in malitigi, malirigi, &c., place at the side, that is, beside, near : and

Tigitigi na, s., d., edge (outside or exposed edge or side of a thing), and

Tiki na, and

Tikitiki na, id. ; and

Tiki nrā nin, d., this point (of time), now.

Tika, a strong negative, it is not, no, by no means ;

Tiki (or tikā), neg. ad., not ; i tiki ban he did not go ; and

Tika, and tiki, the same, used, with the verb. pron., as a verb, to be not, to exist not, dd. tsika, nika. rika, tika : neg. ad. ti, and ka. It is thus construed : i tikā sa it is not in it or him, or he has it not, i tika ki nia it is not to

or in him, or he has it not, thus namuruen i tika ki nia there is no laughing in him, i tika ki namuruen he has not laughing. See also under bi enia, *supra*. For ti see ti, ad., *supra* ; ka is to be compared with the E. ko in 'eko not, ko being a contraction of kona (A. kana) to be, and tika with the Talmudic and Mandaische lika not, is not (Nöldeke, Mand. Grammatik). [Fut. jikai, My. tak, Mg. tsia, and diahoe, To. ikai, Sa. i'ai, no, not, not so.]

Tiki-amo, d. takāmo, q.v.

Tiki, v. i., to be soft (of the skin), syn. busa, as nauīli na i tiki, or i busa, his skin is soft (his skin is bad, or has an uncomfortable feeling, as on hearing some dreadful story, or witnessing some fearful thing). See busa. A. 'atika, b), 3), to become soft and tender (of the skin).

Tiki na, and triki na, s., for riki na.

Tiko, s., a staff, a walking stick, a pole by which a canoe is poled forward in shallow water. [Sa. to'o a canoe pole, a stick in which is fixed the perch of a pigeon, to'ona'i to lean on a staff, to lean on anything for support, tootoo a staff, walking stick, toto'o to lean upon a staff, To. toko a post used to make fast canoes to, tokotoko a staff, My. tákân, Mg. tehina, a staff, mitehina to walk with a staff, to walk leaning on a

person.] A. toka'at a staff, a
support, he who leans much
on his side, and props himself
up. Hence, Nm., taka, 8,
itteci to lean upon. Hence

Tiko ki, v. t., to pole (a canoe).
This is done by leaning upon
the tiko, and so throwing
one's weight upon it.

Tila ia, d. til ē a (and ta lisi)
v. t., to wrench, prize (with a
lever), to struggle, wriggle,
wrestle (as through a narrow
place); tilā ki, v. t., to wrench,
sprain, twist (as one's foot by
stepping into a hole); tilatila,
v. t., wrench up with a lever
roots and rocks in making a
hole in which to plant a yam ;
hence

Tīla, s., a lever, crowbar. [Mg.
tolona, mitolona, to struggle
together, to wrestle.] A.
'atala to violently drag and
wrench away, 3, to wrestle
with, atala/, Nm. 'atela, crowbar, lever, hod.

Tila ia, tīla, d. for lita ia : līta.

Tili-mar, v. i., d. for lele maroa,
to revolve or roll turning
round : lele, maroa.

Tilasi a, and redup. tilatilasi a :
lasi a.

Tilai, titilai. See talai, tatalai.

Tili a, v. t., to tell, relate (a
thing). [Sa. tala, v. and s.,
tell, relate, tale, narration,
tala'i, talatala'i, To. tala.]
A. tala', to follow, to relate (a
narrative), read, recite.

Tinom ia, d. for tulum ia.

Tirāgi (tira gi), v., to look at (as
at a spectacle). A. sara, c.
'ali, to look at.

Tirā sa, d. rirā sa. See terā sa.

Tiri, v. i., to fly (of birds), d.
riri ; also to fly into a rage, to
be transported with rage,
flying and jumping about
excitedly ; i tiri, syn. i miti,
as i tiri bas ia, or i miti bas ia,
he (transported with rage)
flies snatching him (the object
of his passion, as if to tear
out his eyes). Hence rīri a
spark, and mitiri a grasshopper (from leaping and
flying), and taroa a pigeon).
[Sa. lele, Ma. rere.] A. tāra
to fly ; to be swift, move
quick.

Tirigi, for ririgi, rigi.

Tirikit, v. i., to begin to drop or
sputter (of rain). [Fi. tiri to
drop.] For tiri see tuturu,
and for kit, kita small, little.

Tiro, v. i., to sink, roll down (as
in the sea, or down a precipice,
or into a pit) ; hence

Tiroa, s., c. art., a precipice, or
deep, steep place. [Fi. tiro,
siro, sisiro, My. turun, turun-
kan.] H. salal, sul, to be
rolled down, sink (as in the
sea), mĕsolah and mĕsulah
depths (of the sea, a river,
clay). See mitaru, toroaki ;
also

Tiro e, d., v. t., to swallow, send
down, make to sink down
(into the stomach) : and

Tiro aki, v. t., make to sink
down (as an anchor,) to anchor,
d. toro aki, tirotiro, redup.

Titiro, v. i., to gaze into the sea
looking for fish or shellfish ;
to look at one's image in
water or a looking-glass. [Fi.

tiro, tiro-va, to look at oneself in the water, peep at, Sa. tilotilo, ps. tilofia, to peep, spy, Ma. tiro, tirotiro, titiro, look, gaze, Ha. kilo to look hard, earnestly, to star-gaze, prognosticate, act as a sorcerer.] A. naf'ara to gaze, look for, consider, spy, to prognosticate, divine.

Tiso, v. i., to exude, d. lisoa, tisō a exude on to (a thing) : toto.

Titi, v., to tread, titia ki nakasu tread on a log (as on a log thrown across a stream). [My. titi.] A. watiya to tread.

Titia, v. i., to slaver, dribble (as an infant), to have saliva flowing, to have the mouth watering, nat'tia na saliva, water of the mouth. [Mg. rora saliva.] H. rir saliva, A. rāla to slaver, dribble (of an infant), riyal' saliva, cf. My. liyor slaver, dribble.

Tiū sa, d., v. t., to sink, dip, matiu, v. i., to sink, d. redup. tutu, d. lulu, v. i., to sink, d. riū sa, v. t., to point out with the finger, d. tuma ia, v. t., to point out with the finger, d. tiū sa, tū sa, d. tū nia, or riū sa, or rū sa, or redup. tiutiū sa, tūtū sa, riūriū sa, or rūrū sa, v. t., to smear, tinge, colour, or paint nafōna (native cloth). See also lolofa, lum, luma, lulum. [Ma. totohu to sink, tohu mark, sign, toi finger, also toe, Tah. tohu to point at with the finger, make a sign, To. tuhu, v., to point with the finger, s., the forefinger, Sa. tusi to

mark (native cloth), to write, to point out, tusitusi striped, Fi. luvu to sink, Mg. tsoboka soaked, drenched, dipped, My. tud'ing to point at with the finger, to indicate. See also under lolofa, luma.] H. taba' to sink (eg. saba'. A. saba'a to dip into, immerse, E. tam'a, id.), to be dipped, plunged, H. saba' to dip in, immerse, to dye, tinge, seba' something dyed, a versicoloured garment, Ch. (see lolofa) sēba', A. saba'a to point out or at with the finger, 'asbi', 'asbu', &c., the finger, H. 'asba' finger, also toe, A. saba"a to dye or colour (cloth), to make a sign, indicate.

To, v. i., contr. for toko, or tok, dd. ti, te, to rest, sit down, dwell, remain, be. [Malo ate, Ml. d. at, Mg. toetra, toatra, toitra.] See toko.

Tō, redup. toto, d. touo, d. tau, s., a measure, equal. [Fi. rau.] And

To-naki, v. t., to compare ; to place, fix; to appoint, determine, establish. See tau.

Tō (and see tofi a), v. t., to push, press upon. A. da"a to push, propel.

Tōa (towa), or tō', s., a (domestic) fowl, also a bird (= manu). [Fi. toa, My. ayam, Ceram dd. toli, towim, Bouru dd. tehui, teput, teputi, Cocos Island ufa, bird, Tag. ībon.] H. 'of bird (gen. name), A. 'a'f' gallus. Note tōa (towa) has t' art.

Troa i. See roa i.

Toitoi a, v. t., also teitei a (and

trei a), to hate. A. 'ada', 2),
n. a. 'adw', b), 'adiya, to hate.

Touo, d. for roua. See roa.

Tōb, d., v. i., or a., to be large,
great. [Epi sombi, Mg. dobe.]
A. 'at'oma to be great.

Tob, s., c. art. natob, spittle.
H. tof, E. tafe' to spit.

Tobag ia. See tabag ia.

Tobaroba. See rabaraba.

Tobet, s., rubbish heap. Cf. H.
tofet spittle. See tob.

Tobu, s., a tumour, swelling.
See tubu.

Tobu na, s., grandfather. See
bobu, bua. [Malo tubu, Ta.
tupu, Epi kumbuo, Ml. P. apu,
Fi. bu, Fut. bua, grandfather
or grandmother, prop. ances-
tor.] H. 'ab (father), pl.
'aboth, A. pl. 'abau, 'ab'u (and
'abuna) ancestors.

Tobua, s., d., a natemate, spirit,
familiar spirit, demon. [Fut.
tupua, Ma. tupua, cf. Sa.
tupua.] See sube (where see
Sa. tupua).

Tōbu, d. nōbu, q.v.

Tofe na, s., native cloth, clothing.
[To. tapa, Ha. kapa, Sa. siapo.]
Num. thiyab clothes, dress ;
sole essential article of Arab
dress, A. tha'b', pl. thiyab'.
And hence

Tofe, v. i., d., to put on the
tofe, to dress.

Tofi a, v. t., to push. A. da'aba
to push.

Toga, d. rog, d. taga, s., a basket.
H. tene', id.

Toga, s., far away, also natoga
a distant place or country.
H. rahok, S. ruhka, E. rēhūk
far off, away.

Togo ia, d. toko ia, v. t, to push,
thrust, and see bakatoko ia.
H. dahak, A. dahaka to push,
thrust.

Troga, for toga, basket.

Trogo, d. nrogo, for rogo, to
hear.

Toki a, tokitoki a, v. t., to
gather up one's things, or pack
up, preparatory to flitting.
See raku, taku ti. [Cf. Fi.
toki a.]

Toko, d. tok, v. i., to rest, sit
down, dwell, remain, be, contr.
to, q.v., sometimes pronounced
tuk. [My. and Ja. duduk,
dodok, Mg. toatra (see to), Fi.
tiko, toka.] H. takah, Pu.
tukah (Deut. xxxiii. 3), A.
waka'a, 8, 'ttaka'a, cf. 5, to
sit (Luke xiv. 8), to remain.
Hence

Tokōn, s., c. art., a village, re-
maining or dwelling place.

Tokei, or tokai, s., c. art., a
prop, or rafter (which reaches
from the ground to the ridge-
pole in an Efatese house) ;
then natokai nafanua the
prop, i.e., chief, of the land.
A. 'atka'ā to prop up.

Tokora, s., a place. [Mota togara
behaviour, togava a station.]
See toko.

Tōki, s., an axe ; and

Tōk, s., violence, force. A.
takka to cut, H. tōk violence.

Tokalau, s., easterly wind : tok
remain, alau on the sea.

Toko ia. See togo ia.

Toko-naki, v. t., to strike on (as
one's foot on a stone, the wind
on a mountain). [Ma. tu-
tuki, To. tugia.] See tuki a.

Tokotoko na, s., a shark's fin : toko ia.

Toko ni, v. t., to kindle, set fire to, redup. tokotoko. A. daka' to kindle.

Tol, s., violence, force. See tila to wrench.

Tola, v. i., to be early dawn : toa i tola the cock crows, lit. crows at early dawn ;

Tola, s., the dim early dawn : the dim distance in the sky ; and

Tolarola, id., redup. ; and, d. tolau, id. Hence matōl, d. tomorrow. H. s'ahar, A. sahara, to be far remote, sahira, to do, or to set out at early dawn, S, the cock crew at early dawn, H. mis'har the morning.

Toli a, v. t., to surpass, to go past, before, bitoli, v. r., d. bilele ; to pass or go before each other, d. toliu sa. See liu, and to.

Tolĕ na, s., c. art., egg (of a bird), d. atol mita na eyeball. [My. tâlor, Mg. atody, Oba toligi, Sulu iklug, Nias ajuloh, Poggi agoloh.] Mahri chali, Amh. 'ankuilal : the radical meaning is round.

Trōm, or tōm, s., turmeric, a reddish curry powder. [Fi. damudamu red, Mg. tamotamo turmeric, tomamotamo yellow, of an orange, saffron colour.] A. 'adoma to be red, H. 'adamdom reddish.

Tōnako, for taunako.

Tontonō sa, v. i., to be perplexed, in pain or distress on account of (something) : tunu.

Tomo na, s., tumu na.

Tomotomoa, v. i., tumutumua.

Toro, v. i., to leak (as a canoe). A. ta''ara to boil, emit water (as clouds), to leak (as a vein or vessel).

Toro, v. t., to lay down, abandon, let down, permit, tor ea lay it down, &c.

Torŏ sa, lit. lays down or abandons on account of it, i.e., gives up his old mind or opinion in consequence of the evil it has brought upon him, rues ; toro bisi a, also dd. turu bisi, and taru bisi, lay down leaving (a thing), permit, &c. ; tor ea put into (as liquid into a vessel), totor ea, id., syn. tutua ki ;

Toroa, v. i., to be rich, toro (lay down, store up, and a. ending a) : matoro-toro, let down, slackened, slack (as a rope), A. wadara (not used in perfect), fut. yadaro, imperative dar, to lay down, leave, permit.

Toro aki, for tiro aki.

Torotoro, for teratera.

Toro na, s., his impulse, onset, power, might. [Ma. tara courage, mettle.] This same word occurs as tere na (comb of cock, &c.), where see the verb. A. tarra to propel vehemently, &c., Nm. tarr free will, arbitrary power ;

Torotoro na, id., redup.

Tore, or tere (natuone), s., the leg below the knee. See tere mast (of ship), column.

Torotoro, v. i., to be hot, to sweat. A. sala' to be hot. Hence

Torutoru, id., and

Tōru, s., sweat.

Tōs, d., v. i., to creep, d. for rosa.

Trot ia. See rot ia.

Totau, dd. tatau, titau, titu, s., a child, infant. [Mg. zaza.] E. sa's'āe, H. se'esa'em off-spring.

Trotro, v., to think ; and

Trotro na, s., thought, mind. See mitroa.

Toto, dd. tiso, lisoa, v. i., to exude (as gum, juice. from plants). [Fi. titi, titi-va, My. titik, Mg. mitete, mitate, tete-vana.] A. nas's'a, n. a. nas'īs', to exude. Hence

Toto, s., a plant abounding in a milky juice, and its juice.

Totofa, d., v. i., to swell: d. tubu, q.v.

Toū gi, d. toū ni, v. t., to measure, to weigh. See tau, d. tau asa, to measure.

Tu, dem., in banotu, matuna.

Tu, verb. pron., 1 pl., incl., dual tā. See nigita, ninita.

Tu, v. i., to stand, dd. tsu, ru, and see su ; also to abide, dwell, be ; tu lena stand up straight, used also of rising up, to rise up ; tu-ri a (ri t. prep.) also occurs, to stand, or abide to (or with) a person, and tu-raki, to stand or abide for (a person or thing). [Fi. tu, tu-ra, turaga, TaSa. turu, Ml. P. tu, tutu (= My. diri), Sa. tu, tutu, faatu, tula 'i, tulaga, Ma. tu, tutu, turanga, Ha. ku (1, rise up, 2, to stand), My. diri, Mg. joro.] H. nasa', so', s'et, imp. sa', cf. Hithp.,

E. nasa'a, A. nas'a'. See su, supra.

NOTE.—This word also occurs as matu, batu, fatu ; and, like toko, matoko, and also ani, it is put after demonstratives, as uane tu, uane matu, nin batu, nistu, &c., lit. this or that standing or being (there or here).

Tu na, s., bones (of fish), and

Tutu, a., bony. [Fi. sui, d. dua, bone, suisuia, lean, bare of flesh, bony, rough, sharp.] Cf. A. s'a'a, 4, to become spiky, to be rayed.

Tua, v. t., to place, put down ; also to give, tua i give him ; tua ki place, put down ; used also of liquids, tua ki nia las put or place it in the vessel (cf. tor ea), make it to fall into the vessel, redup. tutua ki, bitua ki nia, or bituā sa, to put down, also to give (a thing) ; with some verbs it is like "from" as bā tua ki nia go or come from, lit. go or come leaving, or putting it down, or placing it, hence bā bituaki to halt between two opinions (in which the reflexive force of bitua, v. r., comes out), ba bituaki lit. being to go leaving it over and over again. A. was'a'a to place, lay, or put down.

Tū sa (see tiu sa), d. tū nia, to tinge, mark, colour native cloth, hence (e. ending a) tuni-tunia striped, marked.

Tua na, s., name of various relatives, as brother's wife, husband's mother, paternal

grandmother, and her grand-
children, husband's sister.
See under the following word.
[Ml. U. tuan elder brother,
My. mântuwah father-in-law
or mother-in-law.]

Tuai, or tuei, a., old, ancient, and
ad. long ago, also a long time
hereafter. See bakatuai to
make long (of time), matua
old, mature, &c. [Sa. tuai, faa-
tuai, matua, My. tuwah,
Ja. tuwa, bârtuwah, bâtuwah,
mântuwah, Bu. matua, Mg.
antitra, anti (panahy), anto
(andro), matoa, matotra.] A.
'adiyy' old, ancient (has the a.
ending), and 'a'd' from 'ada to
confer a benefit on one, to
favour, &c. (see preceding
word), mo'id' powerful, experienced, accustomed. See
matua.

Tuasil, s., giver of help : tua
place, give, sila.

Tua, d. tue, s., c. art., twins :
rua.

Tua, v. i., to go, redup. tutua.
Hence

Tua na, or tuo na, s., legs, feet.
[An. thuo, Ta. su, legs.] H.
s'uk to run, whence s'ok, Ch.
s'ak, A. sak', pl. suk', the legs.

Tui, pronounced also ti, s., as
tui Tongoa chief of Tongoa.
[Fi. tui.] A. waddu, for
watadu. See tatu, supra.

Tuuti a, v. t., to tie ; hence

Tuut, s., a knot. [Tah. toti,
My. tambat.] E. s'abata,
Arm. sĕbat and sĕwat, id.

Tubu, or tub, d. totofa, or totoba,
v. i., to swell. [Oba tutumbu,
Ml. timb.] Arm. sĕba, H.

sabah to swell, sabeh a swelling. See tobu, supra. This
word also means to will, as
Arm. sĕba to will, to wish,
properly to be inclined, prone,
so H. sabah ; hence in Efatese
(cf. S., John iii. 27 and 8)
tuma, d. tumbu (ndumbu),
with the nom. suf. denotes
will, sua sponte, as i tuma-na
he of his own will or accord,
as " Who told him to do
this " ? i tumana bat ia " He of
his own will or accord did it."

Tuba ia (see tiba ia, tibèa, which
is the same word), to thrust,
impel, hence tuba ki to send,
and natuba, s., an arrow,
also a prick, sting, or thorn ;
tuba goto fi (to thrust breaking) to condemn, or adjudge
to die, tuba gori (thrust over or
in front of) to forbid, tuba gasi
(thrust wiping) to wipe, and
redup., tubatuba ia, to impel,
propel, send off : from the idea
of thrusting comes that of
reaching to, touching, hence
bitub, bitubetuba, v. r., to be
touching (thrusting, lit.) each
other, i.e., throughout, wholly,
continually, as tale firi bitub
all round wholly, tatisafisa
bitubetuba pray continually
(one prayer touching an-
other as in a series), and
i mate tuba nasefa ? he died
on account of what ? lit.
touching what; ru tumara tuba
ra they touch each other (as of
any two things, also of one
thing done in retaliation for
another). See tiba ia.

Tubara. See tabara.

Tubatua, v. i., to kneel, lit. to stand on the knees : tu, batua.

Tubut, d., s., rainbow: lit. stand in the middle (i.e., of the sky) : tu, but.

Tugo fi a, d. for toko ia, togo ia.

Tuk ia, or tuki a, v. t., to strike, beat, pound, redup. tukituki a; and uru tukituki run quickly, lit. run beating (the ground with the feet). [Fi. tuki-a, To. tugi, Ma. tuki, tukituki.] H. duk, dakak, A. dakka, dakka, &c., beat, pound, Nm. daqdaqa sound of horses' feet beating (the ground).

Tuku, v. i., to go down, sink down, also v. t., tuku nalai lower the sail (of a canoe), tuku bia kiki put a child in a cloth basket to be carried on the back. [Ma. tuku, To. tugu, Sa. tuu, Ha. kuu, Fi. tuku-ca.] H. s'uah, A. sah'a, sah'a (cf. thah'a, tah'a) to sink down, H. s'uhah, s'ihah a pit, s'ahat pit, cistern, the grave. Hence

Tuk, s., a hole, enclosure like a hole or pit : and

Tukituki, s., the seven stars (because like an enclosure); and

Tūk, s., uora tūk, place of the pit, i.e., Hades ; and

Tukituki, or tukutuku, s., name of a place on the western side of Efate, where is the entrance to Hades ; and

Tuku, s., a fence, stake, or post (because sunk in the ground and firm).

Tuki, in matuki, s., q.v., and Mau-tukituki, or Mau-tiki-

tiki, name of a mythical person, one of the first men. [Mg. toky, matoky. See matūki, supra.] See under taki a, supra, and see mau.

Tukunua, s., a story, tradition, d. syn. kakai. [Fi. tuku-na, v. t., and tukuni, s.] A. nataka to speak.

Tu-ki-roa ki, v. t., to give in commission : roa as in boroa ki, and tua, or tu, to give.

Tuletule, v. i., to swing ; and

Tule aki, v. t., to swing ; and

Tula, s., d. a swing, v. i., to swing. H. dalal, dalah, talal, A. daldala and taltala to swing.

Tula, s., wax of the ear. [Fi.. tule, id., daligatula deaf, Sa. tuli deaf, My. tuli deaf.] A. salah' deafness.

Tuli for tili, to tell, relate.

Tuluku for taluko.

Talūm ia, or

Tulūm ia, v. t., to swallow down, dd. tulug ia, tinom ia, tunug ia, talug ia. [An. atleg, My. tālān, cf. pârlân, târlân, Mg. telina.] A. lahima, n. a., lahm', 5, 8, Nm., 5, telehhem, to swallow down.

Note.—Sa. and To. "to swallow" is folo, A. bali'a, id.

Tu-lake, v. t., to give in commission: tua give, and lake, q.v.

Tuma, d. tumbu (see under tubu). S. sĕbu will.

Tuma ia, v. t., to point out with the finger, bituma v. r.; d. riū sa. See tiū sa.

Tuma ia, v. t., to knock (as a door), as a sign to open it And

Tumatuma ia, id., redup. [Sa. tuma, cf. My. antam.] For tuba ia.

Tuma, or tama sok, for taba soka : taba.

Tumàlu, for tamàlu : taba.

Tūma, d. rūma, q.v.

Tuma ni, v. t., d., to cook (in a particular way), redup. tutuma ; and

Tumu na, d. nubu na, q.v., also tomo na ;

Tumutumua, v. i., or a., formed from tumu by a. ending a. See noba nia, and nobanoba, and matumutumu, and manubunubu.

Tumana, s., a parcel : taum ia, tam ia.

Tumi a, or tomi a, v. t., to suck. [Motu toboa.] E. tabawa to suck.

Trumi a. See rumi a, i.e., ru-mi a.

Tuni, v. t., to heat, tuni fatu to heat red hot the oven stones. [Fi. tunu, tunutunu, vaka-tunu-na.] And

Tunu, v. t., to heat, to oppress or make to suffer (as heat does) ; bitunu to be hot, painful, dd. bitin, bitsin (see also sinu, sisinu, and tontono) ; tutun to light up (torches, the evening cooking fires) ; and

Tunu, s., heat (of fire, or of the sun). See sīnu.

Tuni a See tani a.

Tunika, s., place where the watchers at a koro (fish trap) noiselessly remain : tu to stand, and see nikenika.

Tunitunia (see tiū sa, tū sa, d. tū ni a), a., striped, marked.

Turà sa, v. t., to lengthen (as by splicing) ; tutur ki, to delay for (as for a sick man unable to walk quickly), d. tutura ki, bakatura ki, id. A. tāla 1, 2, 4, make long, lengthen, to delay.

Turausi. See tera usi.

Tur ia, d. turu sa, v. t., to sew : also to nail ; to go through an opening (as a ship through the entrance of a harbour) : turu sa ;

Turi, and turituri, s., needle, also nail ;

Turua (a. ending a), full of holes (as a rock of holes through which rain percolates) :

Tuturu, v. i., to drip (as eaves), leak (roof) ;

Tuturu, s., a drop, a dripping, c. art. ; and

Turu ki, drip or leak through. See also tiri-kit. [Sa. tulu'i, tulutulu, faatulutulu, To. tulu. tului, To. tulu he mata = riri mita (tears), Fi. tiri, turu. titiri, tuturu, tiri-va, turu-va.] A. s'alla, 3), to sew, 2), shed tears, s'als'ala to drip, fall in drops, was'ala to drip, drop, leak out.

Turu bisi. See toro bisi.

Turuk, d., v., to permit. A. taraka, id.

Tūsi, s., book, writing, Sa. word. See tiū sa, tū sa, for its origin.

Tutu, v. i., to sink : tiū sa.

Tutua ki, redup. of tua ki, to place.

Tutua, redup. of tua, to go.

Tutuma, redup. of tuma ni, to cook.

Tutun (redup. of tunu, q.v., to heat), to light up (torches and cooking fires, as in the evening).

U, verb. pron., 1 pl., excl. (contraction for au), d. bu (dual moa), we (and) they. Mahri hem, or habu, they (Ef. bu = habu = 'mi in kinami, nami).

U, s., in näu, d. for usu ; also in bitëu, for bitesu.

U. verb. pron., 3 pl., they : d. for ru (r elided).

U, v., d. for ba, q.v. ; in umai to come here.

Ua (wa), dd. ua (uwa), ui (wi), interj., ad., yes : ua, dem.

Ua (u-a, and u-wa), s., oven, dd. um, ubu, of (ov).

Ua (wà), d. uè, q.v., inter. ad.

Uā, s., c. art. naua (nawa), veins, or muscles (so called from swelling out or up). [Fi. ua, Sa. ua.] See ua'a.

Uā, v. i., d. for ba, and böua, to rain : ba.

Uā ki, v. t., d. böuā ki, to yield fruit ; and

Uā, s., c. art. näuā, or nuā na, its fruit. [Ta. v., auwa, s., nowa, Oba, v., mo ai, Sa., v. and s., fua, My., s., buwah, Ja. uwoh, woh, My., v., barbuwah, Mg., s., voa, v., mamoa.] Arm. 'eb, 'ub, 'iba, 'ëbo, Assy. (inbu) imbu, fruit, and Arm. abeb to produce fruit.

Ua, dem., this : with other demonstratives suffixed, either this or that, uāna, uane, ua naga, uai, uase, uai na, uai naga, and with tu (to stand,

to be) uane tu, dd. uo, nose, nintu. Connected with this word are ua, uua, ui, uisa, niko, uila, uanā. Compare O, dem., supra, which is identical with the u in ua. The S. also suffixed other demonstratives to hu, or 'u, thus huhana, cf. St., p. 23, owa (oa, wa = Ef. ua) this, that. Compare Assy. uma (which, however, has the appended enclitic ma) this or that indeed, also thus.

Ua'a, s., a swelling, rise, i bi ua'a (of, e.g., an island seen from a distance swelling up or rising out of the sea). See fuata, and bua III.

Uābě, inter. ad., d. syn. sābě, where now ? where then ? See bě and ue (d. ua).

Uago, s., d. nåk, pig, swine. [Ta. puka, Fi. vuaka, Sa. pua'a, Malo boi, Epi bue, Bouru babue, My. babi, Mysol boh.] This name seems lit. to denote "grunter," Ta. puka to grunt, puka, s., a pig. Compare supra buka to bark, to cough (also d. buku).

Uai, dem., this, that ; and

Uaia, id., also uai na, uai naga, uai ntu, id. Compare English this here, this 'ere, for this.

Uaka na, s., d. for aka na : aka.

Uako, interj., a mere exclamation : ua and ko, dems.

Uāl, for āli, day.

Uālu, for balu, friend ; and

Uālubota, s., enemy, lit. alien friend.

Uāna, dem., that : ua dem., and another dem. suffixed to

it. Compare S. huhana. See
na, dem.

Uànà, interj.. an exclamation,
see! look out! Dems. ua
and na.

Uan, inter. ad., d., where? This
is dem. n suffixed to ua, inter.
ad. See ue. Santo veai and
even, id.]

Ua-nate natua na, s., d., calf of
the leg, lit. fruit of the belly
(liver) of the leg.

Uane, dem., this: ua, ne.

Uārīk, d. for bātīk, q.v.

Uāsa, ad., d. āsa, the day after
to-morrow. [An. vith, Epi
veūa, Ml. vis, wisa, Am.
bugirua, Santo pogirua, Lo
weria, Mota arisa.] The word
uāsa is ua (for which see ma)
day, and sa (for ra, or rua, 2),
2, or 2nd: in pogirua, pogi is
another word for day, and, in
arisa, ari is still another, Ef. ali.

Uase, dem., this: ua, se.

Uasi a, v., d. for asi a.

Uata, s., a portion: bota ia.

Uataki, v., d. for bitaki; and

Uataki, s., dd. otaki, itaki.

Uateaf, and d.,

Uateam, and d.,

Uateau, s., kidneys: ua fruit,
ate liver (&c.), and amo belly,
lit. fruit of the liver (or inside)
of the belly; and

Uateau-laso, s., testicles, lit.
kidneys of the scrotum.

Uati a, v., d. ati a.

Uatu, v., d. for atu.

Uaua (waua), v. and s., for
baua, q.v.

Uba na, or ube na, s., his day, d.
kuba na.

Ubog, s., day. See bog.

Ubu, s., dd. um, ua, of.

Uè, inter. ad., where? dd. ua
(uan, uabĕ), bai, mbè. [Fi.
vei, Sa. fea.] H. 'ĕ', and,
with n suffixed, 'aiŋ, 'an, A.
'a'na, and, with fi (prep.)
fa'na, Mod. A. fain, or fein
(where? sans mouvement).

NOTE.—In Ef. sā or sĕ (for
safa or sefa) also denote
where, lit. what (place)? sometimes fully expressed sefa
nalia? or sefe tokora? But uè
is an entirely different word,
with a different construction,
being always used with the
verb. pron., with which sĕ or sā
cannot be used. Thus i uè he,
she or it (is) where? This is
because the prep. fi (bi) is used
also as the verb "to be." On
the other hand i baki (ba ki)
sĕ he goes to where (i.e., to
what place)? One cannot say
i sĕ for i uè, nor baki uè for
baki sĕ.

Uei, interj., an exclamation: uai.

Uēlu, v., for bēlu, and

Uēlu, s., a heathen function
in which the men pass days in
the bush, hidden from the
women, under the direction
of the natamole tabu, in order
to ascertain from the natamate,
in dreams, what their future
fortune is to be.

Uen, s., c. art., sand: aran.

Uĕnr, d. for

Uĕre, d. for

Uĕte, d. for fāta, q.v., and fatu.

Ufēa, ad., afar, far away, at a
distance: d. emai, q.v.

Ui, interj., and ad., yes (that's
it): ua, or uai, dem.

Ui, uia, also *bia* (pwia), v. i., or
a., good, well, beautiful, &c.
[Mota wia, Am. wi, Ml. bu,
Santo va, Ma. pai (whakapai-
pai to adorn), Sula pia, Ceram
lia, My. baik.] II. yapah to
be fair, beautiful, Pi. to adorn
(cf. Ma. *supra*), yapeh fair,
beautiful, good, excellent.

Uiko, interj., exclamation : ui
interj., and ko dem.

Uila, interj., exclamation : ui
interj., and la ad.

Uili na, s., d. for kuli na, the skin.

Uiroa, s., a crooked kind of
yam : biria, tafirofiro.

Uis, or uisa, interj., and ad. yes:
ui, and sa dem.

Uisia, v., for bisi a, to take with
the hand.

Uisi, uisiuisi (wisiwisi), d. bisi-
uisi, d. bisi, d. busiwusi, v., to
make, to work, bisi ekobu
make a house, uisiuisi ki work
at, nauisien work, or act of
working. [Sa. osi, Ja. yasa,
Mg. asa.] H. 'asah, n. a.
ma'āseh (work), to make, produce by labour.

Uisiki na, s., elbow, or anything,
as a corner, like an elbow,
uisiki aru na (or naru na)
elbow of the arm, d. mago
naru na heel of the arm.
[My. siku.] A. zugg' elbow.

Ula, s., a maggot. [Sa. ilo, My.
ulat, Mg. olitra.] E. 'es'e
vermis, 'as'ya vermes producere
(Ex. xvi. 23 (4), Acts xii. 23):
cg. A. 'uthat.

Uli, for uili, kuli, skin. Mahri
gotl. See kuli na.

Uli a, or ul ia, v. t., dd. oli a,
auli a, uilia, to take the place

of, to substitute for, to
barter for, buy. See biauli,
d. bioli, v. r., and bauli a,
faulu ; also c. art. naulu, s.,
barter, and redup.,

Uliul, id., and especially in the
phrase uliul nako substitute
the appearance (or face) of
some other person for his own
to deceive (demons were supposed to do this). [Mg. vidy,
mividy to buy, Fi. voli a, id.,
volivoli to trade or barter,
Santo uliul give for, buy ;
Ha. ouli.] A. 'as'a to do or
give something for another
thing, 2, 3, id., 4, id., 5,
accept one thing for another,
8, substitute one for another ;
'awis' one (person or thing) in
place of another, in place of,
ma'us'at what is given for
another thing (*i.e.*, one thing
given for another thing, Ef.
faulu, id.)

Uli na, s., leaf, leaves, also ulu ;
and

Ulua, v. i., or a., to put forth
leaves, to grow up (of plants
and hair), and redup.,

Uluulua, id., also to be full of
leaves, to be hairy, hence
lulu na (for uluulu na) hair,
and uluma, s., a pillow for the
head. [Ha. ulu, uluulu, Fi.
ulu, Ma. uru, Sa. ulu, Malo
ulu, My. ulu ; To. ulunga
(ulu the head), Tah. urua,
pillow for the head.] See lu
lulu, lua, laga, elagi, &c. A.
'ala, n. a. 'aluw', H. 'alah,
whence A. 'ilawat the head,
H. 'aleh leaf, leaves, 'oleh
sprouting forth, growing up.

15

Ululuia, ululia, and lulia. See
alialia.

Um. s., oven, dd. ubu, &c. See
banï a (ba ni a).

Uma, v., to clear for a plantation, cut down the jungle for
this purpose, d. syn. beru.
[My. uma.] And

Uma, s., a clearing, for cultivation, in isuma, q.v. [My.
uma.] A. h'amma to cut;
to sweep out, to clean, h'imm'
a garden vacant of trees and
fruits.

Umai, d. See banomai, babe.
[Sa o mai.]

Umkau, d. makau, or mukau, a
cluster, gathering, hence many,
all (d.) : kau.

Umba ia, v. t., to cast on it,
umbaki, v. t., to cast a thing,
d. bi. E. haypa to cast.

Una, v., to cover or bury itself
in the sand or mud (of a snake,
and an eel-like fish which does
so);

Una ki, v. t., to make to bury
itself in the ground (a post or
fence stake);

Una, s., an eel-like fish that
burrows or buries itself in the
sand;

Una, s., a post, or fence stake;

Un, s., a fish scale (because it
covers);

Unu, s, ghost. See anu. [Sa.
una fish scale or tortoiseshell (covering).] H. ganan
cover over, A. ganna to cover,
bury, egg. H. kanan, 'anan,
A. kanna. See anu.

Uo, dem., d. for ua.

Uo, ad., d. for bo, now, then.
See bo.

Uokati, v., for boka ti : hence

Uoka, chapped, sore (of the
hands, as from striking or
chopping with an axe, &c.)

Uoki, s., an axe. A. waki' a
sharp cutting instrument.

Uol, s., c. art., a bed ; and

Uolis ia, v. See bolis ia, mauol,
&c.

Uol. See bol, bolo.

Uolau. See bolau, böuolau.

Uolo, interj., exclamation. [Fi.
uala.] See uoro.

Uon, dem., d. for uane.

Uon, v., for bon.

Uonda, s., d. uete.

Uontu, dem., and v., uon, tu :
d. for uanetu.

Uora, v., and

Uora na, redup. uorauora na, s.,
and

Uoratan, s. (uora sprout, tano
of the ground) a plant that
springs up of its own accord
(without being planted or
sown); fig. a person without
friends or connections to
avenge him, i bi uoratan ba
faku sa he is a person without friends, pluck him up (i.e.,
uproot, or kill him). See
bora II.

Uorausi a, d. for uru usi a.

Uora, or era, s. See bora ia.

Uori a, uoriuoria, mauori. See
bori a.

Uoro, and auoro, interj., exclamation (d. uolo) : uo, dem.,
and ro, dem., and a as in ako,
ake.

Uosa, nosauosa, uosagoro. See
bosa, bosauosa, bosagoro.

Uose, or uos, d. uohe, s., oar,
paddle. See balu sa. [Ml.

bos, Epi Bi. voho, Fi. voce, Ta. vea, Fut. foi, Sa. foe, My. dayung, Mg. fi-voy, Bisaya bugsai.] A. mikdaf', migdaf', milidaf', mikdaf', Amh. makzaf, A. "aduf', oar.

Uose, dem., d. for uase

Uota, s., c. art., a chief, lord, husband. [Tah. fatu, Ha. haku.] See fatu.

Uota-n-manu, and fatu-n-manu, s., name of a pillar-like rock (Monument Rock) off Efate, lit. pillar or stone of birds.

Uota, uotauota : for bota, botauota.

Uoti a, d. for uti a, oti a : moti a.

Uotu, s., a mark ; hence

Uotuuotu, a., having marks. A. nabathu mark.

Ua (u-à), d. for ua (wa), yes, that's it : ua, dem.

Ura, v., in masi ura ki to scoop up water, sprinkling (someone) ; and

Ura, s., c. art. niura, dew, or rain water on the foliage of plants (from its sprinkling and wetting people). H. yarah to sprinkle, to water, hence yoreh rain, lit. sprinkling.

Uri na, s., the latter or after part, i.q. muri na, s.

Ura, s., lobster, prawn. [Sa., Ha. ula, Ma. koura, My. ud·ang, Ja. urang, Mg. orana (oranorana eating greedily).] H. hawar to be white, become pale, A. hara to be bleached, &c., 4, to eat greedily, hawar', Nm. haur, red leather

NOTE.—Ef. ura seems to be so called because of the red colour which the lobster assumes immediately on being put on the fire to be cooked : hence the proverb i ti bi ura iga miel marafi it is not the lobster to become red immediately (said of wickedness whose punishment does not follow at once, but will come, however slowly and unobserved).

Uru, v. i., to run. A. "ara (H. 'ir) to run.

Uru, uruuru, v. i., to growl, grumble, mutter, murmur. See oro, orooro.

Usi a (for kusi a), v. t., follow in the track of, investigate, ask, question ; and redup.,

Ususi a, v. t., investigate, ask. See takusi a. [My. usir, mangusir, tarusir.]

Usi, v. i., to hasten, usŭ-naki, v. t., hasten about, or as to. H. hus' (and 'us'), A. hās'a, to hasten.

Usiraki, or usereki, i.e., usi-raki (usi to follow), v., to follow through, hence, as ad., through-out.

Usŭ, s., c. art. nausu, d. iu, or u, a reed. [Ml. ui, Epi yi, Sa. u, Fut. gasau, To. kaho.] E. hasĕ, H. hes, reed, arrow.

Us, d. for su, v. t., to take up.

Uta, s., land, euta ashore, on land, by land. [Sa. uta, My. utan (hutan).] A. "utal' land planted with trees ; and

Uta i, or uta ki, v. t., to load (make sink, immerse) a canoe. [Ma. uta, Mg. ondrana.] And

Uta, s., c. art. nauta, a canoe load, cargo. [Sa. uta, Ma. utanga.] And

Utu, ut ī a, v. t., to fill (by immersing) a water vessel. [Sa. utu, utu-fia, Ha. uku-ki.] A. "āta ("a'tu), 4, to immerse.

Uti a. See oti a, moti a.

Uti na, prep., after, following; originally v., i.q. usi a.

Uulu, v. i., also uilu (wulu, wilu), for bilu, q.v., to dance. [Ml. U. velu, Malo velu, Motu mavaru, Ha. mele.] H. mahol, and mholah dance, dancing, from hul, or hil to go round, also to dance (in a circle).

Uusike, and uisiko, or uisiki, q.v., elbow.

Uui (uwi, and u-i), s., c. art. naui (nau-i, or nau-wi), the yam. See afa ki.

www.ingramcontent.com/pod-product-compliance
Lightning Source LLC
Chambersburg PA
CBHW030734280326
41926CB00086B/1375